Julian of Norwich
and the
Mystical Body
Politic of Christ

STUDIES IN SPIRITUALITY AND THEOLOGY 5
Lawrence Cunningham, Bernard McGinn, and David Tracy
SERIES EDITORS

Julian of Norwich and the Mystical Body Politic of Christ

Frederick Christian Bauerschmidt

University of Notre Dame Press
Notre Dame

Copyright © 1999 by
University of Notre Dame
Notre Dame, Indiana 46556
www.undpress.nd.edu
All Rights Reserved

Manufactured in the United States of America

Paperback edition printed in 2008

Library of Congress Cataloging-in-Publication Data

Bauerschmidt, Frederick Christian.
　Julian of Norwich and the mystical body politic of Christ / Frederick Christian Bauerschmidt.
　　p.　cm. — (Studies in spirituality and theology : 5)
　Includes bibliographical references and index.
　ISBN 13: 978-0-268-01194-9 (cloth : alk. paper)
　ISBN 10: 0-268-01194-X (cloth : alk. paper)
　ISBN 13: 978-0-268-02208-2 (pbk. : alk. paper)
　ISBN 10: 0-268-02208-9 (pbk. : alk. paper)
　1. Julian of Norwich, b. 1343.　2. Christianity and politics—History of doctrines—Middle Ages, 600–1500.　3. Jesus Christ—Mystical body—History of doctrines—Middle Ages, 600–1500.　4. Mysticism—England—History—Middle Ages, 600–1500.　I. Title.　II. Series.
BV5095.J84B38　1999
230'.2'092—dc21　　　　　　　　　　　　　　　　98-41339

∞ *The paper in this book meets the guidelines for permanence and durability of the Committee on Production Guidelines for Book Longevity of the Council on Library Resources.*

TO MAUREEN,
who welcomes the stranger

Contents

Introduction and Acknowledgments	ix
1. IMAGINING THE POLITICAL	**1**
A. Theological Politics	3
B. Political Theology	9
C. Between the Times	12
1. The Metaphysics of Order	15
2. The Metaphysics of Freedom	23
2. "I DESYRED A BODELY SIGHT"	**33**
A. The Humanity of Christ	34
B. Bodily Seeing	36
1. Three Requests	36
2. Seeing Jesus	42
C. Event and Interpretation	46
D. The Only Heaven	50
1. Neither Affectivity nor Contemplation	51
2. God's Righteousness Written in the Flesh of Jesus	57
3. "A FEYER AND DELECTABLE PLACE"	**63**
A. Boundaries	64
1. Bodies Smooth and Grotesque	64
2. Dwelling on Margins	73
B. The Grotesque Body of Christ	79
1. Defecation and Degradation	79
2. From Flood to Drought	84
3. A Body of Lack: Christ Our Mother	89
4. Privation and Plenty	96

C. Closed in the Goodness of God	107
1. Dwelling in the Body	108
2. The Scope of the Body	113
D. The Deformation of a Persecuting Society	119

4. "A CONTYNUANT LABORER AND AN HARD TRAVELER"   125

A. A Shewyng Full Mystely	127
1. Sensus Litteralis	129
2. Sensus Mysticus	138
B. Treasure in the Earth	144
1. Reuniting Substance and Sensuality	145
2. Exemplarism and Election	153
C. A Drama without Footlights	162
1. Theo-drama	162
2. Lords and Servants	173
Conclusion: Performing the Book	191
Appendix: Who Was Julian of Norwich?	203
Notes	213
Bibliography	267
Index	283

Introduction
and Acknowledgments

This book consists of an argument for a single claim—that Julian of Norwich may fruitfully be read as one who "imagines the political." However, the argument is rather obliquely made, because the explication of what that claim means and the evidence to support it require several journeys down what might seem to a reader to be lengthy detours. So I offer here a very brief map of what lies ahead, followed by acknowledgment of those who have helped me follow this sometimes twisting path.

In the first chapter I argue that all political and social theory and practice is undergirded by a "metaphysical image" that is, broadly speaking, "theological." I then briefly display the metaphysical images supporting both feudalism and modernity and argue that the fourteenth century was a volatile mixture of feudal and modern structures and ideas that provided Julian with the opportunity to put forward a metaphysical image that is quite different from the images of both feudalism and modernity. In the remaining chapters I gradually unfold the alternative that Julian offers: the mystical body politic of Christ. In chapters 2 and 3 I examine the way Julian sees the body of Christ, and argue that her image of that body as an open and generative one both runs counter to the persecutory imagining of the body of christendom that was prevalent in the later Middle Ages, and presents us with the possibility of a social body infinite in scope. Using the language of traditional theological categories, one might say that chapter 2 deals with issues of christology and the epistemology of revelation, while chapter 3 focuses on ecclesiology and soteriology. In chapter 4 I turn to the *exemplum* of the lord and servant to see how Julian rereads feudal social relations through the trinitarian relations of Father, Son, and Spirit so as to reimagine them as a reciprocal exchange of gifts. Again in traditional theological terms, one might describe this chapter as continuing to pursue the question of soteriology by means of an exploration of Julian's theological anthropology as well as her understanding of the Trinitarian life of God. In the conclusion I argue briefly that there is a certain thwarted quality to Julian's imagining of the social because it was a *mythos* that was virtually impossible to perform under the conditions of late medieval christendom, and I point to ways in which that *mythos* might be performed today. More technical issues of who Julian was are discussed in an appendix.

I do not claim to have unlocked the "real" significance of *A Revelation of Love*. There are many important issues in Julian's book, both theological and otherwise, that I do not touch on, at least not in the depth they deserve. Other productive approaches could be and have been offered. What I have tried to present is a reading of her *Revelation of Love* that brings into the foreground Julian's images of Christ's body and her *exemplum* of the lord and servant as ways in which her understanding of God both grows out of and recommends a particular understanding of human community. But beyond this, I am not so much trying to read the text of Julian's *Revelation of Love* as I am trying to read the text that Julian herself read, the text of Christ's crucified body that she describes. It is in this sense that I seek to enter into Julian's imagining of the political and her rendering of the *mythos* of power beyond violence, both the violence of "order" and the violence of "freedom."

* * *

This book is my attempt to say something about Julian of Norwich and her theology. But, as Gilles Deleuze and Felix Guattari have noted, behind every direct discourse there is a "collective assemblage" that is "the murmur from which I take my proper name, the constellation of voices, concordant or not, from which I draw my voice." Some of those voices can be discerned from perusing the notes and bibliography of this book; others, however, are not so apparent.

I first wish to acknowledge the tremendous debt of gratitude that I owe to the teachers I have had over the years, especially James Clayton and James Peterman at the University of the South, George Lindbeck and the late Hans Frei at Yale Divinity School, and Kenneth Surin, Stanley Hauerwas, and Sarah Beckwith at Duke University.

INTRODUCTION AND ACKNOWLEDGMENTS / xi

I would also like to thank those who have read all or a substantial portion of this book in its various manuscript forms and have offered suggestions with regard both to particular points and to the overall shaping of the argument: David Aers, James Buckley, Lawrence Cunningham, L. Gregory Jones, Susan Keefe, D. Stephen Long, Bernard McGinn, Geoffrey Wainwright, and Nicholas Watson. I am particularly grateful to Michael Baxter, C.S.C., and William Cavanaugh, who have offered not only helpful comments, but also intellectual companionship and spiritual friendship.

I have attempted to write this book with concrete Christian communities in mind, for it is only such manifestations of the mystical body politic of Christ that make the claim that "all shall be well" intelligible. During the time of writing this I have been sustained by many different communities: Holy Cross Catholic Church in Durham, North Carolina, the Trappist monastery of Our Lady of Mepkin in Moncks Corner, South Carolina, and the Monastery of the Carmelite Sisters in Baltimore. During my time in North Carolina I was also blessed to be part of an ecumenical prayer group that met weekly to challenge and support one another. To these "even christians," and countless others, I owe an immeasurable debt.

Finally, I would like to thank my family. My parents and brother continue to inspire me with a love for both the life of the mind and the life of the church. My children, Thomas, Sophia, and Denis, have been to me a means of grace and a source of wonder. My wife Maureen read this manuscript in an early form and helped to deflate a bit of its academic hot air. But more importantly, in both her work and in our family life she has been a vivid reminder of the divine compassion of which Julian speaks so eloquently. It is to Maureen that I dedicate this book.

NOTE ON TEXTS AND CITATIONS

Unless otherwise noted, I have used Edmund Colledge and James Walsh's edition of both the short text (British Museum MS Additional 37790) and the "Paris" manuscript of the long text (Bibliothèque Nationale MS Fonds anglais 40), found in *A Book of Showings to the Anchoress Julian of Norwich*, 2 vols. (Toronto: Pontifical Institute of Medieval Studies, 1978). Parenthetical citations of the short text are to chapter (roman numeral) and line number (arabic). Citations of the long text are to chapter and line numbers (both arabic). On occasion I have quoted or cited the "Sloane" manuscript of the long text (British Museum Sloane MS 2499), using Marion Glasscoe's edition (3rd rev. ed., Exter: University of Exeter Press, 1993). Citations to this edition are made by chapter and page number. With the exception of chapter fifty-one, Julian's chapters are fairly short, so it should be possible for a reader using any edition or one of the many modernizations available to locate quotations. The Paris manuscript will be referred to as "P" and Sloane 2499 as "S."

Though Julian's Middle English, at least in the extant manuscripts, is on the whole comprehensible to modern readers, I have provided modernizations in square brackets following each quotation. For readers unfamiliar with Middle English, I would note the use of two archaic characters found in the short text and the Paris manuscript: þ, which corresponds to a "th," and ȝ, which corresponds to a "y" or "gh." Other Middle English texts have been quoted in the original, where I have had editions available, and these too are translated, with the source of the translation (where it is not my own) provided in square brackets in the notes. Latin texts are quoted in translation. In general, I have cited ancient and medieval texts according to their book and chapter divisions, so as to facilitate locating references in the various editions and translations available. The particular translation I am using is given in square brackets in the first citation, and page numbers from that translation are given in square brackets in subsequent citations. An exception to this is the citations from Thomas Aquinas's *Summa Theologica*, for which I do not give page numbers.

* * *

A small portion of chapter 1 appeared in slightly different form in "Julian of Norwich—Incorporated," *Modern Theology* 13, no. 1 (1997): 75–100. Sections of chapter 2 appeared as "Seeing Jesus: Julian of Norwich and the Text of Christ's Body," *The Journal of Medieval and Early Modern Studies* 27, no. 2 (1997): 189–214.

1

IMAGINING THE POLITICAL

> A document is a witness; and like most witnesses, it does not say much except under cross-examination. The real difficulty lies in putting the right question.
> —Marc Bloch[1]

Julian of Norwich's day was a long time in coming. The modern popularity of the fourteenth-century anchoress and the author of *A Revelation of Love*[2] follows upon several centuries of neglect, during which copies of her book were rare, and there was little scholarly or popular interest in it. When the first printed edition of her book was published in 1670 (just less than three hundred years after the visionary experience that occasioned the book), it was by no means greeted with universal accolades. The Anglican bishop Edward Stillingfleet saw it as an example of "the Fantastic Revelations of distempered brains"[3] so highly regarded by the Roman Church—a church that forbade the reading of scripture, yet commended "the blasphemous and senseless title tattle of this Hystorical [*sic*] Gossip."[4] Times certainly have changed. Since the turn of this century, there have been three editions of Julian in her original Middle English, at least eight modernizations, and countless collections of excerpts.[5] The choice of Edmund Colledge and James Walsh's 1978 modernization, *Julian of Norwich: Showings*, as the inaugural volume in the series *Classics of Western Spirituality*, indicates not only its current status as a "classic," but also its popularity with a wide audience. Thomas Merton, one of this century's most famous contemplative writers, called her "the greatest of the English mystics" and, rather than seeing in her writings mere "senseless tittle tattle," describes her work as "a coherent and indeed systematically constructed corpus of doctrine."[6] Even Stillingfleet's Anglican Church seems to have come around: a shrine to her has been built at St. Julian's Church in Norwich, where she was enclosed and from which she took her name, and recent years have seen the foundation of the Order of Julian of Norwich in the American Episcopal Church.

Such interest should give one pause, particularly in its more "popular" manifestations. Though Julian's summary of the meaning of her revelation—"Wytt it wele, loue was his menyng" (86.16)—seems simple enough, her thought is in fact complex and, in a number of places, quite obscure. Apart from the probably unresolvable question of what written sources, if any, lie in the background of her text, she clearly draws upon a host of medieval theological conventions with which most of her modern readers are unfamiliar. In some ways her piety is typical of late medieval affective devotion, with its emphasis on the human sufferings of Christ and the royal majesty of God, themes that seem distinctly unfashionable today. The central image around which her visions cluster—the crucifix that is placed before her and that she sees bleed copious amounts of blood—seems excessively morbid when compared with the contemporary religious iconography of Western Europe and North America.

Nor is the point of attraction the events of Julian's life. Whereas many who do not particularly care for or about Augustine's theology are still captivated by the life story of the sinner turned saint, Julian offers us no such narrative. We know virtually nothing about her except the meager information that she herself gives us: born probably in early 1343, she fell ill in May of 1373 and was the recipient of a series of sixteen visions, or "showings," upon which she meditated for at least the next twenty years of her life. We know from the texts that have been preserved that she wrote at least two accounts of the visions, the "short text," which was written at some point before 1388, and the greatly expanded and theologically more developed "long text," which was written at some point after 1393, and perhaps as late as the early fifteenth century. Apart from a few external witnesses who tell us that she had been enclosed as an anchoress by 1393, served at least on occasion as a spiritual guide to those who sought her out, and was still alive in 1416, this is about all we know.[7]

The question of who Julian of Norwich was is a controversial one, but the related question of who she *is* is no less controversial. What I mean by this is that, in part, Julian's popularity is a result of the variety of ways in which she is read and purposes to which she is put. Should she be read as a theologian, who can aid us in probing and expanding the Christian theological tradition?[8] Should she be read as someone who is both a victim of and resistant to medieval misogyny, who can help us understand the status of women in medieval society and culture?[9] Is she a devotional writer who can help today in tending to our prayer life?[10] These differing interests with which readers approach the text produce radically different, and at times even incommensurable, readings.

What follows is an extended and diffuse argument for what is perhaps, at least initially, a counterintuitive claim: Julian should be read as *one who theologically imagines the political*. This means that my chief concern is not with Julian as a writer of inherent theological or sociocultural interest, nor as a devotional writer, but with Julian as a resource for thinking about the relationship between theology and social theory and practice. My reading of Julian will have, I hope, affinities with more purely theological or sociocultural or devotional approaches, but will differ from them in attempting to show that the more truly theological the reading of Julian, the more political, and vice versa. What this claim means cannot be explained immediately, but can only be unpacked as the thesis is argued by means of a close reading of the long text of Julian's *Revelation of Love*. In the remainder of this chapter I will sketch what I take it to mean to "imagine the political," how this task is an inherently theological one, and two of the alternative imaginings of the political in Julian's day.

A. THEOLOGICAL POLITICS

My reading of Julian depends on two axiomatic claims: that all politics is "theological" and that all theology is "political." While it is beyond the scope and purpose of this book to fully defend these axioms, I will explain what I mean by them, since such claims are subject to misunderstanding.[11] Reading Julian as one who theologically imagines the political faces the difficulty of the presumption forced on us by modern Western political orders that theology and politics are or should be something distinct. Theology is concerned with either private realms of religious inwardness or the semiprivate realm of the church as a voluntary association, whereas politics is concerned with the state and the exercise of public authority. To mix the two is to put modern pluralistic society at risk.

This view of things is underwritten by a particular narrative of the genesis of the modern nation-state. The standard claim of liberal social theorists is that Europe, recoiling in horror from the excesses committed in the name of God during the sixteenth and seventeenth centuries' Wars of Religion, came to construe religion as an essentially private matter, handing over the public realm, or at least the apparatus of power by which the public realm was governed, to a secularized state. It was the violent fragmentation of the Christian world that necessitated the institution of secular nation-states. However, as William Cavanaugh has argued, "this story puts the matter backwards. The 'Wars of Religion' were not events which necessitated the birth of the modern State; they were in fact themselves the birthpangs of the State."[12] In other words, it is not simply that the "Wars of Religion" were not *really* motivated by religious beliefs, but rather that they were part of a larger intellectual and political battle being waged against the medieval understanding of the church as the source of *religio*—that virtue that binds a community together. The secular state was not instituted as an answer to a problem already posed by the fragmentation of Christianity, but that very fragmentation was necessitated by the genesis of the nation-state. Pierre Manent notes, "Whereas in the Middle Ages political bodies were enveloped or incorporated by the Church, every monarchy tending toward absolutism tended to incorporate the Church within its borders. The Kingdom became the supreme political body, the human association par excellence."[13] Thus the *religio* of the church is displaced by a *new* principle of *religio*—the state. Manent claims that the subsequent development of liberal political thought is driven by a problematic that can be represented "in an almost mathematic form: 'given the characteristics of the Catholic Church, find the political form X that makes it possible to ensure the secular world's independence.'"[14]

If we narrate the rise of the secular state as a displacement of the church as the human community par excellence, then the state perhaps does not appear quite so innocently secular. The state can only displace the *mythos* of the church by supplying its own *mythos*, its own version of salvation, its own account of reality. Carl Schmitt wrote in 1922 that "All significant concepts of the modern theory of the state are secularized theological concepts."[15] But saying that these concepts are "secularized" is not to say that they have become innocent with regard to transcendence, for they form a political metadiscourse or, one is tempted to say, a political metaphysic. Schmitt notes, "The metaphysical image that a definite epoch forges of the world has the same structure as what the world immediately understands to be appropriate as a form of political organization."[16] Schmitt himself—his grounding of the notion of sovereignty in the notion of "the exception" and of the political in the distinction between friend and enemy—hints at a dark and violent metaphysical image in which primacy is given to unconstrained will, an image finding historical form in Schmitt's support of the Nazi Party, but an image that, as shall be argued later in this chapter, is all too common in modernity.[17] The space inhabited by the modern state is not void of sacrality; it is rather the temple of Leviathan.

The notion that the political is structured by a "metaphysical image" underlies my description of Julian as one who "imagines the political." What I mean by imagining is twofold. In perhaps the more conventional modern sense, I mean something like the acts of the imagination (which are not necessarily "imaginary" in the sense of unreal) that shape our understanding of existence as a whole and of the existence that we share within some bounded group in particular. Central to my argument in this book is the contention that *all* politics is "imaginary," in that all societies are "founded" on a *mythos*, an ideological coding that makes the political entity what it is. Let me repeat, this is not true of only some societies, as if some political orders are based on mystification and some are not, but of *all* societies. As Benedict Anderson puts it, "In fact, all communities larger than primordial villages of face-to-face contact (and perhaps even these) are imagined. Communities are to be distinguished, not by their falsity/genuineness, but by the style in which they are imagined."[18] One might think of this as the Marxist base–superstructure scheme stood on its head, or perhaps on its side. For the material social processes that (a certain kind of) Marxism would claim are the *real* and *fundamental* determinants of society are always already accompanied by an ideological (perhaps one should say "metaphysical") coding. They are always already given meaning and significance. They are always already located within an overarching construal of reality.[19] The two are so inseparably intertwined that while they *may* be distinguishable, they cannot be separated.

This inseparability of material social processes and of the process of imagining societies leads me to the other sense in which societies are imagined. It was clearer in the medieval period than it is today that the function of the faculty of the imagination is the production of images. But this imagining, this production of images, is not simply something that individuals do; it is something societies do. Raymond Williams argues that "thinking" and "imagining" are from the beginning social processes (of course including that capacity for "internalization" which is a necessary part of any social process between actual individuals) and that they always become accessible only in unarguably physical and material ways: in voices, in sounds made by instruments, in penned or printed writings, in arranged pigments on canvas or plaster, in worked marble or stone.[20]

In other words, the *mythos* that always accompanies material social processes in a kind of mutual overdetermination is itself sustained and communicated through those very social processes, through shared rituals, monuments, holidays.[21] An imagining of the political always involves concrete media through which that imagining can become common property. Thus one may often read the metaphysical image off of such concrete images as buildings, works of art, or literary (or theological) texts.

It is perhaps a peculiarity of modern states that they so resolutely hide their metaphysical underpinnings, resulting in the general understanding of "secular" as "religiously neutral." We can see this in Max Weber's distinction between an ethic of responsibility, which is the truly political ethic, and an ethic of ultimate ends, which is private and can at best provide an unattainable ideal.[22] For Weber, as for modern liberal theorists in general, politics is equivalent to statecraft and statecraft is a matter of pragmatics. While acknowledging that "politics" could be broadly understood as encompassing various "policies"—such things as a union's strike policy, the Reichsbank's monetary policy, a town's education policy, and even the policy of a wife who tries to guide her husband—Weber seeks to provide a more narrow and precise definition, i.e., "the leadership, or the influencing of the leadership, of a *political* association, hence today, of a *state*."[23] Weber goes on to point out that a "state" cannot, sociologically speaking, be defined in terms of its *ends*—it has no specific ends—but must rather be understood in terms of the *means* peculiar to it, which is the use of physical force. Thus,

> a state is a human community that (successfully) claims the *monopoly of the legitimate use of physical force* within a given territory.... The state is considered the sole source of the "right" to use violence. Hence, "politics" for us means striving to share power or striving to influence the distribution of power, either among states or among groups within a state.[24]

Weber captures well here the modern image of politics. The *agon* of the political arena is not a historical contingency, but is of the very *essence* of the political. At the same time, by bracketing the question of ends, the violence of the state, unlike "religious" violence, can be justified because it allegedly rests on a purely pragmatic basis.

However, in places Weber hints that the violence of politics is something more than mere pragmatics. The tension between responsibility and ultimate ends is ultimately the tension inherent in trying to worship conflicting gods:

> He who seeks the salvation of the soul, of his own and of others, should not seek it along the avenue of politics, for the quite different tasks of politics can only be solved by violence. The genius or demon of politics lives in an inner tension with the god of love, as well as with the Christian God as expressed by the church.[25]

The state is not without its end—its god—but this end is the preservation of the state itself (or, perhaps, the interests of a particular class within society) and thus necessitates violence as an ultimate recourse. This end, this god, is the antithesis of the god of love. Weber believes that both of these gods must be worshiped by anyone who has a "calling for politics" (the god of love serving to mitigate the more rapacious aspects of the god of state-preservation), yet they must be segregated into the private god of love and the public god of pragmatic violence. Given the scheme that Weber has set up, it seems that in the end the demon of violence must always emerge victorious from this uneasy truce, because the only way to avoid violence is to renounce any pragmatic concerns and retreat entirely into religious interiority. In fact, the only way to avoid the alternatives posed by Weber is to reject the metaphysical image underlying this concept of the political and thus to use the term "politics" in a quite different sense.

I am proposing, at the risk of being quaint, a more "classical" definition of politics as the art of seeking the good of the *polis*, which is the common good.[26] The pursuit of this good involves, of course, the employment of power, understood as the capacity for action. But this power is not the monopoly of the state, nor is it inevitably violent (or backed up with the threat of violence). Though Weber mentions other forms of "politics" that extend into the realms of the economy, civil society, and even the family, it seems that he considers them political only in the most extended metaphorical sense, no doubt because they concern themselves with ends. If, however, we take a broader notion of the political, we can see that in addition to the "macroscopic" operations of state power there are also the "microscopic" politics by which power is distributed throughout systems of social relations that extend beyond the scope of the state.[27] The micropolitics of power work without surfacing in the form of a state, through a multitude of obscure and occluded practices that perpetually trace patterns of meaning in human lives. These microscopic forces may serve as constituent elements of the macroscopic politics of state power, or they may trace patterns of resistance. The *polis* that is the site and agent of this micropolitics may well work for an end that it cannot specify, that it does not "have in view," but that is registered in the form of resistant concentrations of power that subsist but momentarily in the interstices of macropolitics. The point is that politics need not be reduced to the working of the state, but exists anywhere some shared end is pursued, even an unseen or unspecifiable one.

Similarly, the power that is associated with the political need not take the form of violence or the threat of violence. The association of power with politics is undeniable, but Weber's association of political power and violence is arbitrary. He may well be right that any politics associated with a state, in which no particular end is pursued except the maintenance of the state itself by means of continual domination of a particular territory, is inextricably bound up with violence. However, if we imagine a *polis* that is not bound to a specific territory, there is no *necessity* in the link between violence and the political. There are forms of political power that operate as "poachers" in alien territory, that have no stake in domination, but that are still capacities to act toward a shared end.[28] And even if that action meets resistance, this conflict need not be understood in terms of violence, but as momentary diminishments that can be transformed into greater capacities. Put simply, there is no necessary reason why the common pursuit of the good cannot, at least in principle (and Weber's linking of violence and politics is made in principle), be nonviolent. The formation of a workers' cooperative is no less political because it is outside of the state apparatus and not governed by the threat of violence.

Implicit in this broader understanding of politics that I am adopting is a rejection of the usual distinction that political and social theorists make between the state as the realm of the "political" and civil society as the realm of the "social." According to this distinction, something like a workers' cooperative belongs, along with churches, charitable organizations, and various voluntary groups, to civil society, and thus is not really within the realm of the political. Yet this distinction only serves to establish clearly the state's monopoly on coercive force and to forge a seemingly natural link between politics and violence. What consigns social groups to civil society is their exclusion from access to violent means to establish their control. The only way to unthink the connection of politics with violence is to blur, if not erase, the distinction between "political" and "social," for this ironically serves to marginalize the significance of mediating institutions, and in the end simply underwrites what John Milbank has called "the monotonous harmony of sovereign state and sovereign individual."[29]

All politics is theological, and in many ways the theology of the state has such a tight grip on our political imaginations that it has come to seem natural to us. I have tried to indicate that the modern conception of politics as statecraft and of statecraft as defined by the *pragma* of violence is not natural or necessary (and certainly not theologically innocent) but is rather a contingent construction, one that can be unthought.

B. POLITICAL THEOLOGY

If all politics is theological, so too all theology is political. I do not mean this in the banal sense that all theology has political consequences somewhere (who knows where?) down the line, nor that theology is an ideological mystification masking political machinations. What I mean is that the metaphysical image, the *mythos*, proffered by Christian theology is one that finds its political correlate in the church as the exemplary form of human community. Such a claim obviously raises a difficult question. How can one speak of *the* metaphysical image proffered by Christianity? Clearly such language can be homogenizing, betraying both the reality as well as the ideal of legitimate theological pluralism as well as masking the ideological warfare that goes on within Christianity. Similarly, how can one speak of *the* church, given the manifest fragmentation of Christianity? Minimally one must say that in Christianity exactly what one means by the Christian *mythos* is and always has been a contested point, and this contestation is carried on both within and across communities that claim the name church. Part of the purpose of reading Julian as one who theologically imagines the political is to discern how *she* understands and figures that *mythos*, how she enters into this contest, and what form of community she imagines, and this will be developed in the subsequent chapters of this book. At this point I simply mean to stress that theology is always already political because it is the "social theory" underlying the distinctive forms of life of concrete, historical communities that make up the church.

As noted, in the modern era Christianity has come generally to be confined either to the privacy of spiritual inwardness, or to the semi-private space of the churches, understood as being among the voluntary institutions that make up civil society. This obscures the inherently social and political character of Christianity. Georges Florovsky writes, "Christianity entered history as a new social order, or rather a new social dimension. From the very beginning Christianity was not primarily a 'doctrine,' but exactly a 'community.' There was not only a 'Message' to be proclaimed and delivered, and 'Good News' to be declared. There was precisely a New Community, distinct and particular, in the process of growth and formation, to which members were called and recruited."[30] Henri de Lubac pointed out earlier in this century that just as in Israel so too in early Christianity, salvation was conceived of "as essentially social."[31] Sin had destroyed not simply the bond between God and humanity, but the unity of the human race as well. Through the covenant with Abraham and the renewal of that covenant in the death and resurrection of Christ, God is bringing about the reconciliation of humanity in a new social reality. Thus the importance for Paul that Christianity be a community of Jew and Gentile, male and female, slave and free.

That the church was seen as a political reality can be seen in the word *ekklesia* itself. The term that was taken over by the early Christian community to describe itself was not a cultic term, but a political one that referred to the assembly of free men, called together to deliberate on issues concerning the civic good.[32] This understanding of the Christian community as a *polis*—a distinctive social space—can also be seen in the second-century *Epistle to Diognetus*, which claims that Christians possess a distinctive "constitution of their own citizenship [*politeias*]," while at the same time continuing to live in the midst of their pagan neighbors.[33] This fundamental political reality of the church, however, is radically different from other earthly polities because it is the foretaste and promise of the heavenly *politeuma*

(Phil. 3:20), and as such qualifies the loyalties of Christians to any earthly polity, so that "every foreign country is their fatherland and every fatherland is a foreign country."[34] Yet this did not prevent this new community from posing a political threat. Thus when Pliny the Younger set about persecuting Christians around A.D. 114, he did so on the basis of an edict by the Emperor Trajan that "banned all political societies."[35] Later in that century the pagan writer Celsus charged that Christians were "rebellious" and "suffering from the disease of sedition."[36] Celsus sees the exclusive monotheism of Christians as a revolt that is at once both metaphysical and political.[37] And when faced with such charges, Christians did not seek to evade them by claiming a private, nonpolitical status for their community, but, as N. T. Wright puts it, "continued to proclaim their allegiance to a Christ who was a 'king' in a sense which precluded allegiance to Caesar, even if his kingdom was not to be conceived on the model of Caesar's."[38]

By a long and very complex historical process, this sense of the church as a distinctive political community comes to be occluded, first by its gradual identification with the Roman Empire in the entity of christendom, then (in the wake of the eleventh-century controversy over lay investiture) by the distinction within christendom between the spiritual realm, which was the purview of the church, and the temporal realm, which was governed by kings and princes. For our purposes, suffice it to say that by the seventeenth century the church was on the whole not seen as a distinct social entity, but was rather one element among others in the body politic. And with the beginnings of self-consciously secular societies in the eighteenth century, that element is gradually purged from the body, to take refuge in various apolitical spheres.

One reason for taking this hop, skip, and a jump through Christian history is to make clear that reasserting the political character of theology is not the same thing as calling for a return to christendom. It may well be that christendom itself was but the beginning of Christianity's depoliticization.[39] For christendom ended up identifying Christianity with European society, thus tending to militate against the church as a distinctive, and discomforting, social presence in the midst of the nations. The church's political status was no longer a result of being the foretaste and effective sign of the heavenly *politeuma*, but of its role in the project of christendom. With the breakup of christendom into nation-states the church becomes, at its worst, simply one branch of government, charged with giving a sacred aura to the interests of the state. Or, put in terms of "imagining the political," the church comes to see its task as developing and promulgating whatever metaphysical image underwrites the particular society in which it finds itself. Lost is the imagining of the heavenly *politeuma* that makes every foreign country a homeland and every homeland alien territory.

In some small way I am seeking to recover in this book a metaphysical image that is distinctive to the Christian community, though perhaps not without analogue in other communities. By reading Julian as one who imagines the political, I hope to show how she takes up the task of telling the story of God's dealings with the world in a way that explicates and makes resound again the distinctively Christian metaphysic of divine love become incarnate, and how she does this with striking newness. In other words, I hope to show that she is a theologian.

C. BETWEEN THE TIMES

My reading of Julian is shaped in part by an interpretation of the fourteenth century as a point at which a metaphysical image that we might describe as "modern" begins to emerge. At the same time, the metaphysical image that underlies the form of life that we retrospectively call "feudal" is waning.[40] Thus Julian writes at one of those points of historical transition in which the operation of what Cornelius Castoriadis calls the "radical imaginary" comes into particularly clear view.[41] Here we must move with caution, albeit quickly, for while it is widely agreed that Julian lived in a time and place of transition, the nature of this transition is hotly contested. What we find in the fourteenth century is a bewildering mixture of residual and emergent cultural forms that makes its characterization as "modern" or "feudal" difficult.[42] This can be seen in scholarly disputes over the question of the "discovery of the individual," which have embedded within them questions about the beginnings of "modernity."[43] Also, the tendency in the intellectual historiography of the Middle Ages for a long time, particularly among Catholics, was to see the fourteenth and fifteenth centuries as the "dissolution of the medieval outlook," in which the synthesis of high scholasticism, represented by Thomas Aquinas, dissolved into the nominalism of William of Ockham, characterized by skepticism, pelagianism, and theologism.⁴⁴ Yet recently, late medieval philosophy and theology have been more positively characterized by scholars.⁴⁵ Similarly, medieval liturgical and religious practice has been portrayed for a long time as debased, superstitious, and individualistic,⁴⁶ but more recently has appeared as a powerful and quite sophisticated means by which communal identity was formed.⁴⁷

Was England in the fourteenth century in fact a society undergoing fragmentation? Certainly many modern writers take this to be the case, and on many different levels. Regarding the philosophical and theological scene, Janet Coleman writes, "[c]haracteristic of the fourteenth century was the lack of a development toward a synthesis; there was instead a fragmentation of an earlier constructed whole."⁴⁸ Christopher Dyer writes that patterns of employment after 1349 "became even more fragmented, as employees broke away from the long-term commitments of annual contracts, preferring to work by the day."⁴⁹ Barbara Hanawalt notes that peasant communities that had depended on such institutions as village bylaws, manorial courts, and even royal courts to order their communal life gradually lost this framework, so that "[b]y the fifteenth century the traumas of the previous century began to erode these institutions of village regulation, and neighbor became estranged from neighbor."⁵⁰ Likewise, various late medieval sources exhibit a concern over the unity and vitality of England. The late fourteenth century was marked by the reigns of a very old (Edward III) and an initially very young (Richard II) king, neither of whom seemed capable of leading England effectively. The constantly shifting fortunes of England in the Hundred Years' War with France produced periodic uncertainty about the strength of the nation. Certainly William Langland's visionary allegory, *Piers Plowman*, has as a constant undertone Langland's sense that England is dangerously fragmented and must be reunited.⁵¹ Perhaps more importantly, this fragmentation was not simply a national one, but extended to christendom as a whole. The protracted conflict of the Hundred Years' War heightened national loyalties over and against a common European identity, and with the advent of the Great Schism in 1378, the unity of the church, which since the end of John the XXII's reign had grown tenuous under the weak Avignon popes, was visibly shattered. When Langland describes how Christ built a house, "And called that hous Unite—Holy Chirche in Englissh,"⁵² he gives to the church "unity" as its proper name, something that, in the face of the Great

Schism and increased national identity, might not have been so apparent.

At the same time, one must not be too quick to presume that what was taking place in late fourteenth-century England is best described as fragmentation. If Marc Bloch was correct to describe fragmentation of authority as one of the fundamental characteristics of European feudalism, then the "crisis of feudalism" can be seen not as a process of fragmentation, but the beginning of consolidation of authority by the state.[53] Similarly, while the Hundred Years' War strained the fabric of English society through the insecurity it generated and the financial burdens it placed on the populace, it also provided the English with a newly strengthened sense of national identity.[54] Likewise, the fragmentation of the church under mutually excommunicate rival popes weakened the principal rival of the emergent nation-state, allowing the state to emerge as a new focal point of unity, in which the church functioned *de facto* as a branch of the state.[55]

In short, it is a debatable point whether the fourteenth century should be seen primarily in terms of what was passing away—a certain "organic" social order—or in terms of what was emerging—the nascent "modernity" to which we are heirs. What we are in fact confronted with in the fourteenth century, as perhaps in any time, is a cultural matrix within which no single factor or set of factors should be set up as determinative of the whole. The picture we get remains puzzling—a pastiche of residual and emergent forms, medievalisms and modernisms, that signal a culture in a particularly crucial period of transition. The cultural matrix seems fragmented in a way that renders any point at which we seek to grasp it uncertain, liable to break if held too tightly or pulled too hard. Yet it is precisely this fragility of the cultural matrix that provides the conceptual space within which Julian of Norwich rethinks the Christian *mythos*.

But before proceeding to the exegesis of Julian, I beg a bit more indulgence from the reader. I wish to present first two alternative metaphysical images, both of which were (at least putatively) live options in Julian's day, and to which Julian provides an alternative. The first is the metaphysics of organic ordering that imagines traditional feudal society. The second is the new metaphysics of freedom that is articulated in nominalist theology. My treatment of both of these will necessarily be cursory, and rests on the shoulders of scholarly giants, but I hope by sketching these two metaphysical alternatives to make Julian's own metaphysic of divine love stand out with greater clarity.

1. The Metaphysics of Order

In the Middle Ages the idea of the body politic was not simply a metaphor but *was* the political and social theory of christendom.[56] As John of Salisbury put it in the twelfth century, "a republic is . . . a sort of body which is animated by the grant of divine reward and which is driven by the command of the highest equity and is ruled by a sort of rational management."[57] In this body, each member has its own, divinely ordained role, grouped roughly into three "estates" or "orders." The clergy, who direct the worship of God, are like the soul; the rulers are like the head, subject only to the direction of the soul; and the peasants are like feet, bound to the earth yet moving the body forward. The health of the whole body depends on the members fulfilling their proper roles, which include attending to the well-being of the other members of the body. Thus John writes:

> The health of the whole republic will only be secure and splendid if the superior members devote themselves to the inferiors and if the inferiors respond likewise to the legal rights of their superiors, so that each individual may be likened to a part of the others reciprocally and each believes what is to his own advantage to be determined by that which he recognizes to be most useful for others.[58]

John presents us with a vision of social order that is in no way a mere convention, but is rooted in the meticulous observation of roles that are determined by the divinely ordained, essential natures of the various groups in society.

This organic vision, with its division of the three estates and a strong notion of the common good toward which they were oriented, thus uniting this tripartite division, was widespread in the ancient and medieval worlds and found echoes in the imagining of both the cosmos and the individual.[59] This image was constantly reinforced in sermons and other popular religious forms.[60] The metaphor changes; sometimes it is the body and its members, sometimes it is the three orders of husbandmen laboring in the vineyard, sometimes the elements of an architectural edifice, or the various parts of a ship, but the vision remains one of a single entity defined by a divinely-given common end, yet made up of distinct parts with distinct roles—roles that must not be confused if the whole is to function properly. In John Mirk's *Festial*, a popular collection of sermons that were probably composed in the 1380s, we find:

> So most yche good seruand enforse hym forto laboure yn þe degre þat God hath sette hym yn. Men of holy chyrche schuld labour bysily prayng and studiyng forto teche Godys pepull; lordys and oþr rented men schuld labur bysyly, to kepe holy chirch yn pees and rest, and all othyr comyn pepull; the comyns schuld labour bysyly, forto gete lyflode to homselfe and to all oþir.
>
> [So must each good servant strengthen himself to labor in the estate in which God has set him. Men of Holy Church should labor busily praying and studying in order to teach God's people; lords and other endowed men should labor busily, to maintain Holy Church in peace and rest, as should all common people; the commons should labour busily in order to provide livelihoods for themselves and all others.] [61]

Similarly, Thomas Brinton, bishop of Rochester, in a sermon preached on July 17, 1377, the day after Richard II's coronation, reminds his hearers of the mutual obligations of rich and poor. While he does not invoke the image of a body or refer to the three estates, the vision offered is still an organic one in which rich and poor are united by their common father, Adam, by their common redemption by the blood of Christ, by their sharing of one baptism and partaking of one eucharist, and by the one beatitude that they all seek. At the same time, one must not confuse rich with poor, for each has a distinct role to fulfill within the social body:

> Although the rich and poor appear to be contraries, this is necessary. For if all were poor, no one would be able to support another. If all were rich, no one would labor, and thus the world would collapse. Thus, the rich exist on account of the poor and the poor on account of the rich. The rich must offer alms, and the poor must pray.[62]

Brinton's sermon shows how the difference between rich and poor is described in a non-conflictual way, so that both coexist within a harmonious, organic whole.

The sermon is also typical of late medieval denunciations of social injustice, which were made within the context of an organic society that presumed wealth and poverty were divinely assigned roles. Within the social body, the burden falls primarily on the rich; as one author notes of Brinton's social vision in general, "[t]he nub of Brinton's argument is that, given a society that it is inconceivable to change fundamentally, the greater the position occupied the greater the obligation to the wider community."⁶³ All will be provided for in society so long as they fulfill the duties of their roles. In Brinton's view, rich and poor are divinely fixed stations that not only ensure the stability of society ("thus the world would collapse") but also are part of God's plan of salvation: "[God] willed that the poor should remain in want so that by them God might see which of the rich were His friends and which His enemies."⁶⁴ Social organicism is theologically coded by this notion of a divinely established order among the three estates, so as to make "religion" and "politics" indistinguishable. As I argued earlier, there is no political theory that is not a political theology.⁶⁵

In this metaphysics of organic order the body plays a central role. Mary Douglas notes, "[t]he physical experience of the body, always modified by the social categories through which it is known, sustains a particular view of society."⁶⁶ In other words, there is an intimate mutual relation between how bodies are understood and how society is understood; culture shapes our experience of the body, which in turn shapes our understanding of culture. Whether or not this claim is universally true, it was certainly true of Europe in the Middle Ages. And it was not simply the experience of a generic human body that was socially shaped and shaping, but the experience of the human body of the God-man, Jesus Christ. Even more important than sermons in reinforcing the organic social vision of the medieval world was its public, ritual enactment in the sacrament of Christ's body, the Mass.

Despite the common and not inaccurate perception of late medieval eucharistic practice and devotion as increasingly individualistic, the celebration of the mass still had a powerful corporate dimension. While the laity normally received communion at mass infrequently (only one to three times a year), these communions of the whole parish on high feast days, prepared for by fasting and confession, were intensely communal occasions, and therefore opportunities both for inclusion and for exclusion.⁶⁷ It was in the celebration of the mass and in other rituals associated with it, such as processions on the feast of *Corpus Christi*, that inhabitants of late medieval England participated in the enactment of their identity as that corporate body of which Thomas Brinton spoke: children of a common Father, sharing a common supernatural destiny. It was in the context of the eucharistic sacrifice that members of the social body became heirs of a common redemption: "blody bretheren, for God boughte us alle."⁶⁸ At least in theory, the paradigmatic body by which relations among the members of the social body were understood was the suffering, generative, eucharistic body of Christ.

This strong sense of correlation between the Eucharist and the body politic can be seen from a speech given by the speaker of the Commons, Sir Arnold Savage, toward the close of Parliament in 1401, in which he compared parliamentary procedures to the celebration of the mass.[69] In particular, the king's repeated promise to protect the church and to see that all, both rich and poor, abide by the laws of the realm, is compared by Savage to the offering of the sacrifice of the mass. The king's promise was one of peace and unity, like the eucharistic sacrifice that promised to the community, in the words of the Secret (offertory) collect for the liturgy of Corpus Christi, "the gifts of unity and peace, which are mystically represented in the gifts we offer."[70] The eucharistic body of Christ was the paradigm not only of the English nation, but of smaller social groupings such as villages or guilds. It was in human social relations that God's redeeming work in Christ, the restoration of the unity lost in the garden of Eden, was enacted, and the Eucharist was the pattern and agent of that salvation.[71] Just as sacramental doctrine held that each fragment of the host was the body of Christ in its totality,[72] so each element of the social body reproduced within itself the christomorphic structure of the whole. The macrocosm was reproduced in the microcosm, reinforcing the organic unity of the whole.[73]

The very nature of the mass and other eucharistic rituals—hierarchically structured while at the same time uniting the participants as one—emphatically underscored the social body's complex organic structure of differentiation and unity.[74] The rituals associated with Christ's eucharistic body, like the social body that it signified and created, were not egalitarian, but ordered by differences of rank and dignity. The celebration of the mass, particularly the High Mass in which the priest was assisted by a deacon, subdeacon, and clerks, was a complex rite that depended on the participants properly performing their distinct functions. The hierarchical nature of the rite was vividly expressed in the way that subdeacon, deacon, and priest were ranged on increasingly higher steps before the altar,[75] as well as the complex order of precedence in which the choir was censed and the Gospel book kissed.[76] This hierarchy was not simply established among the clerics who assisted in the celebration of the mass, but was extended, at least at the parish mass on Sundays, to the lay participants through the ceremonial kissing of the paxbred, which was a flat image of the crucifix or *Agnus Dei*. Before the priest's communion this image was kissed first by the priest, then by the deacon and subdeacon and the choir.[77] After this it was taken to the congregation, the members of which kissed it in order of social precedence. This ceremony, which for the laity substituted for the actual reception of communion on most Sundays, reveals quite clearly the nature of the medieval mass as a ritual of bodily unity and peace—a unity predicated on the maintenance of a certain social taxonomy.[78] This taxonomy can also be seen in the physical space of the church building within which the mass was celebrated. The rood screen, a carved wooden or stone screen surmounted by a crucifixion scene consisting of Christ, John the Evangelist, and the Virgin Mary, stood between choir and nave and separated clerical and lay participants, at least during masses celebrated at the high altar. In some churches, the screen took the form of a veritable wall that effectively cut off the laity's view of the altar. This wall of separation would therefore have been dramatically ruptured by the ceremony of the paxbred; the kissing of the pax was a transgression of the social division between clerical and lay Christians, yet for its ritual impact it depended on that very social division. As Michel de Certeau writes, "It is as though delimitation itself were the bridge that opens the inside to its other."[79]

This combination of hierarchical differentiation within a ritual of unity can also be seen in the eucharistic processions that took place on or around the feast of *Corpus Christi*. The feast itself, which took place in early summer on the Thursday after Trinity Sunday, developed into a great community festival celebrated with meals and plays and other entertainments. Chief among the events was the procession in which the eucharistic bread was carried through the town. This procession, like the mass, was a hierarchically structured event. The priest himself, walking under a canopy and surrounded by flags or banners so as to mark ritually the center of sacramental and sacerdotal power, carried the Eucharist in a monstrance. The higher one's place in the community's social structure the closer one was to the Eucharist, with the community's most illustrious members having the privilege of carrying the canopy over the sacrament. In some communities the processions were ordered by craft, with members of various guilds marching together, the more prestigious guilds walking closest to the priest with the monstrance.[80] The progress of the ordered procession through the town, city, or village acted as a way of renewing the organic, hierarchical unity of the social body by defining its boundaries and internal structure.

Various modern interpreters have offered differing accounts of what is in fact going on in these eucharistic rituals. Some, such as John Bossy, Eamon Duffy, and Mervyn James, present them as establishing what Victor Turner called *communitas*, "a state of pre-political, undifferentiated human affinity, which dissolved tensions and bound people together despite the differences between them in the non-ritual space and time."[81] In this interpretation, the Eucharist resolves the tensions inherent in a hierarchically ordered social body by mirroring those differences in a ritual of unity. Other interpreters, such as Miri Rubin and Sarah Beckwith, see the rituals of the Eucharist not as resolving tensions created by hierarchy, but as functioning to construct hierarchy and boundaries of exclusion, thus serving as the field in which social conflict is played out.[82] It is certainly the case that eucharistic rituals were not simply occasions of serene *communitas* but were sometimes boisterous eruptions of simmering communal tensions. We hear of cases of masses at which parishioners threw the paxbred to the ground, enraged because others had kissed it before them, thereby establishing their higher social position. One irate man even used the paxbred to pummel the clerk who offered it to him, having warned him the week before, "Clerke, if thou here after gevist not me the pax first I shall breke it on thy hedd."[83]

The connection between the eucharistic body and the body politic, and the threat that was posed to the latter by attacks on the former, can be seen in the case of those followers of John Wyclif known as Lollards. It is difficult to determine what *positive* eucharistic beliefs Lollards held—positions range from Wyclif's consubstantiation to later Lollard views that seem to approximate a kind of memorialism—but it is clear that they were *against* the medieval doctrine of transubstantiation and the view of clerical power that attended it. They also rejected other communal practices associated with the feast of *Corpus Christi*, particularly the religious dramas, as well as the quasi-sacramental veneration of images.[84] Despite the fact that Lollards often explicitly connected their critique of certain religious practices with concern for the poor—complaining that people spent money to buy images for churches yet "þei may not fynde at her herte to gif þere almes to quicke ymagis of God, þat ben pore folc [they cannot find it in their heart to give their alms to living images of God, that is, to the poor]"[85]—they were frequently attacked as enemies of the social body. The rejection of the symbolic structure of the community was perceived as such a threat to social cohesion that the political menace posed by the Lollards was inseparable from their theological menace, as can be seen by the statute *De haeretico comburendo* passed by Parliament in 1401, which commanded the burning of Lollards. Religious belief and practice, and specifically eucharistic belief and practice, once again formed the arena of conflict.

Yet the fact that eucharistic rituals were occasions for social disruption does not in any way reduce their powers of social incorporation. Nor should the fact that the social body imaged as an extension of the *Corpus Christi* was possessed of a hierarchical structure lead us to suppose therefore that it was experienced by its members as inherently oppressive. Maurice Keen has noted, "in the minds of the men of that age [i.e., the later Middle Ages], the relations of deference and service that persisted between grades were the basis of social order, of its essence: they had not yet come to regard social distinctions as divisive, as forces with potential to tear society apart, as Rousseau and later Marx were to do."[86] Certainly there was oppression in late medieval English society, and certainly people experienced themselves as oppressed. But, not being burdened as we are with an egalitarian ideology, they believed that social inequalities could serve to relieve the material and social deprivations of people as well as impose them. What Marc Bloch says of the feudal relations of lord and vassal was at least in theory and often in practice true of medieval hierarchies in general: "whatever the inequalities between the obligations of the respective parties, those obligations were none the less mutual: the obedience of the vassal was conditional upon the scrupulous fulfillment of his engagements by the lord."[87] Bloch also makes the point that medieval hierarchy was not a single ordering system, but in fact a complex aggregate of differing taxonomies, so that "to contemporaries the structure of the society in which they lived did not possess clear-cut contours. The fact was that very different systems of classification cut across each other."[88] For example, one might note in terms of the ecclesiastical hierarchy the different structures within which secular and regular clergy operated, the overlapping of ecclesiastical and royal jurisdictions, and the fragmentation of royal authority by franchises granted to the church.[89] The social body was perforated by spaces that escaped any single system of classification, yet could exist within the encompassing image of the body politic.

Put in terms of the metaphysical image underlying this organicism, one might say that social space is intrinsically and complexly ordered. Unlike modern political theory, in which, typically, the chaos resulting from an essentially *un*ordered "state of nature" gives rise to the human creation of political structures, in this medieval vision the state of nature bears within it its own intrinsic ordering.[90] One might see this as the political correlate of the metaphysical realism of the era: just as universals such as "goodness" or "whiteness," by which we classify and categorize particular entities, were not mere human constructions but had an independent ontological status, so too the classificatory scheme of peasant, noble, and cleric was not merely a human construction but a divinely-given and teleologically-ordered reality.

R. H. Tawney noted of medieval society: "The gross facts of the social order are accepted in all their harshness and brutality. They are accepted with astonishing docility, and, except on rare occasions, there is no question of reconstruction."[91] This "harshness and brutality" is accepted as intrinsic to the social order in a way that makes one suspect that the unity of the three orders is bought at the price of the exclusion of elements alien to the social body—such as Jews, lepers, heretics, and unruly women. The social body imaged in feudalism can only exist when tightly bounded. Likewise, the harshness and brutality within the social body of the ruling orders is justified in the name of the common end shared by the three orders. Yet if that end were indeed common to all three orders, then the rule by force of the commons would hardly seem necessary. Again, one suspects that the metaphysics of organicism masks a gap that can only be filled with coercive rule of the lower by the higher.[92] Thus one must ask, to what extent was the sense of unity and order provided by this organic metaphysics predicated on violence toward outsiders and deviants? From a theological point of view, feudalism offered an organicism of the *corpus christianum* that was not exactly identical with the ecclesial *Corpus Christi* and that supplanted the body of the church with christendom. In doing so, it limited the imagining of the possibilities of Christ's body as a counterpolitics by wedding it to the politics of Europe. The social body is imaged as smooth and contained, not broken and generative.

Still, I think it is important to realize that the organic social vision that was preached from pulpits, inscribed in prose and poetry, and enacted in ritual performance was as full of possibilities as it was of constraints. It did not simply breed passivity, but also fostered acts of charity. It did not simply assign social stations, but also imposed mutual obligations between rich and poor. If nothing else, it had at least the potential of fostering a sense of unity and participation that to us moderns might seem oppressive, but which in medieval society was positively salvific. It is precisely this sense of unity and participation that was threatened in various ways in the fourteenth century. We find in this period an increased invocation of the theme of the three orders of society, yet these invocations are taking on a more clearly fictional character as social structures begin to change.[93] Maurice Keen notes that up until about 1300 "the three-estates description of social relations could still enjoy some appearance of relevance to real circumstances" but that by the end of the fifteenth century this was no longer so.[94] Anomalous members—wealthy peasants, literate laymen (and women), powerful monarchs who stood apart from other lords—disordered the body in such a way that it could no longer channel and control the vital powers of the social whole.

2. The Metaphysics of Freedom

Above I said that the metaphysical image of feudal society was akin to medieval "realism," in which terms of classification and ordering referred to extra-mental realities. Extending this analogy, we might say that the dissolution of medieval society and the birth of modernity are grounded in a metaphysical image that is akin to the "nominalist" metaphysics of the later Middle Ages.[95] The nominalist understanding of the status of universals and of the nature of divine omnipotence lays the foundation for modernity's *mythos* of amoral, nonrational *potentia*; along with this shift occur concomitant shifts in how the human exercise of power, the autonomy of creatures, and the structure of human social relations are conceived.[96]

Part of the problem in evaluating nominalism lies in determining exactly what constitutes it as something distinctive. The term "nominalism" technically identifies a philosophical position that holds that universals are names and not independent realities, and this position is often presented as nominalism's definitive characteristic. Ockham's reduction of universals or common natures to names (*nomina*) that have no extra-mental existence means that a concept such as "humanity" or a relation such as "fatherhood" is robbed of its status as an ontological reality; the only independently existing things are individual particulars, such as specific human beings, that are related to each other by spatial and temporal proximity or simply by a degree of similarity.[97] Put differently, only speech about singulars is denotative; speech about relations is connotative. In the statement "X has relation Y to Z," the term "relation Y" has no ontological status apart from the juxtaposition of X and Z.

Attractive as it is for its clarity, this view of nominalism as a philosophical view with theological consequences has been questioned in the past fifty years. Heiko Oberman, among others, has argued that certain theological convictions shape nominalist philosophical positions and not vice versa.[98] Oberman also argues that nominalism was not a single thing, but there were in fact several distinct "schools" of nominalism that might be characterized as a spectrum stretching from "left-wing" to "right-wing."[99] Both within and between these schools there was a great deal of theological and philosophical diversity.[100] Nominalism is thus a more complicated and diverse phenomenon than previously thought. What enables us to unite these diverse positions under the rubric "nominalism" or *via moderna*, according to Oberman, is not primarily a common ontology of individual existents, but the shared emphasis on the omnipotence of God, and in particular the exploitation of the distinction between God's "absolute power" (*potentia absoluta dei*) and God's "ordained power" (*potentia ordinata dei*).[101] Oberman notes, "Nominalism is not a doctrinal unity, but a common attitude, on some points at least, of remarkably different strands."[102]

Profession of God's omnipotence was not in itself anything unusual in Christian theology, and even the distinction between the *potentia absoluta* and the *potentia ordinata* had appeared in such a representative of the *via antiqua* as Thomas Aquinas as a way of distinguishing divine capacity and volition.[103] However, there are subtle differences between his use of this distinction and that of a nominalist such as Ockham. Aquinas understood everything that occurred in the actual, existing world as within the order of the *potentia ordinata*; even miracles that went against the normal laws of nature were effected through God's ordained power, so long as God actually performed them.[104] As Marilyn McCord Adams puts it:

> For Aquinas, God's ordered power is His power to do what conforms to the completely determinate plan of action that He actually

chooses, where this plan consists, not of a system of general laws, but a series of determinations of what to do in each and every case throughout the whole of world history.[105]

Thus for Aquinas, to speak of God's *potentia absoluta* is not to speak of a power that ever is in fact exercised, a kind of reserve that might be utilized in exceptional circumstances. Exceptional circumstances are all foreseen and foreordained by God. The *potentia absoluta* is a manner of speaking about hypothetical things that God has not, in fact, done; it is a way of acknowledging that God's capacity is not exhausted by the realm of actual existents. There is not really a "dialectic" between the *potentia absoluta* and the *potentia ordinata* because the order of things willed by God is a true, if incomplete, expression of the divine *ratio:* "the divine wisdom includes the whole potency of the divine power."[106] Omnipotence can include the inability to do certain things, both things that are logically impossible as well as things that would not be in accord with divine perfection.

In later scholastic thinkers it is not so clear that this is the case. In the thirteenth century the canonist borrowed the absolute-ordained distinction from the theologians to speak of the way in which the pope, by his plenitude of power (*plenitudo potestatis*), could change church law for the good of the church. William Courtenay notes that such a use of the terms "did violence to the basic meaning of the theological distinction" because it understood absolute power as "a sphere of *action*, however rarely it might be used" rather than the realm of possibility that is logically prior to *any* action.[107] In defining the distinction John Duns Scotus (c. 1265–1308) adopts the canonists' legal metaphor: "every agent ... can act in conformity with some right and just law, and then it is acting according to its ordained power ... or else it can act beyond or against such a law [*potest agere praeter illam legem vel contra eam*], and in this case its absolute power exceeds its ordained power."[108] The use of the canonists' legal metaphor makes it possible to think of a general system of laws *changing*, in a way that Aquinas's determinative divine judgements could not.[109]

William of Ockham (c. 1285–1347), though frequently presented as the nominalist par excellence, is an extremely ambiguous figure on this issue. Sometimes he speaks in a way similar to Aquinas of the *potentia ordinata* as a series of determinate judgements eternally made by God; in other places he speaks, following Scotus, of God's *potentia ordinata* as a system of general laws.[110] Thus some argue that Ockham's understanding of God's power is the same as that of Aquinas and adamantly opposed to the canonist understanding employed by Scotus,[111] while others see his usage as closer to the canonist one.[112] One can indeed see in Ockham a desire to maintain, along with Aquinas, the stability of the *ordinata* and to deny that God's *potentia absoluta* is ever a mode of action. Thus in *Quodlibeta* VI.1, addressing the question "can a human being be saved without created charity?", Ockham says first that he does not mean by the distinction between absolute and ordained power that there are two powers in God (which would compromise divine simplicity), or that God does anything "inordinately" (*Deus nihil potest facere inordinate*).[113] This would seem to be in agreement with Aquinas. However, as he begins to discuss the question, Ockham adopts Scotus's legal language to speak of what was possible under the Old Law of Israel, and what is possible under the New Law of Christ. Not only is it within God's absolute power to grant eternal life without created grace (even if this never occurs), but God can and *has* altered the general laws that have been decreed according to God's *potentia ordinata,* as in the transition from the Old Law to the New. Then, Ockham uses the example of papal power to illustrate the absolute-ordained distinction: "In the same way, there are some things that the Pope is unable to do in accordance with the laws established by him, and yet he is able to do those things absolutely."[114] This seems to move toward the definition of the canonists and Scotus whereby the *potentia absoluta dei* is a mode of action *praeter legem vel contra legem*.

Ockham clearly exploits the distinction with greater frequency than earlier scholastics, putting it to work on a variety of philosophical and theological problems.[115] And while the difference between Ockham's and Aquinas's understandings of divine power may be slight—perhaps merely a shift in metaphors from judgement to law—it is a significant difference. One might say that whereas for Aquinas the *ordinata* is the expression of God's *potentia absoluta,* in Ockham it becomes the self-imposed rule by which God binds God's *potentia absoluta*. The dialectical relationship of *absoluta* and *ordinata* at the very least initiates a movement toward an understanding of God's ordained power as something that could be overruled by God's absolute power—toward a God who can and does act "inordinately."[116] By the end of the fourteenth century, Pierre d'Ailly has identified God's *potentia ordinata* with the "natural" and God's *potentia absoluta* with the "supernatural" or "miraculous."[117] The miraculous becomes a manifestation of God's absolute power erupting into the normal order of things. What Heiko Oberman says of Gabriel Biel is also applicable to many later scholastic thinkers:

> The realm of the *potentia absoluta* is not merely hypothetical and the sum of all noncontradictory possibilities. It is also founded on conclusions drawn from a few deeds which God in fact performed, according to biblical authority, when he deviated from the laws now in force, the *potentia ordinata*.[118]

The general trend of the nominalist understanding of divine omnipotence correlates with an understanding of human freedom in a way that initially seems surprising. One would think that the expansion of divine power in the form of an unbridled, nonhypothetical *potentia absoluta* would consequently cause the sphere of human power to shrink. In fact, the opposite appears to have been the case. In Aquinas, God's ordered power is the detailed scripting of events in accord with divine reason; in nominalism it is the establishment of general laws that human beings can know (if only through divine revelation) and within which they can operate with a limited but "pure" autonomy. Aquinas presents an account of causality in which divine and human agency do not need to be segregated in order to preserve genuine human freedom, claiming that the immediate determination of all things by divine providence did not imply necessity, since the categories of necessity and contingency are concerned with proximate causes, not the primary causality of providence.[119] As David Burrell puts it, "On Aquinas' analysis, the power which rational creatures have to move themselves does not cease to be originative by the fact that the power must itself be moved."[120] Nominalism offers a more clearly delineated sphere of human freedom in which rational creatures act *ex puris naturalibus* as what Oberman describes as God's "covenant partners" to whom grace will be given if they do what is in them (*facere quod in se est*).[121] The distinction between absolute and ordered power becomes, in Oberman's words, a "dome" that "shuts out the world of God's non-realized possibilities and provides room on the inside for man's own realm, in which he, as the image of God, thinks and acts in freedom."[122]

As Hans Blumenberg reads the role of nominalism in the creation of modernity, there is an irony in the way in which the absolute sovereignty of God produces a liberation of the human will. As reason is blinded, the will becomes increasingly free and faith becomes its rationally ungrounded movement. Blumenberg writes, "Under the enormous pressure of the demands made upon it by theology, the human subject begins to consolidate itself, to take on a new overall condition, which possesses, in relation to ambushes set by the hidden absolute will, something like the elementary attribute of the atom, that it cannot be split up or altered."[123] This atomistic subject eventually becomes the agent of modernity's project of human self-assertion. As Louis Dupré puts it, nominalism's voluntarist account of God "prepared the modern concept of moral autonomy in presenting the divine lawgiver as a model for the human one. Even as God's essence consists in unrestricted, self-sustaining power, so is the person a self-sufficient center in his own right."[124]

All of this brings us back to "nominalism" *per se*—the denial that universals have any extra-mental ontological status. Certainly recent scholarship is correct in drawing attention to the nominalist use of the distinction between God's *potentia absoluta* and God's *potentia ordinata*. However, this distinction, and the consequent understanding of divine and human freedom, is not unrelated to nominalism's emphasis on particulars. To put it perhaps oversimply, as the *potentia absoluta dei* increases in importance as an explanatory category, the world created through the *potentia ordinata dei* comes to be seen not as an immanently structured whole, but a collection of particulars that occur together by the divine *fiat*.[125] Each particular is what it is independent of its relation to any other particular. As Ockham puts it, "every absolute thing that is distinct in place and subject from another absolute thing can by God's power exist when that other absolute thing is destroyed."[126] This radical dependence of entities (rather than the order of entities) upon God means their radical *in*dependence from each other. Amos Funkenstein notes that for nominalism, "'[o]rders' of all kinds are connotative, not denotative notions: God creates only *things*, and real things can always exist without each other; hence statements about aggregates of things, about structures and natural sequences, can never be much more than protocol statements without any intrinsic necessity."[127] The category of relation, and therefore of order, has no extra-mental status.

Ockham himself acknowledged that his position on relation was open to the accusation "that those who speak thus undo the substantial connection of the universe," though he did not believe the charge held.[128] Whether, materially speaking, Ockham's position does in fact undo "substantial connection" is debatable; what is clear is that Ockham proceeds in such a way that the contingency of the created order is foregrounded in order to ensure both divine and human freedom, yet it also introduces a notion of the arbitrary exercise of divine sovereignty. This arbitrary sovereignty is no more intelligible than blind chance, which, as Blumenberg notes, will eventually come to replace it.[129]

It is very tempting to seek a direct line running between the consolidation of the atomistic subject under the pressure of divine absolutism and Ockham's social thought. But the issue of the connection between Ockham's theological works (almost all written before 1328) and his political writings (all written after 1324) is a vexing one. Ockham himself seems to make no reference in his political writings to any sort of "nominalistic" philosophical or theological grounding. While this in itself might be philosophically and theologically significant, any direct connections between the two bodies of writings must be inferred.[130] Still, I believe it is possible to discern a certain homology between the two.

Ockham has been described, no doubt anachronistically, as a "constitutional liberal," and Blumenberg notes that the nominalist God, who restricts himself to the *potentia ordinata*, is "like a partially constitutional monarch."[131] While one should be careful about too close an assimilation between Ockham's views on divine power and his views on the powers of earthly rulers,[132] it certainly seems possible that the use and abuse of political and ecclesiastical power that Ockham experienced shaped his reflections on divine power, and vice versa. More importantly, Ockham's thought is typical of late medieval anxiety over an increasing absoluteness and arbitrariness of power and the attempt to limit that power through law. Ockham himself uses the example of the powers of the pope to illustrate the distinction between God's absolute and ordained powers. This illustrative example, probably dating from the autumn of 1323, is particularly interesting in light of events five years later, when Ockham joined Michael of Cesena, the Minister General of the Franciscans, in breaking with Pope John XXII over the question of the poverty of Christ and the apostles. One might also note that the early fourteenth-century England in which Ockham lived had seen the Ordinances of 1311, in which a king who was perceived as irrational and unreliable, Edward II, had his absolute royal powers bound by ordinances imposed on him by the aristocracy, though under the legal fiction of royal self-binding.[133] While one cannot ascribe Ockham's position on divine and human power to these events, we should at least note that Ockham's milieu was one characterized by the relatively new phenomenon of rulers, both temporal and spiritual, who possessed power of sufficient scope to make absolute sovereignty a real possibility. This also made the abuse of power threatening in a new way. Dupré notes that "[o]ne of the immediate consequences [of the voluntarist conception of freedom] was that the will of the lawgiver, rather than the intrinsic rationality of the law, determined the legal order."[134] In a world in which sovereign power was seen as unbounded by any intrinsic reason, that power must be extrinsically bound and limited in its exercise by will so as to secure some measure of private freedom for those subject to that power.[135]

Indeed, there is a sense in which Ockham's understanding of the human creature's freedom beneath the "dome" of the *ordinata* is analogous to a citizen's private freedom within the confines of the law in a liberal social order. Peter Fitzpatrick argues that "the predominant story of modern law, one told now in the perspective of the nation-state, attributes precedence to the god of will and revelation."[136] The formal sovereignty of the nominalist God is the metaphysical image underlying the formal sovereignty of the king who imposes positive law through an act of will. The omnipotent royal will can do anything, but it does not do everything, reserving a "'private' domain of the subject." Fitzpatrick goes on to note:

> So, law's power of positive and universal determination turns, as it were, against social relations to which law was once integrally tied. Law constitutes and empowers the realm of so-called civil privatism which replaces the myriad "public" realms of pre-modern regulation.[137]

Ockham's political position is not one of radical individualism, but rather, as Arthur McGrade characterizes it, a "pre-political" corporatism. He still understands Christianity as communal, but it is a part of something analagous to the modern notion of civil society (indeed, Ockham may well be helping to develop that notion) and thus not political. McGrade writes:

> it is impossible to describe Ockhamist political institutions as purely conventional constructions of permanently isolated individuals. . . . In both suitable and adverse conditions, however, the specifically

political component in human affairs, the apparatus of law and government, will be distinct from and secondary in value to the larger human *corpus* which it regulates.[138]

In other words, human sociality is something that is in principle separable from the political, rooted in human sentiments of affinity, not unlike Victor Turner's notion of *communitas*. According to Ockham, in the pre-political community established by Christ among his followers, Christ denies rule to his apostles, "not only worldly rule that is tyrannical, but also rule which is just, legitimate, and secular."[139] In practice one still needs government to exercise a regulative, coercive function, but this political aspect of community must be "secularized" in the sense of being removed from the jurisdiction of Christians *as* Christians. It does not in any positive sense move one toward the good, but simply regulates conflicts, particularly through the punishment of evildoers. Its very *secularity* serves its minimal function of punishment, because it can coerce evildoers more severely, being freed from the constraints imposed upon the apostles' successors.[140] Ockham does not propose eliminating rule or hierarchy; he simply denies it any positive moral or religious significance.[141] We see here the lineaments of the distinction that we saw in Weber between, on the one hand, the violence-wielding, pragmatic state and, on the other hand, the value-bearing and essentially peaceful civil society.

In nominalism we see displayed most vividly a complex set of relationships by which a certain image of divine power both mirrors and is mirrored by particular understandings of human autonomy, the nature of ecclesial and political community, the relationship between knowledge of God and knowledge of the world, and ultimately the nature of power itself. This complex of interlocking elements constitutes what we might call the metaphysical image of modernity, in which order finds its foundation not in itself, but in the will of those with the power to instantiate and maintain a particular order through the arrangement of discrete bodies.[142] Of course, as the modern world developed it came to see that the God of absolute power was superfluous, cordoned off as he was by the "dome" of the sublunar order, and mirrored as he was by the human subject. But the shape of the metaphysical image of modernity is as resolutely "theological" as that of the metaphysical image of feudal organicism. What Julian offers us, and what we shall proceed to explore in the remaining chapters, is a metaphysical image that is neither that of feudalism nor that of modernity.

2

"I Desyred a Bodely Sight"

> The Cross of Christ is the only source of light that is bright
> enough to illumine affliction.
> —Simone Weil[1]

Julian's *Revelation of Love* speaks of the divine nature in a way that stands in stark contrast both to the feudal account of order and to the nominalist account of freedom, for it discerns God's nature from the divine wisdom and love displayed in Jesus Christ. God's power is neither enshrined in a putatively natural order of human subjugation nor bound to an arbitrarily posited order. Rather, it is structured as it is revealed, and it is revealed in all its fullness in the infinite compassion of Jesus.[2] The power of God is coextensive with God's redemptive desire; or, as Julian says, "as myghty and as wyse as god is to saue man, as wyllyng he is [God is as willing as he is powerful and wise to save humanity]" (40.44). In her belief that God's power is not contentless omnipotence, but rather a capacity with a particular structure and orientation, Julian is harkening back to a theological vision older than nominalism.[3] As Louis Dupré notes, "spiritual attitudes change at a slower pace than most cultural transformations do."[4] Yet she develops a theology that is not simply a repetition of the *mythos* of feudalism, in which society is eternally fixed by God in the three orders of lords, clergy, and peasants, but presents something different in its vision of human unity. The counter-*mythos* of Christ's kingdom that Julian imagines in the inter-space between feudalism and modernity is mapped onto the contours of her particular vision of the crucified *Corpus Christi*, which forms the backdrop of her revelations or "showings."

In this chapter I will explore the significance of Julian's language of "bodily sight" as a way of showing both the significance for her theology of the humanity of Jesus in overcoming the division between "affective" and "contemplative" pieties, and the particular understanding that she has of what it means to "read" her showings. Julian speaks of bodily seeing in such a way as to put forth a participatory model of knowing, in which there is a mutual interpenetration of subject and object. In this knowing by participation, stress can be placed *both* on the fullness of God's revelation in Christ *and* on the unknowability of that fullness. The incomprehensibility of God lies not in God's hiddenness, but in the fullness of God's revelation in the paradoxical sign of the crucified. Julian provides a way quite different from nominalism of understanding the omnipotence of God as a power revealed in the weakness of the cross.

A. THE HUMANITY OF CHRIST

It is commonly accepted that in the later Middle Ages there was an increased emphasis, in both theology and devotion, on the humanity of Christ.[5] In theology, Anselm's *Cur Deus Homo?* argued that it was the *human* nature of Christ that was crucial in our salvation, for it was by virtue of his human nature that he was able to act as our representative before God.[6] We also find Aquinas saying that it is the "flesh [*caro*]" of Christ "and the mysteries accomplished therein [*et mysteria in ea perpetrata*]" that is both instrumental and exemplary cause of grace.[7] In both of these cases the relative emphasis is on Christ as a human agent rather than as the divine pantocrator.

Similarly in devotional literature, one sees, also beginning with Anselm, an emphasis on affective devotion to the humanity of Christ. In his widely circulated and much imitated prayers and meditations, we find a voice expressing the devotion to Christ's crucified humanity that would become so typical of late medieval religion.[8] Contemplating vivid imaginings of Christ's suffering served to heighten the sense of Christ's love and the self's unworthiness, so as to produce a response of what, at least since Gregory the Great, was called "compunction": a divinely inspired piercing of the heart by sorrow for sin and longing for God.[9] This "affective piety" was propagated, particularly by the Franciscans, through vernacular aids to such devotion, often translations of the pseudo-Bonaventurian *Meditationes vitae Christi*, that catalogued in minute detail the dying agonies of Christ so as to arouse a response of compunction in the reader, a response by which one subjectively appropriated the objective work of Christ.[10] There is an insistent emphasizing in these meditations not simply of Christ's human nature, but of the embodied quality of that nature, and the suffering of that body, and of bodily suffering of the one meditating as a response to it.

In addition to the theological and devotional aspects, there is also a third aspect of the medieval emphasis on the humanity of Christ: Christ as a model for imitation. There is clearly an element of *imitatio Christi* in affective piety, in which the experience of compunction mirrors the sufferings of Christ on the cross that are recollected in meditation.[11] However, there is another, less frequently identified, mode of Christ as exemplar, in which it is not Christ's sufferings that are exemplary, but his prophetic activity. This can be seen in the early Franciscan movement, whose members took the poverty of Jesus, and its implicit social criticism, as the norm for their common life. After the controversy over the nature of Franciscan poverty and the condemnation of the "radical" or "Spiritual" Franciscans, this particular way of understanding the imitation of Christ became suspect, associated not only with the Franciscan Spirituals but with other condemned groups, such as the Waldensians and the Cathars.[12] Yet the imitation of Christ as prophet and even, to speak anachronistically, as social critic does not disappear entirely. As David Aers has recently argued, we can find in various texts by Wyclif, the Lollards, and Langland an emphasis on the humanity of Christ that highlights his prophetic role as a critic of the political and religious establishment rather than his sufferings on the cross.[13] Aers notes that the affective piety promoted by the leaders of the church did not completely ignore Jesus the prophet, but "it certainly sidelined that Jesus through its intense concentration on Passion, crucifixion, and the tortured body."[14] Similarly, while figures like Wyclif do not ignore Christ's passion, they refuse to separate it from his life, seeing his execution at the hands of the Roman and Jewish leaders as intrinsically linked to his ministry as a prophet.[15]

We can see that the historical, bodily humanity of Christ was an object of intense interest in the late Middle Ages that functioned in a variety of ways, and it is not easy to pull the various strands together. In any particular figure one is liable to find diverse and even divergent elements. This is certainly true of Julian. In what follows we shall see that Julian's approach is rooted in the strongly somatic tradition of affective piety: Jesus' humanity is significant for her because it entails bodiliness, and thus the ability to suffer pain. Yet Julian goes beyond the affective tendency to turn Christ's body into an icon of *pathos*, a kind of catalyst for meditation on one's sinfulness. Rather it is Jesus' crucified body that Julian "reads" as her revelatory text; what is primary is not the subjective response aroused by meditation on Christ's body, but the message of love that is revealed there. In this "textual" understanding of Christ's body, Julian moves away from the experiential emphasis of affective piety, yet we shall see that she does not succumb to the "contemplative" temptation to consign all that is sensual and historical to a merely preparatory stage of prayer. In a way at once like and different from Francis of Assisi, we find in Julian's use of the embodied humanity of Christ a stubborn refusal to submit to any account of divine power that turns our eyes away from the revelation of divine power as love shown in the weakness of the cross. And in her constant attention to her "onehede of cheryte with alle my evyn cristen [unity of love with all my fellow Christians]" we see this love displayed not simply as an individual's consolation amidst the brute forces of a heartless world, but as the social bond that grounds "the lyfe of alle mankynd that shalle be savyd [the life of all humanity who will be saved]" (9.10–11). Salvation depends on incorporation into and union within the suffering, generative body of Christ, and this incorporation and union is as much "political" as it is "spiritual."

B. BODILY SEEING

The agony of two bodies features prominently at the outset of Julian's visionary experience of 1373. The first of these bodies is Julian's own. Tortured by a sickness for which she had once prayed, Julian's body lies for three days at the boundary between life and death. The second of these bodies is Christ's, specifically the representation of Christ's body that hangs upon the cross that is set before her by the priest who comes to attend her dying. The drama of redemption upon which Julian will meditate for the rest of her life is performed in the space established by the intersection of these two bodies in pain.

1. Three Requests

Julian writes at the outset of both the short text and the long text that she had desired "thre gyftes by the grace of God [three gifts by the grace of God]." The first was "mynd of the passion [recollection of the passion]," the second was "bodily sicknes," and the third was the gift of three "woundes": contrition, compassion, and ardent longing for God (2.5–46). She had asked for these things at some time in her youth (2.38–39) and the first two had passed from her mind, though the third "dwellid contynually [dwelled continually]." In all three of her desires there is a startling physicality, predicated on a view of bodies as malleable, transformable realities, a view that blurs the line between soul and body. This view is not, of course, peculiar to Julian; the author of the *Ancrene Wisse*, a widely disseminated guide for female recluses, notes the close connection between soul and body: "through the soul's sublimity, the flesh shall become very light, lighter than the wind is and brighter than the sun."[16] The traditional picture of medieval Christian culture as animated by a hatred of the body is far too simple.[17] Bodies, closely entwined with the soul, were indeed a source of temptation and a drag upon the soul, but they were also a means by which the soul could be transformed for the better. This ambivalence is captured by the *Ancrene Wisse*:

> Though the flesh is our enemy, we are commanded to uphold it. We must cause it grief as it very often deserves, but not destroy it altogether, since however weak it is, it is so joined and so tightly fixed to our precious soul, God's own image, that we could easily kill the one with the other.[18]

To work on the body through fasting and other ascetic practices is to work on the soul. As Talal Asad characterizes the medieval view: "Disciplined gesture is thus not merely a technique of the body . . . it is also the proper organization of the soul—of understanding and feeling, desire and will."[19] As mentioned earlier, affective piety in particular focused on bodily practices, engaged in contemplation of the bodily humanity of Jesus, and sought bodily manifestations of God's activity within the soul, whether in "private" sensations such as a burning feeling in the breast or the hearing of angelic song,[20] or more "public" phenomena such as stigmata, levitation, miraculous elongation of the body, or the exuding of healing liquids.[21] There is thus a kind of knowledge of God that is not so much an epistemological event as it is a reflux upon the soul of a corporeal transformation that is effected through bodily events. Despite constant warnings from spiritual writers not to place too much emphasis on such extraordinary phenomena[22] or to engage in extreme forms of corporal penance, the body was still considered an integral part of the life of the spirit. As Caroline Walker Bynum says of this affective piety: "In such piety, body is not so much a hindrance to the soul's ascent as the opportunity for it. Body is the instrument upon which the mystic rings changes of pain and delight."[23] Even when dead, the bodies of the holy were venerated, traded and sold, and used to effect miraculous cures; it was as if the holiness or merits of the saint had saturated the material stuff of their bodies. This view was not restricted to women or to "popular piety" but was embodied in such official forms as the requirement that every altar have a relic in it.[24] Theologians toiled over questions of embodiment such as the nature of the material continuity of our present bodies with the bodies we will receive in the general resurrection at Christ's return.[25] What one might call "somatic" religion was the common, though not uncontroversial, spiritual currency of the day.

All this should be kept in mind when thinking about Julian's three desires. Julian's first request is for "mynd of the passion [recollection of the passion]," in the form of "a bodely sight." She desires this so as to "haue more knowledge of the bodily paynes of our saviour [have more knowledge of the bodily pains of our savior]" by suffering with Christ, just as did Mary Magdalene and the others who were at the crucifixion. In the short text she makes clear that in this desire she was not rejecting "the payntyngys of crucyfexes that er made be the grace of god aftere the techynge of haly kyrke to the lyknes of Crystes passyonn [the paintings of crucifixes that are made by the grace of God according to the teachings of holy Church in the likeness of Christ's passion]" (i.16–18) (thus protecting herself from charges of Lollardy), but rather sought something more, something that would put her at the very foot of the cross, so as to obtain a kind of solidarity in suffering: "I wolde have beene one of thame and suffrede with thame [I would have been one with them and suffered with them]" (i.23).[26]

As noted, vernacular devotional literature fostered intense meditation on the humanity of Christ, and particularly on the passion, with the goal of achieving sorrow for sin, through which one attained a kind of subjective appropriation of Christ's objective atoning work by participation in his redemptive pains. The Virgin Mary was the paradigm for this vicarious sharing in Jesus' suffering: gazing with her bodily eye upon her crucified son she feels his passion in her own body. Robert Mannyng's early fourteenth-century English translation of the pseudo-

Bonaventurian *Meditationes de Passione* describes how Christ, hanging on the cross, sees his mother's pain and cries out to God,

> Fadyr! seest þou nat my modyr peynes?
> On þys cros she ys with me,
> Y shulde be crucyfyed, and nat she; . . .
>
> [Father! do you not see my mother's pains?
> She is with me on this cross;
> I should be crucified, and not she; . . .]²⁷

The eye is an avenue not simply of perception, but of communication and communion with Jesus' pain. To gaze with the same intensity of love as Mary upon Christ crucified was to be with him on the cross, to the point where perception lapses over into imitation, so as to reproduce in one's own body his salvific suffering. In the same way, Julian seemed to desire not simply a vivid imagination of Christ's crucifixion, but something akin to actually being present at the historical event, just as Mary was, so as to identify with Christ's suffering. One might go so far as to say that Julian wanted to "see" the crucifixion with her body and not simply with her spiritual eyes; she desired a sensual point of contact. What seems clear is that Julian was requesting some sort of extraordinary knowledge of and sharing in the pains of Jesus on the cross.

Julian's second request, for "a bodily sicknes," is one that she says comes to her mind "with contricion" (2.20). She desires a sickness "so hard as to the death [severe enough to be fatal]" (2.22), so that she and those with her would believe that she was dying, and she would face all the pains of death, "saue the out passing of the sowle [except the departure of the soul]" (2.28–29), in order to be purged of all sin and to serve God more faithfully once she recovered. It is only when Julian actually becomes sick that she seems explicitly to connect her second request to the first, so that the pain of her bodily sickness becomes part of her identification with Christ. Noting that Jesus, out of love, became "deadly man [a mortal person]," she says, "With him I desyred to suffer, liuyng in my deadly bodie, as god would giue me grace [I desired to suffer with him, living in my mortal body, as God would give me grace]" (3.51–52). Her desired sickness is not simply purgative; it is, like her "mynd of the passion [recollection of the passion]," a form of imitation.

Julian seems to have felt that there was something unusual or suspect about these two desires, so she asked for them only on the condition that they were God's will (2.34–38). Certainly "bodily sight" of Christ's passion and near-death experiences were not typical, and along with her requests Julian, at least in retrospect, seems to have brought to God a suitable amount of humility. Her third desire—the threefold request for contrition, compassion, and longing for God—inspired a bit more confidence in her, since it did not go beyond the ordinary teachings of the church. Here we see perhaps a more "spiritualized" version of the kind of somatic identification with Christ sought in the first two desires (though it is still couched in the somatic image of "wounds"), and Julian notes that it is *this* that persists until the time of her sickness; the others pass from her mind. By the time that she actually falls ill, she does not seem to see it as an identification with the suffering of Christ, but simply a painful shortening of her life. Her body goes numb from the waist down and her curate is sent for, to attend her dying.

When he comes and sets a crucifix before her face,[28] her eyes are firmly fixed on heaven (3.20–25), as if she had surpassed her earlier focus on the carnal love of Christ and its physical manifestations.[29] She only consents to look at the crucifix because she figures that she can last longer looking straight ahead rather than up. But when she does this the room grows dark, save for a mysterious light around the image of the cross. This sight seems to set off a kind of sympathetic reaction in Julian, stripping away any misgivings she may have had about something so carnal as the humanity of Christ. First, the numbness extends itself from the lower into the upper part of her body; her breath grows short; and she believes she is about to die. Then, her pain suddenly passes and feeling returns to her upper body. This seems miraculous to Julian, though she still believes that she is going to die. At this point, it occurs to her to ask God for the second of the three wounds, the wound of compassion:

> Then cam sodenly to my mynd that I should desyer the second wound of our lordes gifte and of his grace, that my bodie might be fulfilled with mynd and feeling of his blessed passion, as I had before praied, for I would that his paynes were my paynes, with compassion and afterward langyng to god.
>
> [Then it suddenly came to my mind that I should desire the second wound, by our lord's gift and his grace, that my body might be filled

full with recollection and feeling of his blessed passion, as I had prayed before, for I wanted his pains to be my pains, with compassion and, afterward, longing for God.] (3.43–47)

The way she describes this seems to identify this wound of compassion with the more explicitly corporeal quality of the first two desires, which she had forgotten. Presented at what she believes to be the point of death with an image of the suffering Christ, she seeks to obtain the spiritual wound of compassion through the identification of her own tortured body with Christ's. Still, though she desires that her body "might be fulfilled with mynd and feeling of his blessed passion," she goes on to note, "in this I desyred never no bodily sight ne no maner schewing of god [in this I never desired any bodily sight or any kind of revelation from God]" (3.48–49).

But Julian finds what she has not sought. The crucifix in front of her begins to bleed from beneath the crown of thorns. She notes that the blood ran down "hote and freyshely, plentuously and liuely, right as it was in the tyme that the garland of thornes was pressed on his blessed head [hot and fresh, plentiful and full of life, just as it was when the crown of thorns was pressed on his blessed head]" (4.4–6). At the same time that she looks upon the bleeding crucifix, "in the same shewing sodeinly the trinitie fulfilled my hart most of ioy [in the same revelation the Trinity suddenly filled my heart most full of joy]" and she understands this not simply as a showing of Christ's suffering humanity, but of the Trinity, thus establishing a basic hermeneutical principle for all the showings:

> For the trinitie is god, god is the trinitie. The trinitie is our maker, the trinitie is our keper, the trinitie is our everlasting lover, the trinitie is our endless ioy and our bleisse, by our lord Jesus Christ, and in our lord Jesu Christ. And this was shewed in the first syght and in all, for wer Jhesu appireth the blessed trinitie is vnderstand, as to my sight.
>
> [For the Trinity is God, God is the Trinity. The Trinity is our maker, the Trinity is our keeper, the Trinity is our everlasting lover, the Trinity is our endless joy and our bliss, by our lord Jesus Christ and in our lord Jesus Christ. And this was revealed in the first vision and in all, for where Jesus appears the blessed Trinity is understood, as I see it.] (4.9–16)

Julian seems to be saying that at the same time that she has a "bodily sight" of Christ crucified, something else—a revelation of the Trinity—

is being shown in some other mode, a mode that is "ghostly" or spiritual. And as she proceeds with her description of the first revelation, especially in the long text, it seems that the bodily sight of the crucified Jesus forms a backdrop, a horizon, against which various "ghostly" revelations are displayed: the virgin Mary (4.28–40), "a little thing, the quantitie of a haselnott [a little thing, the size of a hazelnut]" (5.9–33), a teaching on the use of "meanes [intermediaries]" in prayer (6.1–28), and so forth. Julian notes, "And in alle þat tyme that he schewd thys that I haue now seyde in gostely syght, I saw the bodely syght lastyng of the pituous bledyng of the hede [The whole time that he showed in spiritual sight what I have described, I saw the bodily sight of the piteous bleeding of the head continue]" (7.12–14).

2. Seeing Jesus

What sort of vision was Julian in fact having? What was the nature of her "bodily" sight? On the face of it, Julian is "seeing something," but what is distinctively "bodily" about these sights? How can we understand this category?

At the end of her description of the first showing, Julian notes, "All this was shewed by thre partes, that is to sey by bodyly syght, and by worde formyde in my vnderstondyng, and by goostely syght [All this was revealed in three parts, that is to say by bodily sight, by words formed in my understanding, and by spiritual sights]" (9.29–30; cf. 73.1–3). Julian seems to be trying to give some order to what is taking place in the showing. These categories are perhaps an indirect derivation of Augustine's scheme in *De Genesi ad Litteram* for classifying prophetic visions as corporeal, spiritual, and intellectual.[30] Yet Julian's seeming precision is deceptive, and readers who attempt to apply these categories too strictly are inevitably frustrated by showings such as that of the Virgin Mary in chapter four, which Julian describes as "ghostly in bodily lykenes [spiritual in bodily likeness]," or by the way in which Julian seems occasionally to blithely ignore her scheme and simply say "I saw" or "it appeared to me," never specifying in what mode the vision occurred.[31] As Nicholas Watson has noted, Julian's use of this classificatory scheme is probably simply an attempt to connect her visions with a visionary tradition so as to reassure her readers (and perhaps herself).[32] It does not have the kind of precision that many interpreters have ascribed to it, and it can be misleading in attempting to understand the nature of the showings.

Yet Julian's use of the language of "bodily sight" is not indiscriminate. In using it she is indicating both a *mode* of seeing—something involving physical sensation, though in a way that to her is clearly different from the usual perception of a material object[33]—and an *object* of vision—Christ's body, specifically the body on the crucifix that the priest has placed before her. Julian speaks of "bodily sight," without further qualification, *only* in reference to this specific representation of Jesus' body and the various permutations that she sees it undergo.[34] This accords with Julian's first desire as originally stated: she seeks a vision of Jesus and his suffering (2.8–20). And Julian's first description of what is happening to her, which she offers to the "relygyous person [i.e., priest]" who visits her between the fifteenth and sixteenth showings, is simply, "The crosse that stode before my face, me thought it bled fast [I thought the cross that stood before my face bled profusely]" (66.16–18). Nothing else is mentioned.

For readers familiar with *A Revelation of Love*, this claim will no doubt strike them as mistaken, in large part because most commentators have assumed that what Julian means by "bodily sight" is primarily a mode of subjective apprehension—a mode that engages, or seems to engage, the senses—which leads them to try to categorize any "vision" Julian has as a bodily sight. Thus Brant Pelphrey says that the vision of the "hazelnut" was "probably a corporeal vision," though Julian in fact nowhere describes it as such.[35] Pelphrey also lists as "corporeal" her dream of demonic attack in the sixteenth revelation,[36] though she clearly states that this was different in kind from any other revelation she experienced (67.2–12). Similarly, he describes as "corporeal" the smoke and fire that Julian sees, on the grounds that she says, "I went it had been a bodely fyer [I thought it was a bodily/actual fire]" (67.18–19), but her point seems to be that she was mistaken about this. A bit later in the same revelation she speaks of "bodely heet [bodily heat]" and "bodely talkyng [bodily talking]" (69.3–4), but this does not seem to indicate the same thing as a "bodily sight," not least because she is speaking of a demonic temptation and not a divine showing. She does describe her vision of the virgin Mary during the first revelation as "ghostly in bodily lykenes [spiritually in bodily likeness]" (4.29), but notes later that in fact during that time the bodily sight of the bleeding of Christ's head persisted and that all the other showings were "gostely [spiritual]" (7.12–14).

If one looks carefully at what Julian describes as bodily sights, it seems that they were in fact rather obscure transformations associated with the crucifix upon which she was gazing, what Nicholas Watson describes as "a disparate series of glimpses of Christ's Passion, strung like beads along her life-saving gaze at a crucifix, and interspersed with other, more abstract sights, as well as with a few pregnant words passed from Christ to her and sometimes back again."[37] In other words, the bodily sights are distinguished from the other sights because they are of Christ crucified and are closely related to the material object of the crucifix, not because they simply involve the senses, nor because they are particularly vivid or detailed or even realistic. In fact, some of the bodily sights have an exaggerated quality, such as the blood pouring out from underneath the crown of thorns like rain running off of the eaves of a house in a heavy rainstorm.[38]

At the same time, Julian does seem to be indicating that there is something distinctive about the *manner* in which Christ's body is perceived. It is as if there were a resonance between Julian's body and the body of Christ on the cross, communicated through the medium of sight. Just before the bodily sights commence, Julian is in extreme pain and is convinced that she is about to die. Her body is numb from the waist down and her curate has set the crucifix before her face. As she looks at it her sight begins to fail, and she can see nothing but the crucifix. Her upper body begins to grow numb and she believes she is at the point of death. Then, "sodenly all my paine was taken from me, and I was as hole, and namely in þe over parte of my bodie, as I was befor [suddenly all my pain was taken from me, and I was as whole, particularly in the upper part of my body, as I was before]" (3.35–37). At this point it occurs to Julian to ask "that my bodie might be fulfilled with mynd and feeling of his blessed passion [that my body might be filled full with recollection and feeling of his blessed passion]" (3.44–45). She identifies this as the second wound for which she asked, the wound of compassion, but it is also the first of the gifts that she said she had desired, "mynd of the passion" (2.5). For Julian, "compassion" takes the quite literal form of sharing in Christ's passion by having her body "fulfilled"—literally "filled full"—with Christ's pain: "for I would that his paynes were my paynes [for I wanted his pains to be my pains]" (3.46). Though Julian notes "in this I desyred never no bodily sight ne no maner schewing of God [in this I never desired any bodily sight or any kind of revelation from God]" (3.48–49), it is at this point that Julian has her first bodily sight of the crucifix bleeding from underneath the crown of thorns.

Thus if there is a particular "mode" of seeing that can be described as "bodily sight," it is one that involves the physical displacement of Julian's pain by Christ's. Julian does not mention feeling Christ's pains in her account of the first showing, and at the beginning of her description of the sixteenth showing she refers back to her earlier statement that all her pain was taken from her and further notes "of whych payne I had no grefe ne no dysesses as long as þe xv shewynges lastyd in shewyng [I had no grief or discomfort from this pain as long as the fifteen revelations continued to be shown]" (66.7–9). Yet despite what she says, Julian seems to have continued to experience pain, for in her recounting of the eighth showing she tells us that "the shewyng of Cristes paynes fylled me fulle of peynes [the revelation of Christ's pain filled me full of pain]." But the pain is no longer *her* pain, rather it is *Christ's*: "in alle thys tyme of Christes presens, I felte no peyne, but for Cristes paynes [during the entire time of Christ's presence, I felt no pain except for Christ's pain]" (17.52–53). Following the same dynamics of beholding, when Christ's demeanor changes to one of joy, Julian's changes as well: "The channgyng of hys blessyd chere channgyd myne, and I was as glad and mery as it was possible [the changing of his blessed appearance changed mine, and I was as glad and merry as possible]" (21.7–9). Similarly, after the fifteenth showing Julian says "alle was close, and I saw no more [all was concealed, and I saw no more]," soon after which "sodeynly all my body was fulfyllyd with sycknes lyke as it was before . . . and as a wrech [I] mornyd hevyly for feelyng of my bodely paynes . . . [suddenly my whole body was filled full of sickness like it was before . . . and like a wretch (I) mourned greatly because of my bodily pains that I felt . . .]" (66.9–15).

There thus seems to be a close association with "bodily seeing" and the experience of Christ's physical sensations. In a sense, one can say that this conforms to the basic medieval model of knowledge of sensible objects, in which it was commonly thought that the image or phantasm of the object perceived was, as it were, brought into the perceiver through the senses.[39] Already in Julian's day, this model of perception through participation was undercut by the nominalist approach to perception as a matter of efficient causality.[40] But Julian, at least in her bodily sights of Jesus crucified, retains a participative model of knowing. Looking upon Christ's passion, she is possessed by his suffering in such a way that her suffering is displaced, and when Christ's suffering is transformed to joy, she participates in that joy as well. One might say that Julian's bodily seeing is the adequation of her disease-wracked body to the object of her perception: Christ's suffering, generative, crucified body.[41]

Perhaps most significant about Julian's bodily seeing is that for her, Christ remains irreducibly "other"—thus the significance of the association of the bodily sights with the brute materiality of the crucifix—yet at the same time can never be objectified by her gaze. She does not "see" simply with her eyes, but with her entire body. She cannot maintain the distance that the eyes allow, but sees Christ's suffering by participating in it. At the same time, while the otherness of the crucified comes to inhabit her in compassionate intimacy, he still maintains his otherness. The bodily sight is always the sight of another, never Julian's possession.

C. EVENT AND INTERPRETATION

It is impossible, in my judgement, to reconstruct precisely what transpired in May of 1373—what Julian *really* saw in her bodily sight. Further, I believe that the attempt at such a reconstruction fundamentally misunderstands the nature of Julian's revelation by focusing it in the events of those few hours. Julian is quite clear that those events in and of themselves are not of ultimate importance; what matters is the revelation that she is given—the message of the nature and scope of God's merciful love. And Julian does not conceive of that revelation as bounded by her visionary experience in 1373. For Julian, the visions were simply her initiation into a life of seeking and thus of unending "showings," a life in which others could participate as readily as she.

One of the initially puzzling things about Julian's two accounts of her visionary experience is that the earlier short text lacks much of the detailed visual richness of the later long text. One expects that with the passage of twenty or more years there would be considerable development of theological insight from the short text to the long text, as indeed there is, but one would also expect that Julian's remembrance of the visual details of the bodily sights would, if anything, grow dimmer, or at least more stylized. Yet while this is true of certain details of the external circumstances of her visionary experience,[42] the long text's descriptions of her bodily sights are in many cases strikingly more vivid and detailed than those in the short text. Thus in the first showing the short text states laconically that "the bodylye syght lastande of the plentyuouse bledynge of the hede [the bodily sight of the plentiful bleeding of the head persisted]" (v.2–3), whereas the long text adds a description of the great quantity of blood flowing from underneath Jesus' crown of thorns, its thickness and brownness, how it vanished when it reached his brows, and how the roundness of the drops of blood made her think of the scales of a herring (7.14–26). Similarly in her account of the eighth showing, the short text gives a brief account of the drying of Christ's body as it hangs on the cross (x.13–23), whereas the long text elaborates on how at first Christ's tender flesh was torn by the nails and his body sagged under its own weight, almost to the point of falling from the cross, and then began to dry, turning a tawny color, the face being a darker shade than the body (17.1–37). Perhaps the simple explanation is that in composing the short text Julian omitted details that she still recalled and recorded later. Or perhaps Julian was possessed of a particularly morbid imagination that liked to elaborate upon the gorier parts of her memories. In that case, one might claim that such elaborations constitute something of a falsification of the original experience.

But Julian herself offers another explanation. In her account of the "wonderfull example" of the lord and servant, which is entirely absent from the short text yet which forms the pivot upon which the long text turns, she says that she was at the time unable to fully comprehend the meaning of the example, and "sawe and vnderstode that euery shewyng is full of pryvytes [saw and understood that every revelation is full of secrets]" (51.73–74). The revelations or "shewings" are not simply messages delivered to Julian, either for her edification or her sanctification, but rather are images before which she "stode mekyl in onknowyng [stood much in unknowing (i.e., was very confused)]"[43] and around which her entire life is gathered. She goes on to distinguish "thre propertes [three properties]" of the revelation:

> The furst is the begynnyng of techyng that I vnderstode ther in in the same tyme. The secunde is the inwarde lernyng that I haue vnderstonde there in sythen. The thyrd is alle the hole revelation fro the begynnyng to the ende whych oure lorde god of his goodnes bryngyth oftymes frely to the syght of my vnderstondyng.
>
> [The first is the beginning of the teaching that I understood from it at that time. The second is the inward instruction that I have since

understood. The third is the entire revelation from beginning to end, which of his goodness our lord God brings frequently and freely to the sight of my understanding.] (51.76–80)

Having distinguished these three, however, Julian goes on to say:

And theyse thre be so onyd, as to my vnderstondyng, that I can nott nor may deperte them. And by theyse thre as one I haue techyng wherby I ow to beleue and truste in oure lorde god, that of the same goodnesse that he shewed it and for the same end, ryght so of the same goodnes and for the same end he shall declare it to vs when it is his wyll.

[And these three are so united, as I understand it, that I neither can nor may separate them. And by these three as one I have instruction as to how I ought to believe and trust in our lord God, that from the same goodness and for the same purpose that he revealed it, so too from the same goodness and for the same purpose he shall declare it to us when he so wills.] (51.80–85)

Julian spells out here the mutual indwelling of the three elements of the revelation as analogous to the *perichoresis* of the persons of the Trinity—"theyse thre as one." The event of the visionary experience of 1373 is for Julian distinguishable but inseparable from her subsequent reflection on it, and neither of these is separable from the significance of God's entire revelatory activity, which extends beyond the confines of a few hours in May of 1373 to encompass and shape Julian's entire life.

As Nicholas Watson has noted, text and commentary in Julian's writing are perhaps provisionally distinguishable, but not ultimately separable. Watson notes: "This combination—of a format that always seems *about* to be that of text and accompanying commentary, with slippages between the two that continually undo this distinction—is . . . a virtual hallmark of Julian's exegetical practice."[44] Julian's initial bodily sight passes and she is left with "neyther sygne ne tokyn where by I myght know it [neither sign nor token whereby I might know it]" (70.19–20). The revelation as a whole must be renewed constantly by Julian's clinging to it in faith, which for her is not so much unquestioning trust as it is a constant seeking to overcome "oure owne blyndnesse and our gostely enemys within and withoute [our own blindness and our spiritual enemies both within and without]"

(71.6–7). This corresponds to Julian's emphasis on sight as a means of knowing God (though one must take into account the nature of "seeing" as discussed above) and on sin as "blindness" that constantly threatens knowledge of God. For Julian, what she sees—Christ's body—is like an inexhaustibly detailed landscape that requires more than a lifetime to comprehend, and her subsequent interpretation of what she saw is always more seeing, by which the revelation is shown again and again "with more fullehed with the blessyd lyght of his precyous loue ... [with more fullness in the light of his precious love ...]" (70.32).

One might say that this "text" of Julian's visionary experience of the bleeding corpus on the crucifix, and the locutions and insights that cluster around it, is one that proliferates through her interpretation of it, to the point where it is perhaps misleading even to speak of the interpretation of an experience, as if there were some sort of "pure" experience that is subsequently transformed (for better or for worse) by an interpretive clarification. Rather, the process initiated in May of 1373 extends through the whole of Julian's life, becoming richer and more complex. Julian's *Revelation of Love* is not a link in a signifying chain that delivers to the reader a message from Julian, who has received a message from God. It is rather the textual trace of the process of Julian's constitution as a particular kind of subject before God, a trace that implicates the reader in that process, thus seeking to create an appropriate recipient of its message in the very activity of delivering the message.[45] This is why the seemingly simple meaning of the revelation—love—can only be stated at the end of the book (86.20). Julian, and her readers, must become capable of hearing properly such a message. Experience and interpretation are alike encompassed in a practice of prayer into which Julian is initiated by God and into which Julian initiates those who take up her text.

If such a description of the action of the text is persuasive, it may help us short-circuit various debates over the relationship of interpretation and experience that sometimes arise in the interpretation of mystical texts. These debates are often couched in terms that presume the circumscription of the field of "consciousness" as the site of both experience and interpretation. Disagreements over the role of subsequent interpretation in accounts of mystical experience for the most part presume that what is at issue is the nature of a particular kind of consciousness.[46] Yet "experience" and "consciousness" are not of particular interest to Julian, nor to many of those we call mystics.[47] In Julian's case, the intensely somatic character of her "seeing" and "knowing" makes it impossible to restrict perception and knowledge within the domain of "consciousness." Julian's concern is much more about the content of the revelation as a whole, and how assimilation of its message of love and trust might contribute to the living of a holy life, both for her and her fellow Christians. In other words, the revelation is a process constituted by certain intellectual and bodily practices.[48] "Consciousness," on the other hand, is an interest of post-Cartesian philosophy that some modern interpreters impose on the sources (the mystical texts) by the application of particular rules or analytical procedures.[49] Perhaps then our puzzles over the relationship of "original experience" and "subsequent interpretation" are simply produced by our particular way of using the text of Julian's *Revelation*. If so, this is not in itself an illegitimate undertaking, but I would simply note that it has proved a singularly unfruitful one, at least in part because the text as it comes to us is so resistant to the separation of experience and interpretation. It is all part of what is shown to Julian, thus it is all part of the "original experience." And for us to interpret Julian's text is to find ourselves implicated as participants in her experience: "it is Gods will that ye take it with a gret ioy and likyng as Iesus had shewde it on to you all [it is God's will that you receive it with a great joy and pleasure, as if Jesus had revealed it to you all]."[50]

D. THE ONLY HEAVEN

Julian thus is not interested in the experience of her bodily seeing, but in the body that she sees, and in the cultivation of the form of life necessary for seeing it rightly. Julian's revelation is of the divine nature as revealed in the works of God, for in the sight of Jesus crucified she claims to have been presented with all of the "pryvytes [secrets]" of the Godhead, short of the bliss of heaven. As she says at the very beginning of the long text, along with the revelation of Jesus' crowning with thorns,

> ther in was conteined and specified the blessed trinitie with the incarnacion and the vnithing between god and mans sowle, with manie fayer schewynges and techynges of endlesse wisdom and

loue, in which all the schewynges that foloweth be grovndide and ioyned.

[in this was contained and specified the blessed Trinity with the incarnation and the uniting between God and man's soul, with many fair revelations and teachings of endless wisdom and love, in which all the revelations that follow are grounded and joined.] (1.4–7)

The whole of the revelation is contained in the sight of Jesus' suffering humanity, in that it forms the comprehensive horizon that is the *sine qua non* for the other insights. This sight is a continuing source of both consolation and puzzlement to Julian; Jesus' crucified body is the concrete reality to which she clings for solace and the mysterious hieroglyph that she insistently probes and questions. It is a body whose mysteries seem beyond articulation, not because it is beyond words (for it is precisely as the Word of God that Jesus is crucified), but because in the image of the crucified, Julian is presented with what Paul calls the *logos tou staurou* (1 Cor. 1:18), which may be read as both "the word of the cross" and "the crucified Word," God's disarticulated eloquence. As Jean-Luc Marion writes, "On the cross, the Word is killed, but thus is manifested, in a totally paradoxical light, an *other* discourse."[51] This is the language through which God speaks to Julian and to her "evyn cristen." It is the icon of divine love.

1. Neither Affectivity nor Contemplation

For all of the sharp christocentric focus of much medieval devotion, there were countervailing tendencies that sought to moderate the excesses of certain forms of affective piety. In particular, there was a strongly apophatic theology of contemplation that was highly critical of the "experiential" emphasis of piety focused on the passion, with its concern for the subjective response aroused by meditation on the historical humanity of Jesus.[52] In this apophatic theology, such meditation was simply a prelude to a higher form of contemplation that did not focus on images, but put them behind, beneath a "cloud of forgetting" so as to stand before what is famously called "the cloud of unknowing."[53] It was presumed that such higher contemplation was by and large reserved for those living under religious vows, and many devout lay people would never proceed beyond mere meditation on Jesus' historical humanity.[54]

As noted earlier, there are certain indications that, by the time of her visionary experience, Julian herself had come to desire "true contemplation" and had rejected the affective emphasis on Jesus' humanity. Julian says at the end of the second chapter of the long text that the first two of her desires—for bodily sight of the passion and for sickness to the point of death—"passid from my mynd, and the third," her request for the wounds of contrition, compassion, and longing for God, "dwellid contynually [dwelled continually]" (2.45–46). Simon Tugwell makes the interesting suggestion that the first two desires "indicate clearly that at the time Julian's piety was of an affective, devotional kind" and that their passing from her mind "probably reflects a movement away from 'carnal love' of the humanity of Christ towards something supposedly more elevated."[55] This "more elevated" contemplation would be represented in *The Cloud of Unknowing* and Hilton's *The Scale of Perfection*, which are strongly suspicious of extraordinary bodily experiences and present meditation on the humanity of Christ as a necessary but penultimate stage in the spiritual life.

In point of fact, we know very little about developments or changes in Julian's approach to spirituality. However, two things can be pointed out here in support of Tugwell's suggestion. The first suggests something of a shift in Julian's perspective between the composition of the short text and that of the long text. In the short text's account of the revelation of the "little thing" the size of a hazelnut, Julian says that it contains important information for those men and women "that desyres to lyeve contemplatyfele," by which she seems to mean the vowed contemplative life. She goes on to say: "For this es the cause why thaye þat er occupyede wylfullye in erthelye besynes and euermare sekes warldlye wele er nought here of his herte and in sawlle; for thaye love and seekes here ryste in this thynge that is so lytille [For this is the cause why those who are willingly occupied in earthly business and forever seek worldly well-being are not, heart and soul, his heirs, for they love and seek rest here in this thing that is so little]" (iv.42–47).[56] In the long text the references to contemplatives are excised, and rather than singling out those in the world for criticism, Julian simply says "*we* seeke heer rest in this thing that is so little [*we* seek rest here in this thing that is so little]" (5.27, my emphasis). Similarly, when describing the vision of Jesus "mare gloryfyed [more glorified]" in the twelfth showing, the short text says with regard to the vision of Mary, "in this was I lerede that ilke saule contemplatyfe to whilke es gyffen to luke and seke god schalle se hire and pass vnto god by contemplacionn [in this was I taught that each contemplative soul to which it is given to look and seek God shall see her (Mary) and pass on to God by contemplation]" (xiii.26–28). The long text, on the other hand, reads "wher in I was lerned that oure soule shalle nevyr haue reste tylle it come into hym, knowyng that he is full of joye, homely and curteys and blessydfulle and very lyfe [in this I learned that our soul shall never have rest until it comes into him, knowing that he is full of joy, familiar and courteous and blessed and true life]" (26.4–6). Not only does Julian eliminate the reference both to the vision of Mary and to contemplatives, she also transforms the passage so that it no longer speaks of contemplative prayer but of trust in the plentitude of God's life. In other words, the emphasis shifts from the person praying to the attributes of God. These changes would seem to strengthen the impression that at the time of the revelation, and for a considerable period of time afterward (at least until after the composition of the short text), Julian identified with the aspiration of contemplatives rather than of the practitioner of affective piety. They also indicate that between the composition of the two texts Julian had broadened her audience to include all of God's lovers, not just "contemplatives." They perhaps *also* indicate that in the interim she had gained some insight into the ways in which even those who "lyeve contemplatyfele [live contemplative lives]" can "seekes here ryste in this thynge that is so lytille," and saw that the focus of the Christian life should not be the act of contemplation but its object. Julian has taken up the contemplative critique of the experiential emphasis of affective piety and radicalized it, so as to turn it back upon the contemplative tradition itself.

The other point to mention is the discussion of "meanes," which Julian adds in chapter six of the long text. Julian begins with a critique of "the custome of our praier [our customary way of praying]" and how "we vse for vnknowing of loue to make menie meanes [we use many intermediaries because we do not know love]" (6.4–5). Here Julian speaks of the various devotions and intercessory prayers to the precious blood, Jesus' passion, etc., as well as devotions to Mary, the Holy Cross, and the saints (6.12–22), that were popular in the Middle Ages. Criticism of such devotions might be found in any number of "advanced" spiritual texts. But Julian does not criticize devotional religion as somehow lower, to be abandoned for something supposedly higher. Her concern is that we not let the "meanes" we employ make us think that we have somehow to persuade God to help us. Rather than being implements with which we may pry favors out of God, these intermediaries are humble signs of God's desire for us. Julian says of the use of these intermediaries, "it is to litle and not ful worshippe to god; but in his goodnes is all the hole, and ther fayleth right nought [it is too little and not the highest worship of God, but his goodness encompasses them all, and there nothing fails]" (6.9–11). As Simon Tugwell puts it, "they are not ways of procuring God's favour, they are precisely gifts of his favour."[57] If these intermediaries employed in devotional religion are acts of divine condescension, the proliferation of devotions and intermediaries can be seen as a sign of the abundance of God's love: "For the meanes that the goodnes of god hath ordeineth to helpe vs be full faire and many [For the intermediaries that God's goodness has ordained to help us are very lovely and many]." And chief among the "means" that God employs is "the blessed kynde that he toke of the maiden [the blessed nature that he took of the Virgin]" (6.22–25). The incarnation of God in human flesh is for Julian a sign of divine humility, God's willingness to come to us, so that we might be enclosed in God.

It is only through God's goodness, which "is the highest praier, and . . . cometh downe to vs to the lowest party of our need [is the highest prayer and . . . comes down to us in the lowest part of our need]" (6.29–30), that we may come to the vision of God, and the most exalted spiritual state is as much an act of divine condescension as the humblest devotion. This is why we find in Julian little interest in stages of spiritual progress. Though there is a certain resemblance between the three wounds that she requests—contrition, compassion, and longing for God—and various medieval schemes of spiritual progress,[58] one finds, particularly in the long text, that these three become something more akin to recurrent themes in a piece of music, rather than distinct movements; they are enduring aspects of the Christian life, not stages to work through. Julian makes much the same point in her discussions of the experience of woe and weal: in this life, we are in constant alternation between the two, and the pain of this life exists in a kind of simultaneity with the bliss of heaven (15.1–35; 21.1–28).

Julian's lack of interest in stages of spiritual development is of a piece with the shift in emphasis away from the experience of revelation to the object or content of the revelation, which is not an esoteric meaning reserved for higher initiates but the event of Jesus Christ. In the first revelation, Julian speaks of the "grette homelyness [great familiarity]" of God, noting "[b]ut this marvelous homelynesse may no man know in this lyfe, but yf he haue it by specialle schewyng of oure lorde, or of gret plenty of grace inwardly yeven of the holy gost [but no one may know this marvelous familiarity in this life, except by a special revelation of our lord, or by a great plentitude of grace given inwardly by the Holy Spirit]" (7.55–58). This seems at first glance to be designating a "higher" type of contemplative experience, and Julian certainly understands her "schewyng" to be extraordinary and to be an experience that is only had by the grace of God. But she goes on to say that "feyth and beleue with charyte deserue the mede [faith and belief with love deserve the reward]" (7.58–59), and by "faith" Julian seems to mean both *fides qua creditur* (the subjective act of faith by which one believes) and *fides quae creditur* (the content of faith that is believed). This showing does not teach a "higher" knowledge than the content of faith, nor is it an experience that eliminates the need for faith: once the experience is passed, "than fayth kepyth it by grace of the holy goste [faith preserves it by the grace of the Holy Spirit]" (7.64. Cf. 32.51–55; 33.16–17). In other words, both in its content and in its apprehension, the showing "is none other than the feyth, ne lesse ne more [nothing apart from the faith, neither less nor more]" (7.65–66). Julian does not here distinguish, as S. S. Hussey claims, "a more advanced stage of contemplation . . . available not to all but to those who have received infused grace."[59] Rather, she marks an extraordinary grace that is given for the sake of others—in scholastic terminology, *gratia gratis data*.[60] Julian stubbornly refuses to focus her attention on her own contemplative experience, lest this separate her from her fellow Christians.

This is particularly true of her refusal to look "beyond" the humanity of Christ. In her account of the eighth showing, Julian says that she wanted to take her eyes off of the cross before her face, no doubt because "[t]he shewyng of Cristes paynes fylled me fulle of peynes [the showing of Christ's pains filled me full of pains]." But she was afraid to look away for fear of demonic attack. Then she had "a profyr in my reason [a suggestion to my reason]" saying "Loke vppe to hevyn to hys father [look up to heaven to his Father]," and she realized that she had nothing to fear from demons. But Julian still refused the temptation to take her eyes from the cross: "I answeryd inwardly with alle the myght of my soule, and sayd: Nay, I may nott, for thou art my hevyn [I answered inwardly with all the power of my soul, and said: No, I may not, for you are my heaven]." Then she says, "I had levyr a bene in that payne tylle domys day than haue come to hevyn other wyse than by hym [I would rather have been in that pain until the day of judgement than to have come to heaven in any way except by him]" (19.1–14). Julian rejects any path to heaven that would circumvent the humility of God made flesh, including any contemplative or affective "technique" for spiritual advancement. She goes on to say:

> Thus was I lernyd to chese Jhesu for my hevyn, whom I saw only in payne at that tyme. Me lykyd no nother hevyn than Jhesu, whych shalle be my blysse when I come ther. And this hath evyr be a comfort to me, that I chose Jhesu to be my hevyn by his grace in alle this tyme of passion and sorow. And that hath ben a lernyng to me, that I shulde evyr more do so, to chese Jhesu only to my hevyn in wele and in woe.
>
> [Thus was I taught to choose Jesus for my heaven, whom I saw only in pain at that time. I was pleased by no other heaven than Jesus, who shall be my bliss when I am there. And this has continually been a comfort to me, that I chose Jesus to be my heaven by his grace in all this time of suffering and sorrow. And that has been a lesson to me, that I should always do so, to choose only Jesus as my heaven in well-being and in distress.] (19.15–20)

If in fact Julian had rejected or surpassed her earlier devotional aspirations to share in Christ's pains in favor of aspirations to higher contemplation, now she names a new aspiration, which is neither affective nor contemplative, though containing elements of both.

As in contemplative prayer, Julian seeks immediate union with God; as in affective piety, the focus is on the crucified Jesus. As I indicated earlier, Julian takes up and radicalizes the apophatic tradition's critique of experience by turning it against even "elevated" contemplative experience. She realizes that union with God is inseparable from the solidarity of the human race in the humanity of Jesus; there is nothing "higher" than participation in Christ's compassion, for that *is* the divine nature, unfolded in time and space. Thus she speaks of "a grett onyng betwene Crist and vs . . . for when he was in payne we ware in payne, and alle creatures that myght suffer payne sufferyd with hym [the great union between Christ and us . . . for when he was in pain we were in pain, and all creatures that could suffer pain suffered with him]" (18.14–16). In choosing Jesus, whom she sees at that time only in pain, Julian identifies union with God as union with Christ in his suffering. Simon Tugwell captures well the significance of this moment: "This is a decisive move, even if it is only long afterwards that Julian appreciates its full significance: the 'upward' movement towards God, towards heaven, is redirected towards the suffering humanity of Christ. *That* is where heaven must be sought."[61] Julian abandons any contemplative aspiration that would circumvent the humble "meanes" of Christ's humanity. However, she does not do this because of fear of confronting God apart from the humanity of Jesus,[62] but because she is confident that in the suffering humanity of Jesus, the Father and the Son and the Holy Spirit are truly revealed.

2. God's Righteousness Written in the Flesh of Jesus

Julian takes up again the theme of the humanity of Jesus as "heaven" in chapter twenty-two of the long text. Jesus speaks to Julian, saying that his suffering of the passion was "a joy, a blysse, an endless lykyng [a joy, a bliss, an endless delight]" to him and if he could have suffered more, he would have (22.5). These three—joy, bliss, and endless delight—are described by Julian as "iii hevyns, and alle of the blyssedfulle manhed of Christe [three heavens, and all of the most blessed humanity of Christ]" (22.9). These three heavens are correlated with the three persons of the Trinity[63] and the revelation of the persons in the humanity of Jesus. Julian focuses on the first: how God the Father is revealed in the suffering of Jesus on the cross. "I saw in Crist that the father is" (22.14). She writes that the Father is shown to her by Christ "in no bodely lycknesse but in his properte and in hys wurkyng [not in any bodily likeness, but in his property and his working]," by which she means that the Father is known through his relationship to the Son, as revealed in the human nature of Jesus, for the working of the Father is "that he geavyth mede to hys sonne Jhesu Crist [he gives reward to his son Jesus Christ]" (22.12–15). The Father "is wele plesyde with alle the dedes that Jhesu hath done about our saluacion [is well pleased with all the deeds that Jesus has done for our salvation]" (22.19–20) and gives him the human race, healed from sin, as his reward and crown.[64]

We have here a complex semiotics of the invisible Father's becoming visible in his relationship to the Son, as revealed in the redemption of the human race by the suffering humanity of Jesus. The mutual embrace of Father and Son is temporalized in the economy of salvation, so that one might say that what is shown to us in the redemption of humanity, even in the suffering of Jesus on the cross, is the relationship between Father and Son. Because the Father is not simply *in* relationship to the Son, but *is* the relationship to the Son (what Aquinas calls a "subsistent relation"),[65] in the human suffering of Jesus the Father is truly revealed. And what this redemption through suffering reveals is divine love poured out into the world. Julian sees in the suffering of Jesus the infinity of the love that is God's nature:

> The loue that made hym to suffer it passith as far alle his paynes as hevyn is aboue erth; for the payne was a noble precious and wurschypfulle dede done in a tyme by the workyng of loue. And loue was without begynnyng, is and shall be without end.
>
> [The love that made him suffer surpasses all his pains, as far as heaven is above earth; for the pain was a noble and precious and worthy deed accomplished in time by the working of love. And love was without beginning, is and ever shall be.] (22.46–49)

The love that surpasses the suffering of the cross reveals God working according to the fulness of the divine capacity.

> This dede and thys werke abowt oure saluation was ordeyned as wele as god myght ordeyne it. It was don as wurshypfully as Crist myght do it; and heer in I saw a fulle blysse in Crist, for his blysse shuld nott haue ben fulle yf it myght ony better haue ben done than it was done.
>
> [This act and this work of our salvation was ordained as well as God might ordain it. It was done as worthily as Christ might do it; and in this I saw complete joy in Christ, for his joy would not have been full if it might have been done any better than it was done.] (22.53–57)

The cross is, if you will, the real presence of divine power as intrinsically shaped and formed by God's eternal will to bring humanity into the divine life.

We therefore find in Julian's Christocentric vision an alternative to the nominalist account of divine power as formal omnipotence. The will of God is always the will to love, even to the point of suffering and death, because it is grounded in God's nature as love. Thus there is no conflict between God's power and God's goodness. One way in which we might think about this is through Julian's wordplay with the Middle English term "kynd." In Julian's *Revelation* this word is used in roughly the same way as our modern word "kind," but also means "nature" or "essence" (as in our modern term "humankind")—the essential property that makes a thing what it is. In some instances the word clearly carries one or the other of these senses, but in a number of cases Julian exploits the dual meaning of the term in such a way as to depict the nature of God as "kindness" itself. She accomplishes this in particular through the association of "kynd" and motherhood. Thus she writes of our restoration to our "kyndly stede [natural place]," which was created for us "by þe moderhed of kynd loue [by the motherhood of kind/natural love]" (60.4–5). Jesus is "[o]ure kynde moder, oure gracious modyr" (60.7), which might be glossed either as "our kind mother, our gracious mother" or as "our mother by nature, our mother by grace." Our "kynd" is associated with the second person of the Trinity (who, as we shall see later, is central both in the creation and the redemption of that nature), who is revealed to Julian as our "kynde moder." From this she concludes that "God is kynd in his being; that is to sey that goodnesse that is kynd, it is god. He is the grounde, he is þe substance, he is the same thyng that is kyndnesse, and he is very fader and very moder of kyndnys [God is kind/nature in his being; that is to say, that goodness that is kind/natural is God. He is the ground, he is the substance, he is the same thing that is kindness/nature, and he is true father and true mother of kindness/nature]" (62.13–15). Here Julian offers us a complex knot of metaphysical terms, made even more complex by the ambiguity of "kynd." Yet she exploits this ambiguity in order to depict God's nature as "kindness" itself, and furthermore to claim that this kindness is shown to us in our mother Jesus, giving birth on the cross to the new creation. In contrast to the nominalist principle that God is "debtor" to no one, unless God so ordains it,[66] Julian goes so far as to say, "hym behovyth to fynde vs, for the deerworthy loue of moderhed hath made hym dettour to vs [it is fitting that he nourish us, for the most dear love of motherhood has made him our debtor]" (60.28–29). Christ our mother nourishes us not on the basis of an act of will, but out of the love that flows from his very nature.

A similar point might be made with regard to what Julian says regarding God's "ryghtfulhed [righteousness]." In chapter thirty-five of the long text she speaks of it as "that thyng þat is so good þat may nott be better than it is [that thing that is so good that it may not be better than it is]" (35.26–27). This righteousness is both the character of God *in se*, "for god hym selfe is very ryghtfulhed [for God himself is true righteousness]," and descriptive of the works that God has ordained: "and all hys werkes be done ryghtfully, as they be ordeyned fro withouʒt begynnyng by hys hygh myght, hys hygh wysdom, hys hygh goodnesse [and all his works are done righteously, as they are eternally ordained by his high power, his high wisdom, his high goodness]" (35.27–29). In other words, the *ordinata* is not grounded in God's omnipotent will, but in God's nature as righteous, particularly as that righteousness is revealed in the pattern of human life enacted by Christ on the cross. This human pattern is not a first step that must be transcended in contemplation, but is a means by which we have an immediate apprehension of God's nature. And in imitating this pattern, through God's grace, we participate in the divine nature. This is why Julian says with regard to Christ's command to love and "to do good aʒenst evylle [to do good against evil]" that "Crist hym selfe is ground of alle the lawes of cristen men [Christ himself is the ground of all the laws of Christians]" because "he is hym selfe thys charite [he himself is this charity]" (40.45–47). The command to love even our enemies is in no way a contingent provision of the *ordinata*, an arbitrary law that a hidden God declares righteous and rewards to the extent that we fulfill it. Rather, love is commanded of us because it flows from the very nature of God and therefore conforms the soul to God: "he wylle that we be lyke hym in hoolhed of endlesse loue to oure selfe and to oure evyn cristene [he wants us to be like him in wholeness of endless love toward ourselves and our fellow Christians]" (40.47–48). The law of love is "read" by Julian from the text of Christ's body.

One finds in the later Middle Ages several examples of Jesus' crucified body portrayed as textual. Richard Rolle writes, "swet Jhesu, þy body is lyke a boke written al with rede ynke [sweet Jesus, your body is a book written all over with red ink]."[67] And in the image of the "Charter of Christ," Jesus' body was seen as a promissory note from God, with his flesh as the parchment and his wounds as the inscription that promised redemption. *Fasciculus Morum*, a fourteenth-century preacher's manual, provides a good example of this:

> Notice that a charter that is written in blood carries with it extreme reliability and produces much admiration. Just such a charter did

Christ write for us on the cross when he who was "beautiful above the sons of men" stretched out his blessed body, as a parchment maker can be seen to spread a hide in the sun. In this way Christ, when his hands and feet were nailed to the cross, offered his body like a charter to be written on. The nails in his hands were used as a quill, and his precious blood as ink.[68]

Julian does not speak explicitly of Christ as a book, nor of the Charter of Christ, though her description of the drying of Christ's body in the wind (16.13–20) bears some resemblance to the description just quoted of its preparation as a parchment. But on a deeper level, Julian's entire *Revelation* is a reading of that text of Christ's cross, and presents us with an understanding of God's law as something more than divine legislation, but as the love and bliss that may be read in the marks of the tortured humanity of God.

One of Julian's concerns is that while we may believe in the power of God, we might doubt God's love: "for some of vs beliue that god is allmyghty and may do alle, and that he is alle wysdom and can do alle, but that he is alle loue and will do alle, there we fayle [for some of us believe that God is all-powerful and may do all, and that he is all-knowing and can do all, but that he is all-loving and will do all, there we fail]" (73.28–31). This is the great danger of an account of God that posits a contentless divine omnipotence "behind" the God revealed in the events of the economy of salvation, and of a form of prayer that would seek to transcend the humanity of Jesus. The content of Julian's revelation—the text of Christ's body upon which God, as the *Fasciculus Morum* puts it, "wrote a promise when he allowed his blessed body to be carved and inscribed with many wounds"[69]— is simply the love of God revealed in the cross of Jesus, the love that "makyth myght and wysdom fulle meke to vs [makes power and wisdom quite gentle to us]" (73.44). Both contemplation that transcends the humanity of Christ and understandings of divine power that abstract from God's nature as revealed on the cross risk losing the nature of God as love, or reducing "love" to a contentless abstraction, for what we see in the cross is the shape that the divine nature as love takes in a world of sin.[70] God's power is the power of the cross, and in her bodily sights Julian looks upon the reality of the divine nature, shown in God's redemption of humanity. For God to be almighty is inseparable from God being all good; God's power to save is identical with God's will to save. God's power and freedom are precisely the power and freedom to be the God whose nature is revealed in cross and resurrection. It is the power to heal and bind up that which is broken, to incorporate wounded and divided humanity into the mutual embrace of the Father, Son, and Spirit.

Julian's bodily sight is representative of neither affective devotion nor imageless contemplation. It is rather the inauguration of a process of formation of a new identity shaped by "mynd of the passion." This means that to be "fulfilled" by "feeling of his blessed passion" is to become a fellow sufferer with Christ who has taken on the sufferings of humanity, and thereby to receive the wound of compassion. And to receive such a wound is to enter into immediate participation in God's own nature; "atonement" and contemplative "union" meet in Julian's vision of the crucified, whose thirst shall end only with "the onyng of al mankynd that shalle be save into the blisful Trinite [the union of all humanity that shall be saved into the most blessed Trinity]."[71] If anything, to focus on her "experience" would betray the solidarity in suffering that has been given to her in the *memoria passionis*. Julian's task is not recollection of her experience, but recollection of Jesus as the appearance of divine power.

Julian concludes her account of the first showing by noting that she is not good for having the visions, but only if she loves God better because of them, and that there are surely "meny that never hath shewyng ne syʒt but of the comyn techyng of holy chyrch that loue god better than I [many that have never had revelations or visions, but only the common teaching of holy church, who love God better than I]." She then goes on to say, "For yf I looke syngulerly to my selfe I am ryʒt nought; but in generall I am, I hope, in onehede of cheryte with alle my evyn cristen. For in thys oned stondyth the lyfe of alle mankynd that shalle be savyd [For if I look at myself as unusual (or, exclusively) I am quite nothing, but in general I am, I hope, in union of love with all my fellow Christians. For this is the ground of the life of all humanity that shall be saved]" (9.7–11). The sufferings of Jesus' human body inaugurate not simply a life-project for Julian, but a historical task of atonement for the body of Julian's "evyn cristen," Christ's body "in which alle his membris be knytt [in which all his members are knit]," in which "he is nott ʒett fulle glorifyed ne all vnpassible [he is not yet fully glorified nor impassible]" (31.35–36). It is the contours of this body that we must next attempt to chart.

3

"A Feyer and Delectable Place"

> Behold him, "this new being in the world," the masterpiece of the Spirit of God. Henceforward one living being grows under the action of a single life-force, and vivified by one Spirit attains to the stature of perfection. Its scope remains God's secret.
>
> —Henri de Lubac[1]

The human flesh of Jesus is central both to Julian's revelation and to her understanding of the nature of God. In contrast to the nominalist emphasis on God's omnipotence as the formal capacity to do *any*thing that does not involve logical contradiction, Julian presents us with a picture of divine power that is, in a sense, the capacity to do only *one* thing—the capacity to love—and the nature (*"kynd"*) of this love is further specified in the cross of Jesus. God's power is in this sense knowable: to know this power is to know Christ crucified, to have "mynd of the passion." Julian chooses Jesus as her only heaven in this life, and does not offer us any infinity apart from that which is imaged in the infinite suffering, love, and bliss of the cross. Thus, for Julian, the power of God is not a capacity without content or limit, but has a specific "shape" that can be, at least provisionally, mapped. We might say that what Julian presents us with in her *Revelation of Love* is the morphology of divine power. At the center of this morphology is Christ's body, both as the content of the revelation and the form imparted to those who receive God's revelation in Christ, who dwell within that body and thereby receive the wounds of contrition, compassion, and longing for God. Therefore the specific shape of divine power has a correlative social shape, and for Julian this too is the form of Christ's crucified body. In other words, Julian imagines the political as the mystical body politic of Christ. Therefore, it is to Julian's images of the human body, specifically Jesus' human body, that we must look in order to understand both the nature of divine power and the social form that embodies it in the world.

A. BOUNDARIES

The actual images of bodies employed by Julian are both like and unlike those found in other late medieval sources. In particular, while she shares with her contemporaries a sense of the way in which embodied existence is fragile and thus necessarily subject to pain and suffering, her images of the human body seem to exploit that fragility's capacity for openness and generativity in a way that is remarkably positive. To be embodied is to have boundaries, but to have boundaries is also to have thresholds, points of opening into which others may enter and from which new things may proceed. It is this possibility that Julian highlights.

1. Bodies Smooth and Grotesque

There are two seemingly conflicting tendencies in late medieval piety. One is a tendency to try to keep the boundaries of the body—in particular the senses, but also all of the orifices of the body—tightly policed in order to preserve the purity of the soul. We see this in the *Ancrene Wisse*, which prescribes a regimen that minutely orders the bodily life of the anchoress, including dress, diet, and postures of prayer. While this "outer rule" is subordinated to the "inner rule" of charity, and may be modified at the discretion of the anchoress's confessor (thus allowing adaptation to specific needs while maintaining the hierarchy of soul over body, and of confessor over anchoress), the detail in which the outer rule is specified indicates the importance of "external" discipline. In particular, the physical enclosure of the anchoress is both symbolic of and an aid to the project of creating a body in which the openings of the senses are carefully regulated in order to protect the heart from temptation.[2] One finds something similar in Julian's contemporary, Walter Hilton, when he advises an anchoress:

> you should know that the cause of your bodily enclosure is that you may the better come to spiritual enclosure; and as your body is enclosed from bodily association with men, just so should your heart be enclosed from the fleshly loves and fears of all earthly things.[3]

The anchoress was in a particularly favorable position with regard to this undertaking, since the things with which she came into sensible contact were limited by the walls of her anchorhold, yet such care for the thresholds of the body was also commended to the laity, both in popular preaching and in various devotional manuals. For example, the mid-fourteenth-century work *The Abbey of the Holy Ghost* offers instructions to those who, because of circumstances (i.e., poverty, family objections, or marriage), could not enter religious life, on how to construct an "abbey within." It recommends:

> if you wish to keep yourself in spiritual religion and be at peace of soul and sweetness of heart, keep yourself within, and guard your gates, and so carefully keep watch over your cloister that no outer or inner temptations can gain entrance to cause you to break silence or incite you to sin. Guard your eyes from foul sights, your ears from foul hearings, your mouth from foul speech and from unclean laughter, and your heart from foul thoughts.[4]

As this passage shows, the body's thresholds were points of danger both in what they let in and in what they let out. And while temptations might enter through the senses, from the mouth might also issue forth lies or blasphemies or "unclean laughter" that could endanger the soul. As a homily in Mirk's *Festial* puts it, "mannys flesche ys . . . wyld and lusty to synne [man's flesh is wild and desires to sin]."[5]

Alongside the view that the body's margins were points of danger through which temptation could enter, there was a countertendency that saw those margins as sites through which *God* could enter to take possession of the soul. We have already seen how the tradition of affective piety stressed the opportunities of embodiment and how for Julian the fragility of her body in its sickness was an occasion for identification with Christ's suffering body and for possession by his pain through the medium of sight. The Middle Ages were rife with the possibility of holy transgressions. The entire medieval sacramental system centered on the mass, in which (at least on occasion) the faithful took Christ into themselves through their mouths—his body transgressing the boundaries of theirs. This eucharistic transgression could, at least in legend, assume an even more dramatic form, as in the story from a sermon for *Corpus Christi* in Mirk's *Festial*:

> Then taket þis ensample of syr Auberk þat was erle of Venys, and louet þe sacrament of þe auter, and dyde to hit al þe reuerence þat he

couþe. But when he schuld dye, he myȝt not receue hit for vpcasting. Then made he to clanse his syde, and hull hit wyth a clene clote of sandelle; and layde þeron Godys body, and sayde þus to hym: "Lorde, þou knowes well þat y loue þe, and wold fayn receue þe wyth my mouþe, and I durst; but for I may not, I lay þe on þe place þat is next myn hert, and so schow þe my hert and my loue." And þerwyth, in syȝt of al men, þe syde opened, and þe ost glode into þe body; and þen þe syde closet aȝen, hole as hit was befor, and so sone aftir he ȝaf þe gost vp.

[Then take this example of Sir Auberk, who was earl of Venice, and who loved the sacrament of the altar and paid to it all the reverence that he could. But when he was dying, he was not able to receive it for fear that he would throw it up. Then he washed his side and covered it with a clean silk cloth, and he laid on it God's body and said to him, "Lord, you know well that I love you and would joyfully receive you with my mouth, and I so desire; but because I cannot, I lay you on the place that is next to my heart, and so show you my heart and my love." And at that, as everyone could see, the side opened and the host glided into the body, and then his side closed again, as whole as it had been before, and shortly thereafter he died.]⁶

Auberk's body and Christ's body confront each other not across the impenetrable boundary of two essentially self-contained entities, but through an act of union between bodies that miraculously open toward each other. Thus at the same time that we find in medieval piety an emphasis on policing the boundaries of the body, we also find techniques that are designed precisely to exploit the permeability of those boundaries, using sensual experience (the sight of a religious image, the taste of the eucharistic host, the pain of corporal penances) as a means for the soul's encounter with God.⁷

This interest in and anxiety over the body's boundaries has a social as well as an individual significance. Mary Douglas has argued that the body is a powerful symbol of the social body, particularly with regard to boundaries: "We cannot possibly interpret rituals concerning excreta, breast milk, saliva and the rest unless we are prepared to see in the body a symbol of society, and to see the powers and dangers credited to social structure reproduced in small on the human body."⁸ Further, she argues that bodily margins are symbolic of "danger." She writes:

> ... all margins are dangerous. If they are pulled this way or that the shape of fundamental experience is altered. Any structure of ideas is vulnerable at its margins. We should expect the orifices of the body to symbolise its specially vulnerable points. Matter issuing from them is marginal stuff of the most obvious kind. Spittle, blood, milk, urine, feces or tears by simply issuing forth have traversed the boundary of the body. So also have bodily parings, skin, nail, hair clippings and sweat.[9]

In a society such as medieval England, in which bodily margins are seen as "dangerous" or, as Mirk put it, "wyld," one might expect that the margins of the social body would also be of considerable concern. It is across the boundaries of the social body that foreign invaders—whether military, economic, or intellectual—threaten, and boundaries mark the point of expulsion of internal threats to the body politic. A desire to police the body's boundaries is a desire to create and maintain a certain *status quo*.

The purity of the social body of christendom was a major concern of the medieval world, which in the late Middle Ages is overlaid with a concern for the purity of emerging national bodies. This period was heir to the ideology and apparatus of what R. I. Moore calls a "persecuting society," which emerged in the period between A.D. 950 and 1250 as a way of policing social boundaries. As the traditional "segmentary societies" of the early Middle Ages were superseded by the emerging bureaucratic states, there was an increasing regulation not only of the internal structures of christendom, but also of the boundaries of that social body, primarily through the construction of categories of exclusion: the Jew, the leper, and the heretic. The Third Lateran Council (1179) had mandated that lepers should be segregated in separate communities,[10] and the Fourth Lateran Council (1215) saw not only legislation concerned with the life of the faithful, such as the enforcement of yearly confession and communion, but also legislation against heresy, as well as the emergence of the Jew as a marked category, set apart by special clothing and exclusion from certain professions.[11] What Jews, heretics, and lepers shared was not any specific characteristic save that, as Moore puts it, "they were all victims of a zeal for persecution which seized European society at this time."[12] This zeal, which identified Jew, heretic, and leper under the rubric of "threat," was at the service of the creation of a unified identity for christendom; the purity of the *corpus christianum* was secured by the identification and exclusion of sources of pollution. "Jews were . . . held to resemble heretics and lepers in being associated with filth, stench and putrefaction, in exceptional sexual voracity and endowment, and in the menace which they presented in consequence to the wives and children of honest Christians."[13]

While the apparatus of persecution took shape well before the fourteenth century, the categories of exclusion that were part of it remained a structural feature of the medieval world. Jews were expelled from England by Edward I in 1291, but the Jew persisted as a marked category of defilement in the social imagination. For example, the cult of William of Norwich, the twelfth-century child martyr who was said to have been tortured to death by the Jews, kept alive the memory of the Jew as child murderer and, as such, a threat to the continued existence of the community.[14] Similarly, in the East Anglian *Croxton Play of the Sacrament*, which probably dates from the mid-fifteenth century, Jews function as a symbol for unbelief in general, and in particular for lack of belief in the presence of Christ in the eucharistic elements—and hence a symbol of the Lollard.[15] The specifics of belief, whether of Jew or Lollard, are in this sense unimportant: Jew and heretic function simply as the "other" against which the community defines itself. At the same time, the *Croxton Play of the Sacrament* ends not with the death or expulsion of the Jews, but with their conversion, displaying the assimilative power of the eucharistic/social body. The body opens to engulf the threat.

Just as in late medieval piety one finds a dual emphasis on bodily closure and bodily opening, so one also finds a dual emphasis on the way in which the social body is imaged. We find a desire to present christendom as a unified whole, possessed of a smooth surface that can repel any invasion, from which all possible sources of internal dissonance have been expelled, if not literally (as with the Jews in England), at least symbolically. This is the body of Christ imaged by the smooth, white, unbroken host elevated by the priest after the consecration—the host as object to be adored rather than food for consumption. On the other hand, the host was also understood as food—food that must be broken to be eaten, food that was the presence of the crucified body of Christ, food that was not assimilated by those who consumed it, but that rather assimilated them.[16] There coexists within the one symbol of the Body of Christ both an emphasis on unity and the necessity of transgression.[17] Accompanying the smooth, unbroken unity of medieval christendom there is a persistent whisper of what Mikael Bakhtin has described as the "grotesque," which undermined accounts of unity as the integrity of a self-contained body by counterposing another kind of social body, that of the carnival. Bakhtin's description of the "grotesque body" of medieval folk culture is in certain ways strikingly similar to Julian's imagining of the mystical body politic of Christ.

In his analysis of the "folk culture" of the Middle Ages and Renaissance, Bakhtin identifies this folk culture by placing it in opposition to the "official culture." Thus, where the official culture is characterized by the rigidly fixed hierarchy of being, folk culture is rooted in becoming and relativity. Where official culture is "spiritual," folk culture is characterized by what Bakhtin calls "grotesque realism" in which "the bodily element is deeply positive." Perhaps most important for our purposes at this point is that the body in folk culture is a corporate body. Bakhtin writes:

> the body and bodily life have here a cosmic and at the same time an all-people's character; this is not the body and its physiology in the modern sense of these words, because it is not individualized. The material bodily principle is not contained in the biological individual, not in the bourgeois ego, but in a people, a people who are continually growing and renewed.[18]

The grotesque body is a body in flux, thus its boundaries with the world are highly permeable:

> Contrary to modern canons, the grotesque body is not separated from the rest of the world. It is not a closed, completed unit; it is unfinished, outgrows itself, transgresses its own limits. The stress is laid on those parts of the body that are open to the outside world, that is, the parts through which the world enters the body or emerges from it, or through which the body itself goes out to meet the world. (26)

In Mary Douglas's terms, it is a "dangerous" body, and the danger, in Bakhtin's view, is to "official" culture. It is the social body of the peasant festival, with its mocking of the forms and institutions of official culture; it is, in Bakhtin's term, "carnivalesque." The festival constitutes "the world's second truth" (84), which is the negation of official culture, but is at the same time a renewal of collective sociality—not simply the negation of order, but a new, utopian kind of order. "It is the people as a whole, but organized *in their own way*, the way of the people. It is outside of and contrary to all existing forms of the coercive socioeconomic and political organization, which is suspended for the time of festivity" (255). This new order, "the utopian kingdom of absolute equality and freedom," is not, however, deferred for some future age (as if it were a mere modification of the gloomy eschatology of official culture), but is enacted within life itself—a theater, as Bakhtin says, "without footlights," in that there are no spectators; *all* are actors (264–265). For the time of the festival, the social order without hierarchy (or, perhaps better, that order in which hierarchy is reversed) is an actual, existing, material reality (265).

Folk culture reverses the structure of official culture by means of what Bakhtin calls "degradation." All that is high, spiritual, and abstract is made low, material, and concrete—it is, in his term, carnivalized—simply because it can be laughed at or cursed. Mockery is a key trope in the language of festival; one response to the overwhelming power of official culture is simply to laugh in its face. The point is not to destroy the object of derision, but to bring it down to earth, to rob it of its mystique by an artful and mocking exploitation of that very mystique, to recreate the power of that mystique in a historical and popular form. As Bakhtin puts it, "[t]rue ambivalent and universal laughter does not deny seriousness but purifies and completes it" (122–123). In this process of degradation is revealed the tremendous ambiguity that is the power of the "material bodily lower strata."

> To degrade means to concern oneself with the lower stratum of the body, the life of the belly and reproductive organs; it therefore relates to acts of defecation and copulation, conception, pregnancy, and birth. Degradation digs a bodily grave for a new birth; it has not only a destructive, negative aspect, but also a regenerating one. To degrade an object does not imply merely hurling it into the void of nonexistence, into absolute destruction, but to hurl it down to the reproductive lower stratum, the zone in which conception and a new birth take place. Grotesque realism knows no other level; it is the fruitful earth and the womb. It is always conceiving. (21)

One must bear in mind that Bakhtin's sharp distinction between "official" and "folk" culture is drastically overdrawn, particularly in the medieval context. His attempt to distinguish "official" from "folk" culture along the divide between Latin and the vernacular (465) stumbles not only over the burgeoning vernacular devotional literature that was quite "official" and "orthodox" in its theology, but also over macaronic works such as Hilton's *Scale of Perfection*, which can hardly be considered an attempt at "degradation" of official culture (though Langland's *Piers Plowman* might be).[19] Certainly after Archbishop Thomas Arundel's *Constitutions* of 1409 placed tight restrictions on the creation and dissemination of vernacular texts, the contours of a divide between official-clerical culture and popular-lay culture were constructed that traced at least in part the line between Latin and English. But what is clear is that this distinction had to be *constructed*; there was not a "natural" fault line between official latinate culture and popular vernacular culture.[20] In fact, the construction of this fault line is testimony to the anxiety produced by a culture in which it has become increasingly difficult to make such a distinction.

Also, certain forms of "official culture" in the Middle Ages, whether in the form of residual feudalism or hierarchically sanctioned Christianity, would not seem to be primarily imaged by the individualized body that Bakhtin describes, though in the newly emerged and emerging bureaucratic states there was certainly a preference for "orderly" bodies; there was also an increasing pull toward "closed" and "purified" social bodies, manifesting itself both in the increasing dominance of national identities, and in the endemic xenophobia that led to the vicious though sporadic persecution of heretics and the expulsion of Jews. However, it is not at all clear that a preference for "smooth" over "grotesque" bodies easily divides along the lines of "official" versus "folk" culture. At the very heart of that most official formula of official culture, the canon of the mass, there is, as John Bossy notes, "a certain element of the *carnivalesque*" in its logic of extirpation of violence through public manifestation.[21] Likewise, carnival time was not a spontaneous erruption of peasant life, but was normally orchestrated by representatives of "official" culture. Without painting too homogeneous a picture of the Middle Ages, one must still maintain that the lines of division and conflict, as well as the bonds of unity, cut across the division between social classes.[22] The situation was simply much more complex and the conflicts more multi-sided than Bakhtin indicates. As Peter Stallybrass and Allon White point out, Bakhtin does not sufficiently distinguish between the grotesque as the excluded "other" against which the group is defined, and the grotesque as "a boundary phenomenon of hybridization or inmixing, in which self and other become enmeshed in an inclusive, heterogeneous, dangerously unstable zone."[23] The *Croxton Play of the Sacrament*, for example, combines elements of the grotesque and the carnivalesque with the project of creating the smooth body of christendom by the eradication through assimilation of the impure Jews. One might well ask, is the story ultimately one of locating alien elements of the social body in their proper place, or is it about that body's grotesque capacity for assimilation and generativity? Is the play finally an example of "official" culture—a clerically constructed morality tale—or is it an occasion for carnival? One can only say that it is both, for in its representation of the excluded other, the play hybridizes and therefore carnivalizes itself.

With this caveat offered, I believe that Bakhtin still provides important insights into the social valence of certain bodily images. In particular he draws our attention to the persistence in medieval culture of positive value given to dangerous images in which the margins of the body are transgressed and the safe interior is opened to the world. The social body so portrayed is grotesque because it has no way of preventing mixture with other bodies, yet in its grotesqueness it has a generativity, a fecundity that is always accompanied by risk of death or pollution. The material bodily lower stratum is the site of both dirt and birth, of the anus as well as the genitals. Similarly, Bakhtin shows us that images of degradation, in which those things that are symbolically coded as "high" or "spiritual" are made "low" or "material," are not simply images of destruction but are also images of renewal and birth.

Given what I have said about the nature of Julian's "bodily seeing," one might aptly describe the revelation as a whole as an event of the grotesque sphere. It is precisely such bodies as Bakhtin describes that we find in Julian's *Revelation*. Julian is like Rabelais' physician, of whom Bakhtin writes: "The body that interests him is pregnant, delivers, defecates, is sick, dying, and dismembered" (179). In particular, the unfinished character of the bodily sights, blurring the line between text and interpretation, indicates that the revelation, like the grotesque body, "is not a closed, completed unit; it is unfinished, outgrows itself, transgresses its own limits" (26).[24] It is a drama without footlights, in which one can never objectively delineate the boundaries of a performance that turns spectators into actors. Similarly, identities are not neatly fixed by corporeal or other boundaries, rather there is a salvific "hybridization" of identity that occurs between God and humanity, and among all of humanity that shall be saved, particularly centering around the figure of Adam. Full explication of this must await discussion of the *exemplum* of the lord and servant in the next chapter; at this point I wish to examine the grotesque images of the body that form the backdrop for such hybridization.

2. Dwelling on Margins

At the very outset Julian describes the third of her requests for which she had prayed in terms of three "woundes in my life" of "verie contricion [true contrition]," "kynd compassion [kind/natural compassion]," and "willfull longing to god [the will's longing for God]" (2.40–43). The very language of "wounds," reinforced in the short text by reference to the physical wounds of the martyr Cecilia (i.46–49), evokes both the violence of wounds inflicted upon the body and the salvific image of Christ's wounds. Such terminology was not unusual in affective piety,[25] and no doubt Julian's request was inspired by such piety; she prays for a kind of transformation through transgression of the body's closed spaces. As I have argued in the last chapter, Julian interprets her "bodily sight" as the means by which she is "fulfilled with mynd and feeling of his blessed passion." The revelation is one of what Bakhtin describes as "events of the grotesque sphere," that "are always developed on the boundary dividing one body from the other and, as it were, at their points of intersection."[26]

Julian's revelations are marginal events in part because they are given to one who is herself in some sense a "marginal" figure, whose very existence displays the complexity of the relationship of margin to center. Perhaps the most obvious sense in which Julian is marginal is her gender. The misogyny of mainstream medieval thought is well enough known not to need detailed rehearsing here. Such theoretical commonplaces as Augustine's allegorical identification of woman with the lower part of the soul (the part turned toward material things) and her subordination to man, who represents the higher part of the soul (the part turned toward God),[27] as well as Aquinas's statement that "[a]s regards the individual nature, woman is defective and misbegotten" (the force of which is not quite undone by the later statement, "as regards human nature in general, woman is not misbegotten, but is included in nature's intention as directed to the work of generation"),[28] have been well worked over by feminist scholars. Less theoretically, and more powerfully, we are confronted with events ranging from the economic marginalization of women (despite claims for a "golden age" for women's work in the later Middle Ages)[29] to the politically expedient burning of Marguerite Porete.[30] The identity of woman was derivative of and secondary to the identity of man; the female was a figure at the edge of a scene in which the male was central. As Joan Cadden writes of medieval medical theories, "Men were clearly central, primary, and standard.... Among the reasons for [woman's] marginality is her incompleteness, from which arises not only a social dependence on man but also a conceptual dependence on the masculine standard."[31] And to disrupt the order of center and margin is to pose a threat.

Yet within this misogynist tradition, certain women used their marginalization as a means by which they could follow and imitate Christ, precisely because of the way in which marginal status is encoded within the image of Jesus himself, who, as the letter to the Hebrews puts it, "suffered outside the city gate" (Heb. 13:12a). This is no doubt cold comfort to those who would dismiss religious beliefs as superstructural. But theologically, the marginalization of women must take on an ambiguous character inasmuch as it makes possible certain forms of relationship to and identification with Jesus that were closed to those who eschewed the margins. Women's piety flourished despite, and in some sense *because of,* the regime of marginalization under which they lived. This does not mean that we can romanticize these women or their marginal status. The unfortunate tendency of someone like Bakhtin is to so romanticize "folk" culture and to valorize marginalization that it can be forgotten that marginal status was most often imposed on people (not sought by them), frequently under threat of violence, and sometimes by the strictures of "folk" culture itself. It may sound exciting to be an oppositional figure on the margins, but as Caroline Walker Bynum writes:

> We must never forget the pain and frustration, the isolation and feelings of helplessness, that accompanied the quest of religious women. For all her charismatic empowerment, woman was inferior to man in the Middle Ages; her voice was often silenced, even more frequently ignored. Not every use of the phrase "weak woman" by a female writer was ironic; women clearly internalized the negative value placed on them by the culture in which they lived.[32]

Julian's status as a woman made her even more marginal in late-fourteenth-century England than it would have elsewhere in Europe. England produced no female figures who were equivalent to Catherine of Siena or Birgitta of Sweden, who led religious renewal movements and rebuked emperors and popes. Women in England seem to have been severely limited even in their charismatic religious leadership, perhaps because women leaders left themselves open to charges of Lollardy.[33] It seems hardly an accident that what are today the two most significant works written by women in late medieval England—Julian's *Revelation of Love* and Margery Kempe's *Book*—had virtually no impact or circulation during the Middle Ages themselves.[34] The fact that Julian and Margery produced books at all is perhaps a result of continental influences, which were greater in East Anglia (and in particular Norwich) than elsewhere, and the relative lack of heresy (and thus the persecution of suspected heretics) in the area.[35] But whereas we know from Margery's own writings that she was familiar with the continental tradition of holy women,[36] there is no concrete evidence that Julian had access to any of their writings, or even knew them by reputation. This makes Julian's marginality and isolation, as well as her achievement, all the greater.[37]

One indication of how Julian perceived herself as a woman is a passage in the short text that she excised from the long text. She offers an *apologia* for daring to speak of religious matters, which is worth quoting in its entirety:

> Botte god for bede that ȝe schulde saye or take it so that I am a techere, for I meene nouȝt soo, no I mente nevere so; for I am a womann, leued, febille and freylle. Botte I wate wele, this that I saye, I hafe it of the schewynge of hym that es souerayne techare. Botte sothelye charyte styrres me to telle ȝowe it, for I wolde god ware knawenn, and mynn evynn crystene spede, as I wolde be my selfe to the mare hatynge of synne and lovynge of god. Botte for I am a womann, shulde I therfore leve that I schulde nouȝt telle ȝowe the goodenes of god, syne that I sawe in that same tyme that is his wille, that it be knawenn?

> [But God forbid that you should say or think that I am a teacher for that is not what I mean, nor is it what I ever have meant, for I am a woman, unlearned, feeble and frail. But I know well that what I say I have by revelation of him that is sovereign teacher. But it is truly

love that moves me to tell it to you, for I want God to be known and my fellow Christians to profit, as I would myself, for the greater hating of sin and loving of God. Simply because I am a woman, am I supposed to believe that I should not tell you about the goodness of God, since I saw at the same time that it was his will that it be known?] (vi.40–48)

Julian defends herself with a combination of self-abnegation (she is "a womann, leued, febille and freylle") and the rather gigantic claim that she is not presuming to teach, but simply recounting what she was told by "hym that es souerayne techare." Should her inadequacy as a woman thwart Christ's message? If Julian truly acts as a channel of divine communication, then she will become transparent to Christ who teaches through her.[38] Thus paradoxically, her marginality as a woman enhances the authority of her text, because it is not *she* who authorizes the text—something that she, as a woman, is incapable of doing—but Christ. Christ's authorization has an immediacy that is necessitated by Julian's inadequacy as a medium.

There is no reason to think that Julian is being disingenuous when she speaks of herself as a feeble and frail woman; such a view of herself would simply reflect her culture's prevailing views. What is interesting is that Julian drops this *apologia* in the long text. Can we take this as an indication that Julian no longer sees her gender as an obstacle to speaking about God? Does she now present herself as exercising at least a proximate causality in the composition of the *Revelation*? Or does she still see her femaleness as a problem, but seeks to mask it by removing this reference? Or is her omission of this passage simply an example of her tendency in revising the short text to downplay the specific circumstances of the revelations and of herself as an individual so as to heighten the universality of her message? Did she begin to think that showy displays of self-denigration merely called attention to oneself? As with so much about Julian, it is impossible to know. However, in view of the development in the long text of her understanding of Jesus as mother it certainly seems possible that she had come to a more positive assessment of femaleness than normally prevailed in late medieval England. While femaleness was still coded as marginal and dangerous, the margin and the danger were now mapped onto Christ's bodily humanity.

If Julian's marginality as a woman was imposed on her, her marginality as an anchoress was one which, we may presume, she in some sense freely chose.[39] This is a form of marginality—perhaps liminality would be a better term—which is also ambiguous, though in a different way than the marginality of being a woman. An anchorite was simultaneously at the center and at the margin of the community. On the one hand, the anchorite, unlike the hermit, did not completely withdraw outside the gates of the city, so as to live apart. He or she remained in the midst of the city, both to offer spiritual counsel to those in need (as Julian herself apparently did) as well as to be a symbolic "anchor" for the community.[40] The community likewise provided the anchorite with material support through various channels. On the other hand, the anchoritic life rooted its spiritual power, from which the community drew, in the material as well as symbolic erection of a boundary between the anchorite and the community. Contact with the world was channeled through the window of the anchorhold and, at least in theory, tightly regulated. As Ann Warren describes it,

> Encouraged, applauded, and supported by society and church, they undertook their solitary life by encamping in the heart of the community. Enclosed and yet exposed, hidden and yet visible, shadows behind the curtains of their access windows, medieval English anchorites were daily reminders of the proper focus of Christian existence.[41]

The anchorite served the community by creating an enclosed space of order and purity over and against the chaos and pollution of the world; paradoxically, this space of order and purity stood out within the social body like an alien intrusion, offering a visual jeremiad that both atoned for the community's sins and called it to conversion.

In some ways this ambiguity is mirrored by the anchorite's similarly ambiguous position within the hierarchical structure of the church. As Norman Tanner has noted, even though an anchorite's enclosure was normally officially sanctioned by the church, "[a]s men and women trying to lead religious lives outside the normal framework of the priesthood and religious orders, anchorites and hermits were in a sense an anti-order."[42] Not unlike the Beguines on the continent, anchoresses took up a mode of existence that combined elements of secular and religious life.[43] Being an anchorite was not necessarily tied to the religious state, but neither was it belonging to the lay state; the anchoritic life worked the line between the two.⁴⁴

The symbolic marginality of anchorites is further seen in the various associations between anchoritic enclosure and death. Extreme unction (which had become by this point an anointing of the dying, not of the sick) was a frequent part of rituals of anchoritic enclosure, as was the celebration of the mass for the dead, and marked the anchorite as a liminal figure who dwelt in the boundary between this world and the next.⁴⁵ It is impossible to know with our current information when Julian became an anchoress, so it is difficult to know how, if at all, living such a life of symbolic death would have affected her writings. Yet one might say that even if Julian became an anchoress only relatively late in life, this was in substantial continuity with her early desire for bodily sickness to the point of death, and in particular her desire to receive the last rites, which can be read as a desire for some of the same symbolic liminality as the anchorite. In popular understanding, such an experience would have set her apart from her "evyn cristen." Eamon Duffy notes:

> It was widely and erroneously believed that the solemn anointing of all the senses involved in the reception of Extreme Unction was a sort of ordination or consecration, cutting the recipient off from the normal activities of life, even should they recover. They would have to live thereafter as a sort of animated corpse, as it was widely thought that 'stinking Lazarus' had done after Jesus had raised him from the tomb. Despite all the authorities could do to reassure them, many lay people believed that an anointed person could never again eat meat, or have sexual relations with his or her spouse.⁴⁶

Extreme unction made of one an "animated corpse," a peculiar kind of body, a body much more susceptible to occupation by Christ. Perhaps Julian's statement that she hoped to "liue more to the worshippe of God by cause of that sicknes [live more to the worship of God because of that sickness]" (2.30–31) indicates that she saw her reception of the last rites as a kind of consecration. In any case, regardless of the point at which Julian became an anchoress, if her fellow citizens shared the common view of the effects of extreme unction, then even prior to her enclosure as an anchoress she would have been marked for them, if not for herself, as a kind of marginal figure, a sacred intruder from the land of the dead.

B. THE GROTESQUE BODY OF CHRIST

Whatever Julian's personal circumstances might have been and however she might have perceived herself in relation to the concrete community in which she lived, her *Revelation* displays an intense interest in bodily margins, both of individual human bodies and of the communal body of her "evyn cristen." Julian repeatedly describes bodies in terms of their openings, the orifices and exudings through which interior and exterior communicate. The image of Christ that she sees is one in which the bodily margins are foregrounded through their transgression. The key theological problematic with which she wrestles—how it could be true that "alle shalle be wele" if some are damned, excluded from enclosure in God's goodness—is a question of how the boundaries of salvation are delimited. All of this makes Bakhtin's description of the grotesque body particularly apt for understanding the character of the body of Christ as seen by Julian, for it provides a way to think about the communal significance of mutable and transgressed bodies.

1. Defecation and Degradation

One of Julian's most clearly "grotesque" images is found in chapter six of the long text, in which she describes how the goodness of God comes down to us in our lowest need. After speaking of how God "hath vs all in hym selfe beclosyde [has us all enclosed in himself]," Julian, in a seeming nonsequitur, goes on to speak of another kind of enclosing: "A man goyth vppe ryght, and the soule of his body is sparyde as a purse fulle feyer. And whan it is tyme of his nescessery, it is openyde and sparyde ayen fulle honestly [A man walks upright, and the food in his body is enclosed, as if in a well-made purse. And when it is his time of necessity, it is opened and closed again quite decently]" (6.35–37).[47] She goes on to make the point that even in such humble activity as defecation, God is acting; nothing concerning human beings is outside the sphere of God's concern: "For he hath no despite of that he made, ne he hath no disdeyne to serue vs at the symplest office that to oure body longyth in kynde, for loue of the soule that he made to his awne lycknesse [For he does not despise what he has made, nor does he disdain to serve us in our body's simplest natural function, out of love for the soul that he made in his own likeness]" (6.39–41).

Julian's image, as oblique as it is, is a somewhat startling one—startling enough that it is omitted in the Sloane manuscripts.

While Julian does not seem to be using the image deliberately to shock (her use of the by then obsolete word "soule" to mean cooked or digested food indicates that Julian herself was attempting to state her point with a certain delicacy),[48] it is impossible to ignore some of the connotations of such a scatological image: feces is taboo, excluded, associated with our mortality as a sign that we are made of earth. At the same time, it is associated with the fecundity of the lower material bodily stratum. A sermon from the late fourteenth or early fifteenth century exploits precisely these dual associations to put forward a conventional *momento mori* theme:

> Consider your body: how vilely, how weakly, how full of care you come into this world, weeping and wailing, and without any mirth. Afterwards, what you are and what you shall be at the end: you are but a sackful of dirt, covered by clothing, and if what was within were to be turned outwards, he who makes the most of himself would be treated as nothing by the world. Afterwards, look all over your body: what filth comes out of each orifice in it, what at the eyes, what at the nose, what at the mouth, also the ears, and beneath in other privy places. This is no reason for pride, if it is considered properly![49]

The rhetoric of this passage is one of mortification, in the dual sense of death and embarrassment. Not only is feces an indication that we are created from the earth and thus one of the signs of our mortality, but the inevitable exteriorization of the filth with which the body is filled is also a source of social mortification, humbling the proud and showing them to be ultimately no greater than the humblest member of society.[50] At the same time, feces has a positive connotation as the manure used for cultivation; it is associated with generativity and growth. The same sermon goes on to say: "With your mind on this matter, you will make good manure to make the root of righteous works grow all the better."[51]

Julian makes similar connections between the body and dirt, noting that "whan god shulde make mannes body, he toke the slyme of the erth, whych is a mater medelyd and gaderyd of alle bodely thynges, and therof he made mannes body [when God went to make man's body, he took the slime of the earth, which is a material mixed and gathered from all bodily things, and from this he made man's body]" (53.42–45). Similarly, in her vision of the soul departing the body, the body is "lyeng on þe erth [lying on the earth]" and is described as "a swylge stynkyng myrre [a pit stinking of mud]" (64.31–33). However, for Julian the humbleness of physical existence does not engender shame, but gratitude. For her, the human being's "tyme of his nescessery" is an occasion to meditate not on death, but on the enfolding love of God. Immediately after her remarks on the marvels of the alimentary canal she returns to discussing our enclosure in God: "For as þe body is cladd in the cloth, and the flessch in the skynne, and the bonys in þe flessch, and the harte in the bowke, so ar we, soule and body, cladde and enclosydde in the goodnes of God [For as the body is clothed in the cloth, and the flesh in the skin, and the bones in the flesh, and the heart in the torso, so are we, soul and body, clothed and enclosed in the goodness of God]" (6.41–44). God's love can be seen in the concern that God shows for even the humblest detail of human life.[52]

The larger context in which this image of defecation occurs is a discussion of the place of "meanes" (i.e., various prayers and devotions) in the spiritual life. While it may be tempting to read this as a parody of such intermediaries between the soul and God (as one might find in Lollard literature), Julian in fact assigns to them a limited yet real place as signs of God's goodness. As I said in the last chapter, for Julian these forms of mediation are properly understood as God's way to us, not our way to God. She goes on to note that "the chiefe and principall meane is the blessed kynde that he toke of the maiden [the chief and principal intermediary is the blessed nature that he took from the virgin]" (6.24–25). Thus, rather than deploying the image of defecation as a way to humble the proud human spirit or to ridicule the simple devotions of her fellow Christians, Julian uses it to indicate the "homelynesse [familiarity/intimacy]" of God, which can be seen in creation but is chiefly displayed in the incarnation.

Julian speaks just before this in terms of a movement from "high" to "low": "For to the goodnes of god is the highest praier, and it cometh downe to vs to the lowest party of our need [For the highest prayer is to the goodness of God, and it comes down to us in the lowest part of our need]" (6.28–30). If God's seemingly inordinate interest in the lower material bodily strata is employed here to mark an act of "degradation" (in Bakhtin's sense), it is God's mysterious self-degradation in creation and, above all, redemption that is being registered. As Bakhtin notes:

> Degradation here means coming down to earth, the contact with earth as an element that swallows up and gives birth at the same time. To degrade is to bury, to sow, and to kill simultaneously, in order to bring forth something more and better.[53]

In her next chapter, Julian's language becomes one of inverted oppositions between "high" and "low" as she attempts to describe the kind of reverence and dread that is inspired by her vision of God's self-degradation. Thus she sees in "gostely syght" the "hyghe wysdom and truth [high wisdom and truth]" that the Virgin Mary had "in beholdyng of her maker [in the contemplation of her maker]." "This gretnesse and this nobylnesse [This greatness and this nobleness]" of Mary's beholding of God, which leads her to see herself as "so lytylle and so lowe, so symple and so poer [so little and so low, so simple and so poor]," is seen by Julian against the background of "the plentious bledeing of the hede [the plenteous bleeding of the head]" of Jesus (7.6–14).[54] In her beholding of God, Mary has a wisdom that is *high*, yet which enables her to see herself as *low*; it is *great* and *noble*, and causes her to see herself as *simple* and *poor*. At the same time, however, Julian is beholding the bodily sight of Christ's bleeding head, which continues "tylle many thynges were sene [until many things were seen]," an act of divine degradation that she, seemingly to her own surprise, finds beautiful.

In the long text, Julian greatly expands the short text's description, noting in particular the tremendous quantity of the blood: "The plentuoushede is lyke to the droppes of water that falle of the evesyng of an howse after a grete shower of reyne, that falle so thycke that no man may number them with no bodely wyt [The plenteousness is like the drops of water that fall off the eaves of a house after a great shower of rain, that fall so thick that no one may number them with any natural intelligence]" (7.22–24). The image is a grotesque one of a body exteriorizing its liquid interior, of borders becoming fluid and malleable. The comparison to rain water contributes to the generative overtones of the image—the great quantity of Christ's blood waters the earth to bring forth new life. She goes on to note, again combining terms normally found in opposition, that:

> Thys shewyng was quyck and lyuelu and hidows and dredfulle and swete and louely; and of all the syght that I saw this was most com-

fort to me, that oure good lorde, that is so reverent and dredfulle, is so homely and so curteyse, and this most fulfyllyd me with lykyng and syckernes in soule.

[This revelation was living and vibrant and hideous and dreadful and sweet and lovely; and of all the visions that I saw, this was the greatest comfort to me, that our good lord, who is so to be revered and feared, is so familiar and so courteous, and this filled my soul full of the greatest delight and security.] (7.30–34)

For Julian, God is revealed in the dying of Jesus as both "homely" and "curteyse," the former term indicating familiarity and the latter a kind of feudal *noblesse oblige*. Joan Nuth notes the overtones of "curteyse": "The word thus captures something of the relationship which ideally existed between lord and vassal in feudal society, a relationship based on personal love, mutual respect, and fidelity to the obligations willingly assumed by both parties."[55] She goes on to say, "[w]hile 'courtesy' allows for friendliness and hospitality, it also evokes notions of majesty and worship."[56] The word "homely," on the other hand, is a more intimate term and carries implications of dwelling together or, as Julian employs it, of dwelling within: "Julian interprets the homeliness of God's love quite literally. God's love is simply our home."[57] But we do not simply dwell within God, God also dwells within us: "The place that Jhesu takyth in oure soule he shall nevyr remoue withouten ende, as to my syght, for in vs is his homelyest home and his endlesse dwellyng [The place that Jesus takes in our soul, he shall never leave, as I understand it, for his most familiar of homes and his eternal dwelling is in us]" (68.15–17).

One should carefully note that Julian is not saying that God's courtesy is in some sense supplanted by homeliness; God's relationship to the soul is such that the relationship of fealty between a lord and vassal remains a valid analogy. The perdurance of courtesy signals that this relationship is still one of asymmetrical power. There is a genuine "reverent drede," fully pleasing to God, that corresponds to God's courtesy and that persists even in heaven (74.43–47). The proper relationship of the soul to God is one in which God is seen as sovereign power itself, but in such a way that God is also an intimate companion.

> For oure curtese lorde wylle þat we be as homely with hym as hart may thyngke or soule may desyer; but be we ware þat we take not so rechelously this homelyhed for to leue curtesye. For oure lorde hym

selves is souereyn homelyhed, and so homely as he is, as curtesse he is; for he is very curteyse.

[For our courteous lord desires that we be as familiar with him as the heart can conceive or the soul can desire; but we must beware that we do not accept this familiarity so carelessly that we abandon courtesy. For our lord himself is sovereign familiarity, and he is as courteous as he is familiar, for he is true courtesy.] (77.51–55)

One can speak simultaneously of God's power and God's self-degradation only through the hybrid language of incarnation. It is the sight of Jesus' bleeding head that occasions Julian's hybridization of language, mixing high and low, majesty and familiarity, and indeed, Christ's crucified and risen body is the grotesque backdrop against which all of Julian's revelations take place. Christ's body is the site of the degradation of God, where the very interior of God is opened up to Julian and her fellow Christians, and as such is characterized, beyond all other bodies, as imbued with infinite generative power.[58]

2. From Flood to Drought

In his description of the grotesque body, Bakhtin stresses that it is a body of perpetual becoming, which constantly mutates into new forms as it assimilates and is assimilated by those other bodies with which it comes into contact. We see a similar emphasis on bodily mutability in Julian's descriptions of Christ's body.[59] Not only is it a body that, as the site of the self-degradation of God, hybridizes oppositions, but it is a site that seems to undergo constant visible changes, which Julian notes in detail. In particular, the suffering that Christ endures on the cross, as the assimilation of human suffering, transforms his body, and this transformation is intrinsic to his salvific generativity, whereby his body assimilates us, even in our sinfulness.

One of the transformations that Jesus' crucified body undergoes that is of passionate interest to Julian is its transition from wetness to dryness. We have seen how in the first showing Julian compares the blood coming from Christ's head to a great shower of rain falling from the eaves of a house. In her account of the fourth showing in chapter twelve she returns to the great quantity of Christ's blood, this time explicitly associating it with the violent transgression of the boundaries of his body in the scourging at the pillar.[60] Whereas in the first showing the blood came from the head, in this vision it is the blood from his body that she sees, and with this move downward, toward the lower bodily strata, we have an even more vivid description of the moistness of Christ's body. She says that the amount of blood is so great that she could see neither the skin nor the wound from which the blood flowed, "but as it were all blode" (12.7). Jesus' "tendyr flessch [tender flesh]" is abused to the point that his body liquefies. In a way typical of her close association of creation and redemption, Julian goes on to say that the blood brings to her mind God's gift of the earth's plentiful waters, which it infinitely surpasses in healing properties and cleansing powers. For Julian, the blood of Jesus is charged with regenerative power for humanity, for it is both plentiful by the power ("vertu") of his divinity and yet is still *human* blood, *our* blood.[61] Divine power is released by being brought low, so as to be spread abroad by the human blood of Jesus. It is this human blood that harrows hell, that "overflowyth all erth, and is redy to wash all creatures of synne which be of good wyll, haue ben and shall be [overflows all the earth, and is ready to wash from sin all creatures that are, have been, and will be of good will]," and that ascends in Christ's body into heaven, where Jesus continues to bleed "as long as vs nedyth [as long as we have need]" (12.22–31). For Julian, the intercessory power of Christ's blood has overtones of the power of infinite and eternal fecundity.

Jesus speaks to Julian and says, "Here with is the feende ovyr come [With this the devil is overcome]" (13.7). The power of the blood Christ pours out in his passion overcomes the power of Satan. Revealed in this outpouring is a fullness to divine power that leaves no room for any real power of evil, so that Satan's power is shown to be in fact "vnmyght [unmight]"—or in Augustine's terms, "privation." God's power is not one that must struggle for dominance over other powers, or one that has a delimitable sphere proper to it that it might seek to expand.[62] It is a power present in all its fullness—not in some "bound" or "muted" form—in the death of Jesus, in the opening to the world's suffering of his body. The confrontation of divine power and demonic "vnmyght" is not therefore agonistic but "carnivalesque"; it is not so much a defeat as an unmasking of demonic pretensions. Julian's response to Christ's words is also articulated in the language of the carnival: she laughs (13.25). And those around her laugh. The power of Satan, which seemed in the late medieval imagination to be at times perhaps more vivid and more real than God's power, is overturned by the grotesque effluence of Christ's blood, and Julian joins in this effluence through the laughter which flows from her. She writes, "I thought that I wolde that alle my evyn crysten had seen as I saw. Then shoulde all they a lawchyd with me [I thought that I wished that all my fellow Christians had seen what I saw. Then they all would have laughed with me]" (13.27–28). In the face of the demystification of the power of evil, one loses the compulsion to identify and expel dangerous impurities and christendom takes on the aspect of a carnival. Julian sees God appear as the lord of a feast, filling his house with joy and mirth, "to glad and solace hys derewurthy frendes fulle homely and fulle curtesly [to gladden and comfort his dear friends with great familiarity and courtesy]" (14.9–10).

But the carnival makes only a brief appearance in this life. Julian experiences a sudden sense of divine abandonment, followed by a rapid alternation of consolation and desolation, "now that oonn and now that other, dyuerse tymes, I suppose about twenty tymes [now the one and now the other, many times, I suppose about twenty]" (15.16–18). Julian understands this as a revelation that "God wylle that we know that he kepyth vs evyr in like suer, in wo and in wele [God wants us to know that he keeps us always in the same security, in trouble and in well-being]" (15.23–24). The carnival of God's victorious unmasking of demonic power is real, but so is the suffering inflicted by the unmight of evil. While Julian and those around her laugh, Christ does not laugh (13.28–29), because the overcoming of the devil is an unmasking that is irrevocably tied to "the blessydfulle passion and deth of oure lorde Jhesu Crist, that was done in fulle grette ernest and with sad traveyle [the most blessed passion and death of our lord Jesus Christ, which was done with the greatest seriousness and with somber labor]" (13.39–41).

Immediately after this follows the eighth showing, in which Christ reveals "a parte of hys passyon nere his dyeng [a part of his passion near his dying]" in which his face is "drye and blodeles with pale dyeng [dry and bloodless with pale dying]" (16.3–4). Julian proceeds with a gruesome catalogue of the transformation of Jesus' body from a fountain of healing power to a dry, desiccated corpse. Focusing on Christ's lips, she notes the discoloration changing from the paleness of the dying to a blue and then a brownish blue, "as the flessch turned more depe dede [as the flesh turned more deeply dead]" (16.6). Julian describes this as "a peinfulle chaungyng to see [a painful changing to see]" (16.9–10),⁶³ and continues describing how Christ's nose shrivels and his body turns black, "alle chaungyd and turned ouȝte of þe feyer fressch and lyuely coloure of hym selves in to drye dyeng [all changing and transformed from his own beautiful fresh and vivid color into dry death]" (16.11–13). A cold wind blows, drying the body from the outside, while loss of blood and pain dry it from within, though some moisture remains. And as long as any moisture remains the pain continues, for what seems to Julian like seven nights, "contynually dyeng [continually dying]" (16.29).

If the great quantity of Jesus' blood is salvific, what can this drying mean? Is its salvific power in fact limited? The change in Christ's body seems anticipated by Julian's sudden experience of desolation in the previous chapter. However, Julian had taken away from that experience the message that "blysse is lastyng withouȝt ende, and payne is passyng, and shall be brought to nowght to them that shall be savyd [bliss is eternal, and pain is passing, and shall be brought to nothing for those who shall be saved]" (15.31–32). Yet her vision of Jesus' pain seems to go on and on. As much as she stressed the plenty of Christ's blood, she stresses this "deep drying." The pain is not only Jesus', but all humanity seems imperiled by the vanishing of the saving blood. Of the former flood of salvific power there appears to remain only enough to perpetuate Jesus' pains.

The carnival seems by nature something that arrives riding on the flow of time to interrupt "business as usual." It seems inevitably to be a deviation from the normal construction of relationships of power, never to be permanently instituted as itself the norm. As it arrives with the season or the saint's festival, so too the carnival departs, establishing a pattern of feast and fast, of weal and woe. It is subject to the very flow of time that carries it. So too Julian's image of the power flowing forth with Christ's blood *seems* a merely temporary respite from the grip that privation and pain have on humanity. What does it mean to invest one's salvation in something so mutable, so time bound, so subject to pain and death, as a human body? The image presented to Julian of the ruin of Christ's corpse seems to betoken the ultimate failure of his power.

As if to drive home the fragility and transitoriness of Christ's power, Julian returns to her description of the drying process, focusing this time on the wounds made by the crown of thorns and emphasizing the way in which the wounded skin was stretched open by the nails and thorns. It is at this point that Julian says, "in alle thys tyme of Cristes presens, I felte no peyne, but for Cristes paynes [in all this time of Christ's presence I felt no pain except for Christ's pain]," and she realizes that her desire to share in his suffering has been granted her. But it seems that she begins to have second thoughts, for this pain is so great that it appears more destructive than salvific:

> than thought me I knew fulle lytylle what payne it was that I askyd, and as a wrech I repentyd me, thyngkyng if I had wyste what it had be, loth me had been to haue preyde it. For me thought my paynes passyd ony bodely deth. I thought: Is ony payne in hell lyk thys?
>
> [then I thought, I had so little knowledge of what pain it was that I had asked for, and like a wretch I regretted it, thinking that if I had known what it was, I would have been reluctant to pray for it. For I thought my pain passed any physical death. I thought: is any pain in hell like this?] (17.53–57)

Julian momentarily regrets her desire to share the pains of Christ on the cross, because it seems to her that these are not purgative pains preparing her for heaven, but rather the torments of hell. Julian is answered that "Helle is a nother peyne, for ther is dyspyer [Hell is a different pain, for there is despair]." In other words, this pain is not bereft of the hope that it might be in some sense salvific, that it might be "peyne þat leed to saluacion [pain that leads to salvation]" (17.58).[64] In Christ's sufferings on the cross, pain is comprehended within hope. Thus it is not the joy of the carnival that is the interruption, but the pain of loss, which interrupts the plentitude of God's infinite goodness only ultimately to be encompassed within the horizon of God's salvific will.

Here the dynamics of bodily seeing become important, as Julian notes her great sorrow occasioned by her sight of Jesus' pain. This sorrow is a sign of a union, "a grett onyng betwene Crist and vs [a great union between Christ and us]," because "when he was in payne we ware in payne [when he was in pain, we were in pain]," and this union extends beyond the human so that "alle creatures that myght suffer payne sufferyd with hym [all creatures that could suffer pain suffered with him]" (18.14–16). As the forces of nature fail because of the suffering of their sustaining cause,[65] the cosmic dimensions of this event begin to appear, moving us beyond the simple devotionalism of Julian's initial desire to be filled with mind of the passion, yet not, as we have seen, to a "contemplative" transcending of the humanity of Christ as the soul strains toward the ineffable. The suffering of the humanity of Christ is *itself* "ineffable" because it has a depth beyond what she could have imagined, just as his blood is plentiful beyond her powers of description. And it unites her not only to Jesus, but also to the world that suffers along with its crucified Lord.

The sorrow elicited by the event of Christ's passion, not only in Julian but in all creatures, is an atoning sorrow that bears salvation within it. In its drying on the cross the body of Jesus is a "failed" body. It is a body deprived of its proper form, because it did not prudently police its boundaries but rather squandered the limited supply of its precious blood. Yet the failure of that body is encompassed within the larger story of its creative act of becoming. It is only in its failure, in its dissolution, that the great atonement that unites all creatures in the compassion of God comes to pass. In order to be a salvific body, Christ's body must in some sense be a failed body.

3. A Body of Lack: Christ Our Mother

Julian's *Revelation* presents Jesus' body as an ambiguously "failed" body even beyond its crucified suffering. Julian also sees Jesus as having a body that is, according to the prevailing medieval view, in some sense *inherently* degraded and inferior: a female body, a body that is nature's failed attempt at creating a male. The medieval tendency to view female bodies as characterized by lack and failure, while at the same time seeing them as fertile and nutritive, is exploited by Julian in her teaching on the motherhood of Jesus. The motherhood of Jesus is, along with the tag line "alle shalle be wele," certainly the best known thing about Julian and frequently considered her chief contribution to theology. While the importance of the theme of Christ as mother in Julian's theology as a whole can be overstressed—and to my mind *has* been in recent years—it is certainly true that she takes and develops what was a minor theme in medieval devotion into a theologically fruitful way of understanding divine love.[66] Yet I would argue that Julian's primary interest is not in the femaleness or "femininity" of Jesus *per se*, but in femaleness as a code for humanity and for "degradation," in Bakhtin's sense. This is not to say that she sees the motherhood of Jesus as only a negative indicator of his weakness; as we shall see, motherhood obviously has a deeply positive value for Julian. Yet God's humanity and humility revealed in Christ our mother are inseparable from the "failed" body of Christ as the site of our redemption.

As was typical of medieval women writers,[67] Julian's gendering of Jesus as female is accomplished for the most part not by what we today would think of as "gender roles" (woman as helpmate or compassionate intercessor with a powerful male figure), but by biological roles (gestation, birth, lactation), thereby highlighting the central importance of corporeality to the identity of Jesus.[68] However, one must be careful in making a distinction between gender roles (the feminine) and biological sex (the female), as if to say that the former is simply "constructed" and the latter "natural." In medieval cultures, the gender roles and inferior status of women were seen as flowing "naturally" from their inferior biology.[69] Thus while Julian displays little overt interest in woman in her gender role and is extremely interested in woman as "flesh," it is difficult to separate the fleshiness of women from their low social status. Jesus' corporeality is female precisely *because* the lowly status of the female body is a suitable site for the self-degradation by which God renews and restores humanity. Jesus takes flesh so that "alle shalle be wele"—even such a "little thing" as the (female) flesh. At the same time, by appealing to woman as flesh, and particularly as maternal flesh, Julian is invoking a very ambiguously coded set of symbols that speak both of power and of passivity.

The portrayal of Christ's humanity as "female" is not something peculiar to Julian. Indeed, the twelfth-century abbess Hildegard of Bingen wrote, "man signifies the divinity, woman the humanity of the Son of God."[70] It was commonly believed in a very literal sense that Christ's flesh was created from the female flesh of the virgin Mary, thus accounting for its greater tenderness and susceptibility to pain. A not untypical argument went as follows:

> For this reason [Christ's] suffering was even more painful, because the tenderer a part of our body is, the more painful is the suffering it experiences, as can be seen in the eye. And keep in mind that the flesh of man is tenderer than that of a wild animal, and among men the flesh of a woman is tenderer than that of a man, and among women, that of a virgin more so than that of a woman who has lost her vir-

ginity. But Christ's flesh was taken and formed out of the most pure blood [*purissimis sanguinibus*] of the Virgin, and he himself lived in the most pure virginity until his death.[71]

Thus Christ's flesh is quite literally made out of female flesh (or rather, as the account quoted above would have it, female *blood*), there being no male "seed" as the active generative principle.[72]

On the whole, women were thought to be physically, intellectually, and morally weaker and inherently more passive than men; the female body was, in short, a body characterized by lack. The flesh of women was thought to be colder than that of men and constantly in need of heat. This lack was related to an excess: women's greater moistness.[73] Tears, menstrual blood, milk, all were excess fluids exuded by female bodies and were highly charged symbols both of growth and fertility as well as of pollution. A fifteenth-century gynecological text notes: "you must understand that women have less heat in their bodies than men and have more moisture because of lack of heat that would dry their moisture and their humors."[74] Because of this coldness, women were drawn to men, who were warmer, and a good deal of heat could, according to medieval medical theory, be generated by sexual excitement.[75] The body of Jesus, taken from female flesh, would seem therefore more subject to desire than male flesh. But Christ's body is not only female flesh, but virgin female flesh, which is even more at risk. As the *Ancrene Wisse* puts it:

> This brittle vessel, which is woman's flesh—though the balm, the ointment, is maidenhood held within it (or chaste purity, once maidenhood is lost)—this brittle vessel is nonetheless as brittle as any glass, for if it is once broken, it is never mended to the wholeness it had, any more than glass. But it breaks more easily than brittle glass does. For glass does not break unless something hits it, but with respect to the loss of maidenhood the flesh can lose its wholeness with a stinking desire, if it go far enough and last long enough.[76]

The flesh of the virgin is fragile, easily shattered by desire and by the assaults of the devil.

At the same time that it was a sign of weakness and lack, women's flesh and its liquidity were also symbolic of nourishment and power. The much-cited medieval legend of the mother pelican who feeds her young with her own blood (and was therefore seen as a type of Christ) testifies to the nutritive qualities that were ascribed to female blood.[77] Beyond this, all of the fluids of the body were thought to be essentially interchangeable, and in particular, according to Galen's widely accepted theory of delabation, breast milk was thought to be a transformed type of blood.[78] This was perhaps the root of seeing the blood of Christ related to a mother's milk.[79] It is clear that Christ's body was seen as a nutritive body, eaten by the faithful in the Eucharist, and therefore a female body. The image of Christ as the mother who nourishes with his own body was a fairly common one in late medieval piety and preaching.[80]

In addition to the female body being nutritive, it was also seen as generative, though in a passive manner and through great pain. The perceived passivity of woman in the reproductive process seemed to fit well with Christ, who eschewed "manly" virtues such as bravery in battle in order to undergo his passion. Also, the pain with which women brought their children into the world was seen as an apt symbol for the great suffering undergone by Jesus in order to bring forth sons of God. Anselm writes in his well-known "Prayer to St. Paul,"

> And you, Jesus, are you not also a mother?
> Are you not the mother who, like a hen,
> gathers her chickens under her wings? . . .
> It is by your death that they have been born,
> for if you had not been in labour,
>   you could not have borne death;
> and if you had not died, you would not have brought forth.
> For, longing to bear sons into life,
>   you tasted death,
> and by dying you begot them.[81]

The medieval image of female corporeality is therefore simultaneously one of excess desire and a fundamental lack. Joan Cadden has argued that various medieval medical views of women, despite their differences, "share the underlying suggestion that women are empty, void, lacking—that by not having the male principle they both lack masculine activity and need (and therefore desire) men's active principle, semen."[82] At the same time, women's bodies are images of fertility. The woman's body is generative and nutritive, while also being cold, fragile, and suffering. The contradictions in this image give it the grotesque quality so common in images associated with generation and renewal.

We can see why Julian would use the language of Christ as mother, and indeed she deploys many of these images of femaleness in depicting the corporeality of Jesus. When Julian wants to make clear that the *humanity* of Jesus suffers, and not the divinity, she says, "only the maydyns sonne sufferyd"; Christ's humanity is associated with that which is taken from Mary (23.31–32). Thus, rather than emphasizing "feminine" attributes in her various depictions and descriptions of Jesus, Julian has above all a sense of the sheer biological femaleness of his body. While the sex of Jesus is clearly male—Julian nowhere hints that what she is seeing is a female or even androgynous figure[83]— his bodiliness itself is portrayed, in a variety of ways, as female. For example, the excessive moistness of Julian's image of Christ's body, the sheer quantity of his blood, is symbolically coded as female.[84] The reversal effected by Christ's descent into hell and defeat of evil is all the more striking because the great abundance of blood that defeats Satan and demystifies evil flows from a body that is in essence female. We see here again a grotesque reversal of high and low in which transcendent generative power is ascribed to the blood pouring forth from a lowly female body.

Jesus' body is not only characterized by excessive moisture, it is nourishment for his children: "The moder may geue her chylde sucke hyr mylke, but our precyous moder Jhesu, he may fede vs wyth hym selfe, and doth full curtesly and full tendyrly with the blessyd sacrament, that is precyous fode of very life [The mother can give her child to suck of her milk, but our precious mother Jesus can feed us with himself, and does so most courteously and most tenderly with the blessed sacrament, which is the precious food of true life]" (60.29–32). He also brings these children to birth through his dolorous passion, but in a reversal of what we know of human mothers, Julian notes that the children of Christ do not come out of his body, rather they remain enclosed within him for eternity: "oure savyoure is oure very moder, in whome we be endlessly borne and nevyr shall come out of hym [our savior is our true mother, in whom we are eternally carried and we shall never come out of him]" (57.49–50).[85] His motherhood surpasses all others both because its pain was sharpest and its gestation is unto eternity:

We wytt that alle oure moders bere vs to payne and to dyeng. A, what is that? But oure very moder Jhesu, he alone beryth vs to joye and to endlesse levyng, blessyd mot he be. Thus he sustenyth vs with in hym in loue and traveyle, in to the full tyme þat he wolde suffer the sharpyst thornes and grevous paynes that evyr were or evyr shalle be, and dyed at the last.

[We know that all our mothers bear us for pain and dying. Ah, what is that? But our true mother Jesus, he alone bears us for joy and eternal living, blessed may he be. Thus he sustains us within him in love and labor, until the full time that he would suffer the sharpest thorns and most grievous pains that ever were or ever will be, and died at the last.] (60.18–23)

Julian also discusses less obviously biological aspects of motherhood, in particular the association of motherhood and mercy and the role of the mother in rearing the child.[86] Thus there *is* a certain "femininity" to Christ our mother. However, several things might be noted here. First of all, as I have said, it is very difficult, if not impossible, to separate the symbolic coding of woman's gender roles from the symbolic coding of woman's biology. Thus Julian associates the mother's tenderness with "the kynde and condycion of moderhed [nature and condition of motherhood]." Second, Julian never seems to balance the mercy of the mother and the wrath of the father. Nowhere in Julian's *Revelation* do we find an image like that in the *Ancrene Wisse* in which Jesus our mother interposes himself between us and the enraged Father, who proceeds to beat Jesus to death in our stead.[87] Such a use of motherhood would be entirely counter to Julian's position that there is no wrath in God. Finally, Julian attributes to Jesus as mother qualities that were not stereotypically female or feminine. Thus she writes, "our hevynly moder Jhesu may nevyr suffer vs þat be his chyldren to peryssch, for he is almyghty, all wysdom and all loue [our heavenly mother Jesus can never allow we who are his children to perish, for he is almighty, all wisdom and all love]." Attributing power and wisdom to women was certainly not typical of the Middle Ages' picture of the feminine, despite divine Wisdom's feminine personification in scripture.

Julian's chief interest remains Jesus' suffering corporeality as salvific, and femaleness as a code for "degraded" corporeality that is yet fecund.[88] In Julian's teaching on Jesus as mother, the notions of gestational enclosure, labor, and lactation are primary. All of these distinctively female activities are clearly bodily, tied to the lower strata and replete with associations of fecundity, and thus incarnational. In chapter sixty-three Julian explicitly associates Christ's taking of human nature with these activities:

> And in the takyng of oure kynd he quyckyd vs, and in his blessyd dyend vppon the crosse he bare vs to eternal lyfe. And fro þat tyme, and now and evyr shall in to domysday, he fedyth vs and fordreth vs, ryght as þe hye souereyne kyndnesse of moderhed wylle, and as þe kyndly nede of chyldhed askyth.
>
> [And in taking of our nature he gave us life, and in his blessed dying upon the cross he bore us to eternal life. And from that time, now and to the day of judgement, he feeds us and fosters us, just as the high sovereign kindness/nature of motherhood wills, and as the natural need of childhood asks.] (63.30–34)

One might note the connection between "kyndnesse" and motherhood in this quotation, and indeed throughout Julian's discussion of Jesus as mother. Diane Krantz has shown that in Middle English the term "kynd" not only had the dual meaning of "kindness" and of "nature," but also could refer to sexual organs and in particular to the womb.[89] She goes on to argue that Julian's association of "kyndnesse" with motherhood is grounded, at least partially, in this sense of "kynd"-as-womb.[90] Christ is our mother not simply because of stereotypical feminine characteristics—because he is merciful or tenderhearted or an intermediary between us and a wrathful Father God—but because his is a body that gives birth through suffering and that is food that communicates its very substance.

Jesus as mother—as a suffering body characterized by "failure" and "lack," yet bringing forth life out of a desire of infinite expanse and intensity—is crucial to Julian's mapping of the contours of Christ's body. Within the body of Christ our mother is the infinite expanse of his empty womb, which is the shape of his desire for us. Julian exploits the tensions and contradictions inherent in medieval views of the female body to produce an image that in its grotesqueness and hybridity combines failure and renewal, emptiness and excess, so as to speak of God's salvation effected through Jesus' death. In doing so, she forces a reinterpretation of our understandings of failure and emptiness, renewal and excess.

4. Privation and Plenty

How can Julian understand the drying of Christ's body as salvific when it seems that it was his plenteous blood that held out hope for redemption? How can she understand the "failed" body of Christ our mother to be possessed of infinite generativity, bringing forth children from the emptiness of his womb? Julian must find some way to locate absence within the economy of God's saving work so as to understand the role of privation in human life. It is in the context of reflecting on sin as it registers itself in the pain of Jesus' crucified body that Julian explores the nature of privation. Julian walks a fine line in developing an extremely subtle account of negation, weaving together ideas of sin as privation and of desire as lack, along with images of secrecy, purgation, breaking, and wounding. Nothingness is both the essence of sin and also that from which God creates; it is the ontological poverty of creatures apart from the sustaining love of God. God's overcoming of sin is tied to the wounding of Christ on the cross and the "breaking" of the church. And all of this is somehow tied to a secret deed that is hidden in God.

At the beginning of the thirteenth showing Christ brings to her mind "the longyng that I had to hym before [the desire I had for him before]," and she reflects that nothing hindered her except sin, thinking that if there had never been sin, then "alle shulde haue be wele [all would have been well]" (27.9). But Jesus responds, "Synne is behouely," which might be glossed "sin is necessary" or, perhaps better (if less pithily), "sin has a place in the economy of salvation," and then he adds perhaps the most famous words in Julian's *Revelation*: "but alle shall be wele, and alle shalle be wele, and alle maner of thynge shalle be wele" (27.13–14). My somewhat torturous gloss on "behouely" is designed to make clear that Julian's use of the theme of *felix culpa* is not equivalent to the claim that God somehow *needs* sin to accomplish God's intentions for creation, for sin is in fact the nothingness that God's creative act transforms "in the beginning." Rather, sin is "fitting" in an almost aesthetic sense; it can be located within the divine "art" in such a way that it is incapable of destroying the goodness of everything, because it is fundamentally lacking in positive existence. It is incorporated as a shadow is incorporated into a landscape. Thus even in the face of sin, "all shall be well."

Julian offers a dual interpretation of the words "all maner of thyng shalle be wele." On the one hand, she takes this to mean that God "nott oonly . . . takyth heed to nobylle thynges and to grett, but also to lytylle and to small, to lowe and to symple, and to oone and to other [not only . . . concerns himself with noble and great things, but also with little and small, lowly and simple, this one and that]" (32.5–7). In making well, God makes *all* things well: "he wylle that we wytt that the lest thyng shall nott be forgeten [he wants us to know that the least thing will not be forgotten]" (32.8–9). This emphasis on God's attention to the "lest thyng" harkens back not only to her reflections on God's concern for the humblest of human activities, but also to her vision in the first showing of "a little thing, the quantitie of an haselnott," which she is told "is all that is made" (5.9, 12–13). The littleness of all things is an indication of the ontological poverty of creation— "me thought it might sodenly haue fallen to nawght for littlenes [I thought it might suddenly fall into nothingness on account of its littleness]"—and this poverty simply highlights for Julian the richness of God's sustaining love: "It lasteth and ever shall, for god loueth it; and so hath all thing being by the loue of god [It continues in existence, and always will, because God loves it; and thus do all things exist by the love of God]" (5.13–16). As Vincent Gillespie and Maggie Ross have noted, the very nature of the vision is "apophatic," highlighting in a sense precisely that which is *not* seen:

> [W]e are being offered an image which does not exist. What Julian sees is not a hazelnut but an unspecified thing, about the size of a hazelnut if it were in the palm of her hand (which it is not), and as round as a ball. The 'little thing' is described by gesture toward material objects but its true properties, as perceived by Julian, are *not* its materiality or referentiality but rather aspects of God's relationship to it.[91]

Thus, intertwined in Julian's vision of the littleness of creation is knowledge both of the essential nothingness of all things, as well as of God's love, which communicates existence to nothingness. Julian takes from this the Augustinian point that while creation can be an indicator of God who created it—she sees in the little thing the Trinity's work of making, loving, and keeping (5.17–18)—human beings cannot rest in creatures but only in God.[92]

> For this is the cause why we be not all in ease of hart and of sowle, for we seeke heer rest in this thing that is so little, wher no reste is in, and we know not our god, that is almightie, all wise and all good, for

he is our verie reste.... And this is the cause why that no sowle is in reste till it is noughted of all things that is made.

[For this is the reason why we are not completely at ease of heart and of soul, because we seek rest here in this thing that is so little, where there is no rest, and we do not know our God, who is all mighty, all wise, and all good, who is our true rest.... And this is the reason why no soul can be at rest until it is stripped of every created thing.] (5.26–32)

To encounter the "little things" of this world is both to see God's goodness toward the least of creatures and also to experience a restless desire that, if referred to God as its proper end, becomes not a desire to accumulate or possess things, but a desire to pass through things to the love that undergirds them, to be "noughted of all things that is made" so as to "come to him naked, pleaynly and homly [naked, plainly, and familiarly]" (5.35). This "noughting" is the cultivation of "meekenes": "that a creatur see þe lord meruelous great and her selfe mervelous litle [that a creature see the lord marvelously great and herself marvelously little]" (65.10–11). Such a soul sees herself and all things as "little," and at the same time as sustained in their existence by God's infinite love, which makes *all* things well. This is another version of the hybridization of courtesy and homeliness that we saw earlier: God's courteous gift of existence to creation is grounded in a fundamental asymmetry of power between creator and creature, yet this gift takes the form of a homely intimacy between creatures and God as their sustaining cause.

The other meaning that Julian gives to the locution "all maner of thyng shalle be wele" is that God shall make well even the evil that to our sight is beyond repair (32.10–12). She employs the same language of negation to speak of sin that she used for the stripping away of attachments to creatures. As I have pointed out, for Julian, sin is quite simply *nothing*. She explained in the third showing that she saw that "alle thynges that is done is welle done, for our lord god doth all.... for he is in the myd poynt of all thynges, and all he doeth [all things that are done are done well, for our lord God does all.... for he is the midpoint of all things, and all that he does]," and therefore "synne is no deed [sin is not an action]" (11.18–22). Whereas we might analogically speak of divine and human actions, evil is not even analogously a "deed" in relation to God's activity. Julian is again making an Augustinian point that sin is that privation of the act by which God communicates being to creatures. The overcoming of the nothingness of sin in God's redemptive activity is not some sort of "new" activity that God undertakes, but is simply *creatio ex nihilo* played, if you will, in another key. "For ryght as the blessyd trinite made alle thyng of nought, ryght so the same blessyd trynyte shalle make wele alle that is not welle [For just as the blessed Trinity created all things from nothing, just so shall the same blessed Trinity make well all that is not well]" (32.35–37).

Though sin is in this sense "no deed," there is still a manifest opposition between the deeds of God and the undoing of those deeds by sin, for whereas God calls creatures out of nothingness, evil (at least within the flow of time) negates that creative activity. The essential nothingness of sin cannot be seen, but can be registered by the damage it inflicts on creatures; sin, since it has "no maner of substance, ne no part of beyng . . . myght not be knowen but by the payne that is caused therof [no manner of substance, nor any part of being . . . cannot be known except by the pain that is caused by it]" (27.27–28). Sin is revealed preeminently in the sufferings of Jesus on the cross, which is "the ymage and the lyknes of owr fowle blacke dede where in our feyer bryght blessyd lorde hyd his godhede [the image and likeness of our foul black deed, within which our fair, bright, blessed lord hid his divinity]" (10.59–61).[93] However, Julian believes that if all in fact shall be well, then even this pain, which obscures Christ's divinity and shows to us our own sin, must somehow be locatable within the creative and redemptive intention of God: "It is tru that synne is cause of alle thys payne, but alle shalle be wele, and alle maner of thyng shalle be wele [It is true that sin is the cause of all this pain, but all shall be well, and all manner of things shall be well]" (27.33–34). Walter Hilton will speak similarly of the "image of sin" as a "darkness" and a "nothing" in which "Jesus is hidden in his joy."[94] In the cross Julian sees the depth of human sin revealed as that which hides the divinity of Christ, yet which is paradoxically enfolded within the saving flesh of Jesus.

How the origin of sin within a good creation fits into the intention of God remains "an hygh mervelous prevyte hyd in god, whych pryuyte he shalle opynly make and shalle be knowen to vs in hevyn [a high, marvelous secret hidden in God, which he will make plain and shall be known to us in heaven]" (27.39–40). Note here the secrecy theme: in this life our knowledge of God is a kind of disciplined lack of knowledge, a *docta ignorantia*. This is different both from the ignorance that results from sin, and from the nominalist idea of a God of absolute power who is hidden behind the "dome" (to use Oberman's metaphor) of the *ordinata*. It is a particular way of knowing that is correlative to the grotesque body. Intertwined with the transformations in Christ's appearance that Julian describes in chapter ten of the long text are her reflections on the relationship between "seeking" and "seeing," so that her vision of his transfigured face is taken by her to be "a lernyng to my vnderstandyng that the contynually seeking of the soule plesyth god moch. For it may do no more than seke, suffer and trust [a lesson to my understanding that the continual seeking of the soul is very pleasing to God. For it may do no more than seek, suffer, and trust]" (10.68–70). In part the need to seek grows out of her inability to see this image well, for it appears "swemly and darkely [frightening and dark]" (10.11) and she must thus persist in seeking. But it also grows out of the very nature of the image that she beholds. On the one hand, the sufferings of Christ are "the ymage and the lyknes" of our sin, the becoming visible of evil. At the same time, the crucified body of Jesus is, to use Bakhtin's phrase, "a body in the act of becoming,"[95] the saving incarnation of immutable, infinite divinity in mutable, finite, suffering flesh. The tensions within this single image are not subject to resolution in this life, thus it is an image that can be beheld only through endless seeking, an image by which one must be "led"—a verb Julian habitually uses to describe how God gives her insight[96]—along its various transformations. Because our seeing in this life is always also a seeking, we cannot know the reason why God allowed sin. But we can know that it is consistent with the divine love displayed in creation and cross and thus can behold in the crucified both the becoming visible of sin and the manifestation of God's saving love.

While Julian does not downplay the seriousness of sin—she calls it an "oygly syȝt [ugly sight]" (27.26)—she consistently blurs the distinction between "natural" evil (such as sickness) and "moral" evil (i.e., sin *per se* and its effects).[97] For Julian, sin is less like a willful transgression (perhaps this is one of the nuances of her claim that "synne is no deed") and more like a sickness or accidental injury that afflicts us, weakening us and blinding us to God's love. And like sickness, sin too is (at least potentially) a "nowtyng" by which the soul is stripped of earthly affections. But most of all, sin is pain, and preeminently the pain that she sees in the dying of Jesus. Julian writes:

In this nakid word 'synne,' our lord browte to my mynd generally al that is not good, and the shamefull dispite and the utter nowtyng that he bare for us in this life, and his dyeng, and al the peynys and passions of al his creatures, gostly and bodyly—for we be all in party nowtid, and we shall be nowtid followyng our master Iesus till we be full purgyd: that is to sey, till we be fully nowtid of our dedly flesh and of al our inward affections which arn not very good—, and the beholdyng of this, with al peynys that ever wern or ever shal be; and with al these I understond the passion of Criste for most peyne and overpassyng.

[In this naked word 'sin,' our Lord brought to my mind the general idea of all that is not good, and the shameful cruelty and the utter stripping that he bore for us in this life, and his dying, and all the pains and sufferings of all his creatures, spiritual and corporeal—for we all are in part stripped, and we shall be stripped in following our master Jesus until we are fully purged: that is to say, until we are fully stripped of our mortal flesh and of all our inward affections that are not truly good—and the contemplation of this, with all the pains that ever were or ever shall be; and among these I understood the passion of Christ to be the greatest and surpassing pain.][98]

"Synne" encompasses all that is not good: not only the "peynys and passions of al His creatures," but also Jesus' crucifixion, "the utter nowtyng that He bare for us in this life." But the "nowtyng" of Jesus in the passion is also the redemptive deed of God, and as such a source of joy to God: "It is a joy, a blysse, an endlesse lykyng to me that evyr I sufferd passion for the; and yf I myght suffer more, I wolde suffer more [It is a joy, a bliss, and endless delight to me that I suffered the passion for you; and if I might suffer more, I would suffer more]" (22.5–7). The suffering and death of Jesus is the instance of "most peyne and overpassyng"; both the clearest manifestation of sin and the site of redemptive solidarity (thus the possible play on words of "overpassing" and "passover") with the suffering of creatures.

Thus, Julian says, we must behold the passion of Jesus in three ways. First, we must look at the pain he suffered and feel both contrition (seeing Christ as our victim) and compassion (seeing him as one who has united himself to us in suffering) (20.34–35).[99] Second, we must see how the tremendous suffering that he undergoes, which is greater than the suffering of all of humanity, is surpassed by his motive for suffering: the infinite divine love for creatures (22.45–49).

Third, we see in the passion the joy and bliss that it brings to God by bringing about our salvation (23.6–8).[100] The suffering remains a reality even though Julian is shown that both the antecedent love and the consequent joy far surpass the pain suffered.[101] The first manner of beholding the passion, and therefore the need for contrition and compassion, remains even in the face of the others, as an irreducible aspect of the event. At the same time, it is located as an interruption within the horizon of the eternal festival of God's joy and bliss.

The passion of Christ allows a reinterpretation of the "nowtyng" of sickness and sin and all the privations of life, so that they become a means of following Jesus that "purgyth and makyth vs to know oure selves and aske mercy [purges and makes us know ourselves and ask for mercy]" (27.29–30). Sin is nothing other than preferring creatures to the love of God that sustains them; thus to experience the pain of sin is an occasion for contrition, by which we come to know our own ontological poverty. Like Julian's sickness, sin is a breaking that operates within "goddes servannts" as a participation in the sufferings of Christ and in his compassion and as an opportunity for God's healing. As Hans Urs von Balthasar puts it, Julian sees sin, in light of the cross, "as initiation into the self-dispossession, into the love, of the forsaken Son, who is accused of no offense."[102] Julian does not say that sin afflicts us in precisely the same way that it is inflicted by us on the sinless Jesus. The cross remains the sight of our foul black deed; we are both the victims and the perpetrators of evil. Yet our sin does not have the final word. Because Jesus willingly suffers the effects of our sin in solidarity with sinners, the greatest sinners can become the greatest saints, and wear the scars of sin as badges of honor, testimonies to the power of God's grace (38.10–36).

The idea of sin as a kind of purgative breaking and opportunity for God's saving work raises the question of Romans 6:1—"What then are we to say? Should we continue in sin in order that grace may abound?" Julian anticipates such a question and replies that sin is itself painful to creatures; it is, indeed, the hardest pain, and no soul would knowingly sin (40.37–40; cf. 39.2–7, 76.11–12). We sin out of ignorance of God's love and because of the "bestely wylle [beastly will]" that operates in the lower part of the soul (37.17–18). And the punishment that sin brings is the pain inherent in it. The point she attempts to understand and communicate is that God's redemptive work in Jesus' death, resurrection, and ascension goes beyond a simple restoration of creation.

Julian is not interested in speculating about possible situations in possible worlds that have never been afflicted by sin; she is only interested in what in fact is the case: sin has damaged and continues to damage creatures, and God repairs that damage in such a way that "thys asseeth makyng is more plesyng to the blessed godhed and more wurschypfulle for mannys saluacion with oute comparyson than evyr was the synne of Adam harmfulle [without comparison, this making of reparation is more pleasing to the blessed Godhead and more honorable for humanity's salvation than the sin of Adam ever was harmful]" (29.12–14).

So the "nowtyng" involved in pain, including the pain of sin, *is* a kind of *felix culpa*, but it is one that must first be understood in terms of the pain experienced by Jesus on the cross. In discussing how it is that sin is "behouely," Julian returns to this image of Jesus' body drying on the cross and his words, "I thurst."[103] Julian had mentioned earlier that Christ's thirst was both bodily and spiritual, and she goes back to this to explain Christ's spiritual thirst (following a traditional exegesis of John 19:28) as his longing for the salvation of humanity.[104] This is an eternal thirst, which "was in hym from withouȝt beg(y)nnyng [was in him eternally]" (31.38–39) and which shall last until judgement day. It is "a love longyng to have us al togeder hole in him to his blis [a love-longing to have us all together, healed in him, to his bliss]."[105] But it is not simply a desire rooted in lack, rather it is desire that grows out of the fullness of the life of the Godhead: "and aneynst the godhed he is hym selves hyghest blysse, and was fro without begynnyng, and shalle be without end, whych very endlesse blesse may nevyr be hyghed nor lowyde in the selfe [and as regards the Godhead, he is himself the highest bliss, and was from without beginning, and shall be without end, a true eternal bliss that can never be increased or decreased in him]" (31.22–25). Thus there is a plenitude of bliss coextensive with this thirst—"evyr he drawyth and dryngkyth, and yett hym thurstyth and longyth [eternally he draws and drinks, and yet he thirsts and longs]" (75.7–8). Within human history this fullness is seen paradoxically as privation, displayed in the passion of Jesus, and extended through history in the suffering of his body, the church (31.34–36).

The "nowtyng" of Jesus' body on the cross is replicated in the tribulations that his servants undergo, and in particular that his body the church undergoes. Earlier Julian had written, "Holy chyrche shalle be shakyd in sorow and anguyssch and trybulacion in this worlde as men shakyth a cloth in the wynde [in this world, holy church shall be shaken in sorrow and anguish and tribulation, like men shake a cloth in the wind]" (28.6–7). The image of a cloth flapping in the wind harkens back to her image in the eighth showing of Christ's body hung up like a cloth dry in the wind (17.39–40). The church becomes more perfectly Christ's body when it is "lowhyd and dyspysed in thys worlde, scornyd and mokyd and cast out [lowly and despised in this world, scorned and mocked and cast out]" (28.13–14). But this perfecting through suffering also brings Christ's members to the perfection of his bliss. The church must be degraded so as to be created anew by the God who says: "I shal alle to breke yow from yowre veyne affeccions and yowre vyscious pryde, and aftyr that I shalle gader you and make yow meke and mylde, clene and holy by onyng to me [I will break you all from your vain affections and your vicious pride, and afterward I will gather you and make you meek and mild, clean and holy through union with me]" (28.17–20).

Julian does not seem to think of the "breaking" that Christians undergo in terms of a life of deliberately undertaken penance. Life itself, lived in our damaged human nature, brings its own "penance"—privations and diminishments that strip us naked of our human attachments. Toward the end of the *Revelation* Julian tells of Jesus saying to her: "I telle thee, how so evyr thou do, thou shalle haue woo. And thefore I wylle that thow wysely know thy pannannce whych thou arte in contynually, and that thou mekely take it for thy pennannce profytable [I tell you, whatever you do, you will have woe. And therefore I desire that you wisely know the penance that you are in continually, and that you meekly accept it as a profitable penance]." And Julian goes on to say: "This place is pryson, this lyfe is pennannce, and in þe remedy he wylle that we enjoy. The remedy is þat oure lorde is with vs, kepyng vs and ledyng in to fulhed of joy [This place is prison, this life is penance, and God wants us to enjoy the remedy. For the remedy is that our lord is with us, keeping us and leading us to the fullness of joy]" (77.36–43).[106] Penance becomes for Julian the redescription of human suffering in terms of participation in the passion of Jesus.

> [W]e shulde mekely and pacyently bere and suffer þat pennawnce þat god hym selves gevyth vs, with mynde of hys blessed passion.

For whan we haue mynde of his blessyd passion, with pytte and loue, then we suffer with hym lyke as his frendes dyd that saw it.

[We should meekly and patiently bear and suffer the penance that God himself gives us, with recollection of his blessed passion. For when we have recollection of his blessed passion, with pity and love, then we suffer with him like his friends did that saw it.] (77.28–32)

"Mynde of his blessyd passion" is no longer for Julian a pious devotional exercise, but it is a way of understanding the coincidence of suffering and salvation. The death of Jesus transforms the privations of earthly life into an open space, a place "nowted" of earthly attachments, into which God's servants can be gathered so as to share in the plentitude of the divine life. In the tenth revelation, Julian's understanding is "led forth" by the gaze of Christ into the wound in his side, which is "a feyer and delectable place, and large jnow for alle mankynde that shalle be savyd and rest in pees and in loue [a fair and delectable place, and large enough for all humanity that shall be saved and rest in peace and in love]" (24.6–7). The wound that human sin inflicts upon Jesus' body is healed, not through closure, so as to restore his body to smoothness, but by transformation into the open site of God's salvific work. In "the swete beholdyng [the sweet beholding]" of "hys blessyd hart clovyn on two [his blessed heart split in two]," Julian is shown "in part the blyssydfulle godhede [a part of his blessed/blissful divinity]" (24.9–11). In this space of Christ's wounded side, the foul black deed of human sin touches "the endlesse loue that was without begynnyng and is and shal be evyr [the endless love that was without beginning and is and ever shall be]" (24.13–14).

The thirst of Jesus, no less than the copious rivers of blood flowing forth from him, is salvific: "in thys standyth the poynte of gostly thyrst, which is lastyng in hym as long as we be in need, vs drawyng vppe to his blysse [in this stands the point of spiritual thirst, which lasts in him as long as we are in need, drawing us up to his bliss]" (31.47–49; cf. 75.5–8). The thirst is a lack that is simultaneously an excess of desire. The side of Christ torn open by human sin, not the tightly policed body of heroic virtue, is the appearing of the Godhead's infinite love. In this coinherence of privation and plenty, the passion—of both Jesus and his body the church—is renarrated as compassion: "than saw I that ech kynde compassion that man hath on hys evyn cristen with charyte, it is Crist in hym, that ych maner noughtyng that he shewde in hys passion, it was shewde aȝene in thys compassion [then I saw that every loving/natural compassion that one has for one's fellow Christian with love is Christ in him, that every kind of stripping that he showed in his passion was shown again in this compassion]" (28.21–23). Compassion is the fullness born out of participation in the "nowtyng" of the cross of Jesus.[107] One might say that the greatest of penances is attentive compassion directed toward the suffering of others. As Simone Weil noted, "Not only does the love of God have attention for its substance; the love of our neighbor, which we know to be the same love, is made of this same substance."[108] This attention is not a simple gaze, but a "negative effort [that] . . . consists of suspending our thought, leaving it detached, empty, and ready to be penetrated by the object."[109] Turned toward one in pain, "[t]he soul empties itself of all its own contents in order to receive into itself the being it is looking at, just as he is, in all his truth."[110] Compassion is a hollowing out of the self; it is "mynde of his blessyd passion," in which one's suffering is displaced by Christ, who is possessed of all of creation's suffering.[111]

Thus rather than placing plentitude and privation in opposition, Julian offers in her descriptions of Christ's tortured and salvific body an image in which they are coextensive.[112] It is what Gillespie and Ross have called an "apophatic image," in which absence and privation are discernible as they are presented (and not simply "represented") in the presence and plentitude of the crucified.[113] It is the image of a "nowted" body, a body that has been transmogrified by suffering into an icon of God's compassion, the coincidence of our foul black deed and the bliss of God, forming an infinite space enclosing all who will be saved. Julian's audacity is stunning. Her descriptions of Christ's body present us with a God who stakes the salvation of the cosmos on something as abject and humiliated as a crucified body. She can only be seen as presenting a message of simple "Christian optimism"[114] if one ignores the vivid reality of the tortured body that is the content of her visions. She will not pretend that pain is not pain or that our sin is not the cause of Christ's pain. Any "optimism" on her part takes the form of believing that she can read in this failed body the power of God to choose "what is low and despised in the world, things that are not, to reduce to nothing things that are" (1 Cor. 1:28).

The body of Christ, like Bakhtin's grotesque body, is an "unfinished and open body (dying, bringing forth and being born)" that "is not separated from the world by clearly defined boundaries; it is blended with the world, with animals, with objects." Julian's *Revelation* employs various medieval forms of devotional piety as well as conventions about femaleness to present us with a clearly grotesque pattern, in which Christ's body envelops wounded humanity, damaged by sin, so as to recreate within his body a restored humanity that will be born into life with God. Christ's body is a body of flesh that desires our flesh, that indeed is shattered by desire for us, a body moist and labile, generative and nutritive. This is the home God has prepared for humanity.

C. CLOSED IN THE GOODNESS OF GOD

Images of enclosure and envelopment run throughout Julian's writing, and indeed the very substance of her writing seems to fold back upon itself as various words and phrases reappear, linking the reader back to earlier occurrences.[115] Even within individual passages the words seem to enact an enfolding that mirrors the enfolding within divine love that they describe. For instance, in the fifty-fourth chapter she writes:

> For the almyghty truth of the trynyte is oure fader, for he made vs and kepyth vs in hym. And the depe wysdome of þe trynyte is our moder, in whom we be closyd. And the hye goodnesse of the trynyte is our lord, and in hym we be closyd and he in vs. We be closyd in the fader, we be closyd in the son, and we are closyd in the holy gost. And the fader is beclosyd in vs, the son is beclosyd in vs, and the holy gost is beclosyd in vs, all myght, alle wysdom and alle goodnesse, one god, one lorde.
>
> [For the almighty truth of the Trinity is our father, for he made us and keeps us in him. And the deep wisdom of the Trinity is our mother, in whom we are enclosed. And the high goodness of the Trinity is our lord, and in him we are enclosed and he in us. We are enclosed in the Father, we are enclosed in the Son, and we are enclosed in the Holy Spirit. And the Father is enclosed in us, the Son is enclosed in us, and the Holy Spirit is enclosed in us, all power, all wisdom and all goodness, one God, one lord.] (54.20–27)

Form and meaning conspire as Julian presents a theology of divine goodness in which the mutual indwelling of the divine persons spreads forth into the mutual indwelling of God and humanity through the incarnation of the second person of the Trinity. God dwells in humanity first and foremost because God has taken flesh in Jesus, and thereby God dwells eschatologically within the souls of those who will be saved. Similarly, humanity dwells in God first and foremost by Christ's assumed human nature, which he took into heaven in his ascension, and in which God's lovers participate by dwelling in the body of Christ on earth, the church. This mutual indwelling is the good for which human beings were created, and though there is a sense in which the hypostatic union of divine and human nature in Christ exists from the first moment of creation, central in all of this is the actual, historical assumption of humanity by the Son of God. Therefore, Julian's vision of the good is irrevocably tied to the material flesh of Jesus' body and our enclosure in it.

1. Dwelling in the Body

What then is involved in enclosure in God? How does one live in Christ's body? Given Julian's refusal to seek God apart from the human body of Jesus, crucified at a particular time and place in history, it is perhaps not surprising that she refuses to understand dwelling in that body apart from the concrete act of dwelling within Christ's ecclesial body. Salvation as the "onyng [union/atoning]" of God and humanity is inseparable from the union of human beings with each other. Thus she hopes to be "in onehede of cheryte with alle my evyn cristen [in unity of love with all my fellow Christians]" because "in thys oned stondyth the lyfe of alle mankynd that shalle be savyd [in this unity is grounded the life of all humanity that shall be saved]" (9.10–11). Charity involves not simply affectivity, but concrete acts that create visible bonds of unity, thus the church for Julian *is* that union. She does not, as Wyclif does, have recourse to an invisible church of the elect but rather maintains the church as a visible, institutional entity exerting an authority that is divinely sanctioned. At the same time she, like Wyclif, does not completely identify the visible church with Christ's body. But where Wyclif would have the body of Christ be much smaller than the visible church—composed only of the elect—Julian would seem to hint that it is perhaps much *larger*.[116]

Julian, like Wyclif and so many others in the fourteenth century, recognized the failures and fractures within the church. Living as she did in the time of the Avignon papacy and the Great Schism, her image of the church being shaken in the wind has a vivid concreteness. Closer to home, Henry Despenser, the bishop of Norwich for much of Julian's adult life (1370–1396), is almost a paradigm of the rapacious medieval bishop, waging war in a crusade against the French in order to fill his coffers.[117] Nor does Julian fail to see that the revelation granted her at times skirts perilously close to, and perhaps beyond, the limits of church teaching. Her constant affirmations of loyalty to the church would seem to indicate that she is quite aware of the temporal as well as the spiritual peril that might be occasioned by a lapse of orthodoxy. But just as Julian stubbornly refused to lift her eyes from the suffering body of Jesus, so too she will not let go of the church as a visible, historical entity in which she can dwell in unity with her fellow Christians.

Julian closely identifies the church with Christ, as a kind of extension of his humanity. This is the case particularly with regard to suffering, motherhood, and teaching. The sufferings of the church are the extension in time of the salvific spiritual thirst of Christ. Just as Jesus' body is tortured and broken and is left "hangyng vppe in the eyer as men hang a cloth for to drye [hanging up in the air, like people hang a cloth to dry]" (17.39–40), so too "Holy chyrch shalle be shakyd in sorrow and anguyssch and trybulacion in this worlde as men shakyth a cloth in the wynde [Holy church will be shaken in sorrow and anguish and tribulation in this world, like people shake a cloth in the wind]" (28.6–8). Julian maintains that "as truly as ther is a properte in god of ruth and pyte, as verely ther is a properte in god of thurst and longyng [as truly as there is a property in God of mercy and pity, so truly there is a property in God of thirst and longing]" (31.41–42), which property is seen in the sufferings of Jesus. With the resurrection, the humanity of Jesus has been glorified and become incapable of suffering, but he still suffers in his body the church.

> For as aneynst that Crist is oure hede, he is glorifyed and vnpassible; and as anenst his body, in whych alle his membris be knytt, he is not ȝett fulle glorifyed ne all vnpassible.
>
> [For regarding Christ as our head, he is glorified and incapable of suffering; and regarding his body, in which all his members are bound together, he is not yet fully glorified nor entirely incapable of suffering.] (31.34–36; cf. 20.24–26)

The longing of God for the salvation of humanity is an event that occurs not within God (Julian is quite orthodox in maintaining that God, being eternal, does not have "events") but within humanity—first in the humanity of Jesus in his suffering on the cross, and after his resurrection in his body the church.[118] Longing is the action of God—"for our lord god doth all [for our lord God does everything]" (10.18–19)—yet carried on within creaturely reality, "for he is the myd poynt of all thynges, and all he doth [for he is the midpoint of all things and all that he does]" (10.20–21). The divine activity of longing for humanity is decentered into creatures as humanity's longing for God: "of the vertu of this longyng in Crist we haue to long aȝene to hym, without whych no soule comyth to hevyn [because of the power of this longing in Christ we must long for him in return, and without this no soul comes to heaven]" (31.42–44). Christ communicates his own spiritual thirst to those who belong to his body; Christ's lovers are, as it were, caught up in the desire of Christ, and thereby share in his compassion.

In participating in his desire, the church participates in Christ's work of atonement, thereby participating in his office of motherhood. That Julian should refer to "my modyr holy chyrch [my mother, holy church]" (46.50) is scarcely surprising, since the image of church as mother is an ancient one and was a common image in preaching.[119] However, Julian's teaching on the motherhood of Christ allows her to push this further, to establish an even closer identification. The motherhood of the church is an extension of the motherhood of Christ, particularly through the sacraments of baptism and the Eucharist. Thus she writes,

> a sekir thing it is, a good and a gracious, to willen mekly and mytyly be susteynd and onyd to our moder, holy church, that is Crist Iesus. For the foode of mercy that is his dereworthy blood and pretious water is plentious to make us faire and clene. The blissid wound of our savior ben open and enioyen to helyn us.
>
> [It is a secure thing, a good and gracious thing, to will humbly and powerfully to be sustained and united to our mother, holy church, that is Jesus Christ. For the food of mercy that is his dear blood and precious water is plentiful to make us fair and clean. The blessed wounds of our savior are open and delight to heal us.][120]

The motherhood of Jesus is exercised through the sacraments, entrusted to the church. In fact, the Eucharist serves Julian as a primary example of the motherhood of Jesus: like a mother, Jesus feeds us out of his own bodily substance (60.29–32). Similarly with all of the church's sacraments, the faithful may trust that in receiving them they are truly fed by Christ:

> and with all the swete sacramentes he susteynyth vs full mercyfully and graciously, and so ment he in theyse blessyd wordys, where he seyde: I it am that holy chyrch prechyth the and techyth the. That is to sey: All the helth and the lyfe of sacramentys, alle þe vertu and þe grace of my worde, all the goodness that is ordeynyd in holy chyrch to the, I it am.
>
> [and with all of the sweet sacraments he sustains us most mercifully and graciously, and this is what he meant in these blessed words, where he said: I am what holy church preaches and teaches you. That is to say, all the health and life of the sacraments, all of the power and grace of my word, all the goodness that is ordained in holy church for you, I am.] (60.32–37)[121]

As this passage indicates, the identification of Christ and the church extends beyond the church's sacraments, to its teaching office. In discussing the thirteenth showing, Julian writes: "God shewde fulle grett plesannce that he hath in alle men and women that myghtly and wysely take the prechyng and the techyng of holy chyrch, for he it is, holy chyrch. He is the grounde, he is the substance [God showed the full, great pleasure that he takes in all men and women who strongly and wisely accept the teaching of holy church, for he is holy church. He is the ground, he is the substance]" (34.15–17).[122] The teachings of the church are not groping human articulations of an ineffable experience of the sacred—such a notion is peculiar to modern theology—but they have God as their ground (basis) and their substance (content).[123] God is the content of the church's teaching, as well as the one who, as *ecclesia docens*, teaches through the church: "he is the techyng, he is the techer" (34.18).[124]

It is primarily in this identification of Christ with the church as teacher that one senses the greatest tension in Julian. She does not simply assume a concord between her *Revelation* and the teachings of the church; this is rather something that she must argue for and constantly reiterate. She is anxious to make clear that nothing that was shown to her took her away from orthodox church teachings. At the outset, she states that her desire for the wounds of contrition, compassion, and longing for God was conceived "by the grace of god and the teeching of holie church" (2.40).[125] She says that knowledge of God's courtesy and homeliness, when given through "specialle schewyng of oure lorde [special revelation from our lord]," is still "none other than the feyth, ne lesse ne more [nothing other than the faith, neither less nor more]" (7.57, 65–66). And at the end of her account of the first revelation Julian offers a kind of general disclaimer regarding any perceived unorthodoxies in her account of her showings:

> in all thing I beleue as holy chyrch prechyth and techyth. For the feyth of holy chyrch, which I had before vnderstondyng, and as I hope by the grace of god wylle fully kepe it in vse and in custome, stode contynually in my syghte, wyllyng and meanyng never to receyve ony thyng that myght be contrary ther to. And with this intent and with this meanyng I beheld the shewyng with all my dyligence, for in all thys blessed shewyng I behelde it as in gods menyng.
>
> [in all things I believe as holy church preaches and teaches. For the faith of holy church as I had previously understood it, and that I hope by the grace of God I will keep fully and practice, stood continually in my sight, as I willed and intended never to receive anything contrary to it. And with this intention I contemplated the revelation with all diligence, for I wanted to understand this blessed revelation as God had intended it.] (9.21–28)

Not content with having stated this early on, Julian repeatedly displays her "will to orthodoxy," though perhaps not quite so abjectly as she does in the short text.[126] And not only is it her will that she cleave to the teachings of the church, but she wants us to understand that it is God's will as well. Part of the revelation itself is that she should love the

> comyn techyng of holy chyrch, of whych I was befor enformyd and groundyd and wylfully hauyng in vse and in vnderstondyng. And the beholdyng of this cam nott from me, for by the shewyng I was nott steryd nor led ther fro in no manner poynt; but I had ther in techyng to loue it and lyke it, wher by I myght with the helpe of oure lorde

"A Feyer and Delectable Place" / 113

and his grace encrese and ryse to more hevynly knowyng and hyer lovyng.

[common teaching of holy church, in which I had previously been instructed and grounded and intentionally practiced and understood. And the contemplation of this came not from me, for by the revelation I was not moved or led from it on any point; but I was taught in the revelation to love it and delight in it, by which I might, with the help of our lord and his grace, increase and rise to a more heavenly knowing and a higher loving.] (46.19–25)

On the face of it, Julian seems to be saying that there is a seamless fit between what was revealed to her and what she understood of church teachings, or at least that the teaching of the church provided an unproblematic prolegomenon to her revelation. But this is clearly not the case. Julian's anxiety indicates that in fact she does perceive at least a potential conflict, one that might force her to choose between the teaching she has received in her revelation and the common teaching of the church, a conflict that might place her, in the church's judgement, outside of the boundaries of the body of Christ. Ironically, the question over which Julian experiences this conflict can be understood as precisely that of the scope of Christ's body.

2. The Scope of the Body

Julian's concern for orthodoxy centers on the question of the way in which God regards human sin. Some aspects of this will be taken up in more detail in the next chapter, but one can easily understand the consternation such a thing as her inability to see wrath or forgiveness in God would have caused her (see 47.2–15). More specifically, her understanding of the nature of divine mercy and the promise that all shall be well combine to push Julian toward an understanding of the scope of God's salvific activity that is radically at odds with both the official teaching and popular piety of the medieval church.[127]

The locution "Alle maner of thyng shalle be wele" might not appear at first to be an occasion for conflict, but Julian immediately perceives that in fact this is something difficult to reconcile with what she has understood of the teachings of the church. Her first response to this promise is that it cannot be true because it does not seem to take sin seriously. She says: "A, good lorde, how myght alle be wele for the gret harme that is come by synne to thy creatures? [Ah, good lord, how could everything be well, given the great harm inflicted by sin on your creatures?]" (29.3–5). The reply she receives not only answers her objection, but demonstrates the orthodoxy of the answer. The sin of Adam was "the most harme that evyr was done or evyr shalle in to the worldes end [the greatest harm that has ever been done, or ever will be done until the end of the world]" and "thys is openly knowyn in alle holy church in erth [this is plainly known by all of holy church on earth]" (29.8–10). Presumably this refers to the doctrine of original sin, whereby Adam's sin establishes the context of the subsequent sins of human beings, thus being "the most harme." Julian's reply from God goes on to assure her that the "asseeth makyng [atonement]" of Christ is more pleasing to God than Adam's sin was harmful, a point at least structurally similar to Anselm's in *Cur Deus Homo?*[128] Therefore, "sythen that I haue made welle the most harm, than it is my wylle that thou know ther by that I shalle make wele alle that is lesse [since I have made well the greatest harm, it is my wish that you know by this that I will make well all that is less]" (29.15–17), again, presumably the sins of Adam's descendants.

But Julian recognizes a deeper problem: how can it be the case that all shall be well if some shall be damned?[129] Does the well-being of all things imply a universal restoration or salvation? Even posing the question is something Julian can only do obliquely. Her circumspection makes it difficult to say that she affirms the possibility of universal salvation; any such affirmation is, as Barbara Newman puts it, "unresolved and fraught with contradiction."[130] In fact, what she affirms is her adherence to church teaching, including the teaching that some shall be damned. And yet at the same time it is also clear that Julian is unable to reconcile this with all things being well. In discussing the thirteenth showing, Julian writes:

> one poynt of oure feyth is that many creatures shall be dampnyd, as angelis that felle ouȝt of hevyn for pride, whych be now fendys, and meny in erth that deyth out of the feyth of holy chyrch, that is to sey tho that be hethyn, and also many that recyvyd cristondom and lyvyth vncristen lyfe and so dyeth ouȝte of cheryte. All theyse shalle be dampnyd to helle withouȝt ende, as holy chyrch techyth me to beleue. And stondyng alle thys, me thought it was vnpossible

that alle maner of thyng shuld be wele, as oure lorde shewde in thys tyme.

[one point of our faith is that many creatures shall be damned, such as the angels that fell out of heaven on account of pride and that are now demons, and many on earth that die outside the faith of holy church, that is to say those who are heathens, and also many that were baptized but live unchristian lives and so die outside of charity. All these shall be damned to everlasting hell, as holy church teaches me to believe. And given all this, I thought it impossible that all manner of things should be well, as our lord revealed at this time.] (32.40–48)

This is a problem for Julian because she is convinced that both her revelation and the preaching and teaching of the church are alike gifts to her from God. In the same lengthy locution at the beginning of the twelfth showing in which Julian is told, "I it am that holy church prechyth the and techeyth thee," she is immediately *also* told, "I it am that shewde me before to the [I am the one who revealed myself to you before]" (26.10–11).[131] The God who is preached and taught by holy church is the same God who reveals to Julian things that seem to contradict the church's teaching on damnation. Julian has already hinted at this conflict in her account of the first showing: "I speke of them that shalle be savyd, for in this tyme god shewde me no nother. But in all thing I believe as holy chyrch prechyth and techyth [I speak of those who will be saved, for at this time God showed me no others. But in all things I believe as holy church preaches and teaches]" (9.20–22). Julian believes that the damnation of some is a point of faith and that faith "is groundyd in goddes worde [is grounded in God's word]," which "shall be sauyd in alle thyng [shall be preserved/saved in all things]" (32.38–40). At the same time she must believe her revelation, and her revelation shows her nothing of the damned.[132] The conflict between these two seems to Julian impossible to reconcile and in fact there is no reconciliation offered to her:

as to thys I had no other answere in shewyng of oure lorde but thys: That þat is vnpossible to the is nott vnpossible to me. I shall saue my worde in alle thyng, and I shalle make althyng wele.

[as to this I had no other answer revealed by our lord except this: What is impossible to you is not impossible to me. I will preserve/save my word in all things, and I will make all things well.] (32.48–51)

Julian takes this to mean that she must both hold to the faith that she has been taught through the church *and* believe that all manner of things shall be well. The reconciliation of these two "is þe grete dede that oure lorde god shalle do [is the great deed that our lord God shall do]" (32.55).

Julian realizes that this does not solve the difficulty and she continues to seek a resolution. She says that she desired to see hell and purgatory, so as to see everything that pertained to the faith of the church (though not, she is careful to note, because she doubted that faith and needed proof). But she says that she "ne culde se of thys ryght nouȝt [could see nothing of this]" (33.8–9). Julian is troubled by her lack of vision, perhaps because the contemplation of the fate of the damned was thought not only to be an aid in the cultivation of humility,[133] but also one of the joys of heaven.[134] Not to see the pains of hell or of purgatory might be taken to imply some defect in her revelation. However, Julian understands her inability to see the damned or the suffering of the souls in purgatory to be because "the reuelation was shewede of goodnes, in whych was made lytylle mencion of evylle [the revelation was one about goodness, in which little mention was made of evil]." She goes on to say "ȝett I was nott drawen ther by from ony poynt of the feyth þat holy chyrch techyth me to beleue [yet this did not draw me away from any point of the faith that holy church teaches me to believe]" (33.15–17). She defends the relative silence of her revelation on the subject of damnation by pointing out that silence does not constitute a denial. For example, she says that even though she saw only Jesus' crucified body and did not see the Jews who crucified him, "nott withstondyng I knew in my feyth that they ware a cursyd and dampnyd without ende, savyng tho þat were convertyd by grace [notwithstanding this, I knew from my faith that they were eternally cursed and damned, except for those who were converted by grace]" (33.22–23),[135] and she again affirms that the revelation strengthens her adherence to church doctrine (33.24–27). It is not simply, however, that Julian cannot see the pains of hell or the fate of the Jews, but such things are for her connected with the "grett deed ordeyned of oure lorde god fro withouȝt begynnyng, tresured and hyd in hys blessyd brest, only knowyn to hym selves, by which deed he shall make all thyng wele [great deed eternally ordained by God, treasured and hidden in his blessed breast, known only to him, by which he will make all things well]" (32.33–35). This deed is the "grett prevyte [great secret]" of God, "whych the blessydfulle trynyte shalle do in the last day, as to my syght, and what that deed shall be and how it shall be done, it is vnknowen of alle creaturys whych are beneth Crist, and shall be tylle whan it shalle be done [that the most blessed Trinity will do on the last day, as I see it, and what that deed will be and how it will be done is unknown by any creature beneath Christ, and will remain so until it is done]" (32.23–26). Seeking after such knowledge is not only futile, it can be harmful: "the more we besy vs to know hys prevytes in that or any other thyng, the ferthermore shalle we be from the knowyng [the more we occupy ourselves in trying to know his secrets in this or any other matter, the further we will be from knowing it]" (33.34–36).[136]

In particular, to desire to know the secrets of God with regard to specific creatures is to fail to attend to God's own self. Julian desires to know the fate "of a serteyn creature þat I louyd yf it shulde contynue in good levyng [a certain creature that I loved, whether it should continue in right living]," but she notes that "in this syngular desyr it semyd that I lettyd my selves, for I was nott taught in thys tyme [in this specific desire it seemed that I hindered myself, for I was not taught at this time]" (35.3–6). Julian is instructed not to focus the meaning of her revelation on specific people and things, but to apply it more generally. She once again returns to the Augustinian position that it is dangerous to make any one thing the object of our love, for "it is more worshype to god to beholde hym in alle than in any specyalle thyng [it honors God more to behold him in all things than in any special thing]" (35.8–9). The desire to know the fate of specific people reaches beyond what we can know in this life, and the failure to accept our creaturely limitations paradoxically becomes simply one more barrier that we erect between ourselves and God; the more we occupy ourselves with knowing God's secrets, the further we are from knowing. God wills we know *that* God will work a great deed at the end of time to make all things well, but *what* this deed will be and how God shall accomplish it is hidden from us (32.26–29).[137]

Julian's constant affirmation of her acceptance of church teaching witnesses to the intensity of the conflict between her understanding of what it means for all to be well and her understanding of the church's teaching on hell. We have no reason to think that Julian was not in fact genuine in her affirmation of church teaching and her desire for orthodoxy. As Barbara Newman notes:

> Because the voice of Julian-the-visionary proclaims this consoling message, and because modern readers prefer inner authority to that of Holy Church, it is easy to interpret the protestations of Julian-the-believer as heresy insurance, proof against real or imagined prosecutors. . . . Yet it would be dangerously anachronistic to assume that it was only her "even Christians," and not also herself, that she needed to assure of her orthodoxy.[138]

The greatest source of Julian's desire to maintain the teachings of holy church was a thoroughly internalized one. But the almost obsessive character of her claims to orthodoxy indicate that within the revelation was something that called the church's teachings into question in such a way that a reconciliation or synthesis of the two was impossible in Julian's eyes, even though she knew she must affirm the two together.

The universal restoration of all creatures is the possibility that remains unarticulated within the "grett prevyte" of the deed God will work on the last day. As I have noted, Julian is unable to even bring this possibility to speech, but indicates it obliquely. However, it is a possibility that is implied within the very structure of Julian's understanding of salvation as the "onyng" of creatures in God. As Julian says, "the charyte of god makyth in vs such a vnite that when it is truly seen, no man can parte them selves from other [the love of God makes in us such a unity that when it is truly seen, no person can separate themselves from another]" (65.18–20). This divine charity, binding human beings together as one within the body of Jesus, quite simply *is* salvation, participation in the divine life: God will "make vs all att one with hym, and ech of vs with other in tru lastyng joye that is Jhesu [make us all to be at one with him, and with each other, in the true lasting joy that is Jesus]" (71.23–24). Though Julian repeatedly makes clear that she is only speaking of those "that shalle be safe [that shall be saved]," the boundaries of this elected group seem to constantly stretch to encompass all humanity and ultimately all creation. The spiritual thirst of Christ is his desire for "Adam"—for humanity as a whole—and nothing less than Adam will slake that thirst.

Because Julian understands salvation as the union of those who shall be saved within the body of Christ, for her the question of salvation is one of the scope of Christ's body. While Julian will not separate dwelling in Christ from the concrete, institutional boundaries of the church, which includes acceptance of the church as teaching *in persona Christi*, the claim that all shall be well works its way through the body, pushing out its boundaries, transgressing them by its silent affirmation of the infinity of Christ's "asseeth makyng" in his suffering on the cross. The body of the saved is one that can be whole only in the transgression of its boundaries by its identification with the infinite mercy of God displayed in the crucifixion of Jesus. This body is visible because its center—God's mercy—can be seen with agonizing clarity in the broken body of Jesus. Its boundaries are the "grett prevyte" of God, only to be revealed on the day of judgement.

D. THE DEFORMATION OF A PERSECUTING SOCIETY

At the end of the last chapter I argued that in rejecting the temptation to take her eyes from the crucifix so as to look up to heaven, Julian is in fact refusing to seek God anywhere but in the crucified humanity of Jesus, and at the same time she begins to redefine the significance of that humanity. In doing so she takes up an attitude that is characteristic neither of "affective piety" nor of contemplation; the humanity of Christ is neither a sheltering nor an obscuring veil, drawn between humanity and the deep mysteries of the Godhead. Rather, from its "surface" Julian reads the "depths" as the charter of human redemption. The meaning or content of the revelation is not somehow hidden beneath a veneer; the content of Julian's revelation is manifested quite simply as the human body of Jesus that hangs on the cross. The problem is not one of finding a way to penetrate beyond this surface; it is one of learning to read this surface correctly. For Julian the true vision of God involves not "imagelessness" or "forgetting" but the memory of Jesus who, even as the crucified one, "is the image of the invisible God, the firstborn of all creation" (Col. 1:15). In Christ the mind contemplates the very perfection of God. In both spirit and content this controverts the nominalist distinction between the *potentia absoluta dei* and the *potentia ordinata dei*, for the absolute power of God is not a matter of abstract speculation about what is or is not logically contradictory, but is concretely revealed in the cross of Jesus. God's will, *in se*, is the will to save humanity and this will is grounded in divine love. One might say that the divine will has a concrete and definite structure that is manifested in the cross. For Julian, to claim anything else would be to open ourselves to "doubtful dread" about God's saving will.

This does not mean that, in revealing the nature of God *fully*, the cross reveals something subject to human comprehension. Even once she learns to read the marks of the crucified, his image remains an image of privation; the perfectly noughted (but not annihilated) humanity, which is the expressed image of God. In seeing Jesus crucified, Julian already contemplates the perfection of God, which encompasses the extremes of high and low, circumference and center, cause and effect, and ultimately, creator and creature. It is an image whose contours are expanded into infinity so as to enfold all possible oppositions. It is incomprehensible because it "leads" and "draws" our understanding into the side of the crucified *Logos* of God, confounding and transforming any human *logos*, making thinkable the foolishness of God. It is incomprehensible because it is a carnivalized body: the foolishness of God embodied.

And to imagine this body is to imagine a social body that is, in Bakhtin's terms, "grotesque" and "carnivalesque." The body of Christ as described by Julian is not an "orderly" one; it does not have a smooth surface or tightly policed boundaries that define a governable geography. In a sense, its location is temporal rather than geographical, and its time is carnival, which always comes to *us*, like the Sabbath, as a gift of time. It is a space generated within the stream of compassion flowing from the event of Christ's passion down through human history. It is an assembly that is not yet gathered; Christ says, "I *shalle* gader you" (28.19, my emphasis). It is not a finished project, much as Julian's book is not a finished project. Rather Christ's body is, as Oliver O'Donovan puts it, a "*gathering community.*"[139] It is an image in motion, a body being constituted.

In contrast to the regulated body of christendom, which carefully purified itself from all contagion, eliminating from its geographical boundaries foreign bodies such as Jews and heretics and lepers, the body of Christ as Julian sees it has no specific territory that it must protect because its interior has been exteriorized through its rending on the cross. It is a body constantly in a state of transgression, a body that cannot control its boundaries, a body whose "interior" has become a surface, a body that renders itself passive to forces acting upon it, and thus a passionate body dispossessed of any defense against its enemies, except the ultimate power of God's weakness. But for Julian, as for Paul, "God's foolishness is wiser than human wisdom, and God's weakness is stronger than human strength" (1 Cor. 1:25). The continual transgression of Christ's body is in fact coterminous with its generativity, for in constantly opening itself its scope is infinite; Christ's body is the image of God, "whose center is everywhere and whose circumference is nowhere."[140]

The extremity of Julian's imagining of this body is found in her intimation that hell might not in fact have the final word in the fate of sinners, but that through the incarnation of Christ, *all* might be well. Barbara Newman has suggested that the very capacity to imagine such a thing might be tied to Julian's status as a "freelance," and therefore marginal, religious woman:

> Women in general, but freelance religious women in particular, had little to gain from the enforcement of universal law. Powerless themselves, they had no involvement in the administration of secular justice, and unlike nuns, no opportunity to hold office within a well-established hierarchy of obedience. Sin for them was not a juridical problem, but a way of talking about human pain, estrangement, and lack of love. . . . Hell as the ultimate sanction in a system of cosmic justice, the place that both externalizes rebellion against God's law and forever excludes the rebels, must have seemed superfluous to these women who were, in so many ways, outside the social mainstream yet felt themselves to be profoundly included and even privileged in the realm of God.[141]

To question the sanction of hell, however hesitantly or obliquely, is to twist the persecuting society into a grotesque form.

Make no mistake here: the social body of Christ imagined by Julian is not invisible. But it is possessed of a form that is determined by the crucified Jesus who is at its center. Again, as O'Donovan puts it, "To speak of a 'gathering' church . . . is to speak of a community which, for all the permeability of its skin, has a sharply defined core."[142] For Julian the visibility of the church as the social body conformed to the image of the crucified Jesus is only effected through affirming the existing institutional boundaries of the medieval church, while at the same time appealing to the secret work of God that will transform Christ's body into that "fayer and delectable place" that is "large jnow for alle mankynde that shalle be savyd and rest in pees and in loue." The church's boundaries acquire their visibility as the contours of the body of Christ through the very transgression of these boundaries, by acts of charity and compassion that imitate God's action in Christ's crucifixion and that presage the great hidden deed at the end of time by which God shall make all things well. The visibility of the church is the visibility of the broken sacramental body of Christ our mother, eaten as the bread of pilgrims who journey toward that eschatological deed. This visibility consists in the concrete acts of compassion of Christ's lovers, not as discreet events that interrupt history, but as an unbroken chain of action—a drama—that continues the atoning work initiated by Christ in his passion and reaches forward toward God's completion of that work in the bliss of heaven.

I do not mean by this that Christ's church is a "tolerant" body that respects "otherness." These are modern fantasies; Julian's fantasy is somewhat different. Christ's body is omnivorously seductive in its compassion, assimilating and incorporating all who come within its ambit, intolerantly transforming them into children borne in Christ's body. We might say of Julian what Robert Adams has said of Langland's *Piers Plowman*: "The goal is not something like Sweden: the goal is deification."[143] Julian imagines a social body that quite simply is Christ's body of compassion. But as such, this body itself must be subjected to a discipline, it must be led by Christ and schooled in the wisdom and power of God that is revealed in Jesus. To this body Christ says: "I shal alle to breke yow from yowre veyne affeccions and yowre vyscious pryde, and aftyr that I shalle gader yow and make yow meke and mylde, clene and holy by onyng to me [I will break you all from your vain affections and your vicious pride, and afterward I will gather you and make you meek and mild, clean and holy through union with me]" (28.17–20; cf. 78.23–25). This breaking involves not only the penances imposed by life in its mortifying vagaries, but also the "penance" of life lived with her "evyn cristen" under the discipline of "the comyn techyng of holy chyrch" (9.8).

If the social body imagined by Julian in the crucified body of Jesus is not a tolerant body, neither is it an egalitarian body. Unlike Bakhtin's "utopian kingdom of absolute equality and freedom"—the grotesque body of "the people," which is fully egalitarian because it finds its end in its own endless generativity—the generativity of Christ's body is the extension in history of the infinite generative power of God, which makes and remakes creatures. A fundamental asymmetry of divine and creaturely power—of the "charyte vnmade [uncreated love]" that is

God and the "charyte made [created love]" that is our soul in God (84.12–13)—undergirds Julian's morphology of Christ's body. On the cross, Jesus is subjected to the effects of human evil, yet this evil is in fact the nothingness that is always subjected to God's creative activity. The creaturely humanity of Jesus is sustained in suffering and given atoning significance by the inexhaustible plentitude of God's power. This fundamental asymmetry of power is why there is a proper kind of dread that is felt even in heaven.

In this social, still suffering body, power flows down from Christ the head who is now impassible. Some within the body reflect more intensely the glory of God by being more closely conformed to Christ. However, for Julian this is a hierarchy in which the forgiven sinners—David, Mary Magdalene, Peter, Paul, doubting Thomas, St. John Beverley—hold the highest places, because the scars they bear of the wounds inflicted by their sins have been transformed into signs of God's healing power. The structure of the social body of Christ gives pride of place not to those who possess the most power, but to those who have been most in need and received the greatest mercy.

Julian's focus on the concrete humanity of Jesus as the locus of the revelation of divine power rejects the nominalist God of formal omnipotence in favor of the crucified God of Jesus Christ. The body politic of Christ can therefore never be one of pure sovereignty divorced from the kingship of Jesus who reigns from the cross. As such, the community of Christ's lovers can never purify their communal body, but it remains forever pierced and wounded. This is not an invisible community of the elect, but a community that takes shape through visible acts of compassion. As such, it will not cede dominion to secularized "temporal" structures, where the lordship of coercion can be more freely exercised. Rather, it stakes a claim to embody and display the only true dominion, the lordship of Jesus who was crucified. The social body that is large enough for all of humanity that shall be saved is nothing less than the visible deformation of the persecuting society. Within the persecuting society of medieval christendom Julian beholds the body of one who is persecuted, a body opening out to her, beckoning her to enter.

4

"A Contynuant Laborer and an Hard Traveler"

> Isn't it possible that it was essential in this case to "tell a riddle"?
>
> —Ludwig Wittgenstein[1]

The question of how it could be true that there was no wrath in God, nor blame for sinners, when the church taught that we are, as sinners, deserving of both wrath and blame, poses for Julian a great dilemma. This specific question must be understood within the context of Julian's bodily sight of the crucified Jesus. How does she reconcile her vision of the crucified body of Jesus, whose boundaries have been stretched by suffering to encompass the infinity of God's love, with the ecclesial body of Christ, defined by the seemingly rigid boundaries drawn by the laws and doctrines of medieval Christianity? Unwilling to abandon either of these bodies, yet seemingly unable to reconcile them, Julian writes that she "cryde inwardly with all my myght, seeking in to god for helpe" (50.35–36). But the answer that she is given to this dilemma is almost as disconcerting as the dilemma itself: the "wonderfull example of a lorde that hath a servannt" (51.3).

Along with Julian's images of Christ's body, the feudal image of the lord and servant stands as one of the two great "political" or "social" images in Julian's *Revelation*. We might take these two ensembles of images as means of representing and structuring two different aspects of society. Employing Mary Douglas's terminology, we might see body images as related to the social "group"—"the experience of a bounded social unit"—and feudal images as related to the social "grid"—"rules which relate one person to others."[2] In other words, Julian's images of Christ's body have a particular relevance to questions of the boundaries of the social body, and, as I have argued in the previous chapter,

Julian reads the transgression of Christ's body by the infinity of divine compassion as at least raising the question of where the boundaries which determine who is "in Christ" can be drawn. Her images of lordship, on the other hand, have a particular relevance to questions of relations of power and the fulfillment of roles *within* the society that is imaged as the body of Christ.³ Thus it is to this image that we turn.

The example of the lord and servant, along with the related teaching on Christ as mother, constitutes Julian's most substantial addition to the short text; indeed, it makes the long text not simply a revision or expansion of the short text, but a significantly different work. It in a sense becomes the centerpiece of both her text and of her life, as she spends at least the next twenty years, and possibly the entirety of her life, engaged in intense meditation on this showing.⁴ She writes that "the marveylyng of þe example went nevyr fro me; for me thoght it was gevyn me for answere to my desyer. And yet culde I nott take there in full vnderstandyng to my ees in that tyme [the wonder of the example never left me, for I believed it was given to me in answer to my desire. Yet at that time I could not fully understand it so as to be comforted]" (51.65–67). This example is to her like a strange cipher that promises to answer her dilemma. Yet the answer does not come in a final deciphering of the example that renders a "meaning," but in the activity of deciphering itself. This activity initiates Julian into a particular practice of viewing the world that shapes her capacity to understand love as the meaning of the revelation (86.16) in such a way that a space of meaning opens up before her that is infinite, and yet possesses a determinate shape: "Hold the therin, thou shalt wytt more in the same. But thou schalt nevyr witt therin other withoutyn ende [Remain in this and you will known more in the same. But you will never know in this anything different, without end]" (86.18–19).

This space of meaning is not a space defined by static conceptual antinomies—wrath/forgiveness, divinity/humanity, substance/sensuality, higher doom/lower doom—but is rather a "dramatic" space. In seeking to comprehend the example of the lord and servant, we will be led astray, as Julian was initially, if we fail to approach it as a drama in which the characters are *dramatis personae*, possessed of identities that are dynamic and multiple. To freeze the action of the drama of redemption that Julian's *Revelation* displays for us in this example is to misconstrue it. What Julian learns from her years of meditation is how to view the antinomies of theology as polarities that only appear in defining the space of this drama and setting its action in motion. Even the antinomies of master and slave are brought to a "dramatic" resolution in the exaltation of the servant by the lord. And because the drama can never be resolved into a simple "higher" meaning, the humble "lower" realities of human history, politics, and bodily existence are never left behind, but only redeemed.

The first part of this chapter will consist of a theological analysis of the example of the lord and servant, as well as a somewhat formal analysis of it drawing on Balthasar's notion of "theo-drama." The last part will turn from these more formal analyses to a consideration of what Julian's theology has to say when read against the particular backdrop of the relationship of lords and servants in late-fourteenth-century England. What I hope to show is that Julian's reading of her example as a trinitarian drama implies a very radical critique of the feudal ideology of hierarchy and stability, as well as of modern notions of freedom and liberality.

A. A SHEWYNG FULL MYSTELY

Julian describes her vision of the lord and servant as an "example," by which she seems to indicate that it is something like the *exempla* that were used in medieval sermons to illustrate theological points.[5] These played a major role in medieval preaching, as is witnessed by sermon collections such as Mirk's *Festial* and preachers' handbooks like *Fasciculus Morum*, large parts of which are made up of such *exempla*. Most frequently, *exempla* were stories of miraculous events, though they could also include stories from classical literature and even stories of Greek and Roman gods. On the whole, these stories had a didactic function, specifically as a kind of moralizing illustration. Yet in Julian's hands the example of the lord and servant becomes something other than a didactic illustration. It is rather a "mysty example [obscure example]" in which "the pryvytes of the reuelacyon be yet moch hyd [the secrets of the revelation are still very much hidden]" (51.71–72). It is something like a biblical text with a hidden and polyvalent meaning, to be uncovered through prayerful exegesis.

Colledge and Walsh argue that there is "no doubt that between 1373 and 1393 she had become thoroughly acquainted with, adept in the practice of 'mediaeval exegesis' in the technical sense in which this term has been used by every commentator since Henri de Lubac published his monumental work."[6] By this they mean that she had a technical grasp of the division of a scriptural text into a literal meaning and a spiritual or figurative meaning, and the further division of the spiritual meaning into allegorical (or typological), tropological (or moral), and anagogical meanings, yielding what is sometimes called the "four-fold sense" of scripture. However one need not accept Colledge and Walsh's rather excessive claims for Julian's erudition in order to accept their more general point that Julian sets about interpreting her vision of the lord and servant in a way that is not unlike a learned medieval exegete approaching a scriptural text. Indeed, Julian would not have needed to be particularly learned in theology to have had a basic grasp of at least the spirit of medieval exegesis. The allegorical exegesis of texts was regularly performed publicly in the pulpit, as hidden levels of meaning were teased out of both scriptural passages and *exempla*. Not only were spiritual interpretations gleaned from literal narratives, but the personification of abstract concepts in concrete narrative figures was widely employed both in vernacular literature such as *Piers Plowman* and in preaching.[7]

It is quite clear that part of Julian's difficulty with her vision of the lord and servant is her initial inability to "read" its spiritual or deeper meaning. This seems at least partially a function of her inability to distinguish between the "lower doom" of human judgement and the "higher doom" of divine judgement. A fruit of her years of meditation, which is in a sense the precondition for the vision teaching her anything else, is her realization that the example has a two-fold meaning: "Whych syght was shewed double in the lorde, and the syght was shewed double in the servannt. That one perty was shewed gostly in bodely lycknesse. That other perty was shewed more gostly withoute bodely lyckness [This vision was revealed doubly in the lord, and this vision was revealed doubly in the servant. The one part was revealed spiritually in bodily representation. The other part was revealed more spiritually without bodily representation] (51.4–7).[8] While it is certainly possible, as Colledge and Walsh set out to do, to detect allegorical, anagogical, and tropological aspects of Julian's interpretation of the example, it is primarily this dual division into literal ("gostly in bodely lycknesse") and spiritual ("more gostly withoute bodely lycknes") that is of primary significance to Julian.[9] And the significance of this duality is bound up with other structuring dualities of Julian's theology: higher and lower judgements, substance and sensuality.

1. Sensus Litteralis

Julian's description of the first "perty [part]" of the vision is worth quoting in full:

> For the furst thus I sawe two persons in bodely lycknesse, that is to sey a lorde and a servannt; and therwith god gaue me gostly vnderstandyng. The lord sytteth solempnely in rest and in pees. The servannt stondyth before his lorde, reverently redy to do his lordes wylle. The lorde lokyth vppon his seruannt full louely and swetly and mekely. He sendeth hym in to a certeyne place to do his wyll. The servannt nott onely he goyth, but sodenly he stertyth and rynnyth in grett hast for loue to do his lordes wylle. And anon he fallyth in a slade, and takyth ful grett sorow; and than he gronyth and monyth and wallowyth and wryeth, but he may nott ryse nor helpe hym selfe by no manner of weye. And of all this the most myschefe that I saw hym in was feylyng of comfort, for he culde nott turne his face to loke vppe on his lovyng lorde, whych was to hym full nere, in whom is full comfort; but as a man that was full febyll and vnwyse for the tyme, he entendyd to his felyng and enduryng in woo, in whych woo he sufferyd vij grett paynes. The furst was the soore brosyng that he toke in his fallyng, which was to hym moch payne. The second was þe hevynesse of his body. The thyrde was fybylnesse that folowyth of theyse two. The iiij was that he was blyndyd in his reson and stonyd in his mynde so ferforth that allmost he had forgeten his owne loue. The v was þat he myght nott ryse. The vj was payne most mervelous to me, and that was that he leye aloone. I lokyd alle about and behelde, and ferre ne nere ne hye ne lowe I saw to hym no helpe. The vij[th] was that the place whych he ley in was alang, harde and grevous.
>
> I merveyled how this seruannt myght thus mekely suffer all this woo; and I behelde with avysement to wytt yf I culde percyve in hym ony defauȝte, or yf the lorde shuld assigne in hym ony maner of blame; and verely there was none seen, for oonly his good wyll and his grett desyer was cause of his fallyng. And he was as vnlothfull and as good inwardly as he was when he stode before his lorde, redy to do his wylle.

And ryght thus contynuantly his loueyng lorde full tenderly beholdyth hym; and now wyth a doubyll chere, oone owtwarde, full mekly and myldely, with grett rewth and pytte, and this was of the furst; another inwarde, more gostly, and this was shewed with a ledyng of my vnderstandyng in to the lorde, in restoryng whych I saw hym hyely enjoy for the wurschypfull restyng and noble that he wyll and shall bryng his seruannt to by his plentuous grace. And this was of þat other shewyng.[10] And now was my vnderstandyng ledde ageyne in to the furst, both kepyng in mynd.

Than seyde this curteyse lorde in his menyng: Lo my belouyd seruant, what harme and dysses he hath had and takyn in my servys for my loue, yea, and for his good wylle. Is it nott reson that I reward hym his frey and his drede, his hurt and his mayme and alle his woo? And nott only this, but fallyth it nott to me to geve hym a ʒyfte that be better to hym and more wurschypfull than his owne hele shuld haue bene? And ells me thyngkyth I dyd hym no grace.

And in this an inwarde goostely shewyng of the lordes menyng descendyd in to my soule, in whych I saw that it behovyth nedys to be standyng his grett goodnes and his owne wurschyppe, that his deerworthy servannt, whych he lovyd so moch, shulde be hyely and blessydfully rewardyd, withoute end, aboue that he shulde haue be yf he had nott fallen, yea, and so ferforth that his fallyng and alle his wo that he hath takyn there by shalle be turnyd into the hye ovyrpassyng wurschyppe and endlesse blesse.

[For the first I saw two people in bodily representation, that is to say a lord and a servant; and along with this God gave me spiritual understanding. The lord sits solemnly in rest and peace. The servant stands before the lord, reverently ready to do his lord's will. The lord looks upon his servant very lovingly and sweetly and mildly. He sends him to a certain place to do his will. The servant not only goes, but he sets out suddenly and runs in great haste because he loves to do the lord's will. And immediately he falls into a dell, and is very seriously injured; and then he groans and moans and wallows and writhes, but he cannot rise or help himself in any way. And in all this the greatest misfortune that I saw him in was loss of consolation, for he could not turn his face to look upon his loving lord, who was very near to him and in whom there is great consolation; but like someone who was for the time very feeble and foolish, the servant focused on his feelings and continued woes, in which he suffered seven great pains. The first was the severe bruising that he received in his fall, which caused him great pain. The second was the heaviness of his body. The third was the feebleness caused by these two. The fourth was that his reason was blinded and his mind stunned to such a degree that he had almost forgotten his own love. The fifth was that he could not rise. The sixth was the pain that caused me the greatest wonder, which was that he lay alone. I looked all about and pondered, and neither far nor near nor high nor low could I see any help for him. The seventh was that the place where he lay was narrow, hard and painful.

I wondered at how this servant could meekly suffer all this distress; and I looked carefully to know if I could perceive in him any failing, or if the lord would assign to him any kind of blame; and truly there was none seen, for the only cause of his falling was his good will and his great desire. And inwardly he was as innocent and as good as he was when he stood before his lord, ready to do his will.

And his loving lord continually beheld him with great tenderness, and with a dual demeanor: one outward, very humbly and mildly, with great mercy and pity, and this was of the first; another inward, more spiritual, and this was revealed by a leading of my understanding into the lord, and in the restoring of my understanding[11] I saw him greatly rejoice over the honorable rest and nobility to which he will bring his servant by his plentiful grace. And this belonged to that second part of the vision. And now my understanding was led again into the first, but keeping both in mind.

Then the courteous lord said, "Look at what harm and injury my beloved servant has had and received in my service out of love, and indeed on account of his good will. Is it not reasonable that I should reward him for this attack and his dread, his hurt and his maiming and all his distress? Not only this, but should I not give him a gift that is more valuable to him and more honorable than his own health would have been? Otherwise, I think I would be ungracious."

And in this an inward spiritual revelation of the lord's meaning descended into my soul, in which I saw that it must be the case, given his great goodness and his own honor, that his most worthy servant, whom he loved so much, should be highly and most blessedly rewarded, without end, beyond what he would have been had he not fallen. Yes, and to such a degree that his falling and all his distress that had come to him by it shall be turned into high, surpassing honor and endless bliss.] (51.7–61)

At this point Julian says that the showing vanished and that God "ledde forth my vnderstandyng in syght and in shewyng of the revelacion to the ende [led forth my understanding in sight and in vision of the revelation until the end]" (51.63–64).

Julian says that though she knew that this showing was given to her as an answer to her desire to reconcile the truth that we are sinners deserving of wrath with her inability to see wrath in God, she could not take comfort in it at the time it was shown. She understands the servant to be Adam, yet "I sawe many dyuerse properteys that myght by no manner be derecte to syngell Adam [I saw many different properties that could in no way be attributed to Adam as an individual]" (51.68–69). Denise Baker notes that in this vision there are four points of particular significance: "the servant's good will in responding to the lord's command, the suffering that results from the servant's fall, the lord's refusal to blame the servant for the fall, and the greater reward the servant receives as a result of his suffering."[12] With the exception of the second of these—the servant's suffering incurred by the fall—everything Julian sees seems to go against the teachings of the church, the truth of which God has assured her. Humanity falls because of a perversity of will, not because of a good will. God clearly holds human beings blameworthy. And if the restored state of humanity is in fact greater than its state before the fall, this is not in any sense a "reward" for humanity.

The incongruity of Julian's vision is perhaps best seen if we contrast it with a very similar example used by Anselm in *Cur Deus Homo?* Boso asks Anselm why man should be called unjust for his inability to make restitution to God for sin. Anselm replies:

> Perhaps if his inability has no cause in himself, he can be partially excused. But if there is any guilt in that inability, it neither lightens the sin nor excuses him when he fails to pay his debt. Suppose that a man enjoins some task on his servant, and charges him not to throw himself into a pit which he points out to him, out of which he cannot possibly escape. But that servant despises the command and the warning of his master and, of his own free will, throws himself into the pit that has been shown him, so that he is unable to carry out his assigned task. Do you think that this inability is worth anything as an excuse for not performing the assigned task?[13]

"A CONTYNUANT LABORER AND AN HARD TRAVELER" / 133

What Julian's vision of the lord and servant seems to tell her is that the servant *is* excused, precisely because his fall is something like an accident, incurred while he was zealously performing his lord's will; in fact, the lord describes the servant as the victim of a "frey" or attack.[14] And the suffering incurred by the fall, while grievous, leaves the servant "inwardly" unscathed. This returns Julian to the puzzling insights she had reported earlier: "oure fallyng lettyth nott hym to loue vs. Pees and loue is evyr in vs, beyng and workyng, but we be nott evyr in pees and loue [our falling does not keep him from loving us. Peace and love are always in us, being and working, but we are not always in peace and love]" (39.41–43). Thus the showing seems to leave unanswered her anguished cry, "A, lorde Jhesu, kyng of blysse, how shall I be esyde . . . ? [Ah, lord Jesus, king of bliss, how shall I be eased . . . ?]" (50.36–37). How, in the face of sin, can all be well? How can the fall of Adam not incur God's wrath? So Julian writes: "And thus in that tyme I stode mekyl in onknowyng [And thus in that time I stood greatly in unknowing]."[15]

In the twenty years that follow Julian seems gradually to come to deeper insight into this example. The vision as she initially understood it comes to be inextricably intertwined with both her subsequent "inwarde lernyng" and "alle the hole revelation fro the begynnyng to the ende" (51.76–81). Julian is quite clear as to the nature of this inward learning. God commands her: "It longyth to the to take hede to alle þe propertes and the condescions that were shewed in the example, though þe thyngke that it be mysty and indefferent to thy syght [You should take heed of all the divine and human attributes[16] that were showed in the example, though you may think them obscure and undetermined in your sight]" (51.87–89). Julian is to scrutinize this revelation in all its detail, reconstructing it in her imagination so as to attend to such minutiae as the location and postures of the figures, the color and style of their clothing, their facial expressions, as well as such "inwarde" attributes as the lord's goodness and the servant's innocence. It is this process of "seeing inwardly with avysement [seeing inwardly with deliberation]" (51.90) that Julian understands to be "a begynnyng of techyng . . . wherby I myght come to knowyng in what manner he beholdeth vs in oure synne [a beginning of instruction . . . by which I might come to know how he beholds us in our sin]" (51.115–117).

On the literal level, Julian understands the lord to be God and the servant to be Adam, who is the representative of humanity as a whole, because "in the syghte of god alle man is oone man, and oone man is alle man [in the sight of God every man is one man, and one man is every man]" (51.103–104). The servant suffers grievous effects from this fall, becoming weak and being blinded in his reason because he is turned away from his lord. Yet his will remains whole and it is this that the lord beholds and approves, though the servant cannot know this because of the blindness of his reason (51.104–111). Julian structures her description of the effects of the fall upon the servant according to the triad of power, reason, and goodness of will. These three are attributes of God that are traditionally appropriated to the Father, Son, and Spirit, respectively, and that Julian frequently employs.[17] Her description seems to indicate that the servant's fall damages the divine image as *imago trinitatis* within him.[18] This is a point that she has made earlier, in speaking of how

> Man is channgeabyll in this lyfe, and by sympylnesse and vncunnyng fallyth in to synne. He is vnmyghty and vnwyse of hym selfe, and also his wyll is ovyr leyde in this tyme he is in tempest and in sorow and woe. And the cause is blynnes, for he seeth not god; for yf he saw god contynually, he shulde haue no myschevous felyng ne no maner steryng, no sorowyng that servyth synne.
>
> [Man is changable in this life, and through simplicity and ignorance falls into sin. In himself he is without might or wisdom, and his will is overcome in this time that he is storm-tossed and in sorrow and distress. And the reason is blindness, for he does not see God; for if he saw God continually, he would not have harmful feeling nor any kind of stirring, nor any sorrowing that serves sin.] (47.16–21)

As in her description of the literal sense of the parable, humanity's fall into sin has severely damaged the trinitarian image of God within it, making it weak and foolish, and "overlaying" the will, in effect hiding it from our sight. And the cause of all of this is the inability to see God, which makes it impossible not only to know God, but also to know the true condition of humanity. The will, while its goodness is intact, is unknown to us because of our blindness (51.108–109). This is the famous (or notorious) "godly wylle that nevyr assentyth to synne, nor nevyr shalle [godly will that never assents to sin, nor ever shall]" (37.16–17). This idea of the "godly wylle" seems to be a particularly troubling point for Julian; whatever the degree of her theological knowledge, she would no doubt have been taught that sin has damaged the human will, making it incapable of willing the good. However, she seems to be shown that there remains an element in humanity that is not separated from God, but merely "covered over," and this element is the will.[19] Julian describes this as a provisional understanding, "a begynnyng of techyng" by which she "myght come to knowyng in what manner he beholdeth vs in oure synne." What she sees is that God does not punish us for sin, but "oonly payne blamyth and ponyschyth [only pain blames and punishes]." God "comfortyth and socurryth [comforts and succors]" and always seeks to bring humanity to divine bliss (51.115–119). This presents a difficulty that will only be resolved once she moves beyond the literal understanding of the example.

At this point Julian begins to lead us through a gradual revelation of the deeper meaning, through attentive scrutiny of the details of the literal sense of the example. She attends to both the outward appearance of the figures as well as their "inward" motivations and dispositions. She notes the look upon the lord's face, and his position, sitting on the ground, and the ampleness of his clothing. Within him she sees "an hey ward long and brode, all full of endlesse hevynlynes [a high refuge, long and broad, full of eternal heavenliness]" (51.126). In the lord's face she sees "a semely medelur whych was marvelous to beholde. That one was rewth and pytte, that other joy and blysse [a becoming mixture that was marvelous to behold. One was mercy and pity, the other joy and bliss]" (51.130–131). Both of these are directed toward the servant and Julian anticipates the fuller revelation of the spiritual sense of the example later in the chapter in noting the dual nature of the servant: "The rewth and pytty of the fader was of the fallyng of Adam, whych is his most lovyd creature. The joy and blysse was of the fallyng of his deerwurthy son, whych is evyn with the fader [The mercy and pity of the Father was on account of the fall of Adam, who is his most beloved creature. The joy and bliss was on account of the fall of his most dear Son, who is equal to the Father]" (51.134–136). But she does not at this point dwell on this dual nature, focusing instead on the mercy that is directed to the servant as Adam. She notes that this look of mercy "fulfyllyd all erth, and descendyd downe with Adam into helle, with whych contyn(u)ant pytte Adam was kepte fro endlesse deth. And this mercy and pytte dwellyth with mankynde into the tyme that we come vppe in to hevyn [filled the whole earth and descended with Adam down into hell, and by this continual pity Adam was kept from eternal death. And this mercy and pity dwells with humanity until the time that we come up to heaven]" (51.137–140). God's merciful regard preserves sinful humanity from the final death that sin brings with it, a preservation that extends even to the dead who await the coming of Christ in hell. However, if the life of humanity is preserved by the merciful gaze of God, the suffering of humanity is caused by our blindness, our inability to turn our gaze upon God so as to see God's mercy (51.140–142).

Julian, looking upon the Father in the appearance of the lord, sees him "syttyng on the erth, bareyn and desert [sitting on the barren, deserted earth]" (51.144–145). She understands this to mean that God had created the human soul to be the dwelling place of God, "his owne cytte and his dwellyng place [his own city and his dwelling place]" (51.146), and when humanity fell it was no longer fit for that purpose. Yet God would have no other dwelling and so waited, sitting upon the earth, "abydyng man kynde, which is medlyd with erth [waiting for human nature, which is mixed with the earth]" (51.150), until the day when God's Son had "brought agayne hys cytte in to the nobyll feyernesse with his harde traveyle [brought again his city into the noble beauty with his hard labor]" (51.151–152). His clothing is blue, denoting steadfastness, and ample, signifying that he has enclosed within him heavens, and endless joy and peace (51.153–157). Julian sees again the lord's joy in restoring his servant, yet still she cannot comprehend the meaning of what she sees: "yet I marveyled, beholdyng the lorde and the servannt before seyde [yet I marveled, contemplating the lord and servant as I said]" (51.161–162).

Julian then turns her attention to the servant. Again she refers to the "doubyll vnderstandyng" of the servant, "one without, another within" (51.164–165), and again focuses first on the outward meaning. As with the lord, she attends closely to his positioning and clothing. He stands before the lord, slightly to the side, in a clearly subordinate position. He is dressed in a dirty white tunic that is torn and stained with sweat, tight fitting and short, in contrast to the lord's ample clothing. Julian thinks, "This is now an vnsemely clothyng for þe seruant that is so heyly lovyd to stond in before so wurschypfull a lord [Now this is an unbecoming clothing for the servant that is so highly loved to stand in before so honorable a lord]" (51.171–173). Looking to the inward dispositions of the servant, Julian sees within him "a ground of loue" that the servant has for the lord, which is equal to the lord's love for him (51.173–174). She sees that it is love that motivates the servant to set out, with no regard for himself, "and rynne at the sendyng of his lorde, to do that thyng whych was hys wylle and his wurshyppe [and ran at the sending of his lord, to do the thing that was his will and his worship]" (51.178–180). Julian notes the contrast between the servant's outer appearance and his inward disposition: his clothing indicates that "he had ben a contynuant laborer and an hard traveler of long tyme [he had been a continuous laborer and a hard worker for a long time]" (51.180–181), yet the love and enthusiasm with which he sets out indicates the freshness of one "new begynnyng for to traveyle [just beginning to work]" (51.183).

The task that the servant sets out to accomplish is a bit obscure. Julian states, "[t]her was a tresoure in the erth whych the lord lovyd [there was a treasure in the earth that the lord loved]" and when she wonders what it is she is told "[i]t is a mete whych is louesom and plesyng to the lorde [it is a food that is delicious and pleasing to the lord]" (51.185–187). Julian still seeks to understand the work that the servant must do. As if giving the answer to her seeking, she writes:

> I vnderstode that he shuld be a gardener, deluyng and dykyng and swetyng and turnyng the erth vp and down, and seke the depnesse and water the plantes in tyme. And in this he shulde contynue his traveyle, and make swete flodys to rynne and nobylle plentuousnesse fruyte to spryng, whych he shulde bryng before the lorde, and serve hym therwith to his lykynk. And he shulde nevyr turne ageyne, tyll he had dyȝte this mett alle redy, as he knew that it lykyd to þe lorde; and than he shulde take thys mett with the dryngke, and bere it full wurschypply before the lorde. And all thys tyme the lorde shulde sytt ryght on the same place, abydyng the servant whom he sent oute.

> [I understood that he should be a gardener—digging and ditching and sweating and turning the earth up and down—and seek the depths and water the plants at the appointed time. And in this he should continue his work, and make sweet floods run and noble and plentiful fruit to spring forth, which he should bring before the lord and serve him to his liking. And he should never cease until he has prepared this food completely, as he knew it would please the lord; and then he should take this food with the drink and bring it most reverently before the lord. And all this time the lord should sit

in the same place, awaiting the servant whom he had sent out.]
(51.192–202)

But this insight only leads to greater puzzlement. She sees in the lord "endlesse lyfe and all manner of goodnes, saue the tresure that was in the erth [eternal life and every kind of goodness, except for the treasure that was in the earth]." And although that treasure was "groundyd with in the lord in marvelous depnesse of endlesse loue [grounded within the lord in a wonderful depth of eternal love]," it is "nott alle to his wurschypp [not completely to his honor]" until prepared and presented to him by the servant (51.204–208). But if the lord is God and the servant Adam, what could the lord need that the servant could possibly provide?

On the level of what Julian takes to be the literal sense of the example, she can make no sense of it. And when she seeks more deeply into the literal sense, the example becomes only more puzzling. Could it be true that humanity falls into sin out of zeal to obey God's will? Is this why God does not blame humanity for sin? This seems a perverse inversion of the teachings of holy church, which say that sin is a result of human *dis*obedience. And so Julian concludes her exploration of the literal meaning of the vision by saying, "I vnderstood nott alle what this exampyll ment [I did not understand everything that this example meant]" (51.209–210).

2. Sensus Mysticus

The meaning of the example that is gradually revealed to Julian through her persistent meditation, the *sensus mysticus*, is connected with what she had described as the higher "doom" or judgement, by which God does not blame sinners for sin. She introduces the theme of the difference between divine and human judgement early in the long text, speaking in the third revelation of the need for the soul to be "turned fro the beholdyng of the blynd demyng of man in to the feyer swette demyng of our lorde god [turned from the contemplation of the blind judgement of man to the fair sweet judgement of our lord God]" (11.34–35). Human beings see some things as being done well and other things as evil, but Julian realizes that *all* things are done well because all things are done by God, evil being simply a privation. Human experience of the very real pain caused by evil is shaped by our very partial view of things. One tendency is to see evils as the result of blind fate. Yet, Julian argues, "nothyn is done by happe ne by aventure, but alle by the for(eseing) wysdom of god. Yf it be happ or aventure in the syght of man, our blyndhede and vnforsyght is the cause [nothing is done by chance or by accident, but all by the foreseeing wisdom of God. If it is chance or accident in human eyes, that is because of our blindness and lack of foresight]" (11.8–10). Our blindness is a part of the obscuring of the image of God within us and causes us to fail to comprehend "that alle thynges that is done is welle done, for our lord god doth all [that all things that are done are well done, for our lord God does everything]" (11.18–19). There seems to be a fundamental rupture between "our blyndhede" and "the foreseing wysdom of god."

A second tendency, born out of our blindness, is to see pain as a punishment from God, a sign of God's wrath toward sinners. Yet Julian asserts that "in god may be no wrath, as to my syght [in God there can be no wrath, as I see it]" (13.18–19). She argues for this from her own experience in the seventh showing of the rapid alternation of weal and woe, noting that the woe could not be sent as punishment on account of sin because there was no interval between the weal and the woe in which Julian might have incurred God's wrath. The experience of woe is used by God not for punishment, but, like the experience of well-being, for the perfecting of the soul (15.23–29). From God's perspective the experience of woe is already enfolded within the saving woes of Christ, so that the truth of the situation is that "blysse is lastyng withouȝt ende, and payne is passyng, and shall be brought to nowght to them that shall be savyd [beatitude is eternally lasting, and pain is passing, and shall be brought to nothing in those who will be saved]" (15.31–32).

Later, Julian takes up again the question of divine wrath and makes a more strictly theological argument from the perfection of the divine nature. Wrath is conceived by her as a privation, a passion, that is either a failure of power, or of wisdom, or of goodness. Yet the triune God, which is the very perfection of power, wisdom, and goodness, can have no such failing (46.29–36). In fact, if God's goodness were to fail, so as to turn to wrath, creatures would simply cease to exist:

> For truly, as to my syght, yf god myght be wroth a whyle, we shuld neyther haue lyfe ne stede ne beyng; for as verely as we haue oure

beyng of the endlesse myght of god and of the endlesse wysdom and of the endlesse goodnesse, also verely we haue oure kepyng in the endles myght of god, in the endlesse wysdom and in the endlesse goodnesse.

[For truly, as I see it, if God could be angry for a moment, we would have neither life nor place nor being; for as truly as we have our being by the eternal power of God and of the eternal wisdom and of the eternal goodness, also truly we have our preservation in the eternal power of God, in the eternal wisdom and in the eternal goodness.] (49.15–20)

Thus the failure of power, wisdom, and goodness is something that afflicts *us*, not God (48.7–11); wrath is the failure within us of the *imago trinitatis*. Julian writes, "I saw no wrath but on mannes perty [I saw no wrath except on man's part]" (48.6–7). And if there is no wrath in God, neither, strictly speaking, can there be forgiveness: "oure lorde god as a neynst hym selfe may not forgeue, for he may not be wroth [as regards our lord God himself, he cannot forgive, for he cannot be wrathful]" (49.3–4). Mercy and grace, rather than being a remission of God's wrath, are a remission or reversal of our wrath; to pray for God's mercy is to pray for a transformation in us. As Julian writes earlier: "he [i.e., the soul] by no manner of prayer makyth god suppell to hym; for he [i.e., God] is evyr oon lyke in loue [the soul cannot make God compliant toward him by any kind of prayer, for God is always the same in love]" (43.32–33). The gift of grace is instead the reversal of our fortunes: "grace werkyth oure dredfull faylyng in to plentuouse and endlesse solace; and grace werkyth oure shamefull fallyng in to hye wurschyppfull rysyng; and grace werkyth oure sorowfull dyeng in to holy blyssyd lyffe [grace transforms our dreadful failing into plentiful and endless solace; and grace transforms our shameful falling into high and honorable rising; and grace transforms our sorrowful dying into holy, blessed life]" (48.36–39). How is it possible that our failing, falling, and dying are not punishments inflicted on us by God? Moreover, how is it possible that God could look at fallen humanity with unwavering mercy and without blame? Julian believes that the answer is enfolded within the mystery of the example of the lord and servant.

After exploring the *sensus litteralis* of the example, and concluding by saying "I vnderstood nott alle what this exampyll ment," Julian abruptly returns to the dual identity of the servant that she had earlier mentioned and reveals to us: "In the servant is comprehendyd[20] the seconde person of þe trynyte, and in the seruannt is comprehendyd Adam, that is to sey all men [in the servant is comprehended the second person of the Trinity, and in the servant is comprehended Adam, that is to say, all humanity]" (51.211–212). It is as if the path that Julian follows in her exploration of the example's *sensus litteralis* is suddenly blocked by an impossibility over which she stumbles, forcing her to a new insight into the *sensus mysticus*.[21] Julian's prolonged, intense meditation on the lord and servant leads her to see that while it is clearly showing her something about God and humanity, certain elements of what is shown to her of the servant cannot possibly be true if the servant is taken simply for Adam, and can only be true if the servant is Christ. In order properly to read this vision Julian must discern its dual character, as well as grasp the way in which the different levels of meaning are united in the person of the servant.

Thus the nearness of the servant to the lord signifies Christ the Son who is equal to the Father; his standing to the left signifies Adam (51.215–216). The wisdom and goodness of the servant is the Son; the poor clothing is the humanity of Adam, damaged by the fall (51.225–228). The fact that the servant wears a single article of clothing signifies that in Christ there is a union of divinity and humanity without a mediating third term, and this union of God's Son with Adam means that the different levels of signification in the example are not easily sorted out. Thus the tunic's tightness indicates the poverty of the flesh in which the Son became incarnate and its age shows its years of use by Adam, who has left it sweat-stained from his labor (51.244–247). The tears in the tunic seem to indicate not only the damage inflicted upon human fleshliness by the fall, but also the harm inflicted upon Christ in his passion: "By that his kertyll was at the poynt to be ragged and rent is vnderstond the roddys and (the) scorgys, the thornes and the naylys, the drawyng and the draggyng, his tendyr flessch rentyng, as I saw in some party [By the fact that his tunic was ragged and torn is understood the rods and the scourges, the thorns and the nails, the pulling and the dragging, the tearing of his tender flesh, as I had partially seen]" (51.288–291). The writhing and groaning of the servant after falling is both the misery of sin-damaged humanity and the *kenosis* of the Son of God, who binds himself to human flesh so as only to be liberated in death (51.294–296).

Thus the four points regarding the servant enumerated by Baker as of chief significance—those points that seem so to trouble Julian initially—can all be seen to apply first and foremost to Christ. It is Christ who responds with good will in obeying the lord's command to come to earth; it is Christ who suffers though his "fall" into human flesh; it is Christ to whom the lord assigns no blame; and it is Christ whom the lord will reward for the pains he has suffered. Understood in this way, according to its *sensus mysticus*, the teaching conveyed by the *exemplum* is wholly orthodox. However, for Julian the *sensus mysticus* does not annul the *sensus litteralis*, but transforms it and brings it to its fulfillment. So too, the event of the incarnation reconfigures the meaning of the fall of humanity, and the sufferings of the cross transform the sufferings of sin, so as to enable us to speak of a *felix culpa*.

What is crucial is that while there is a dual significance to the servant, the meaning of the "kirtle" is univocal: it is Adam's flesh. When Christ comes to earth, he takes the worn and rent garment of Adam as his own. The suffering of God's Son is the suffering of Adam's flesh, and the glorification of God's Son in the resurrection is the glorification of Adam's flesh:

> The body ley in the graue tyll Easter morow; and fro that tyme he ley nevyr more. For ther was ryghtfully endyd the walowyng and the wrythyng, the gronyng and the monyng; and our foul dedely flessch, that goddys son toke vppon hym, whych was Adams old kyrtyll, streyte, bare and shorte, then by oure savyoure was made feyer, new, whyt and bryght, and of endlesse clennesse, wyde and seyde, feyer and rychar than was the clothyng whych I saw on the fader. For that clothyng was blew, and Crystes clothyng is now of feyer semely medolour, whych is so mervelous that I can nott discryve, for it is all of very wurschyppe.

> [The body lay in the grave until Easter morning; and after that he lay no more. For there the wallowing and the writhing, the groaning and the moaning, was rightly ended; and all our foul, dead flesh, that God's Son took upon him, Adam's old tunic that was tight, worn and short, was then made by our savior to be beautiful, new, white and bright, and eternally clean, wide and ample, fair and richer than the clothing that I saw on the Father. For that clothing was blue, and

Christ's clothing is now a beautiful and becoming mixture, which is so marvelous that I cannot describe it, for it is made of glory itself.] (51.302–311)

Once glorified through its union with the risen Christ, the servant's tunic—Adam's flesh—surpasses in beauty even the lord's clothing. Human flesh, made from the slime of the earth, "whych is a mater medelyd and gaderyd of alle bodely thynges [which is a matter mixed and gathered from all bodily things]" (53.43–44), becomes a "feyer semely medolour [beautiful and becoming mixture]" of the body transformed into glory itself.

This duality within the character of the servant helps Julian understand why the lord does not blame the servant for his fall. It is the "spiritual" sense of the parable that can be said to surpass, but not negate, the "literal" sense, so that the fate of the servant identified as fallen humanity is taken up into the fate of the servant identified as the incarnate son of God. "And thus hath oure good lorde Jhesu taken vppon hym all oure blame; and therfore oure fader may nor wyll no more blame assigne to vs than to hys owne derwurthy son Jhesu Cryst [And thus has our good lord Jesus taken upon himself all our blame; and therefore our Father neither is able nor desires to assign any more blame to us than to his own most worthy Son, Jesus Christ]" (51.232–234).

As Julian narrates the example, it is only the recognition of the dual nature of the servant as Christ and Adam, joined in the hypostatic union of Christ's divinity and humanity, that allows the example to come to its conclusion. Now she describes the lord, no longer sitting on the earth awaiting the return of the servant, but sitting "on hys ryche and nob(lest) seet, whych he made in hevyn most to his lykyng [on his rich and noblest seat, which he made in heaven, greatly to his pleasure]" (51.312–314). The Son no longer stands before the Father, but sits at his right hand in the glorious clothing of Adam's flesh transformed through resurrection, and upon his head he wears a crown "of precyous rychenes [precious richness]" (51.317) that is humankind. "For it was shewede that we be his crowne, whych crowne is the faders joy, the sonnes wurshyppe, the holy gostys lykyng, and endlesse mervelous blysse to alle that be in hevyn [For it was revealed that we are his crown, the crown that is the Father's joy, the Son's honor, the Holy Spirit's delight, and endless, marvelous beatitude to all who are in heaven]" (51.317–320, cf. 55.2–10). It is humanity that is the "tresoure in the erth whych the lord lovyd" and that the servant was sent to find.

B. TREASURE IN THE EARTH

The humanity that the servant finds, the treasure that is brought to the lord, is understood by Julian to have a dual aspect, mirrored in the difference between God's judgement and human judgement. Writing in the fourteenth revelation, Julian notes: "God demyth vs vpon oure kyndely substance, whych is evyr kepte one in hym, hole and safe, without ende; and this dome is of his ryghtfulhede. And man demyth vppon oure channgeable sensualyte, whych semyth now oone and now a nother . . . [God judges us on the basis of our natural substance, which is eternally kept one in him, whole and safe without end; and this judgement is on the basis of his righteousness. And human beings judge on the basis of our changeable sensuality, which seems now one thing and now another . . .]" (45.2–6). The difference between God's judgement and human judgement is related to a duality within the human person; as Julian says, "we be doubell of gods makyng, that is to sey substannciall and sensuall [we are made by God as a duality, that is to say substantial and sensual]" (58.39–40). This duality is not only roughly correlated with the higher judgement of God and the lower judgement of the church, but also with the depth of meaning of the example of the lord and servant. Julian maps the literal and mystical senses of her exegesis of the example onto an anthropology of "sensuality" and "substance."[22] Thus we have a rough correlation of *literal meaning/lower doom/sensuality* and of *mystical meaning/higher doom/substance*. This is only a "rough" correlation because elements of God's higher judgement, in particular the grace and mercy with which God looks upon sinners, belong to God's judgement upon our sensuality, not our substance. Julian, whether wittingly or unwittingly, never seems able to maintain the distinctions she establishes.[23] Yet one thing remains clear: just as the literal sense of the example must be brought together with its deeper significance, and the lower judgement of the church must be brought together with the higher judgement of God, so too our sensuality must be reunited with our substance if we are ever to find rest. Yet Julian also seems to say that in Christ, both as the exemplar of all created natures and as the

"A Contynuant Laborer and an Hard Traveler" / 145

incarnate and risen servant of God, substance and sensuality, higher and lower judgements, are *already* brought together.

1. Reuniting Substance and Sensuality

Salvation involves the reunification of what Julian calls "substance" (the higher part of the soul) and what she calls "sensuallyte" (the lower part of the soul). She understands the saving significance of Christ's taking flesh to be in this reuniting, first in Jesus' own person and then in us through our incorporation into his person (e.g., 58.47–48). Thus she presupposes what we might call a dualist and hierarchized conception of the soul, the higher substance and the lower sensuality. Some such distinction between the higher and lower aspects of the soul is nearly universal in medieval theology, but Julian develops this distinction in her own way and with her own vocabulary, creating along the way certain difficulties that she must resolve.

She introduces this distinction, though not the terminology, in the eighth revelation, at the key moment when she refuses to raise her eyes from the image of the crucified Jesus, and thus is taught "to chese Jhesu for my hevyn, whom I saw only in payne at that time [to choose Jesus for my heaven, whom I saw only in pain at that time]" (19.15–16). Julian seems puzzled as to *why* she did this. She notes that just prior to this she had regretted ever asking to know Christ's pains, yet now she chooses no heaven in this life but the crucified Jesus. In fact, she indicates that the regretting and the choosing are simultaneous, even though they seem to be unalterably opposed: "Repentyng and wylfulle choyse be two contrarytes, whych I felt both at that tyme [Regretting and deliberate choice are two contraries, both of which I felt at that time]" (19.24–25). She identifies this opposition as one between outward and inward:

> The outwarde party is our dedely flessh, whych is now in payne and now in woo, and shalle be in this lyfe, where of I felte moch in thys tyme; and that party was that I repentyd. The inward party is a hygh and a blessydfulle lyfe, whych is alle in peece and in loue, and this is more pryvely felte; and this party is in whych myghtly, wysely and wyllfully, I chose Jhesu to my hevyn.
>
> [The outward part is our mortal flesh, which is now in pain and distress and always shall be in this life, of which I was very aware at

this time; and this was the part that repented. The inward part is a high and most blessed life, which is entirely in peace and love, and this is more secretly felt; and this is the part by which, with full power, wisdom and will, I chose Jesus as my heaven.] (19.26–32)

It is only later that Julian will identify this outward aspect and this inward aspect of which she speaks in the eighth showing as "substance" and "sensuality" (see 55.50–54). It is our substance that allows us to will as God wills, while it is our sensuality that protests. But this opposition is not a permanent one, for she is promised that "both shall be onyd in blysse without ende by the vertu of Christ [both will be united in bliss without end by the power of Christ]" (19.38–39, cf. 56.34–37).

It is important to remember that the distinction between substance and sensuality is a distinction within the soul, and not a distinction between soul and body. This can be confusing, since at times Julian will speak of the distinction as one between "soul" and "flesh." In the eighth showing, for example, she speaks of the "grugyng and dawnger of the flessch without assent of the soule [grudging and tyranny of the flesh, without assent of the soul]" (19.23–24). But the very way in which Julian speaks of flesh as an agent capable of judgement indicates that her use of the term is not limited to brute bodily materiality but includes elements of human intentionality. In this way, it is not unlike Paul's use of "flesh" or *sarx* in the New Testament,[24] though there are more proximate sources for her use of the distinction, such as Augustine or Julian's contemporary Walter Hilton. Augustine, or the broadly Augustinian theology so prevalent in the Middle Ages, is a probable influence that might have been mediated through numerous channels.[25] Augustine describes the soul as having a dual orientation, toward God and toward the material world, that roughly corresponds to Julian's categories of substance and sensuality.[26] Thus in Julian's terms, substance is that "higher" part of the human person, which is turned toward God. Sensuality, on the other hand, is the "lower" part of the soul, which is turned toward the material world through the senses. Walter Hilton makes a similar distinction within the soul, and like Julian, he employs the term "sensuality," which he contrasts with "reason." But there is a crucial difference from Julian in his use of "sensuality." For Hilton, sensuality is simply "the carnal feeling through the five outward senses which is common to man and beast." It includes no element of human reason or intentionality. Reason, the higher part of the soul, is further divided into a higher and lower part (which are compared to a man and a woman, respectively), which corresponds to Augustine's bipartite *mens*.[27] Julian's understanding of "sensuality" is closer to Hilton's description of the lower part of the soul, in that both are, as Tarjei Park puts it, the "penetrating boundaries between the flesh and that part of the self in which God is reflected or grounded."[28] However, at times Julian goes further and seems to speak of sensuality not simply as the boundary of the soul with the flesh, but as including within it "the carnal feeling through the five outward senses which is common to man and beast" and even our corporeality. Thus "we"—the whole person, not simply the soul—"be made sensuall" in the "knyttyng" of the soul to the body (57.7–8).

There is also a danger in thinking of substance and sensuality as two "parts" or "pieces" of the soul. As Joan Nuth points out, "there is only one soul, and . . . these words designate the soul as related to God and to the body, and are not disjointed 'parts' as such."[29] In this Julian follows Augustine, who writes, "We are, therefore, only discussing a single thing when we discuss the human mind [*mens*]; nor do we double it into these two things that I have mentioned [i.e., higher and lower], except as regard to its functions."[30] Thus it is probably less misleading to speak of two aspects of the soul than of two parts: one aspect being the soul seen in relationship to God and the other being the soul seen in relationship to the mutable, dangerous, material world. But at the same time that she maintains the unity of the soul, Julian also conveys a strong sense of rupture, almost as if the soul had become, as Nancy Coiner puts it, "doubled and split, . . . familiar and yet hidden from itself."[31] This sense of doubling and division within the self is perhaps more intense in Julian than in a figure like Augustine, because she incorporates into sensuality the sensitive soul (Hilton's "carnal feelings"), something that for Augustine *is* different from *mens*, and therefore ultimately not constitutive of the self.

For Julian, this doubled self is as puzzling and paradoxical as the doubled example of the lord and servant; it is a self of privation and plenty—"in oure substannce we be full and in oure sensualyte we feyle [in our substance we are full and in our sensuality we fail]" (57.8–9)—that sees itself articulated in the words of the dying Christ: "I thirst." Substance is "full," as Julian understands it, because it remains united to God in a union so intimate that Julian says, "I sawe no dyfference between god and oure substance, but as it were all god." She quickly corrects the autotheistic implications of this statement by adding, "and yett my vnderstandyng toke that oure substance is in god, that is to sey that god is god and our substance is a creature in God [and yet my understanding grasped that our substance is in God, that is to say that God is God and our substance is a creature in God]" (54.17–20).[32] The rhetorical effect of this pairing of statements is the implication that while Julian understands the distinction between the soul's substance and God's, it is not a difference that she can *see*, because for Julian, as for Augustine, God is *interior intimo meo* [more inward than my inmost part].[33] In fact, our substance is in a sense hidden in God and inaccessible to us in itself; our substance is something which we must see "in God." Julian writes in chapter fifty-six:

> And thus I saw full suerly that it is redyer to vs and more esy to come to þe knowyng of god then to know oure owne soule. For oure soule is so depe growndyd in god and so endlesly tresoryd that we may nott come to the knowyng ther of tylle we haue furst knowyng of god, which is the maker to whome it is onyd.
>
> [And thus I saw clearly that it is quicker and easier for us to come to knowledge of God than to know our own soul. For the soul is so deeply grounded in God and so eternally treasured that we cannot come to know it until we know God first, who is the maker to whom it is united.] (56.2–6)

Yet within the same chapter Julian also maintains, "not withstandyng all this, we may nevyr come to the full knowyng of god tylle we knowe furst clerely our own soul [all this notwithstanding, we can never come to full knowledge of God until we first clearly know our own soul]" (56.32–33). Knowledge of God and knowledge of our souls are so intimately bound together that the sundering of substance and sensuality makes impossible true knowledge either of God or of self. Thus, in speaking of the servant, Julian says, "neyther he seeth clerly his lovyng lorde whych is to hym full meke and mylde, nor seeth truly what hym selfe is in the syght of his louyng lord [he neither sees clearly his loving lord who is fully meek and mild toward him, nor sees truly what he himself is in the sight of his loving lord]" (51.109–111). Our human judgement seems trapped within our changeable sensuality to such an extent that it is unaware of our substance, which is kept whole in God.

"A Contynuant Laborer and an Hard Traveler" / 149

Julian does not say that the judgement passed on the basis of our sensuality is false; in fact, she is convinced that it contains an important truth to which we must attend. For in addition to "a godly wyll in the higher party, whych wylle is so good that it may nevyr wylle evylle, but evyr good [a godly will in the higher part, which is so good that it can never will evil, but only good]," there is also "a bestely wylle in the lower party that may wylle no good [a beastly will in the lower part that cannot will any good]" (37.17–20). Contrition, confession, penance, sorrow at having "defowlyd the feyer ymage of god [defiled the beautiful image of God]"—all of these are necessary for a person's "woundys to heele and the soule to quycken [wounds to heal and the soul to come to life]" (39.6–17). Higher judgement does not trump lower judgement, substance does not negate sensuality, for as Julian well knows, "Pees and loue is evyr in vs, beyng and workyng, but we be nott evyr in pees and in loue [Peace and love is always in us, existing and working, but we are not always in peace and love]" (39.42–43). If the higher judgement that God passes on our substance simply annulled the lower judgement, then Julian would not say "I myght nott by no weye leue the lower dome [I may not in any way abandon the lower judgement]" (45.25–26). Rather, she desires to "se in god in what manner that the dome of holy chyrch here in erth is tru in his syght, and howe it longyth to me verely to know it, where by they myght both be savyd, so as it ware wurschypfulle to god and ryght wey to me [see in God how the judgement of holy church here on earth is true in his sight, and how it pertains to me to know it truly, whereby they may both be reconciled, so that it is to God's honor and the correct way for me]" (45.27–30). She then says that to this desire she had "no nother answer but a mervelous example of a lorde and of a seruannt . . . and that full mystely shewed [no other answer but a marvelous example of a lord and of a servant . . . and that very mysteriously revealed]" (45.30–32). In other words, the only reconciliation of the two judgements given her is that which is enacted in the mysterious example.

But this reconciliation is as yet an unfulfilled desire. Two truths and two responses remain: "we haue mater of mornyng, for oure synne is cause of Cristes paynes, and we haue lastyngly mater of joy, for endlesse loue made hym to suffer [we have reason for mourning, for our sin is the cause of Christ's pains, and we continually have reason for joy, for he suffered out of infinite love]" (52.51–53). Church teachings are a standard by which we judge our fall and amend our lives (52.60–63). God's perspective is "other wyse" than human perspective and consequently humans and God have different tasks with regard to sin: "it longyth to man mekely to accuse hym selfe, and it longyth to the propyr goodnesse of our lorde god curtesly to excuse man [it pertains to man to meekly accuse himself, and it pertains to the proper goodness of our lord God courteously to excuse man]" (52.69–72). Though the example of the lord and servant is "mervelous" (45.31), its marvels are manifested in its oscillations between the "two partyes that were shewde in þe doubyll chere in whych the lorde behelde þe fallyng of hys lovyd servant [two parts that were revealed in the dual demeanor with which the lord contemplated the falling of his beloved servant]" (52.72–73), which do not *quench* desire but *incite* it:

> And yet I stond in desire, and will into my end, that I myte be grace knowen thes ii domys as it longyth to me; for al hevenly, and al erthly things that longyn to hevyn, arn comprehendid in thes ii domys. And the more understondyng be the gracious ledyng of the Holy Gost that we have of these ii domys, the more we shal sen and known our faylyngs. And ever the more that we sen hem, the more kynd[l]y be grace we shal longen to be fulfillid of endles ioye and bliss; for we arn made therto, and our kindly substance is now blisful in God, and hath ben sithen it was made, and shall, without end.
>
> [And still I stand in desire, and will until my end, that I may by grace know these two judgements as they pertain to me; for all heavenly things, and all earthly things that pertain to heaven, are encompassed/understood in these two judgements. And the more insight that we have into these two judgements by the gracious leading of the Holy Spirit, the more we shall see and know our failings. And the more we see them, the more naturally by grace we will desire to be filled full of endless joy and bliss; for that is what we are created for, and our natural substance is now blessed in God, and has been since it was made, and shall be, without end.][34]

In her account of the example of the lord and servant, Julian says that "in that tyme I stode mekyl in onknowyng," but even as she writes the long text years later she must still say "I stond in desire." The doubled, hidden self is an enduring problem: "thus we stonde in this medelur all the dayes of oure lyfe [thus this mixture remains our lot all the days of our life]" (52.33–34). Though she says that by God's revelation her desire was "in perty answeryd [partially answered]" and her "grete fere som dele esyd [great fear somewhat eased]" (53.9–10), Julian must still live within the problem and the promise given to her by God. Confronted with two judgements—the faith of the church and the promise that all shall be well—she must believe God's promise to her: "That þat is vnpossible to the is nott vnpossible to me. I shalle saue my worde in alle thyng, and I shalle make althyng wele [What is impossible to you is not impossible to me. I will preserve/save my word in all things, and I will make all things well]" (32.49–51).

The unfulfilled nature of Julian's desire to reconcile the two judgements is her participation in the "goostly thyrst" of Christ, his desire to gather humanity, and through humanity all created natures, together into him (31.19). It is the suffering of Christ's body "in whych alle his membris be knytt [in which all his members are bound together]," and in which "he is nott ȝett fulle glorifyed ne all vnpassible [he is not yet fully glorified nor entirely impassible]" (31.35–36). Julian clearly articulates a doctrine of the mystical body of Christ in which there is a kind of *communicatio idiomatum* between Christ the head and his members the church based on the incorporation of all within the humanity of Christ: "For all mankynd that shall be savyd by the swete incarnacion and the passion of Crist, alle is the manhode of Cryst. For he is the heed, and we be his membris [For all human nature that shall be saved through the sweet incarnation and passion of Christ, all is the humanity of Christ. For he is the head and we are his members]" (51.254–257). The members of Christ long for the day of their fulfillment in the bliss of Christ, "and all that be vnder hevyn, whych shall come theder, ther way is by longyng and desyeryng [and everyone under heaven who shall come there, their way is through longing and desiring]" (51.260–261). For us to be "in Christ" is to have Christ's thirst in us, which thirst shall only end with the great deed of God at "domys day" when the lower judgement shall be "saved"—reconciled—with the judgement of God. Prior to that day of judgement, when those who shall be saved shall find themselves resting in God, the lower judgement of the church, with its longing and penance, its desire and discipline, remains for Julian a necessary means of salvation (56.25–28).

At the same time that this reconciliation must await the great deed of God at the end of time, there is a sense in which Julian understands this reconciliation to have *already* taken place. She writes, "by the tempest and the sorow þat we fall in on oure perty, we be ofte deed, as to mannes dome in erth. But in the syght of god the soule þat shall be safe was nevyr deed, ne nevyr shall [by the storm and sorrow that we fall into on our part, we are often dead, according to man's earthly judgement. But in the sight of God the soul that will be safe was never dead, nor ever will be]" (50.3–6). Though substance and sensuality are sundered in Adam's falling, they are reunited in Christ's incarnation, and these two are, from God's eternal perspective, simultaneous: "When Adam felle godes sonne fell [When Adam fell, God's Son fell]" (51.218–219). The reconciliation of higher and lower judgements, substance and sensuality, spiritual and literal sense, Christ and Adam—all of this is eternally real in the reality of the Triune God and temporally revealed in the revelation of Christ in human flesh. This seems to intensify the oscillation between higher and lower judgements; the reality of human nature is simultaneously substance and sensuality, Christ and Adam, not as two separate realities, but "a mervelous medelur of wele and of woo. We haue in vs oure lorde Jhesu Cryst vp resyn, and we haue in vs the wretchydnesse and the myschef of Adams fallyng [a marvelous mixture of well-being and distress. We have in us our lord Jesus Christ resurrected, and we have in us the wretchedness and misfortune of Adam's falling]" (52.9–11).[35] This union of higher and lower, bound together in the eternal union of Christ and Adam, is so close that "betwene þat one and þat other is ryght nought [between the one and the other there is truly nothing]" (52.88–89). The knowledge of this union revealed in Christ, combined with the experience of weal and woe as the alternation between the two realities, prevents us from resting either in the higher judgement of God or the lower judgement of humanity: "And now we be reysyde in to that one, and now we are sufferyd to fall into that other. And thus is that medle so mervelous in vs þat vnnethis we knowe of oure selfe or of oure evyn crysten in what wey we stonde [And at one moment we are raised to the one, and at another we are allowed to fall into the other. And thus is that mixture so marvelous in us that we scarcely know about ourselves or about our fellow Christian what our situation is]" (52.20–23). We can only catch a glimpse of how we or our fellow Christians stand before God; and for the most part, we stand in unknowing.

The redemption of humanity, the reunion of substance and sensuality, involves Christ coming to dwell in our sensuality as surely as our substance dwells in God: "For I saw full suerly that oure substannce is in god, and also I saw that in oure sensualyte god is, for in the same poynt that oure soule is made sensuall, in the same poynt is the cytte of god, ordeyned to hym fro without begynnyng [For I saw very clearly that our substance is in God, and I also saw that God is in our sensuality, for at the point (i.e., the time and place) that our soul is made sensual, at the same point is the city of God, ordained by God from eternity]" (55.23–27. Cf. 56.23–25). The city of God is not, for Julian, located solely in our substance, but in our sensuality, the soul's point of contact with the material and historical corporeality of human beings. This is why the lord waits sitting on the earth for the servant's return. The saving work of the incarnation is Christ's reunion of humanity's substance and sensuality, thus enabling our sensuality to become God's city. In this way, while there is a sense in which Julian sees the city of God as having an eternal, ideal existence in God, she maintains this alongside a view of that city as having a real historical genesis as a visible community, born from the side of the incarnate and crucified Son of God. In other words, the city is not simply spiritual, it is also political.

2. Exemplarism and Election

In reuniting substance and sensuality, Christ can be understood as completing the work of creation by bringing all created natures into unity through the incarnation. For Julian, salvation restores within us the trinitarian image of God through the union of Christ the Logos with human nature, reshaping our nature according to its original pattern: "like as we were like made to the Trinite in our first makyng, our maker would that we should be like iesus Criste our saviour, in hevyn without ende, be the vertue of our geynmakyng [just as we were made in the image of the Trinity in our first creation, our maker wills that we should be like Jesus Christ our savior, eternally in heaven, by the power of our re-creation]."[36] This "geynmakyng" is not simply a return to Adam's pre-fall state, but is both a recapitulation and a crowning of creation—not simply a restoration but a perfection in unity. Created natures are reformed in the image of Christ, the Word who is the original pattern of creation, by the Word becoming flesh; yet this incarnation of Christ the exemplar brings about an even greater unity of creation by perfectly enfolding within himself those creatures.[37]

It has been little noticed by commentators on Julian how central neoplatonic notions of exemplarity are to her thought.[38] Julian, whether wittingly or not, has seamlessly integrated commonplaces of neoplatonic thought into her theology, giving an "ontological density" to her understanding of enclosure in God. Enclosure in God is not a subjective feeling about one's relationship with God, but rather it is an account of the being of creatures as reflections of their eternal exemplars, which are enfolded within the second person of the Trinity. Julian adopts the basic neoplatonic scheme of *exitus et reditus*, emanation and return. In chapter sixty-two of the long text Julian describes just this scheme: "alle kyndes that he hath made to flowe out of hym to werke his wylle, it shulde be restoryd and brought agayne to hym by saluacion of man throw the werkyng of grace [all the natures that he has made to flow out of him to accomplish his will, shall be restored and brought again to him by the salvation of humanity through the working of grace]" (62.15–18).

In Julian's descriptions of the exit of creatures from God and their return, there is in addition a third moment, which she describes in terms of enclosure. Thus she speaks of "this feyer kynde out of whom we be all come, in whom we be alle enclosyd, in to whom we shall all goo" (53.32–34). We hear echoes in this of the three moments of enclosure, emanation, and return [*mone*, *prodos*, and *epistrophe*] found in Proclus and adopted by Dionysius the Areopagite.[39] A thoroughly Christianized version of this functioned in the Middle Ages as a kind of theological metanarrative, in which creatures proceed forth from God in creation (and fall) and return to God through the salvific work of Christ. This scheme can be found in the early-fourteenth-century Flemish writer John Ruusbroec, who uses it to explore the way in which the Trinity's simultaneous activity (in the Persons) and rest (in the Unity) provides a pattern for the Christian life which reconciles action and contemplation.[40] It can also be found in Bonaventure in the thirteenth century, who, construing enclosure in terms of the pattern of all things being contained in the Eternal Art of God (Christ the divine Wisdom), makes it the framework of his exemplarist metaphysics: "this is the sum total of our metaphysics: concerned with emanation, exemplarity, and consummation, that is, illumination through spiritual radiations and return to the Supreme Being."[41]

Julian thus shares with others in the Middle Ages a kind of saga of creation: like the prodigal son, creatures take their inheritance of existence and leave their father's house, only to fall, and finally to arise and return; and all the while of this journey *in regione dissimilitudinis* [in the region of dissimilarity],[42] creation is treasured within the Father's heart in the divine exemplars. Perhaps more appositely in the case of both Julian and Bonaventure, we might say that the pattern of creation is enclosed within the womb of divine Wisdom. Bonaventure writes that Wisdom

> is compared to a good woman, not that there is in it anything female or effeminate, but because in eternal wisdom there is a principle of fecundity tending to the conceiving, the bearing and the bringing forth of everything that pertains to the universality of the laws. For all the exemplar reasons are conceived from all eternity in the womb or uterus of eternal wisdom.[43]

Like Bonaventure, Julian identifies divine Wisdom with fecundity, though she feels no need to deny Wisdom's femaleness: "god alle wysdom is oure kyndly mother" (58.12–13). The fecundity of female flesh seemingly codes not only the human nature of Jesus,[44] but also his divine nature as the second person of the Trinity, within whom all created natures are enclosed. Christ as Wisdom bears a hint of a resemblance to the platonic *khora*, the infinite, maternal receptacle containing within itself the possibilities of all forms.

Julian also shares with Bonaventure a view in which the womb of God is the place in which all those elected to salvation, all those who shall ultimately return from the far country to which they have journeyed, are in some sense *already* enclosed. Bonaventure writes that the conception of exemplar reasons (*rationes exemplares*) within the womb of God is true "most of all of predestination." Because the Godhead "conceived the principles of predestination from all eternity, it cannot fail to love us."[45] Similarly, Julian writes, "Thus in oure very moder Jhesu oure lyfe is groundyd in the forseeyng wysdom of hym selfe fro with out begynnyng, with þe hye myght of the fader and þe souereyne goodnesse of the holy gost [Thus in our true mother, Jesus, our life is grounded in the foreseeing wisdom of himself from without beginning, with the high might of the Father, the sovereign goodness of the Holy Spirit]" (63.28–30). For Julian, in each soul that shall be saved is a "godly wylle that nevyr assentyd to synne ne nevyr shall [godly will that never assented to sin nor ever shall]" 53.12–13). She does not mean by this that the elect never sin, but rather that all who shall be saved have their wills somehow preserved within the second person of the Trinity (cf.1 John 3:9). Julian writes: "All the fair werkyng and all the swete kindly office of dereworthy moderhed is impropried to the second person; for in him we have this godly will hole and save withoute ende, both in kind and in grace, of his own proper goodnes [All the fair working and all the sweet kindly office of beloved motherhood is appropriated to the second person, for in him we have this godly will whole and safe without end, both in nature and in grace, of his own proper goodness]."[46] One might go so far as to say that the "godly will" is the human will of Jesus Christ, and those elected to salvation have their wills enfolded within that perfect will of Christ: "we haue all this blessyd wyll hoole and safe in oure lorde Jhesu Crist [we have all this blessed will whole and safe in our lord Jesus Christ]" (53.17–18). The elect are "knytt and onyd [bound together and united]" (53.19) in Christ, so that for Julian, as for Bonaventure, they have been "in the forsyghte of god knowen and lovyd fro without begynnyng in his ryghtfull entent [known and loved in the foresight of God from without beginning in his righteous intent]" (53.29–30).

However, Julian seems to go beyond Bonaventure, for whom the predestination of Christ is essentially different from the predestination of humans, so that his predestination is only an *exemplar exterius* that teaches us "what we are to believe, what we are to hope for, and what we are to do."[47] Bonaventure rejects Christ's predestination as the effective cause of our predestination, while conceding that it might be properly called the dispositive (through his merit disposing God to grant us grace) and excitative (through inspiring us to strive after his example) cause.[48] Julian discusses the causality of Christ's election in very different terms, so comparisons are difficult, but one might say that for Julian, God loves those predestined for salvation because God loves the Son, who encloses them by nature and who is enclosed in them by grace. From eternity those who shall be saved are enfolded in the Father's love for the Son, which is the Holy Spirit: "For or that he made vs he lovyd vs, and when we were made we louyd hym; and this is a lo(u)e made of the kyndly substanncyall goodnesse of the holy gost, myghty in reson of the myghte of the fader, and wyse in mynde of the wysdom of the son [before he made us he loved us, and when we were made we loved him; and this is a love made of the kindly substantial goodness of the Holy Spirit, mighty by reason of the might of the Father, and wise in mind of the wisdom of the Son]" (53.36–39).

Whereas in Bonaventure's understanding the exemplary causality of Christ's predestination with regard to our predestination seems primarily a "moral" one, in Julian the connection seems more "ontological."

In Julian's account of predestination, the human soul of Christ plays a crucial role. When Julian speaks of the "kynde" (nature) out of which we come, in which we are enclosed, and into which we shall all go, she is speaking not of the divine nature itself, but of the created *human* nature of Christ, which is hypostatically united with the Logos.[49] Recall that in her discussion in chapter six of the place of "meanes" as signs of divine condescension, she says that "the chiefe and principall meane is the blessed kynde that he toke of the maiden [the chief and principal mediator is the blessed nature that he took from the Virgin]" (6.24–25). Later, in chapter fifty-three, she seems to push this further, to imply that Christ did not simply take his human nature from Mary, but that all human beings take their natures from him. She writes: "mankynd hath be in the forsyghte of god knowen and lovyd fro without begynnyng [human nature has been, in the foresight of God, known and loved from without beginning]" (53.29–30), and by the eternal accord of the Trinity, Christ, the "myd person" of the Trinity,

> wolde be grounde and hed of this feyer kynde out of whom we be all come, in whom we be alle enclosyd, in to whom we shall all goo, in hym fyndyng oure full hevyn in everlastyng joy by the foreseyeng purpose of alle the blessyd trynyte fro without begynnyng.
>
> [would be ground and head of this fair nature, out of whom we have all come, in whom we are all enclosed, into whom we shall all go, in him finding our full heaven in everlasting joy by the foreseeing purpose of all the blessed Trinity from without beginning.] (53.32–35)[50]

Julian combines notions of exemplarity and election, arguing for a kind of preexistence of Christ's human nature, which contains within it all those who shall be saved:

> God the blyssydfull trynyte, whych is evyr lastyng beyng, ryght as he is endlesse fro without begynnyng, ryghte so it was in his purpose endlesse to make mankynde, whych feyer kynd furst was dyght to his owne son, the second person; and when he woulde, by full accorde of alle the trynyte, he made vs alle at onys. And in our makyng

he knytt vs and onyd vs to hym selfe, by whych oonyng we be kept as clene and as noble as we were made.

[God the blessed Trinity, which is everlasting being, just as he is endless from without beginning, just so it was in his eternal purpose to make human nature, which fair nature first was prepared for his own Son, the second person; and when he would, by full accord of all the Trinity, he made us all at once. And in our making he knit us and united us to himself, by which union we are kept as clean and as noble as we were made.] (58.2–8)

God "made vs alle at onys" not in the sense of creating each individual soul, but in creating the human nature of Christ, for he is the exemplary human being. And in this making the hypostatic union of Christ's divine and human natures was proleptically realized in God's election of the *deus homo*, Jesus Christ. God's noblest creature is humanity, and among humans "the fulleste substannce and the hyest vertu is þe blessyd soule of Crist [the fullest substance and the highest virtue/power is the blessed soul of Christ]." Christ's soul "was preciously knytt to hym in the makyng, which knott is so suttell and so myghty that it is onyd in to god [was preciously knit to him in the making, which knot is so subtle and so mighty that it is united to God]" (53.57–61). In the "endlesse entent [eternal intention]" and "forseyend purpose [foreseeing purpose]" of the Trinity, there is never a moment in which one may speak of a *logos asarkos*, a Word that is not made flesh.[51] It is Christ's eternal role to be the "means," or mediator, between God and creation. In God's foreseeing intent, the human nature of Christ is from the very beginning bound to the second person of the Trinity, thus binding all creation to God in an unbreakable bond, for God "makyth no depertyng in loue betwen the blessyd soule of Crist and the lest soule that shall be savyd [makes no distinction in love between the blessed soul of Christ and the least soul that shall be saved]" (54.3–4).

Julian's position is at first glance a startling one, and indeed there is little precedent for her precise articulation of the existence of the union of divine and human natures in Christ from the first moment of creation, though one can find somewhat similar notions in certain New Testament texts and in both vernacular and scholastic medieval theologies.[52] It is in the context of this eternal election of Jesus Christ in the union of his divine and human natures that we must view Julian's exemplarist metaphysics, because of the centrality of Christ in Julian's understanding of the cosmos. He is the one in whom, from our temporal perspective, God will "gather up all things . . . , things in heaven and things on earth" (Eph. 1:10) and in whom, from God's eternal perspective, all things are *already* held together (Col. 1:17). For Julian, "we ware tresured in god and hyd, knowen and lovyd fro withouȝt begynnyng [we were treasured and hidden in God, known and loved eternally]" because the human soul of Christ was eternally "knytt" to the divine nature, "whych knott is so suttell and so myghty that it is onyd in to god [which knot is so subtle and so strong that it is united to God]" and "made endlesly holy." Our status before God is ultimately judged in terms of our incorporation in Christ: "all the soulys þat shalle be savyd in hevyn with out ende be knytt in this knott, and onyd in this oonyng, and made holy in this holynesse [all the souls that shall be saved in heaven without end are knit in this knot, and united in this union, and made holy in this holiness]" (53.55–64). We are united to God because *Christ* is united to God. Our holiness is *Christ's* holiness. Here we can see the connection between Julian's understanding of the relationship between exemplarity and election, and her putative "universalism." Whereas medieval theologians generally stress the difference between Christ's predestination and ours, Julian stresses their similarity—in fact, their virtual identity. And in this identification between Christ's election and ours, Julian lays the foundation for her belief in God's promise that "all shall be well."

This helps us understand certain claims that Julian makes. One of the striking features of Julian's theology is her meditation on the difference between human perspective, which is bounded by time and space, and God's eternal perspective, in which every moment is eternally present. This is a medieval commonplace, grounded in Augustine's theology: "the order of times is certainly without time in the eternal Wisdom of God."[53] God's knowledge is through the eternal Word, in whom "everything is said in the simultaneity of eternity."[54] This is why "God demyth vs vpon oure kyndely substance, whych is evyr kepte one in hym, hole and safe, without ende [God judges us upon our kindly/natural substance, which is ever kept one in him, whole and safe, without end]," whereas "man demyth vppon oure channgeable sensualyte, whych semyth now oone and now a nother [man judges upon our changeable sensuality, which seems now one thing and now another]" (45.2–6). Our substance is not simply the part of our soul which is oriented toward God—which, as it were, "looks" at God—but it is also the lens through which God "looks" at us. It is our identity as enfolded within the eternal Word. Our sensuality, on the other hand, is characterized by changeability, or what Augustine called *distentio*.[55] Our changeable substance, stretched out in space and time, finds voice in Augustine's cry:

> You are my eternal Father, but I am scattered in times I do not understand. The storms of incoherent events tear to pieces my thoughts, the inmost entrails of my soul, until that day when, purified and molten by the fire of your love, I flow together to merge into you.[56]

For Julian, God does not simply see creatures as enfolded within the eternal Word, but even sees them as enfolded within the *incarnate* Word, in that all created natures are contained within the created human nature of Christ. At the same time, in Christ's human life, and in particular on the cross, God shares human distension in time and space so that history, which is nothing else than "sensuality" as the creaturely experience of time and extension, may be healed from within. The taking flesh of the Word is drawn into God's eternal perspective. Our creation in Christ is of a piece with our redemption in Christ. Christ as mother in creation, God's womb of Wisdom in which the exemplars of all created natures exist, is the same Christ who is our mother in redemption, enfolding us within the body opened to us in the suffering of the cross. It is specifically the motherhood of the second person of the Trinity, Christ, that unites creation and re-creation: "And thus is Jesu oure very moder in kynd of oure furst makyng, and he is oure very moder in grace by takyng of oure kynde made [And thus is Jesus our true mother in nature by our first making, and he is our true mother in grace by taking our created nature]" (59.37–38; cf. 58.37–39). As Nancy Coiner puts it, "The motherhood of grace both repeats and reverses the direction of the motherhood of nature."[57]

Thus God *never* looks at humanity apart from Christ. From creation to consummation in heavenly bliss, God sees all of humanity as enfolded within the humanity of Christ. Even the fall of Adam is seen by God in light of the incarnation of the second Adam. As Julian so strikingly puts it: "When Adam felle godes sonne fell; for the ryght onyng whych was made in hevyn, goddes sonne myght nott be seperath from Adam, for by Adam I vnderstond alle man [When Adam fell, God's Son fell; on account of the true union which was made in heaven, God's Son could not be separated from Adam, for by Adam I understand all humanity]" (51.218–221). Augustine also links the fall (*cadere*) of Adam and the descent (*descendere*) of Christ, but in such a way as to show the contrast between the two: "Quia cecidit Adam, ideo descendit Christus; ille cecidit, ille descendit; ille cecidit superbia, ille descendit misericordia [Because Adam fell, therefore Christ descended; the one fell, the other descended; the one fell by pride, the other descended by mercy]."[58] Julian, by her use of the identical term "fell," seems to emphasize the unity of the two events.[59] And whereas Augustine establishes a causal link (*quia* cecidit Adam, *ideo* descendit Christus), Julian seems to stress the pure simultaneity of the two falls within the eternal knowledge of God.

Julian develops Augustine's insights into the eternity of God's knowing in ways that Augustine himself did not. Augustine writes:

> [God] did not know [creatures] differently when they were created, than when they were to be created, for nothing has been added to His wisdom from them; it has remained the same as it was, while they came into existence as they should and when they should. So it is also written in the book of Ecclesiasticus: "All things were known to him before they were created, so also after they were perfected." The word "so" is used here, meaning that they were not known to Him in a different way, but both "before they were created, and after they were perfected, so they were known to him."[60]

Julian fills out what Augustine sketches here: an understanding of the divine perspective in which creatures are always known protologically through their exemplars and eschatologically through their final perfection. What Julian stresses, beyond Augustine, is that God's knowledge of creation distended in time and space, scattered and changeable, is a knowing through their eternal exemplars, which thus enfolds that distension within the unity of divine Wisdom. And likewise, God sees in creation, and even in its falling, its final perfecting, the bliss of Christ's resurrected and ascended humanity. The fallen servant Adam is always known through his exemplar, the second Adam who falls into the Virgin's womb, who suffers on the cross for love, and who is raised by God to a heavenly bliss surpassing that lost by the first Adam.

C. A DRAMA WITHOUT FOOTLIGHTS

We must at this point step back and ask, is something wrong in all of this? Julian's message is given "for our endles comfort and solace, and also to enioyen in him in this passand iorney of this life [for our endless comfort and solace, and also in order to have joy in him in this passing journey of this life],"[61] but what sort of comfort and solace is being offered? Does Julian's account of the divine perspective end up describing a gaze that both flattens history and obliterates individual identities in the drive to subsume them under the eternal identity of Christ? Is the denial of wrath in God a denial also of the significance of human freedom? Is the claim that God does everything that is done a call to tolerate intolerable evils? Is Julian's revelation a politically conservative one, in the sense that it serves to support the *status quo* of social relations through the claim that this life's troubles should be passively accepted out of hope for heavenly bliss? In short, is the promise that all shall be well in the end simply an opiate of the masses?

Another way to pose this question is to ask whether in the example of the lord and servant Julian presents us with an *allegory* that is simply a convenient vehicle for the delivery of static, timeless truths, and that may be discarded once those truths are arrived at. One of the great temptations of all those who would allegorize is to diminish the significance of human history so that it becomes simply an adventitious clothing of concepts, lacking any true significance of its own. The significance of events is always referred to and redeemed by a *higher* significance. In terms of Julian's *Revelation*, to read it as an allegory would be to read the lower judgement as simply a more or less inadequate pointer to the higher judgement, to see sensuality redeemed by its transformation into substance. But as we have already seen, Julian will not let "higher" meanings trump "lower" ones; sensuality is redeemed through union with substance, not transformation into it. Rather than an allegory, with two static levels of meaning, the example of the lord and servant, which is in fact unintelligible apart from the movement of the action, is better thought of in terms of *drama*.

1. Theo-drama

The "dramatic" character of Julian's thinking is noted by several writers. On a fairly superficial level, Brant Pelphrey remarks on the similarity between the example of the lord and servant and the action of a medieval drama.⁶² Ritamary Bradley points out that Julian understands the "deed" done by God in the life of Christ not as a single event, but as "an action with many parts, moving unerringly, by interlocking causes, to achieve God's purpose, somewhat like the 'action' of a drama."⁶³ Elizabeth Koenig has offered the most sustained analysis of Julian in relationship to the category of drama.⁶⁴ She argues that it was possible that Julian actually saw and was influenced by medieval dramas, which were performed in Norwich at least as early as 1389.⁶⁵ She also presents William of St. Thierry, and especially his reading of the Song of Songs as a drama rather than an allegory, as a possible influence on Julian.⁶⁶ Yet Julian's revelation is not self-evidently "dramatic." As we have seen, Colledge and Walsh make a strong claim for Julian being a self-conscious practitioner of allegorical exegesis, and it is clearly true that this is in some ways the interpretive model she is using. Other writers seem more struck by the static qualities of Julian's visions, the way in which time seems to slow down and even to stop at points to allow her to scrutinize the revelation. Denise Baker argues that Julian's vision of the passion is quite *un*dramatic:

> Julian reads her vision like a picture rather than a story. In contrast to the crowded and bustling scenes described in the *Meditationes* [*vitae Christi*] or depicted in many contemporary paintings of the Crucifixion, both of which are similar to the dramatic and spectacular effects of a motion picture, Julian's style achieves the intimacy of a photographic close-up.⁶⁷

In Baker's reading, Julian's visionary experience, at least of the crucifixion, lacks the movement and interactions characteristic of a drama.

Julian may very well have been influenced by medieval dramas or by theologians who would employ the metaphor of drama, but this does not answer the question of whether Julian's theology itself has a genuinely *dramatic* character, or whether she does not finally collapse time into eternity in her desire to secure God's promise that all shall be well. In order to answer this question we must try to understand what a genuinely theological construal of drama would be. Donald MacKinnon writes that "One is tempted to say that [Julian] wrote as if the future had already happened, indulging in every sort of paradox at once to affirm the reality of time and at the same time to deny it immunity to a certain sort of divine transcending."⁶⁸ I believe that this impulse in her work, the desire to take time and history with absolute seriousness while at the same time seeing them enfolded within and ruptured by God's transcendence of time and history, is the fundamentally dramatic element in her theology.

The work of Hans Urs von Balthasar, and in particular his exploration of what he calls "theo-drama," is singularly useful in attempting to think about the dramatic character of Julian's theology.[69] For Balthasar, the essential characteristic of a theo-dramatic approach is its willingness to take seriously the fact that the eternal God has appeared as an actor—as *the* actor—on the time- and space-bound stage of human history. In theo-drama, both the eternity and universality of God and the temporal and spatial particularity of the humanity which God assumes must receive their due. And not only must both receive their due, but it is the confrontation of eternity and time, universality and particularity, that *is* the drama. Even prior to the scandalous particularity of Jesus, the very existence of human beings, with their genuine yet limited freedom, sets up the drama: "The creation of finite freedom by infinite freedom is the starting point of all theo-drama."[70] Existence itself has a "dramatic" character that is found in the confrontation of absolute infinite freedom and humanity's real but finite freedom. This confrontation is intimated in various philosophical anthropologies of both the ancient and the post-Christian worlds, but only becomes explicit in the "unalterable, twofold postulate" of Christianity:

> first, that the "Absolute" is free (which the philosopher can concede, in a limited sense); and second, that the "Absolute" has a sovereign ability, out of its own freedom, to create and send forth finite but genuinely free beings (which is bound to cause the philosopher the greatest embarrassment) in such a way that, without violating the infinite nature of God's freedom, a genuine opposition of freedoms can come about. (*TD II*, 190)

However this opposition of freedoms is not like an opposition of two distinct "things"; divine and human freedom do not confront each other in the same way that two human wills might. To think in this way is to confuse divine freedom with human freedom. It is to make the error of the nominalists, who felt it necessary, given their understanding of the *potentia absoluta dei,* to carve out an area of human freedom within the *potentia ordinata dei* so as to guarantee that freedom, as if divine and human freedom were somehow placed not simply in opposition but in conflict, "competing for space." Rather, the freedom of human beings is the freedom of the actor who takes upon himself a role in the drama.

In addition to the dramatic tension set up by the "formal datum" of the confrontation of divine and human freedom, Balthasar also sees the very constitution of the human person as "dramatic": structured by the antinomies of spirit-body, male-female, individual-community (*TD II*, 355ff.). These antinomies make the drama "real" for us, "[s]o real that we cannot even attain an external vantage point from which to contemplate and evaluate it; we are caught up in the drama, we cannot remove ourselves from it or even conceive ourselves apart from it" (*TD II*, 335). As with the reunion of substance and sensuality, so too in Balthasar the answer to the tension between these structuring antinomies is not the victory of the one over the other, or a "mean" between two extremes, but a reconciling redemption by the "atoning" incarnation of Christ. Speaking of the antinomy of spirit and body, he writes:

> If man is not to resign himself to a narrow Aristotelian "middle"—in view of the destructiveness of extreme spiritualization and sensualization—he must be given *Lebensraum* in the form of a concrete blueprint that will liberate him from this straitening "middle". Such a blueprint would have to execute fully both movements without hubris and without degradation: it would have to come down to flesh "from above", as the pure breath of God, plumbing the dimensions of "world" and "flesh" to the very bottom. . . . And from below, on the basis of a perfected fleshly being, it must go beyond the realm of the "world" so as to bring both world and flesh with it, in its transcendence, up to God, "transfiguring" it, not "spiritualizing" it in some incorporeal manner. (*TD II*, 364)

The "blueprint" for this reconciliation is, of course, the person of Jesus Christ, and in Balthasar, as in Julian, this redemptive function is grounded in Christ's mediatorship in creation.[71]

In this understanding of the way in which infinite and finite freedom interact, we can see parallels between Julian and Balthasar. Just as Julian claims that "our lord god doth all [our lord God does everything]" (10.18–19) without denying creaturely freedom, so too Balthasar sees infinite freedom not as a threat to finite freedom, but as its enabling ground. Balthasar complains that the modern conception of God, shared by theists and atheists alike, has

> no awareness of the biblical paradox that God can be "everything" (Sir 43:27) and yet man can be "something"; and that God can be absolutely free without robbing man of his genuine freedom; and that, in fact, God shows his almighty power particularly by imparting authentic selfhood to his creatures. (*TD II*, 192)

This "authentic selfhood" imparted by God, of which Balthasar speaks, is not unlike Julian's understanding of the "godly wylle," which is not a faculty that "belongs" to the soul, but "is the werkyng whych is wrought contynually in ech soule that shalle be savyd [the working that is wrought continually in each soul that shall be saved]" (58.10–11). The godly will, the human capacity for genuine freedom, is the freely given gift of God, which can be "in" Christ our mother, "hole and safe" (59.40–41), without implying any heteronomy. Just as Julian says "I sawe no dyfference between god and oure substance, but as it were all god; and yett my vnderstandyng toke that oure substance is in god, that is to sey that god is god and our substance is a creature in God [I saw no difference between God and our substance, but as it were all God; and yet my understanding grasped that our substance is in God, that is to say that God is God and our substance is a creature in God]" (54.17–20), Balthasar offers a caveat to any understanding which univocally positions God as an "other" in relationship to creatures.

> We, for our part, with our finite freedom, must indeed designate ourselves as the "others" when we think of our relationship to God; but we cannot draw the conclusion that we are the "others" as far as God himself is concerned. The question we ought rather to ask is this: Since we owe everything (including our freedom) to the "everything" that God's freedom represents, can we be the "others" when seen from God's vantage point? Does he not recognize and affirm us *in him* and not outside him? (*TD II*, 193; cf. *TD IV*, 373)

Yet to deny *any* sense of God's otherness would be to collapse the theo-drama, for as both Balthasar and Julian recognize, the God who is revealed in the Bible must be spoken to as a "thou." But the "thou" spoken between God and creatures is a reflection of and participation in the trinitarian "thou" spoken between Father and Son, in the Spirit:

> The "not" which characterizes the creature—it is "not" God and cannot exist of itself—is by no means identical with the "not" found within the Godhead [i.e., the Father is *not* the Son or the Spirit]. However, the latter constitutes the deepest reason why the creaturely "not" does not cause the analogy of being between creature and God to break down. The infinite distance between the world and God is grounded in the other, prototypical distance between God and God. (*TD II*, 266)

Julian's view seems quite similar, though perhaps not so clearly stated. The "thou" spoken between God and humanity is "knytt in this knott" that is spoken between the Father and the Word, which is in God's eternal foreseeing purpose bound to the humanity of Christ in a hypostatic union. The unity of divinity and humanity in Christ is the mediating point that creates the analogy between the trinitarian "thou" and the divine-human "thou." This is what Balthasar means when he says that "the divine Son who becomes man is 'the concrete analogia entis'" (*TD II*, 267).

Thus, while the antinomies of divine and human freedom set up the "dramatic tension" of theo-drama, this drama cannot end in tragedy because the opposition of creature and creator is grounded in the (*pace* Hegel) non-tragic opposition of the persons of the Trinity.[72] As Balthasar writes, "we must see the doctrine of the Trinity as the ever-present, inner presupposition of the doctrine of the Cross" (*TD IV*, 319). The cross is the becoming visible of the triune life within a fallen and sinful creation. Christ's cry of dereliction on the cross manifests both the opposition of God and humanity created by sin and the relationship within the Godhead of Father and Son, so that "the Son's eternal, holy distance from the Father, in the Spirit, forms the basis on which the unholy distance of the world's sin can be transposed into it, can be transcended and overcome by it" (*TD IV*, 362). For Julian, her ability to read the cross as both the sight of our foul, black deed *and* the revelation of the Father's love for humanity is grounded precisely in her ability to give to it a trinitarian reading. As she sees the crucifix begin to bleed at the outset of her revelation, "in the same shewing sodeinly the trinitie fulfilled my hart most of joy, and so I vnderstode it shall be in heauen withoute end to all that shall come ther [in the same revelation the Trinity suddenly filled my heart full of joy, and so I understood it will be in heaven eternally to all who will come there]"

(4.9–11). When Julian writes, "wher Jhesu appireth the blessed trintie is vnderstand [where Jesus appears the blessed Trinity is understood]" (4.15), she is offering the interpretive key to her entire revelation: in the suffering of Jesus on the cross we see the mutual love of Father, Son, and Spirit opening out to embrace sinful humanity. Put in terms of the example of the lord and servant, the distance between lord and servant finds its ultimate ground not in human sin, nor even in the incarnation of the Word in history, but in the eternal "distance" between the Father and the Son, who was "the servant before hys comyng in to erth, stondyng redy befor the father in purpos tyll what tyme he wolde sende hym to do the wurschypfull deede by whych mankynde was brought agayn in to hevyn [the servant before his coming to earth, standing ready in purpose before the Father until that time he would send him to do the glorious deed by which humanity was brought again into heaven]" (51.234–237). The procession of the Son, and his "readiness" standing before the Father, is the primal, holy relation of opposition that sublates the opposition of sin. Put in Aquinas's terms, the temporal *missio* of the Son as servant is grounded in the eternal *processio* of the Son from the Father,[73] and in the Son's mission he takes upon himself distance-as-sin in all its pain, bringing it within the distance-as-gift that lies between him and the Father—the space of the Spirit's donation.

Humanity therefore acts upon a stage defined by this confrontation of infinite and finite freedom. According to Balthasar, it is salvation in Christ, and creation accomplished with a view to this salvation, that opens up the "acting area" of the theo-drama (*TD III*, 43). To be a "theological person" in Balthasar's sense is to be "in Christ," to be included in his person by being included in his mission. Christ is not simply "the one *for* whom we now live (and die) but . . . the pattern and archetype of our new vocation" (*TD III*, 248). The selves that we are given by God in our mission are selves in which the individual-community antinomy is healed. The mission, the task of discipleship by which one is "in Christ," is unique to each individual, yet when one receives this unique mission, one is "simultaneously de-privatized, socialized, made into a locus and a bearer of community" (*TD III*, 271). This does not, however, eliminate these tensions between individual and community; Balthasar has a keen sense of the pathos of the individual who must "bear witness to the authentic Church of Christ in the face of an environment that mistakenly imagines that it is the Church"

(*TD III*, 455). He would recognize well the theo-dramatic character of Julian's situation: called by God to deliver to her fellow Christians the seemingly untimely message that all shall be well, living a life of vowed isolation, eschewing anything that would separate her from her fellow Christians, caught between what she has been taught by the church and what she has been shown by God, endlessly meditating on the grotesque body of Christ in the midst of a tragic era.

Part of what a theo-dramatic conception of the self entails for Balthasar is a willingness to renounce the kind of all-seeing viewpoint associated with the genre of epic. Even revelation has a "dramatic" character. It orients one within the drama; it does not lift one out of it. Not only are the scriptures "a word that journeys with us" (*TD II*, 102), but even the incarnation of infinite freedom in Jesus Christ "both constitutes a signpost pointing toward the infinite and accompanies finite being on its journey toward it" (*TD III*, 19). Christ's consciousness is a "mission-consciousness" that can include both the unknowing that allows us to speak of Jesus' "faith," and also the *visio immediata* of his divine nature, because that nature is coextensive with his *missio* from the Father (*TD III*, 166). In this sense, Christ too is a pilgrim: "Insofar as, from all time, he fully embraces and affirms his mission (which does not mean that he has a total and detailed view of it), he is *comprehensor*; but the mission itself sets him upon a path, and, to that extent, he is also *viator*" (*TD III*, 172). Thus even for those who are "in Christ," there is no way to leave the world stage so as to adopt a God's-eye view, and even the revelation of God in Christ is a revelation *on the world stage*, not above it. To step off the stage in the quest for an absolute viewpoint is to remove ourselves entirely from the drama: "In this play, all the spectators must eventually become fellow actors, whether they wish to or not" (*TD II*, 58). Theo-dramatic knowledge is a knowledge that does not require detachment, but engagement through the discipleship of suffering love in union with Christ. "'Absolute knowledge' is the death of all theo-drama, but God's 'love which surpasses all gnosis' is the death of 'absolute knowledge'" (*TD II*, 89).

Julian clearly senses the kind of knowledge appropriate to theo-drama. Like Balthasar, Julian portrays Christ as simultaneously *viator* and *comprehensor*. She will speak in the same breath of Christ suffering the pains of the cross and his enjoying the bliss of heaven. In describing the example of the lord and servant, she says that from his outward clothing the servant appeared to have been "a contynuant laborer and an hard traveler of long tyme [a continual laborer and a hard worker for a long time]" (51.180–181). As Colledge and Walsh note, "an hard traveler" might be read either as an image of a woman in the travail of childbirth (thus foreshadowing Julian's teaching on Christ as Mother) or as an image of a pilgrim, the holy traveler.[74] Near the end of the *Revelation* the image of Christ as *viator* becomes more explicit: "he shewde hym in erth thus, as it were a pylgrymage, that is to sey he is here with vs ledyng vs, and shalle be tylle whan he hath brought vs alle to his blysse in hevyn [he showed himself on earth in this manner: as if it were a pilgrimage. That is to say, he is with us leading us, and will be until he has brought us all to his bliss in heaven]" (81.6–8). While the image of Christ as pilgrim is hardly unusual in the Middle Ages,[75] Julian exploits it to unusually good effect, emphasizing not so much the temporary status of life in this world—though this is certainly a part of it—as the unknowing involved in following the pilgrim Christ. This helps us understand Julian's habitual connection of knowing with divine "leading": to know is to be led by Christ the pilgrim along his path of suffering compassion through the drama of history. The soul in this life "may do no more than seke, suffer and trust" (10.69–70). Yet because seeking is walking the pilgrim path with Christ, and suffering is participation in the cross of Christ, and trusting is sharing in the faith of Christ, "sekyng is as good as beholdyng for the tyme that he wille suffer the sowle to be in traveyle [seeking is as good as beholding during the time that he allows the soul to be giving birth/toiling/on pilgrimage]" (10.74–76).

For both Julian and Balthasar, the renunciation of absolute knowledge entailed by taking up a role within the theo-drama makes certain knowledge of the final destiny of any character impossible. As we have seen, Julian's own thought strains toward universal redemption, yet she is held back by the teaching of the church that some shall be damned. We can now see perhaps more clearly how the teaching of the church is not for Julian a merely external restraint, but rather a sketch of the contours of the drama. To claim to *know* the salvation of all would be to let the drama collapse in on itself; it would be to eliminate the pole of finite freedom that, along with the pole of God's infinite freedom, defines theo-drama at its outset. Though Adam's falling may be placed within the context of the *missio* of Jesus Christ, and even beyond this within the horizon of the *processio* of the Word, Julian cannot claim for her own possession what is God's secret. Likewise, Balthasar notes that "all man's error takes place within the realm of divine love" (*TD II*, 217) and that "the creature's No, its wanting to be autonomous without acknowledging its origin, must be located within the Son's all-embracing Yes to the Father, in the Spirit" (*TD IV*, 329). Yet like Julian, Balthasar pulls back from affirming any knowledge of universal salvation: "Scripture prohibits us from saying that [the creature's] deliberate No is impossible" (*TD IV*, 350). However, he notes that alongside those scriptural passages that threaten dire consequences for sinners are other passages that express a hope for the salvation of all. While these latter passages do not negate the former, they do "give us a right to have hope for all men. . . . Certainty cannot be attained, but hope can be justified."[76] Whereas Julian is holding in tension the teachings of the church and what has been shown to her in her revelation, Balthasar is locating that tension within the word of God itself. However, in both there is a stubborn refusal to give up that tension by claiming certainty, either of the salvation of all or of the damnation of some.[77] This tension, between mercy and wrath, higher and lower judgements, is held together by them in different ways, but both seek to find a way to justify a universal hope.

Their ways of justifying their hope lead to perhaps the most striking divergence between the dramas sketched by Julian and Balthasar. Whereas Julian will deny that there is any wrath in God, but only in us, Balthasar feels compelled by the scriptural witness to give some account of divine wrath. He chooses to do so by speaking of Christ as the recipient of divine wrath in our stead in the event of the cross, whereby divine wrath is transformed through Christ's Yes to the Father: "God's anger strikes him instead of the countless sinners, shattering him as by lightning and distributing him among them; thus God the Father, in the Holy Spirit, creates the Son's Eucharist" (*TD IV*, 348). On the face of it, this sounds more like the image from the *Ancrene Wisse* mentioned in the previous chapter—in which the tender Mother Jesus interposes himself between humanity and the wrathful Father and is beaten to death in our stead—than it sounds like Julian's God, for whom wrath would mar the divine perfection. Whereas for Balthasar, "God's anger at the rejection of divine love encounters a divine love (the Son's) that exposes itself to this anger, disarms it and literally deprives it of its object" (*TD IV*, 349–350), for Julian there seems to be no divine anger to be disarmed. While "blame," in the objective sense of transgression against divine justice, might be ours, and might be taken by Christ upon himself, any subjective sense of "blame" is entirely on the side of humanity: "thus hath oure good lorde Jhesu taken vppon hym all oure blame; and therefore oure fader may nor wyll no more blame assigne to vs than to hys owne derwurthy son Jhesu Cryst [thus our good lord Jesus has taken upon himself all our blame; and therefore our Father cannot and will not assign any more blame to us than to his own most dear Son Jesus Christ]" (51.232–234). Our subjective sense of blame must be always held together with the objective truth of Christ's having taken our blame upon him: "thus gracyously to se and know both to geder is þe meke accusyng that oure good lorde askyth of vs [thus to graciously see and know both together is the meek accusing that our good lord asks of us]" (52.80–81).[78]

Perhaps in the end the difference between Balthasar and Julian is that Balthasar—in order to heighten the drama of wrath, mercy, pain, and death—is willing to bring dramatic elements into the immanent trinitarian relations, and thus risk what Karl Rahner called a "Gnostic" conception of God, whereas Julian would rather risk losing the drama so as to preserve the peace and aseity of the Godhead. Balthasar in a sense sees the pain of the cross projected into the trinitarian relations, whereas Julian sees the tranquility and harmony of trinitarian *perichoresis* in the event of the cross. Yet despite this difference (and I do not mean to minimize it), Balthasar's account of theo-drama remains extremely helpful in reading Julian's *Revelation*. Julian's thought is fundamentally "dramatic" in Balthasar's sense because it is framed by antinomies which are neither static points of paradox nor stable levels of meaning but dynamically related poles that create possibilities that can only be resolved dramatically. Whether she is speaking of lower and higher judgements, the first and the second Adam, sensuality and substance, outward and inward meanings, or the common teaching of holy church and what she has been shown by God, Julian refuses to give up on either pole of the antinomies that she sets up. These antinomies rather define a sphere of action, a "stage," in which the redemption of the world is played out. Only such a theo-dramatic reading of Julian can account for the interplay of temporal and eternal perspectives without collapsing one into the other. This, I believe, is why Julian found the example of the lord and servant initially so unhelpful. Her temptation was to read it as an allegory. Yet such a reading could not account for the significance of the movement of the action. The servant did not simply have a "secret identity" as the second person of the Trinity, which was his "real" identity. Such a resort to allegory would void history of all meaning; it would seem to say that the suffering of sin and the cross was either illusory or insignificant. Before the example can be of any help to Julian she must learn to understand it as drama; the complex identification in the servant of the first and second Adam was one that had to be dramatically enacted upon the world stage. Only such a dramatic understanding could do justice to outward meanings, lower judgements, the common teaching of holy church, the first Adam—all those things that go into making up what we call "history"—while still making sense of the promise that all shall be well. As Balthasar writes:

> what seems ultimate within the human horizon, and is experienced as such . . . , is taken seriously in theo-drama—indeed, it is treated more "absolutely" than in any other drama—and precisely in the way it is transcended. It is transcended in the action of God, *as* the action of God, who, using the hieroglyphs of human destiny, writes his own, definitive word, a word which cannot be guessed in advance. (*TD II*, 95)

2. Lords and Servants

The theo-dramatic reading that I have offered above claims to take seriously the historical specificity of Julian's revelation as a whole and the example of the lord and servant in particular. On a formal level, I have sought to find a way of reading *A Revelation of Love* that could maintain, as Julian wished to maintain, the significance of the *sensus litteralis*, while placing it within a larger context that fundamentally transforms it. Yet, on a material level, what *is* the historical specificity of the example of the lord and servant? What do we see in the "plain sense" of the example? It is quite simply a story of estrangement and reconciliation between a lord and a servant. But the estrangement and reconciliation of a lord and servant in late-fourteenth- or early-fifteenth-century England was by no means simple. In the example of the lord and servant Julian offers us a set of images with resonances that are not only biblical (e.g., Isaiah 42 and 53), but also highly political, as politically charged as her images of Christ's body.

The political nature of this example has not been immediately apparent to some interpreters. Denise Baker contrasts Augustine's and

Julian's views of the fall by noting that both "consider sin a deviation from the original created order, but Augustine's dominant metaphors for this condition are those of political conflict, whereas Julian's are those of physical separation."[79] By this she means that Augustine stresses sin as rebellion against God, whereas Julian claims that the servant's fall is inadvertent.[80] Baker is clearly right to contrast Augustine and Julian on this point; Julian nowhere characterizes the fall as a rebellion. However, this does not mean that Julian's metaphors are not "political." The servant might not be in active rebellion against the lord and thus not be culpable for the separation, but the fact remains that the image of the fallen servant is an image of social and political disintegration. To represent a breakdown, a sundering, of the proper relationship between a lord and a servant, even if that sundering is ultimately overcome, was to raise echoes of the events of the early summer of 1381, often called the "Peasants' Revolt," and all of the social unrest that clustered about them.

The rising of 1381 is itself something of a mystery, both as to its causes and its lasting significance. In early June of 1381, shortly before the feast of Corpus Christi, violence broke out in Essex, apparently in response to the poll tax declared the year before. The tax of 1380, unlike that of 1379, was not graded and fell particularly hard on the poor; evasion of the tax was widespread and discontent brewed. After the outbreak in Essex, the rising quickly spread to Kent, where the town of Canterbury was taken. At this point leaders emerged, most notably Wat Tyler and the priest John Ball (who possibly was liberated by the rebels from the archbishop's prison). Under the leadership of Tyler the rebels entered the city of London on the eve of Corpus Christi (Wednesday, June 13) and controlled the city for several days, executing Simon Sudbury, archbishop of Canterbury. At about this time violence also began to break out in East Anglia. The fourteen-year-old king, Richard II, met with the rebels twice at Mile End, outside London. At the first meeting he granted them a charter (later nullified) granting their request for the complete elimination of villeinage (servile status). At the second meeting (June 15) violence broke out and Wat Tyler was badly wounded by a member of the king's household and later captured and executed (or perhaps killed on the spot—accounts differ). After his death the rebels in London were routed and within a few weeks all of the major leaders had been hunted down and executed, the last of them in Norwich.[81]

Who the rebels were and exactly what it was that they wanted is a vexing question. The surviving accounts of the uprising are all by writers who are on the whole unsympathetic to the rebels, so it is difficult to get a clear image of their motivations and hopes. The anonymous author of the *Anonimalle Chronicle*, while speaking of the "evil actions" of the rebels, acknowledges a certain legitimacy to their complaints about "extortionately levied" taxes, writing: "These subsidies did nothing for the profit of the kingdom but were spent badly and deceitfully to the great impoverishment of the commons—and it was for this reason . . . that the commons arose."[82] Other writers, such as Thomas Walsingham, ascribed purely selfish and base motives to the "rustics," who "sought to better themselves by force and hoped to subject all things to their own stupidity."[83] Froissart speaks of "the ease and riches that the common people were of, which moved them to this rebellion."[84] Despite these ascriptions of stupidity and venality to the peasants, it seems clear that the levying of a third poll tax in four years, along with the unscrupulous behavior of those appointed to collect it, was at least one spark that ignited the revolt. Yet the revolt cannot entirely be described as a response to the poll tax. There is a sense in which Froissart is right that the relative prosperity of the lower classes in the generation following the Black Death had led to rising expectations among them.

But what exactly did the rebels want? All accounts seem agreed that they asked for the universal end of villeinage, but what did they intend by this? Certainly John Ball's famous couplet lends itself to a radically egalitarian reading:

> When Adam dalf, and Eve span
> Wo was thanne a gentleman?

Yet similar sentiments had been expressed before by authors whose theological and political orthodoxy was unassailable; recalling humanity's common source in Adam as a cure for worldly pride and a claim to spiritual equality between rich and poor was fairly common in preaching.[85] However, if Froissart's account of his preaching is to be believed, Ball took this theme further to advocate material equality as a remedy to England's ills: "the matters goeth not well to pass in England, nor shall do till everything be common, and that there be no villains nor gentlemen, but that we may be all united together, and that lords be no greater masters than we be."[86] Whether or not Froissart is correct in ascribing to Ball the advocacy of goods held in common,[87] it appears clear that he and the other leaders of the revolt *did* advocate the abolition of lordship as a kind of radically material reading of spiritual equality. And whether or not the majority of the rebels bought into this egalitarian ideology, these ideas were in the air and they were dangerous.[88] The abolition of lordship would have effected a radical overturning of the social order, a dehierarchicalization of the body politic. One could not hope to find a more radical political program in the late Middle Ages.

How might one read Julian's *Revelation* against the background of these events? It is perhaps tempting simply to hear in Julian's belief that "all shall be well" an echo of the statement from the rebel document known as the letter of Jakke Carter that "if the ende be wele, than is alle wele."[89] But we must avoid the temptation to assign Julian too quickly to a side in the conflict.[90] Though she lived in the town where the last of the rebels made their final stand, we have absolutely no direct indication of what she might have thought of their aspirations. What we do have is Julian's production of a text that uses the image of a lord and a servant, as well as the language of "courtesy," so as to deploy the structuring conventions of feudalism in quite unconventional ways. And the production of such a text in the context of late-fourteenth-century England is a political act. What remains is to try and discern the nature of that politics.

Striking in Julian's use of the figures of the lord and the servant is both their anachronism and their idealized quality. By the time Julian is writing, lords and servants as the defining poles of societal structure, the paradigm of social relations, were a thing of the past in terms of the actual figures on the scene, and were rapidly becoming a thing of the past in the way in which society imagined itself. The Black Death, along with a host of other factors such as the rise of "bastard feudalism," served to loosen the peasant's bond with the land and thus with the lord.[91] One of the resonances that Julian seems to draw upon is the feudal presumption that there is some sort of unbreakable, personal bond between lord and servant. When the servant fails to return, the lord cannot simply go out and hire another. Rather, he is bound to the servant as much as the servant is bound to him. The lord, too, has obligations: "fallyth it nott to me to geve hym a ʒyfte that be better to hym and more wurschypfull than his owne hele shuld haue bene? [should I not give him a gift that is more valuable to him and more honorable than his own health would have been?]" (51.51–52). However, by the latter half of the fourteenth century this pattern of social relation, based on mutual obligation grounded in a personal bond, had been seriously undermined. And even prior to this breakdown, relationships between servants and their lords rarely if ever lived up to the ideal of mutual obligation and goodwill that Julian seems to presume. The relationship Julian portrays between the lord and servant seems to accept entirely feudalism's self-representation as an organic social reality characterized by the absence of conflict, mutual service and protection, faithfulness, and love. Even prior to 1381 such an image was dubious; after, it can only seem like propaganda.

Yet Julian's portrayal of the relationship between the lord and the servant goes beyond medieval idealizations. In fact, as Mary Olson says, "the courtesy of God, by worldly standards, is startlingly inappropriate in its generosity."[92] The idea that a lord would be courteous to a servant is perhaps odd enough, but Julian intensifies the intimacy of the lord and servant through the identification of the servant with Christ, the second Adam. Beyond the apparent inequality of lord and servant is the Son's equality with the Father, which leads the lord not simply to act according to the medieval ideal of lordship, but in fact to transgress the boundaries of that ideal by raising the servant above his proper station.

One place in which this can be seen is in the transformation of the servant-Son's clothing. Perhaps drawing on the parable of the prodigal son, on whom his joyous father placed his best robe, Julian portrays the risen and ascended servant-Son transforming Adam's worn and dirty kirtle into a garment that, like the Father's, is "feyer, new, whyt and bryght, and of endlesse clennesse, wyde and seyde [beautiful, new, white and bright, and eternally clean, wide and ample]." And beyond this, it becomes "feyer and rychar than was the clothyng whych I saw on the fader. For that clothyng was blew, and Crystes clothyng is now of feyer semely medolour, whych is so mervelous that I can nott discryve, for it is all of very wurschyppe [fair and richer than the clothing that I saw on the Father. For that clothing was blue, and Christ's clothing is now a beautiful and becoming mixture, which is so marvelous that I cannot describe it, for it is made of glory itself]" (51.307–311). This transformation of the servant's clothing draws on an established medieval tradition which associates Adam's "flesh," and the pain to which it is subjected, with ragged clothing, and redemption in Christ with the donning of new clothes. We find in the *Ancrene Wisse*: "Our old dress is the flesh which we have from Adam our first father; the new we will receive from God, our rich Father, on the resurrection at Doomsday, when our flesh will shine more brightly than the sun, if it is torn here by adversity and woe."[93] In Julian's use, however, the transformation of the servant-Son's clothing is part of the more general exaltation of the servant to the lord's right hand: "Now stondyth nott the son before the fader as a servant before the lorde, unornely clothyd, in perty nakyd, but he stondyth before the fader evyn ryghte rychely clothyd in blyssefull largenesse, with a crowne vpon his hed of precyous rychenes [Now the Son stands before the Father not as a servant before the lord, wretchedly clothed, partly naked, but he stands directly before the Father, richly clothed in beautiful ampleness, with a crown upon his head of precious richness]" (51.314–317).

The connection of the servant-Son's reclothing with his raising to equality of status with the Father recalls the status significance of clothing in the medieval world. Certain forms of dress were, at least in theory, instantly identifiable with certain social classes—thus Julian's description of the shortness and tightness of the servant's tunic reflects current peasant fashion in the latter half of the fourteenth century,[94] and the transformation of that garment into ample and colorful clothing clearly indicates a change of status. Clothing provided important landmarks guiding one through the social terrain, as can be seen in the sumptuary legislation of 1363 that attempted to regulate the clothing which could be worn by the various social classes. The "outrageous and excessive apparel of divers people against their estate and degree" was unnatural to the point that it threatened "the great destruction and impoverishment of all the land."[95] As Christopher Dyer points out, the sumptuary law was designed precisely to protect against "the dangers to the social hierarchy if lords and servants were to become too similar in their outward appearance."[96] The feudal social ideal would not only take a dim view of the kind of transformation of the servant that Julian describes, but would see it as a positive threat to the divinely sanctioned order of human relations. The servant is not only made equal with the lord, but he is clothed in a garment which is "rychar than was the clothyng whych I saw on the fader."

This exaltation of the servant-Son is reinforced in Julian's sixteenth and final showing. After a vivid dream in which she is attacked by a demon who attempts to strangle her, Julian is shown a revelation of Christ dwelling within her soul.

> I saw þe soule so large as it were an endlesse warde, and also as it were a blyssyd kyngdom; and by the condicions þat I saw there I vnderstode þat it is a wurschypfulle cytte, in myddes of that cytte sitts oure lorde Jhesu, very god and very man, a feyer person and of large stature, hyghest bysschoppe, most solempne kynge, wurschypfullest lorde.
>
> [I saw the soul so large that it was like an endless citadel, and also like a blessed kingdom; and by the properties that I saw there I understood that it is a glorious city and in the midst of that city sits our lord Jesus, true God and true man, a handsome person and tall, highest bishop, most solemn king, most glorious lord.] (68.3–8)

Christ the servant has been exalted to become "hyghest byschoppe, most solempne kynge, wurschypfullest lorde" and dwells not only within heaven, but within the soul, where the godhead "rulyth and ʒe(m)eth withoutyn ony instrument or besynesse [rules and guards without any instrument or activity]" (68.11–12).

The transformation of the servant-Son into the lord is not simply the resolution of a comedic case of mistaken identity. The Son is "servant before hys comyng in to erth [servant before his coming to earth]" (51.234–235) and thus genuinely a servant, not a lord who temporarily puts on a servant's guise. And the exaltation of the Son to lordship is not simply the exaltation of the Son, the second Adam, but also the exaltation of the first Adam: Jesus reigns as "very god and very man." So Julian's claim is not that the resolution to her puzzlement over the example of the lord and servant is her realization that the servant, when understood as Christ, is not *really* a servant. Such a resolution might be possible on an allegorical reading, but it is not possible on a theo-dramatic one. If the servant in the example is taken as an allegorical figure, then the "literal sense" might be discarded once the higher truth, his "real" identity, is known. But in a theo-dramatic reading the servant must be taken for a real servant, who through what he suffers and undergoes is exalted by the lord to a place of equality.

Though Julian portrays Christ reigning in the soul, this is not simply a retreat into the interior and abandonment of the world historical stage, as if Christ's reigning in the soul was opposed to his reign in history; if drama does not resolve itself into epic, neither is it supplanted by lyric. It is true that certain ways in which Julian speaks *do* reflect a movement of interiorization. As noted earlier, Julian's frequent identification of the body of Christ with the elect—"all mankynde that shall be savyd by the swete incarnacion and the passion of Crist [all humanity that shall be saved by the sweet incarnation and the passion of Christ]" (51.254–256)—can seem to move in the direction of Wyclif's "invisible church" of the elect, particularly when seen in light of her emphasis on our inability to judge the eternal fate of any person. Similarly, her qualifying remarks with regard to the use of "means" (6.3–11) might be read as expressing doubts about the visible, concrete practices and structures which characterize and delimit the church as a historical entity. The impression that Julian is positing a purely spiritual church over and against the earthly institutional structures of medieval Catholicism can be strengthened by her depiction of Christ reigning "withoutyn ony instrument" in the soul as "hyghest byschoppe."

Julian could hardly be blamed for preferring the direct oversight of Christ within her soul to the ministrations of Henry Despenser, the bishop of Norwich, who personally led the forces that put down the rebels of 1381, and "gladly stretched his avenging hand over them and did not scruple to give them final absolution with his sword."[97] But she does not retreat from the particularities of historical, embodied, ecclesial existence into a realm of pure "spirituality." Like Wyclif, Julian seems to recoil from the "externalism" to which medieval views of the church and its sacraments could lend themselves. Yet Julian is quite clear that there is an intrinsic relationship between what is learned "inwardly by the holy gost" and what is taught "outward by holy chyrch," for both are "in the same grace" (30.6–7). The rule of Christ without instrument in the soul does not contradict the use of "means" so long as they are understood not as implements by which we gain access to a distant reservoir of grace, but as a direct communication of the divine life and goodness: "All the helth and lyfe of sacramentys, alle þe vertu and þe grace of my worde, alle the goodnesse that is ordeynyd in holy chyrch to the, I it am [All the health and life of the sacraments, all the power and the grace of my word, all the goodness that is ordained in holy church for you: I it am]" (60.35–37). The life of the soul is both substantial and sensual and to reject the visible, "sensual" church in favor of a purely spiritual one would be to reject "oure moder holy church, that is Crist Jhesu [our mother holy church, that is Jesus Christ]" (61.63–64), who meets us sacramentally in the concrete community of the church: "he wylle þat we take vs myghtly to the feyth of holy chyrch, and fynd there oure deerworthy mother in solas and trew vnderstandyng with alle þe blessyd comonn [he desires that we cleave strongly to the faith of holy church, and find there our dearest mother in solace and true understanding, with the whole community of the blessed]" (61.57–59).

For Julian, the realm of history is the realm of the "hazelnut"; it is composed of the "little things" that are held in existence by God's love, and that can only be properly known and loved in relation to God. This is no less true of the church as a historical entity; it too must be seen "spiritually," i.e., in relationship to God. To accomplish this the soul must "comyth aboue alle creatures in to it selfe [rise above all creatures into itself]" (68.31). But this movement of ascent and introversion is not a retreat into subjectivity, but leads to a countervailing movement, in which the soul "may . . . not abyde in the beholdyng of it selfe; but alle þe beholdyng is blyssydfully sett in god, that is the maker, dwelling ther in, for in mannes soule is his very dwelling [may . . . not abide in the contemplation of itself; but the entire contemplation is most blessedly set in God, who is the creator, dwelling therein, for in man's soul is God's very dwelling]" (68.32–34). The soul, rather than being an enclosed space, insulated from history, is radically "exteriorized" by the indwelling of God.[98] The "kyndes" that have flowed forth from God in creation need not be sought *in regione dissimilitudinis*, but may be found by looking "to holy church into oure moders brest, that is to sey in to oure owne soule, wher oure lord dwellyth. And there we shulde fynde alle, now in feyth and in vnderstandyng, and after verely in hym selfe clerely in blysse [to holy church, into our mother's breast, that is to say into our own soul, where our lord dwells. And there we should find everything, now in faith and in understanding, and later in beatitude truly and clearly in himself]" (62.24–27). The soul within which Christ reigns is the restored soul in which the abyss separating substance and sensuality has been bridged by the incarnation of Christ: "in that same tyme that god knytt hym to oure body in the medyns wombe, he toke oure sensuall soule, in whych takyng, he vs all havyng beclosyd in hym, he onyd it to oure substance [at the instant that God bound himself to our body in the Virgin's womb, he took our sensual soul, and in this taking, having enclosed us all in him, he united it to our substance]" (57.41–44). The soul thus healed is not turned in on itself, but is once again exteriorized as a microcosm of creation, by participation in the movement of the drama of salvation: "alle the kyndes that he hath made to flowe out of hym to werke his wylle, it shulde be restoryd and brought agayne in to hym by saluacion of man throw the werkyng of grace [all the natures that he has made to flow out from him to accomplish his will, shall be restored and brought back to him by the salvation of humanity through the working of grace]" (62.15–18). For the soul to be restored as a microcosm, spirit and matter must be brought together through the reconciliation of substance and sensuality.

It is particularly in the soul's sensuality—the changeable realm of history—that Christ dwells: "That wurschypfull cytte þat oure lorde Jhesu syttyth in, it is oure sensualyte, in which he is enclosed [the honorable city that our lord Jesus sits in is our sensuality, in which he is enclosed]" (56.23–24). As Joan Nuth points out,

> The phrase "city of God" is loaded with allusions, first of all to the church, sign of the kingdom of God on earth, obviously dependent upon Augustine's classical work in which the church's historical and corporeal character is developed. . . . While Julian sometimes calls the soul without qualification the city of God, the fact that she often specifically designates sensuality as God's city shows that she was conscious of the historical and bodily implications of the term as employed by Augustine.[99]

One of Julian's overriding concerns is that God be seen as not only "courteous" but also "homely." This means in part that Christ reigns as lord, bishop, and king not only in heaven, but also in that place *we* call home: history. Within this history, Christ reigns from his cross and those within whom he dwells imitate his passion through acts of compassion: "And than saw I that ech kynde compassion that man hath on hys evyn cristen with charyte, it is Crist in hym, that ych maner noughtyng that he shewde in hys passion, it was shewed aȝen in thys compassion [And then I saw that every kind/natural compassion that a person has on his fellow Christian with love is Christ in him; that each kind of stripping that he revealed in his passion, it was revealed again in this compassion]" (28.21–23). Jesus, seated as ruler within the soul as his city, draws together substance and sensuality by conforming the soul to his own atoning passion. For Julian the city of God is in a sense "hidden" within the soul, which is in turn hidden within God. But it is visible and present in its effects: not only in the sacraments as the effective signs of God's grace, but also in the acts of compassion brought about by those who are conformed to the love of God displayed in Christ's cross.

What we have therefore in the example of the lord and servant is not simply an illustration that can be left behind once we have discerned its meaning. This certainly was not how Julian understood it; in fact, she returned again and again, almost obsessively, to the concrete details of the example, attending to them, ruminating over them, as if to discern the meaning revealed in each particular. Within the drama of the lord and servant Julian must discern, in an always provisional manner, the cosmic drama in which sinful humanity is brought to dwell within the trinitarian heart of God by participation in God's compassion. It is within these details that the saga of God coincides with the human story in such a way that our telling of that story must be fundamentally rewritten.

In this rewriting, the pattern of trinitarian relations that is the hermeneutical key to the example becomes the pattern that orders human relations, transposing the sinful separations and oppositions that mar human relations into the infinite harmonious distance of the Spirit that binds Father and Son. Within the trinitarian relations of the Godhead, the Father's unoriginate primacy vis-à-vis the Son and the Spirit is fundamentally dissimilar from human forms of primacy in that the Son can be entirely dependent on the Father, to the point of being from all eternity the Father's "servant," yet can be of equal power and dignity even in his status as servant. As these trinitarian relations are revealed in the economy of salvation, the mission of the servant-Son, grounded in the eternal procession of the Son as servant of God, begins with the Son's fall into Mary's womb and ends with the servant seated at the lord's right hand, in a position of equality, having brought humanity with him as a gift for the lord. In this drama, any human notions of primacy are deconstructed, not by abolishing primacy, but by its rewriting as a "grotesque" hierarchy that is dynamically oriented toward the movement from higher to lower and from lower to higher. The hierarchy of Father over Son, of lord over servant, is not a static one, but rather a taxonomy of power oriented toward the exchange of goods between its poles. The distance between Father and

Son entailed by the primacy of the Father as the source of the Son's divinity is a distance that is infinite, stretching out to encompass the distance of human sin, yet always filled by the infinite gift of the Holy Spirit. This structure is simply the paradox of the Kingdom—in which the last shall be first, the wayward shall be welcomed, the stranger shall be companion—read back into the monarchy of the Father, revealing it to be a monarchy that exists solely to exalt the servant-Son.

As with Julian's images of Christ's crucified body, so too in the parable of the lord and servant, we find a *mythos* of power in which a fundamental asymmetry is the precondition for life lived as a gift. Yet in this case the asymmetry is not simply between creator and creature, but is brought within the very life of God as the asymmetry of Father and Son: the Son's being is an indebted being, received from the Father. This adds a new dimension to the asymmetry of the *mythos*, for in the perfect liberality of the Father's gift of being to the Son, the Son is the fully realized imitative expression of the Father and thus, out of his total dependence on the Father, is capable of in turn giving himself back to the Father, in the Holy Spirit. In this way the asymmetry of the gift becomes paradoxically reciprocal, in that the Father's gift to the Son becomes that which enables the Son to give himself back to the Father. As John Milbank puts it, *agape*—the love by which the Christian God is characterized—is not "pure gift" but "purified gift exchange."[100] This relation of gift exchange—this alternative, prodigal economy of the "carnival"—*is* the divine nature. And as such, it is the "metaphysical image" by which Julian imagines the political.

In this grotesque hierarchy of the exalted servant we see clearly an inversion—even a shattering—of the feudal hierarchy of power. But we see no less a difference from nominalist imaginings of the divine nature and divine power. For a thinker like Ockham, it would be truer to reason and experience to hold that the trinitarian persons are in fact three absolute, individual things, since a relation is in fact nothing but the soul's cognition of the juxtapositioning of two absolute things.[101] It is only on the sheer authority of Christian tradition that he concedes that the persons of the Trinity subsist as real relations, and he denies that anything *else* exists outside the soul except as an individual particular.[102] This means that while we might understand the very being of the Trinity as consisting of real relations of reciprocal giving, these relations are ultimately irrelevant for thinking about human relationships, because in the hands of Ockham the ever greater dissimilarity of analogy between creatures and creator becomes an unbridgeable chasm. The doctrine of the Trinity plays a strikingly small place in Ockham's understanding of God's relationship to the world. That relationship is not one in which we can find *vestigia* of the real relationships of Father, Son, and Spirit displayed in nature and history, but one in which the sheer divine will imparts information about the divine nature through revelation. The trinitarian economy is not something in which creatures can participate. As noted earlier, with regard to creatures Ockham's overriding principle is that God "is no one's debtor."[103]

For Julian, in contrast, the divine nature as an exchange of gifts is imprinted upon the created world. The Father simply *is* the origin of the Son's gift of being: "The werkyng of the father is this: that he geavyth meed to hys sonne Jhesu Crist [the activity of the Father is this: he gives reward to his Son Jesus Christ]" (22.14–15). And the Son *is* the servant, predestined from all eternity to bring the gift of himself, and with himself all of restored humanity, to the Father, and even beyond this to receive it back as his crown. This displays a complex pattern of reciprocal exchange, one that is not simply "contained" within the immanent trinitarian life of God, but that is communicated to creatures through the "forth spredyng [indwelling]" (60.2) of that trinitarian life in the economy of salvation.[104] Humanity is brought within the circle of the trinitarian exchange by our engrafting into the gift that is exchanged between Father and Son through our sharing of Christ's compassion.

> And thus Crist is oure wey, vs suerly ledyng in his lawes, and Crist in his body myȝtely beryth vs vp in to hevyn; for I saw that Crist, vs alle havyng in hym that shall be savyd by hym, wurschypfully presentyth his fader in hevyn with vs, whych present fulle thangkfully hys fader receyvyth, and curtesly gevyth it vnto his sonne Jhesu Crist. Whych gyfte and werkyng is joy to the fader, and blysse to the son, and lykyng to the holy ghost, and of alle thyng that to us longyth, it is most lykyng to oure lorde that we enjoye in this joy, whych is in the blessyd trynyte of our salvation.
>
> [And thus Christ is our way, leading us surely by his laws, and Christ in his body powerfully bears us up to heaven; for I saw that Christ, having all of us within him who shall be saved by him, honorably presents his Father in heaven with us, and this present his Father thankfully receives, and courteously gives it to his Son Jesus

Christ. This gift and action is joy to the Father, and bliss to the Son, and delight to the Holy Spirit, and of all the things that pertain to us, it is the greatest delight to our lord that we enjoy in this joy that is in the blessed Trinity of our salvation.] (55.2–10)

In a sense our participation in this economy must await our final restoration at the end of time, but even prior to this we have the gift of our restored self "tresoured to vs in Jhesu Criste [treasured for us in Jesus Christ]" (57.41). The crown that he wears is the gift of ourselves kept in trust for us: "all the gyftes that god may geue to the creature he hath gevyn to his son Jhesu for vs, whych gyftes he wonnyng in vs hath beclosyd in hym in to the tyme that we be waxyn and growyn, oure soule with oure body and oure body with oure soule [all the gifts that God can give to the creature he has given to his Son Jesus for us, and, dwelling in us, he has enclosed these gifts in himself until the time that we are fully grown, our soul with our body and our body with our soul]" (55.31–35). We participate in this gift of perfected humanity—we in a sense become "our selves"—through our participation in Christ, through sharing in his suffering and compassion, through incorporation into his body "in whych alle his membris be knytt, [in which] he is not ȝett fulle glorifyed ne all vnpassible." There is a continuity between our participation in Christ's body on earth and our participation in the life of God in heaven; the indwelling of Christ in our sensuality is a foretaste of our full and final participation in the trinitarian economy of the gift:

> This dede shalle be begon here, and it shalle be wurschypfulle to god and plentuously profetable to alle hys lovers in erth; and evyr as we come to hevyn we shalle se it in marvelous joy, and it shalle last thus in werkyng to the last day. And the worshyppe and þe blysse of þat shalle last in hevyn before god and alle hys holy seyntes without ende.

> [This deed will be begun here, and it will be to God's honor and plentifully profitable to all his lovers on earth; and when we come to heaven we will see it in marvelous joy, and it will remain operative until the last day. And the honor and the bliss of it will last in heaven before God and all his holy saints without end.] (36.9–14)

To step within the circle of the trinitarian economy is to be implicated in the reciprocity of Father, Son, and Spirit.

This takes us somewhat beyond the analysis of Julian's "bodily sight" that I offered in chapter 2. Seeing Jesus crucified does not simply involve the "negative effort" of attention, but this negative effort becomes, through the "forth spredyng" of the Trinity by the incarnation, a genuine, albeit asymmetrical, reciprocity. Through our sharing with Christ in the suffering of the world through concrete acts of charity and compassion, God "wylle make vs perteyner of his good wylle and dede [will make us a partner of his good will and action]" (43.7–8). Humanity is not simply the passive recipient of grace, but shares in Christ's atoning "deed" through union in him, yet in such a way that Julian can still say "god hym selfe shall do it, and I shalle do ryght nought but synne; and my synne shall nott lett his goodnes workyng [God himself will do it, and I will do nothing but sin; and my sin will not prevent his goodness from working]" (36.5–7). We return the lord's gift by imitating the servant who "falls" into the world of suffering out of zeal to do the lord's bidding. In Bakhtin's terms, the reciprocal gift exchange of the lord and servant is a "drama without footlights" that draws into the exchange all who look upon it, that can in fact only be *seen* by those who accept a role in the drama. As John Milbank puts it, "the divine gift only begins to be as gift to us at all . . . *after* it has been received—which is to say returned with the return of gratitude and charitable giving-in-turn—by us."[105]

In terms of Julian's imagining of the social, this means that sociality is fundamentally a matter of the exchange of the self as gift. Even primacy, rooted in the inequalities of power and ability that seem inherent in "real world" communities, must be understood not as an opportunity for domination, but for self-donation. We might see Julian as having seized the opportunity provided by the dissolution of the feudal taxonomy of social power to offer a trinitarian account of power as reciprocal donation. Her account of divine power lacks the "purity" and freedom of nominalism's omnipotence. Ockham's understanding of justification as God's sheer acceptance of actions done out of obedience to the divine command as meritorious *de congruo*, for all its notorious "semi-pelagianism," is lacking any sense of genuine reciprocity. The meritoriousness of human actions and God's acceptance of them is strictly within the realm of the *ordinata*, but "by his absolute power God could, if it so pleased him, accept a sinner for eternal life without [created] grace."[106] Marilyn McCord Adams notes that for Ockham, "God's redemptive activity is marked, not by maximal rationality, but by liberality!"[107] However, this liberality is one of pure gift born out of God's infinite freedom that, in principle, calls for no response from the recipient, but simply the sheer omnipotence of God. There is no "dramatic" interplay of divine and human freedom; rather they are segregated into distinct spheres, with human freedom protected from divine omnipotence by the dome of the *ordinata*, creating a realm in which humans may exercise their rule.

Julian, while sharing with Ockham an emphasis on divine liberality, also emphasizes the dramatic confrontation of that liberality with finite human freedom in the genuine human response made by Christ the incarnate servant-Son to the Father, which is the economic "unfolding" of the purified gift-exchange that is "enfolded" in the relations of Father, Son, and Spirit, and in which those who shall be saved participate. As much as Ockham, Julian offers a vision of divine omnipotence as a power that need not, cannot, be mastered or regulated by human wisdom, but that obeys its own unique wisdom. Yet this unique wisdom is not the voluntaristic ordering of divine power, but the unfolding of the Wisdom of the divine life that is the Word made flesh. The lord is *bound* to give a gift to the servant—"fallyth it nott to me to geve hym a ȝyfte"—not because of some contingent "decision" within the Godhead, but because the Father's very nature is one of fontal plentitude that gives itself to the Son in the Spirit. To respond in wrath to the servant-Son's fall would only be a diminishment of the divine perfection of power, wisdom, and goodness.

Thus, to put it in the most formal terms possible, the example of the lord and servant offers us a glimpse of a structure of society in which feudal relations of power have been transformed through their reinterpretation in trinitarian categories. It is possible that what we find here is simply an attempt to valorize existing relations between lords and servants, though Julian's portrayal has enough odd features to twist traditional feudal understandings past the breaking point. While there may be in Julian a certain nostalgia for feudal stability as represented by the three orders of society—and who could blame someone living in the last half of the fourteenth century for longing for stability?—there is a sense in which the picture of social relations presented in the example of the lord and servant are extremely *un*stable. Recall that something that to our minds seems as innocuous as a change of clothing was enough to induce what Christopher Dyer calls "moral panic" in the late medieval nobility.[108] Julian, both reflecting the unravelling of the feudal worldview of a social order fixed forever and seizing upon it, imagines Christ's body as a sociality in which the gift-exchange between lord and servant is purified according to the model of trinitarian reciprocity, rendering not the static egalitarianism of modern liberalism, but the drama of the servant's exaltation. What Julian gives us in vignette is something that is neither feudal "stability" nor modern "liberty" but a trinitarian "charity."

Julian's imagining of the political is of a body that is crucified in history—"Holy chyrch shalle be shakyd in sorrow and anguyssch and trybulacion in this worlde as men shakyth a cloth in the wynde"—but raised by God in the person of Jesus Christ. It is a grotesque body: one that mixes what should not be mixed. It is a body that is both a mystical body and a body politic. It is a mystical body, a body whose true parameters can only be discerned in the "mysty example" of the lord and servant, a body that is hidden in God from all eternity and cannot be known apart from the final, eschatological judgement of God in history, a body that must pattern its life on the mystery of the purified gift-exchange that is the life of godhead. It is not simply coextensive with ecclesiastical institutions, but is first and foremost the body that belongs to the risen Christ, its head, to whose judgement the church's judgement must be subordinated. But it is also a body politic, made up of actual concrete human beings—Julian's "evyn cristen"—who dwell within the realm of weal and woe, the realm of sensuality, in order to redeem it through Christ's compassion. Together they form a *polis*, a "city" gathered by Christ, within which he rules as lord, bishop, and king, and marked by sensual practices by which God's servants are sanctified and by which they "be his helpers, gevyng to hym alle oure entent, lernyng his lawes, kepyng his lore, desyryng that alle be done that he doth, truly trustyng in hym [are his helpers, giving him all our intention, learning his laws, keeping his lore, desiring that everything that he does be done, truly trusting in him]" (57.57–59). It is the visible, though at times obscure, realization of the perfect sociality of those who shall share in Christ's bliss at the end of time.

> And therfore whan that dome is gevyn, and we be alle brought vppe aboue, than shalle we clerely see in god the prevytees whych now be hyd to vs. And then shalle none of vs be steryd to sey in ony thyng: Lorde, yf it had ben thus, it had ben wele. But we shalle alle say with one voyce: Lorde, blessyd mott thou be, for it is thus, it is wele; and

now we see verely that alle thyng is done as it was thyn ordynawnce or ony thyng was made.

[And therefore when that judgement is given, and we are all brought up above, then shall we see clearly in God the secrets that now are hidden to us. And then none of us will be moved to say about anything: Lord, if it had only been thus, then it would have been well. But we will all say with one voice: Lord, blessed may you be, for it is thus, it is well; and now we see truly that all things are done as you have ordained before anything was made.] (85.11–17)

Conclusion

Performing the Book

> The wound inflicted on world history by the coming of Christ continues to fester.
> —Hans Urs von Balthasar[1]

At the beginning of the final chapter of *A Revelation of Love*, Julian writes, "This boke is begonne by goddys gyfte and his grace, but it is nott yett performyd, as to my syght [This book is begun by God's gift and grace, but it is not yet performed, as I see it]" (86.2–3). What Julian means here is obscure. In the Sloane manuscripts the scribe has added an interpretive heading: "The Good Lord shewid this booke should be otherwise performid than at the first writing," which seems to be a reference to the supersession of the short text by the long. Colledge and Walsh claim that this "wholly misinterprets the meaning" of Julian's remark, arguing that "[t]he 'performance' of which she now writes is the continuous life-long expression of a Christian's relationship with all aspects of the person of Christ."[2] Whether the Sloane scribe or Colledge and Walsh offer a better interpretation (and the two are not necessarily mutually exclusive), there is surely an aspect of the book's "performance" that they both seem to miss, and this can only be appreciated once one recognizes the "dramatic" quality of Julian's theology.

A Revelation of Love is not simply a medium through which a message is delivered from a speaker to a recipient, but is rather an utterance that actually constitutes both speaker and recipient in the single act of enunciation/reception. At least one sense in which Julian's book is begun, but not yet performed, is that it remains in the uncertain moment of passage from the as-yet-unconstituted speaker to the as-yet-unconstituted recipient. The book is begun by God's grace, but it can only be finished when it is received, and it can only be received by being "performed," by serving as the *mythos* of an actual communal embodiment of the gospel. Nicholas Lash makes a similar point about the scriptures. Noting that "there are at least some texts that only begin to deliver their meaning in so far as they are 'brought into play' through interpretive performance," such as the score of a Beethoven string quartet or the script of *King Lear*, Lash argues that "the fundamental form of the *Christian* interpretation of scripture is the life, activity and organization of the believing community," and that "Christian practice, as interpretive action, consists in the *performance* of texts which were construed as 'rendering', bearing witness to, one whose words and deeds, discourse and suffering, 'rendered' the truth of God in human history."[3] *Mutatis mutandis*, what Lash says about scripture can be applied to Julian's *Revelation*, which is, after all, a kind of gloss on—or perhaps stage directions for—the biblical story. Her *Revelation of Love* must be "put into play," not simply in the lives of individual readers, as Colledge and Walsh seem to imply, but by the "acting troupe" of God's lovers. And if we take seriously Julian's understanding of redemption as the "onyng" of our substance and sensuality, then the site of this performance cannot be a private realm of interiority, but must be the shared realm of history. As Lash writes, "The stage on which we enact our performance is that wider human history in which the church exists as the 'sacrament', or dramatic enactment, of history's ultimate meaning and hope."[4]

This troupe of performers, of Julian's "evyn cristen" who are recipients of the text of her *Revelation*, is constituted in the performance of that text. One of the puzzling things about Julian is *for whom* she thought she was writing.[5] Despite her constant references to her "evyn cristen," *A Revelation of Love* seems to have no ready-made audience. Particularly in the long text, Julian does not seem to have only vowed contemplatives in mind, and her use of the vernacular, though perhaps dictated by her own ignorance of Latin, seems to indicate something of a "popular" audience. At the same time, Julian's use of the conventions of popular devotion seems unconventional enough to have limited the appeal of her book among the lay audience that read such works as Nicholas Love's *Mirror of the Blessed Life of Jesus*. Her book is theologically demanding in a way that is quite untypical of devotional literature.[6] And while her rather gentle remarks on penance and doubtful dread seem to indicate that she has in mind readers whose lives are difficult enough without imposed austerities, what those difficulties might be are unclear.

I would argue that these problems in locating Julian's readership arise from the fact that she seeks to *create* readers who will endeavor to perform the drama of divine love scripted in her *Revelation*, and that in her own day that creation was thwarted. It is striking that Julian's *Revelation*, so popular today, was decidedly *un*popular in the Middle Ages. The reason for this, at least in part, is because it presents a "script" that was extremely difficult to perform under the conditions of late medieval christendom without being accused of heresy. Julian's presentation of Christ's crucified, generative body—"a feyer and delectable place, and large jnow for alle mankynde that shalle be savyd and rest in pees and loue"—and of the inappropriate grace that the lord shows to the servant, could not be performed by a church that saw itself as coextensive with the project of European christendom. This is not to demonize the project of medieval christendom or to portray Constantine's Edict of Toleration as some sort of "fall" from a primal Christian purity. However, christendom was at least an ambiguous undertaking. On the one hand, it took seriously the universal nature of Jesus Christ's claim to lordship. If Christianity is revealed truth, why should not this truth be the basis for the organization even of empires? On the other hand, it forced the church into certain conceptual and practical frameworks—in particular, the relegation of Christ's more radical teachings to "counsels of perfection," the division of the world into "spiritual" and "temporal" spheres, and the virtual identification (particularly after the Great Schism between East and West in 1054) of the boundaries of the church and the boundaries of Europe—that seem an uneasy fit with the gospel. In particular, christendom's linking of the church's identity to a geographical place that must be managed and defended thwarts the performance of Julian's *Revelation*. The body politic of christendom cannot let itself be opened in compassion; rather, it must police its borders. It must be smooth, not grotesque.

The kind of performance that Julian's theology called for was extremely difficult, but not impossible. The first generation of Franciscans stands as witness to the fact that one could, if only for a time, enact a theology that took as its starting point the appearance of the wisdom of God in the folly of the cross, without incurring condemnation by ecclesiastical authorities. For Francis and his followers, Jesus becomes the norm for a new kind of social practice that transforms them into a community of pilgrims, not with regard to the world, but with regard to the body of christendom itself. Early accounts of Francis's life present the Friars as a kind of eschatological sign of the gathering of the People of God. Thomas of Celano depicts Francis saying to his followers:

> I saw [in a vision] a great multitude of men coming to us and wanting to live with us in the habit of our way of life and under the rule of our blessed religion. And behold, the sound of them is in my ears as they go and come according to the command of holy obedience. I have seen, as it were, the roads filled with their great numbers coming together in these parts from almost every nation.[7]

In Francis's vision, with its echoes of the prophetic image of the gathering of the nations into Israel (see Isaiah 2:1–5, Micah 4:1–5, Matthew 8:11, Luke 13:29), the Sermon on the Mount ceases to be a "counsel of perfection" for individuals or a particular group within society (the "religious") and becomes the *regula* of the People of God. The sharing of goods and the evangelical poverty found in the book of Acts are no longer relegated to a golden age of the apostolic church or hidden away in monastic communities, but are lived out in the world as a concrete practice.

However, the Franciscans had the benefit of Francis, who, for all his "simplicity," was in fact a rather shrewd reader of church politics who knew just which tactical maneuvers would allow him to preach and live the radical message of Jesus without alienating the ecclesiastical authorities. The followers of Peter Waldo did not fare so well. And even the Franciscans found that without Francis's leadership it was extremely difficult to walk the fine line he had drawn. By the end of the fourteenth century in England it was only more difficult, as fear grew among church and secular authorities of the Lollard heresy and other vernacular theologies. The performance of a theology like Julian's—with its crucified body of compassion as the instantiation in history of the trinitarian economy of donation—would be quite subversive of the established order of christendom.[8]

Perhaps we can see in Julian's use of the common medieval image of Christ as pilgrim (81.4–8) an inkling of dissatisfaction with the project of christendom, a dissatisfaction shared, in their own ways, by Ockham and Wyclif. As for them, so too for Julian, Christ claims no specific geographical site as his own. However Julian, again like Ockham and Wyclif, does not seem able to unthink completely the logic of christendom. As noted earlier, there *is* in Julian a tendency to retreat into the interior. If the lordship of Christ is a pilgrim lordship because the Son of Man has nowhere to lay his head, she still reserves for him a permanent dwelling in the soul (81.3). The inherent danger in such a move is that it leaves history to be ruled by other lords, as can be seen explicitly in the political writings of Ockham or Wyclif, which seem to lack any critical edge when it comes to lay lords. Against the background of christendom's division of lordship into spiritual and temporal realms, the (rightful) denial to Christ of any lordship based on the coercive use of violence seems inevitably to lapse into a purely "spiritual" lordship that can in no way pose a threat to those who exercise "temporal" lordship. Thus Ockham interprets Christ's statement that his kingdom is not of this world to mean "I am not a king temporally to Caesar's injury, as the Jews falsely impose on me, but I am a king spiritually, because for this I was born and for this I have come into the world, to bear testimony to the truth."[9] In this, it should be noted, Ockham is certainly not unusual.

However, if we take Julian's understanding of sensuality to pertain not simply to the soul, but at least to that frontier where soul is joined to body, then her vision of Christ reigning in our sensuality would seem to undercut any neat division of the world into spiritual and temporal realms. Put another way, for Julian there is no such thing as "pure nature" that may be understood in purely "temporal" categories. The redemption of our sensuality in Christ means that "this lyfe whych is channgeable [this life that is changeable]" (48.6), the realm of history, is no longer insulated from the lordship of Christ so as to be managed by other lords, rather it is brought by Christ as a gift to the Father. The dividing line between time and eternity is ruptured by the incarnation of Christ so that *his* way becomes *our* way in this life. This opens the possibility of a "temporal lordship" that, by following Christ, can trace a peaceful path through history—the paradoxical lordship of Christ who reigns from the cross. Yet this possibility must remain unarticulated, and perhaps even unthought, by Julian.

But it need not remain unthought. For us, living toward the end of the protracted demise of christendom, there open to view other possibilities of the contours of Christ's body, sketched by a social practice characterized by nonviolence and compassion. Such a social practice might appear from one perspective to consist entirely of "deviations" from established norms, a politics of protest and resistance. It would constitute a collective identity that would be grounded not in a geographical "place" that must be defended, but in a "space" defined by an ensemble of narratives—the stories of Jesus and the saints, as well as the memory of those who have suffered, even at our hands—and of practices—hospitality, compassion, the sharing of material goods.[10] As such it would not be utopian, but concrete and visible. The point is simply that one need not always own the land in order to dwell there. From another perspective, such a social practice would not be simply a deviation from established norms—not simply a "sectarian" withdrawal into an enclave of purity—but would be the instantiation within history of the purified gift exchange of the divine life as a new norm, a new horizon against which deviations would be measured. Persecution, violence, abandonment of the poor—these would be registered as privations, deviations from the norm of the prodigal fullness of divine self-donation.[11] Thus sin would be shown to be "unkind,"—i.e., unnatural.

What this means in terms of imagining the political is that both "stability," the feudal ideal, and "freedom," the modern ideal, must be abandoned as controlling *mythoi* in favor of a substantive yet constantly revised account of *caritas* as donation. Rather than seeing possibilities for human beings dwelling together in terms of the antinomy of heteronomy and autonomy—obligation and liberty—Julian opens up the possibility of a freedom that is identical with the obligation entailed in an exchange of gifts in which there is no heteronomy, because what is given and received is nothing less than ourselves. The "obligation" to give myself *to* another is the ground of the possibility of freedom, precisely because the self that I give has been received by me *from* another, indeed, from a host of others. To refuse to give ourselves is not to refuse an externally imposed regulation, but it is a failure of that very self, whose nature is gift.

The site in which this *mythos* of *caritas* would be enacted is what I have alluded to as the "mystical body politic of Christ," and part of the "political" task of those who would seek to perform Julian's book is the actual formation of such a site. Julian calls her "evyn cristen" to become in the world a sacrament of that fair and delectable place that is the infinite heart of Christ. As a "sacrament" Christ's ecclesial body is both a sign and a cause of that place; it indicates under the shadow of a figure the reality that it is to receive, while it also is agent of that reality. As an actualized practice of compassion and forgiveness, it provides a visible sign of an alternative to other visions of human community, visions that are built on metaphysics of domination or conflict or scarcity. At the same time it must be, as Benedict said of the monastic community, "a school for the Lord's service"—meaning the place where the sign becomes reality, where disciples are formed, the *schola* that "performs" the gospel.[12] It is a body that acts in the world in such a way as to call into question the wisdom of the world by showing another way that is in fact livable.

Such a body is "mystical" not because it is "spiritual" as opposed to "temporal," or "invisible" as opposed to "visible." It is a mystical body because it participates in the purified gift exchange that simply *is* the mystery of the triune life of God. Its visibility comes not from its borders, which remain, as Henri de Lubac puts it, "God's secret," but from its center, which is Christ. This means that it is possible to locate people and events in terms of their proximity to or distance from that center, but it is not possible to locate anything outside the mystical body, because "all shall be well" and "everything that is done is well done." Because the saving mystery of God in Christ cannot be contained in boundaries, everyone, including our enemies, must be seen as at least *potentially* a member of Christ.[13] Thus everyone is at least potentially included in the mystical body's participation in the purified gift-exchange of Father, Son, and Spirit. I cannot presume to know in advance from whom I will receive myself, or to whom I will have to give myself.

Such a body is "political" because it forms a new kind of *polis*, a pilgrim city defined not by borders or geography but by the practice of ongoing discernment of the mystery of God in Christ. If the mystical body is not to become simply a way of including everyone within a purely spiritual fellowship, then there must be some faculty within that body for rendering judgement on the shape of the body. This would include both the articulation of the body's "heart"—the central doctrines and moral teachings of the church—as well as locating people and events in relation to that heart—whether through the identification and veneration of the holy or, at an extreme, excommunication of the wicked. The criteria for such judgements would always have to be normed by the love of God revealed in the life of Jesus, lived as a path to the sufferings of the cross and the glory of Easter. And as Julian clearly reminds us, such judgements are always part of the "lower doom," subject to qualification by God's eschatological "higher doom." But, as we have seen, this does not mean that it is invalidated. Rather, it must be located as one of the defining poles of the drama.

I would also maintain that the mystical body is truly a body politic because by its very nature it cannot make peace *in principle* with other politics. This means that while there may be ways of, for example, organizing trade, migration, law enforcement, the dissemination of information, and the growing of food that are *de facto* consonant with the Christian *mythos* (even if animated by another *mythos*), one cannot decide *de jure* in favor of such consonance by consigning these activities to the realm of the "temporal" or "natural" or "secular" where they become theologically irrelevant. The ecclesia and other polities interact within the same plane because the life of the mystical body politic is a life of both substance *and* sensuality: reaching up to the triune mystery that is at the same time "homely," dwelling in history. Again, this is why the "lower doom" is so important—precisely because it is a judgement made on the basis of our sensuality. Made with appropriate eschatological reserve, the judgement of the body of Christ within history must be enacted.

Part of the difficulty in seeing all of this as genuine politics is that it is impossible to derrive any sort of in-principle program of action from this metaphysical image. The programmatic politics of the state is tied to the kind of "gaze" that Julian believes is denied to us by the unknowing in which we stand in this life. Rather, one must grasp the opportunities that come to hand and act in the hope that God does everything that is done. This involves not simply the gentleness of doves, who can fly above to survey the earth without desiring to possess it, but also the wisdom of serpents, who keep close to the ground and know how to follow a path whose end they cannot see. At the same time, a certain glimpse of that end can be attained in the production and narration of "images," real exemplars that can display both for church and world the nature of the politics of *caritas*. This is of course much too abstract to give us an idea of what it would mean to perform Julian's *Revelation* today. However, let me offer an example that is a bit more concrete.

Dorothy Day, founder of the Catholic Worker movement,[14] seems perhaps an unlikely candidate for comparison with a fourteenth-century visionary. In fact, when Day was once asked if she had ecstasies and visions, she snapped back, "[v]isions of unpaid bills."[15] Yet she embodied a theology of divine love revealed in the cross of Christ that in many ways is remarkably similar to Julian's and was at least partly influenced by Julian.[16] But beyond any question of direct theological influence, the example of Dorothy Day is illuminating because she shows us how certain fundamental themes in Julian's theology can manifest themselves in a concrete and visible community of "evyn cristen."

Dorothy Day had a very clear sense that the social practice of the Catholic Worker could not be grounded in any humanistic optimism, but in the Christian hope that Christ has redeemed the world. In times of crisis, Day was known to quote Julian: "The worst has already happened and been repaired."[17] In this reparation, God fundamentally changes our perspectives in two ways. First, Christians can have hope in the midst of despair and disaster. In her first published reference to Julian, in 1947, Day, reflecting on the threat of nuclear war, wrote, "I had been reading Juliana of Norwich, the old English mystic and she had reminded me that the worst that could have happened has already happened, and I do not mean the atom bomb."[18] She expressed similar sentiments two years earlier, after the bombing of Hiroshima: "God permits these things. We have to remember it. . . . He, God, holds our life and our happiness, our sanity and our health; our lives are in his hands."[19] Because the worst had already happened and been repaired, Christians can follow Christ without fear, because they know that whatever evils they confront are within God's capacity to heal. Day shows that Julian's revelation that "all shall be well" is not necessarily a counsel of inaction. Rather, she shows how the belief that every event is enfolded in the being and action of God can liberate Christians from the tedious need to safeguard their lives, thus opening them to the risk of imitating Christ's compassion. In fact, I would dare say that only those who open themselves in such a way can truthfully speak the words, "all shall be well."[20]

Second, in repairing the fall of Adam, Christ has at least potentially incorporated all humanity into his mystical body. Like Julian, Day has a strikingly realist understanding of the mystical body of Christ. In the incarnation, Christ has joined all of humanity to himself, and he continues to work and suffer in his members. In 1951 Day wrote,

> Oh, the loneliness of all of us in these days, in all the great moments of our lives, this dying which we do, by little and by little, over a short space of time or over the years. . . . But we repeat that we do see results from our personal experiences, and we proclaim our faith. Christ died for us. Adam and Eve fell, and as Julian of Norwich

wrote, the worst has already happened and been repaired. Christ continues to die in His martyrs all over the world, in His Mystical Body, and it is this dying, not the killing in wars, which will save the world.[21]

This is not mere confidence, but faith and hope that indeed all shall be well because Christ's suffering on the cross has transformed the meaning of human suffering. Yet this transformation, this identification of human suffering with Christ's suffering, cuts two ways: those who suffer can take hope because they suffer with Christ, but those who inflict suffering on others must also realize that they inflict it upon Christ. Day's vision of Christ's body, like Julian's, is expansive, seeming at times to include the whole of the human race.

Dorothy Day and the Catholic Worker movement, in their willingness to seek Christ in every person, to treat every person as an ambassador of Christ, offer a practical concomitant to the "universalism" of the *exemplum* of the lord and servant. Julian's queries regarding the scope of salvation pose a problem only so long as they are taken as part of a theoretical position on the eternal fate of certain people rather than a very practical inquiry into how we ought to hope and how we should emulate in our lives God's mercy upon sinners. Day was famous for refusing to call the police to deal with unruly guests in the houses of hospitality, not because she did not recognize the damage such people could inflict, but because she believed that God's universal love for all people was bound up with their identification with Christ. In 1960, Day wrote:

> I remember asking Fr. [Pacifique] Roy how God could love a man who came home and beat up his wife and children in a drunken rage (there was one such in our midst) and Fr. Roy shook his head sadly and said, "God loves only Jesus, God sees only Jesus." A hard lesson to take, to see Jesus in another, in the prodigal son, or members of a lynch mob.[22]

We see here what it might mean to actually *believe* Julian when she says that God does not blame sinners, because in looking upon fallen Adam he sees Christ who has taken Adam's flesh. As for Julian, struggling with the implications of the *exemplum* of the lord and servant, so too for Day, this is "a hard lesson to take." Julian wrote, "Thus was I lernyd, þat loue is oure lordes menyng" (86.20), but as Dostoyevsky put it, and as Day was fond of quoting, "love in practice is a harsh and dreadful thing compared to love in dreams."[23] The Catholic Worker is a school for the Lord's service, where we can learn that the love of which Julian speaks—the love of which the Gospels speak—is at times a harsh and dreadful thing.

This may still seem inadequately political. If we view a phenomenon like the Catholic Worker with imaginations shaped either by the modern *mythos* of power as unconstrained liberty, or by a nostalgia for the pre-modern *mythos* of divinely sanctioned stability, we will see only a utopianism characterized by naivete or anarchy. Such a politics can seem to find no place in the earthly city. However, if we can find a way so to shape our imaginations that we can discern that *other* city, the mystical body politic of Christ that is already being enacted in our midst, if we can ponder with Julian her *Revelation of Love*, then we might see something else: love in practice.

"This boke is begonne . . . but it is nott yett performyd." The danger is that we will never perform this book, precisely because we prefer love in dreams to love in practice. We prefer to turn Julian's *Revelation* into a therapy for our sick psyches rather than a summons into Christ's crucified body. The promise of Julian's theology remains in a sense unfulfilled precisely because the demands of the drama are so exacting. And yet Julian also conveys a sense that in its beginning the book is *already* performed, because the book is in fact the text of Christ's body, crucified in pain and risen to bliss in the paschal drama. Christ's exemplary enactment must draw us into the rigors and joys of that drama, which requires a willingness to "stand in unknowing," to abandon fear, and to share in the passion and compassion of the crucified and risen Jesus. This book is begun.

Appendix

Who Was Julian of Norwich?

Despite Julian's wide scholarly and popular readership, she is a figure who is in a certain sense lost to us. Even though *A Revelation of Love* grows out of her own visionary experience, what she has to say about herself is minimal. In fact, if we compare her earlier account of her visions (the so-called "short text") with the later version (the "long text"), it seems as if over time she sought to eliminate, as much as possible, references that would be peculiar to herself and her own circumstances. In her constant insistence on the universality of her revelation, Julian effaces herself. Readers of her *Revelation* seem to come away from their encounter with the text feeling as if they have come to know Julian—her hopes, her doubts, her desires—but the particulars of Julian's life are lost to history. In fact, we do not even know her baptismal name, since "Julian" was almost certainly the name adopted by her after she became an anchoress at St. Julian's Church in Norwich. Any information about her must be gleaned from a few hints that she herself gives us in her book, a few external witnesses, and what we know about late medieval England and its religious and social institutions.

On either the eighth or the thirteenth of May 1373,[1] a thirty-and-one-half-year-old woman, who describes herself as "a symple creature vnlettyrde," received a revelation from God (2.2–4).[2] She fell seriously ill with what was thought to be a life-threatening illness and after three days and three nights she received the last rites (ii.3, cf. 3.3–4). She held on for two more days and nights and on the third night both she and those who were caring for her, which seems to have included her mother (x.29–33), believed that she was about to die. Toward dawn, her "curate" was sent for, to attend her dying, and when he arrived he set a crucifix in front of her face, a standard practice in the visitation of the dying, and said something to the effect of: "Dowȝtter, I have brought the the ymage of thy sauioure; loke there oponn and comforthe the þere with in reverence of hym that dyede for the and me

[Daughter, I have brought you the image of your savior; look upon it and comfort yourself by it, revering him who died for you and me]" (ii.22–28).[3] Shortly after this, around four in the morning (65.38), Julian sees the crucifix begin to bleed, initiating "a reuelacion of loue that Jhesu Christ our endles blisse made in xvi shewynges [a revelation of love that Jesus Christ our endless bliss made in sixteen showings]" (1.2–3). The first fifteen of these visions or "schewynges" continued until "none of þe day" (65.40), which may indicate either noon or the liturgical hour of None, celebrated around 3:00 P.M.[4] During these visions Julian did not feel the effects of her sickness, but once they ceased her illness returned (66.7–11). On the following night Julian received the sixteenth revelation, which she describes as "conclusyon and confirmation of all the xv [conclusion and confimation of all the fifteen]" (66.4–5).

Who Julian was prior to her experience in May of 1373 is a complex question. While there is widespread (though not universal) agreement that Julian was not yet an anchoress at the time of her showings, there is no consensus on what her state in life was. The more traditional view is that at the time of her visionary experience she was a nun, perhaps at the Benedictine monastery at Carrow.[5] The fact that the short text seems intended for the man or woman who "desires to lyeve contemplatyfelye [desires the contemplative life]" (iv.42) argues for Julian's having been a vowed contemplative writing, at least initially, for other vowed contemplatives. However, this only indicates that Julian is living some form of vowed life by the time she wrote the short text, not at the time of the showings. Benedicta Ward has argued that there is in fact no evidence that Julian was any sort of religious prior to being enclosed as an anchoress. She is nowhere mentioned in the extant records of the convent at Carrow, and the various wills that refer to her never associate her with any religious community. The details she gives in the short text, particularly the presence of her mother, do not seem to be consistent with convent life, and certainly not with life in an anchorhold. Ward further argues for the possibility that Julian was a woman who had been widowed at a young age, and had at least one child, who had died.[6] Both views are equally speculative, though Ward's is gaining greater acceptance.

An even more vexing question is the nature and extent of Julian's education. How one assesses Julian's education will clearly affect how one reads her *Revelation*. As Michael J. Write points out, "It is unfortunate, but perhaps inevitable, that the question of Julian's early intellectual formation should become involved in a battle of appropriations."[7] At one end of the spectrum, Colledge and Walsh argue that Julian was "a learned woman and some kind of Latinist" who made her own biblical translations from the Vulgate and was widely read in Latin theological literature.[8] Their critical edition clearly wishes to vindicate the orthodoxy of Julian's theology by placing her firmly within the Western medieval theological tradition. This is accomplished by quite literally imbedding the text of her *Revelation* within extensive notes that point to parallels in both Latin and English theological works. At the other end of the spectrum, Marion Glasscoe takes Julian's description of herself as "a symple creature vnlettyrde" (2.2) at face value, noting, "It is very probable that her account of the revelations was dictated to an amanuensis."[9] It is perhaps no accident that her edition of the long text (in contrast to Colledge and Walsh's edition) is without any critical apparatus or references to other texts. The resulting picture of Julian is one in which she is somewhat loosely connected to the mainstream of Christian theology. Thus, in Glasscoe's estimation, Julian is not concerned so much with Christian doctrines about God, Christ, sin, and salvation as she is with achieving "a depth of insight into the inner realities of human existence as perceived in Christian terms."[10]

Neither of these extremes seems likely to me. The kind of theological erudition that Colledge and Walsh ascribe to Julian would have made her one of the best-read theologians of her day—an unlikely distinction for a woman.[11] In fact, a woman so skilled in Latin theology and rhetoric would have been such an anomaly in medieval England that it seems odd that neither positive nor negative notice was taken of her. Even had she hid her light under a bushel, or within her anchorhold, the effort necessary to obtain books in the medieval world would have attracted *some* attention. On the other hand, it is difficult to read Julian's *Revelation* as the work of an inspired illiterate. While Colledge and Walsh occasionally push their identification of rhetorical figures in the text to the point of absurdity, the text itself shows a kind of polish that would seem unlikely had it been dictated to an amanuensis. In particular, in the transition from the short text to the long text Julian will lift whole passages out of the short text, often with small but important changes, giving the impression of an author revising an earlier version that she has before her.

It is worth keeping in mind that Julian's description of herself as "a symple creature vnlettyrde" can bear several plausible interpretations. Colledge and Walsh claim it is simply a convention of humility, "the rhetoricians' employment of *captatio benevolentiae*."[12] It is also possible that Julian was "vnlettyred" at the time of her revelation but somehow acquired an education later. It is also important to remember that literacy could mean many different things in late medieval England. Being "lettered" meant being educated, not simply being able to read, thus one might read and write English, yet still be considered "vnlettyred." Julian could quite accurately describe herself as unlettered, yet still have been able to read and write English, and perhaps even a bit of Latin.

On the whole I would argue that Glasscoe's presentation of Julian as illiterate in the modern sense is implausible, and Colledge and Walsh's thesis that she was highly educated is unnecessary. Especially given the virtual absence of any direct reference to sources, it is perfectly believable that Julian could have absorbed much of the basic shape and content of the Western theological tradition without any firsthand acquaintance with the texts of Augustine or Gregory or Bernard or William of St. Thierry. This tradition could have been transmitted to her through a variety of channels. If in fact she could read English, as seems to me likely, she might have read popular devotional works and religious lyrics. She would have listened to sermons, which were largely didactic and concerned with conveying the basics of the Christian faith. We also know from Margery Kempe that clerics could be found who were willing (sometimes for a fee) to read and translate Latin works for devout lay people. Doctrine was conveyed in myriad ways. Eamon Duffy writes,

> The teachings of late medieval Christianity were graphically represented within the liturgy, endlessly reiterated in sermons, rhymed in verse treatises and saints' lives, enacted in the Corpus Christi and Miracle plays which absorbed so much lay energy and expenditure, and carved and painted on walls, screens, bench-ends, and windows of parish churches.[13]

As Santha Bhattacharji has argued, it is entirely plausible that a highly intelligent woman, as Julian obviously was, could have used the resources available to a laywoman in devotional literature and practices, and forged the theology we find in *A Revelation of Love*.[14] My general procedure in this book, therefore, has been to seek the "least common denominator" in trying to locate Julian within the Western medieval theological tradition. In other words, there is no reason to posit her having read Augustine's *De Trinitate* when we can find the outline of an Augustinian understanding of the Trinity in a source such as John Mirk's *Festial*, a collection of vernacular sermons.[15] Following this procedure, I believe it is unnecessary to posit for Julian the kind of education described by Colledge and Walsh in order to account for the theological profundity of *A Revelation of Love*.

Julian's account of her experiences comes to us in two forms, which are commonly called the short text and the long text. The short text is almost universally held to be an earlier version of the long text and not an abridgement of it.[16] There is only one manuscript of the short text,[17] which appears to have been copied in the middle of the fifteenth century from a copy made initially in 1413 (see i.4), and was largely unknown until 1909, when it was given to the British Museum. The earliest complete copies of the long text date from only the seventeenth century, although there is a small collection of extracts from the long text copied c. 1500.[18] The complete copies of the long text form two distinct traditions: the Paris manuscript[19] and two manuscripts from the British Library (the Sloane Manuscripts).[20] Both seem to have been preserved by English Catholics who had fled to France at the time of the Reformation. While the two manuscript traditions largely agree, there are significant differences at a few points. Both traditions have their partisans,[21] but no one has been able to establish definitively that either one is a more faithful copy of what Julian originally wrote, and all three manuscripts have their difficulties. In this book I am primarily drawing on the long text, as it presents Julian's more mature theology. I have, in general, followed Paris, and where I have preferred the Sloane reading I attempt to give a reason in the notes. However, it is important to bear in mind that whatever "original" there might have been at one point is no longer extant, and barring the discovery of a new manuscript, we are left with texts which seem to "float" above their now lost *arche*.

The standard accepted account of the composition of the two texts is that the short text was written sometime shortly after May 1373 and the long text was written some twenty years later, prompted by a revelation that led to a deeper understanding of the original vision (51.86–89). In this view, the short text reflects the immediacy of

Julian's original experience, whereas the long text shows the fruits of two decades of reflection. This view has recently been challenged by Nicholas Watson, who dates the short text no earlier than 1382 and no later than 1388. Watson points to two places in the short text, each of which "suggests the passage of some years, at least, between revelation and record."[22] However, the crux of his argument rests on a passage found only in the short text in which Julian interrupts her narrative to assure her readers of her orthodoxy with regard to the use of religious images (i.14–18). This seems clearly an attempt to defuse a charge of Lollardy,[23] but as Watson points out, the critique of images did not become a controversial point until after the Blackfriars Council of 1382, and thus Julian's defensive remark would be difficult to account for during the 1370s.[24] The date of 1388 comes from the fact that in the long text Julian speaks of a second revelation, occurring fifteen years after the first, but nowhere mentions this in the short text (86.13–19).[25] The earliest date of the long text Watson retains as 1393, but argues for a later date, partly on the basis of his later dating of the short text—the long text's differences from the short text are great enough to indicate more than five years separating them. He argues that the fact that the short text was copied as late as 1413 may indicate that she was not yet finished writing the long text at that point.[26]

In terms of practical significance, Watson's later dating would allow for greater influence of continental writers, translations of whose works began to appear in England in the early 1400s. It would also shift our understanding of the short text from being a bare-bones account of visions to a more self-consciously "authored" text. With regard to the long text, such a late date might also indicate why Julian never wrote anything else. It seems clear within the long text that much still seems obscure and unresolved to Julian. If the long text was written in 1393, when Julian was only fifty, it leaves us wondering whether Julian abandoned the minute meditation on her visions. However, if she was still working on it in her seventies (as Watson's dating would indicate), then we would read the long text as a life-project, what Lynn Staley has described as "a text for a life."[27] David Aers has commented that Watson's "interesting attempts to date the long text to the reign of Henry V seem unpersuasive . . . [because] Julian's often radical vernacular theology is most unlikely to have been possible after Arundel's Constitutions of 1407/9."[28] But while Arundel's Constitutions may have made the *distribution* of such a theology most unlikely, they would not necessarily have prevented the *production* of such a theology. Perhaps the absence of medieval manuscripts of the long text (apart from the excerpts in the Westminster manuscript) is an indication that it was never published. Though they do not remove all doubt, Watson's arguments on the dating of the texts seem on the whole convincing.

As the above remarks indicate, we do not know much of Julian's life after 1373. Julian's writings themselves give virtually no information about her subsequent life. They do not tell us at what point she became an anchoress. She does tell us that after fifteen years (1388) she received a secondary revelation, illuminating the original experience: "Wouldest thou wytt thy lordes menyng in this thyng? Wytt it wele, loue was his menyng [Do you want to know your lord's meaning in this thing? Know it well, love was his meaning]" (86.15–16). We also possess some external references to Julian, including several wills. These seem to indicate that Julian had been enclosed as an anchoress at least by 1393 and was still alive in 1416.[29]

A more significant external reference—the only one of these that tells us anything about Julian as a theologian—is Margery Kempe's description of her visit to "an ankres in þe same cyte [Norwich] whyche hyte Dame Ielyan [an anchoress in the same city who was called Dame Julian]" at some point between 1413 and 1415.[30] Margery tells us that Julian "was expert in swech thyngys & good cownsel cowd ȝeuyn [was an expert in such things and could give good counsel]." In typical fashion, Julian advises Margery to judge her extraordinary spiritual experiences according to the criteria of "þe worshep of God & profyte of hir euyn-cristen [the worship of God and the profit of her fellow Christians]." Margery perhaps does not inspire confidence as a reporter of Julian's words, but her account of her conversation with Julian sounds many of the themes found in Julian's own writings: "þe Devyl hath no powyr in a mannys sowle [the Devil has no power in a person's soul]" and "þe sowle of a rytful man is þe sete of God [the soul of a righteous person is the seat of God]."[31]

Both the wills and Margery Kempe indicate that at some point in her life Julian became an anchoress. As I have pointed out, we cannot be sure when this took place, but it seems almost certain that it was after 1373, perhaps as a response to the visions, and prior to 1393, when she is named in Roger Reed's will as "Julian anakorite." If Watson is right in ascribing an early-fifteenth-century provenance to the long text, she was clearly enclosed for many of the years during which she labored over that text. Thus, the anchoress's cell was in many ways the setting for the long text. We can get some indication of what her later life was like from what we know about the life of anchorites in general. Whereas a hermit was a solitary who lived in an isolated place, an anchorite usually lived in a populated area in a cell built on to the side of a church (or perhaps in a church yard). If the cell was built on the side of the church, as it was at St. Julian's in Norwich, there was a window opening on to the sanctuary of the church so the anchorite could see the celebration of mass and receive communion. There was also a window that faced the outside, to which people would come to speak with the anchorite and receive spiritual counsel.[32] That Julian had some reputation as a spiritual guide is clear from Margery Kempe's encounter with her.

Much of anchoritic practice, as well as theory, can be gleaned from the *Ancrene Wisse,* also known as the *Ancrene Riwle,* a thirteenth-century document written as a guide for anchoresses. From this we can reconstruct the typical day of an anchoress:[33]

3:30 A.M.	Rise. Preliminary prayers and devotions
5:00	MATINS LAUDS AND PRIME OF OUR LADY (with other devotions)
8:00	TERCE OF OUR LADY Litany of the Saints Penitential Psalms "Gradual" Psalms Prayers before the Cross
11:30	Mass (with communion fifteen times a year)[34] SEXT AND NONE OF OUR LADY Meal Rest Period
3:00 P.M.	Private Prayers and Meditation Vernacular readings
4:00	VESPERS OF OUR LADY
5:00	COMPLINE OF OUR LADY
7:00	Bedtime prayers and devotions

The prayers were accompanied by various gestures and postures—standing, kneeling, prostration, outstretched arms, signs of the cross, striking the breast, kissing the earth—that sought to effect the complex interplay of outer and inner that is at the heart of the *Ancrene Wisse*.[35] Robert Ackerman estimates that the regimen of prayer set out in the *Ancrene Wisse* would occupy five or more hours a day, with the rest of the time left over for meals, sewing (a chief way in which anchoresses earned money), and at least in the case of Julian, counseling those who came for spiritual guidance.[36] This was in some ways a severe life (though less severe than the life of a peasant), but one that Julian seemed to undertake willingly. The "outer rule" of the *Ancrene Wisse* is an interesting mixture of austerity and moderation, prescribing fasts and corporal penances, but forbidding the extreme severity with which the flesh was punished that we find in stories of some medieval holy women.[37]

This is, in outline, what we know of Julian of Norwich. Much of it is more a delineation of various options (literate or illiterate, nun or widow, writing in the late fourteenth century or the early fifteenth) rather than a description. Interpretive choices must be made at almost every point and these choices have important consequences for how one reads *A Revelation of Divine Love*. Let me reiterate the most important interpretive choices that underlie my reading of Julian.

(1) Claims that Julian was illiterate are hard to square with the carefully constructed literary art of the long text. At the same time, Colledge and Walsh's thesis that Julian was highly educated in any formal sense seems unnecessary. Vernacular sources can, I believe, account for the influence of the Christian theological tradition on Julian.[38]

(2) On the whole, I find Nicholas Watson's redating of the texts, particularly his dating of the long text into the fifteenth century, convincing, if for no other reason than the open-ended, almost "unfinished" quality of the long text. It is difficult to imagine Julian ever having set it aside as a completed work.

(3) While Benedicta Ward's suggestion that Julian was a widow and a mother seems too speculative to me, she does make a convincing case that there is no reason to suppose that Julian was ever a monastic.

(4) The proper milieu in which to locate *A Revelation of Love* is neither monastic theology nor scholastic theology, and especially not "devotional" literature, but rather what Bernard McGinn has recently named as "vernacular theology,"[39] a new genre that emerges in the late Middle Ages. Julian should be read as a theologian who places intense intellectual demands upon her readers.

It is important to identify Julian as a *theologian* rather than a devotional writer because one should approach *A Revelation of Love* without either premature reverence, as if it were the direct outgrowth of a self-authenticating and unassailable religious experience, or premature scorn, as if it were *merely* the direct outgrowth of a self-authenticating and unassailable religious experience. God seldom speaks in Julian's book. The revelation makes little pretense of immediacy and Julian is very conscious of her mediating role as a theologian. We find in *A Revelation of Love* little of the ambiguity of authorship that permeates the writings of other medieval women theologians, such as Mechthild of Magdeburg's *Flowing Light of Divinity* or Catherine of Siena's *Dialogue*, in which God, at least at first glance, seems to be speaking without intermediary. Julian is quite clear that *she* is the author, and as such she is engaged in a complex negotiation of three factors—"mannes kyndly reson [man's natural reason]," "the comyn techyng of holy chyrch [the shared/normal teaching of holy church]," and "the inwarde gracious werkyng of the holy gost [the inward gracious operation of the Holy Spirit]"—by which "we may haue a lyttyle knowyng, where of we shulde haue fulhed in hevyn [we may have a little knowledge, which we shall have fully in heaven]" (80.3–5, 11–12). A fruitful engagement with *A Revelation of Love* requires that we recognize that negotiation, and thus recognize Julian as a theologian who is arguing, however irenically, for a certain set of theological positions.

NOTES

1. IMAGINING THE POLITICAL

1. Marc Bloch, *Land and Work in Medieval Europe: Selected Papers*, J. E. Anderson, trans. (Berkeley: University of California Press, 1967), 48.

2. Julian never gave a title to her book—perhaps a testimony to its perpetually unfinished state. Modern editions are published under various titles, the most common of which is some form of *Revelations of Divine Love*, though the work is also frequently referred to as *Showings*, on the basis of the Edmund Colledge and James Walsh's critical edition, entitled *A Book of Showings to the Anchoress Julian of Norwich*, and their popular modernization, *Julian of Norwich: Showings*, in the *Classics of Western Spirituality* series. I have adopted the title *A Revelation of Love*, which is how Julian describes the work in the opening of the first chapter of the long text: "This is a reuelacion of loue" (1.2). This is the title chosen by Marion Glasscoe for her edition of British Museum Sloane Manuscript No. 2499. I prefer this to Colledge and Walsh's *Showings*, which, while descriptively accurate, has no grounding in the text as a description of the work as a whole, and to the plural *Revelations*, because I believe it better reflects Julian's stress on the unity of the message imparted to her over the diversity of the individual showings.

3. Edward Stillingfleet, *A Discourse Concerning the Idolatry Practiced in the Church of Rome and the Hazzard of Salvation in the Communion of it: In Answer to Some Papers of a Revolted Protestant. Wherein a Particular Account is Given of the Fanaticisms and Divisions of the Church*, 2d ed. (London, 1672), 224.

4. Ibid., 226.

5. For a bibliography of editions and translations up to the year 1984, see Christina von Nolcken, "Julian of Norwich," in *Middle English Prose: A Critical Guide to Major Authors and Genres*, A. S. G. Edwards, ed. (New Brunswick, N.J.: Rutgers University Press, 1984). Since then, Georgia Ronan Crampton has edited a student text for the Consortium for the Teaching of the Middle Ages, *The Shewings of Julian of Norwich* (Kalamazoo, Mich.: Medieval Institute Publications, 1993, 2d ed., 1996)

and at least three translations have appeared: Father John-Julian, O.J.N., *A Lesson of Love: The Revelations of Julian of Norwich* (New York: Walker, 1988); M. L. Del Mastro, *The Revelation of Divine Love in Sixteen Showings: Made to Dame Julian of Norwich* (Tarrytown, N.Y.: Triumph Books, 1994); and John Skinner, *Revelation of Love* (New York: Image Books, 1997).

6. Thomas Merton, "The English Mystics," in *Mystics and Zen Masters* (New York: Noonday Press, 1967), 140–141.

7. For discussion of these issues, see the appendix: "Who Was Julian of Norwich?"

8. In very different ways this approach is represented by Colledge and Walsh in their critical edition, by Denise Baker in her book, *Julian of Norwich's Showings: From Vision to Book* (Princeton, N.J.: Princeton University Press, 1994), and by David Aers in his chapter on Julian in David Aers and Lynn Staley, *Powers of the Holy* (University Park, Pa.: Pennsylvania State University Press, 1996), 77–104.

9. Thus Lynn Staley's chapter on Julian in *Powers of the Holy*, 107–178, Grace Jantzen in *Power, Gender, and Christian Mysticism* (Cambridge: Cambridge University Press, 1995), and Elizabeth Robertson's "Medieval Medical Views of Women and Female Spirituality in the *Ancrene Wisse* and Julian of Norwich's *Showings*," in *Feminist Approaches to the Body in Medieval Literature*, Linda Lomperis and Sarah Stanbury, eds. (Philadelphia: University of Pennsylvania Press, 1993), 142–167.

10. See Ritamary Bradley, *Julian's Way: A Practical Commentary on Julian of Norwich* (London: HarperCollins, 1994), and countless others.

11. For a brilliant argument defending these axioms, particularly the first, see John Milbank, *Theology and Social Theory: Beyond Secular Reason* (Oxford: Basil Blackwell, 1990). Those familiar with Milbank will no doubt see here, as throughout the book, my indebtedness to his work.

12. William T. Cavanaugh, "'A Fire Strong Enough to Consume the House': The Wars of Religion and the Rise of the State," *Modern Theology* 11, no. 4 (October 1995): 398. For examples of the standard liberal narrative, see ibid., 416, n. 3.

13. Pierre Manent, *An Intellectual History of Liberalism*, Rebecca Balinski, trans. (Princeton: Princeton University Press, 1994), 8.

14. Ibid., 9.

15. Carl Schmitt, *Political Theology: Four Chapters on the Concept of Sovereignty*, George Schwab, trans. (Cambridge, Mass.: MIT Press, 1985), 36.

16. Ibid., 46.

17. On sovereignty as the capacity to decide the exception, see ibid., 5–15. On the basis of politics in the friend-enemy distinction, see Carl

Schmitt, *The Concept of the Political*, George Schwab, trans. (Chicago: University of Chicago Press, 1996), 26.

18. Benedict Anderson, *Imagined Communities: Reflections on the Origin and Spread of Nationalism*, rev. ed. (London: Verso, 1991), 6.

19. This reconstrual of "base" and "superstructure" grows out of an internal critique of Marxism, effected by such figures as Raymond Williams. See his *Marxism and Literature* (Oxford: Oxford University Press, 1977).

20. Ibid., 62.

21. See Paul Connerton, *How Societies Remember* (Cambridge: Cambridge University Press, 1989). Connerton points out well the respective function of myth and ritual in transmitting societal memory, though I think his distinction between the two is overdrawn. Rituals are not necessarily any more monovalent than myths are.

22. Max Weber, "Politics As a Vocation," in *From Max Weber: Essays in Sociology*, H. H. Gerth and C. Wright Mills, eds. and trans. (New York: Oxford University Press, 1946), 123.

23. Ibid., 77, emphasis in original.

24. Ibid., 78, emphasis in original.

25. Ibid., 126. Note here the ambiguous mixing of language: politics is secular because it is not concerned with ends—it can do nothing to save the soul—and at the same time it is possessed of a "genius or demon." It is one of the merits of the work of Carl Schmitt that he is fairly explicit about the metaphysical basis for state violence.

26. See Aristotle, *Politica* 1252a [*The Basic Works of Aristotle*, Richard McKeon, ed. (New York: Random House, 1941), 1127].

27. On "macropolitics" and "micropolitics" see "1933: Micropolitics and Segmentarity," in Gilles Deleuze and Felix Guattari, *A Thousand Plateaus: Capitalism and Schizophrenia*, Brian Massumi, trans. (Minneapolis: University of Minnesota Press, 1987), esp. 213–222.

28. See Michel de Certeau, *The Practice of Everyday Life*, Steven Rendall, trans. (Berkeley: University of California Press, 1984).

29. John Milbank, "On Complex Space," in *The Word Made Strange: Theology, Language, Culture* (Oxford: Blackwell Publishers, 1997), 271.

30. Georges Florovsky, "Empire and Desert: Antinomies of Christian History," *Greek Orthodox Historical Review* 3 (1957): 133.

31. Henri de Lubac, *Catholicism: Christ and the Common Destiny of Man*, Lancelot C. Sheppard and Sr. Elizabeth Englund, O.C.D., trans. (San Francisco: Ignatius Press, 1988), 61. The appendix to de Lubac's book offers a convenient compendium of texts—patristic, medieval, and modern—that illustrate and support his "social" account of salvation.

32. See Wayne Meeks, *The First Urban Christians: The Social World of the Apostle Paul* (New Haven: Yale University Press, 1983), 108. The *Theological Dictionary of the New Testament* says that the Christian and secular uses correspond "only in the sense of an analogy, no more no less" (Gerhard Kittel, ed. [Grand Rapids, Mich.: Wm. B. Eerdmans Publishing Co., 1965], 3:514). However, as we shall see shortly, the threat that the Christian community's claim to be an *ekklesia* posed to the Roman authorities indicates that they were widely perceived—and likely perceived themselves—as an *ekklesia* in something more than an analogous sense.

33. *Epistle to Diognetus* V [*The Apostolic Fathers*, vol. 2, Kirsopp Lake, trans. (Cambridge, Mass.: Harvard University Press, 1950), 359].

34. Ibid. [361].

35. Pliny, *Letters* 10.96, quoted in N. T. Wright, *The New Testament and the People of God* (Minneapolis: Fortress Press, 1992), 349.

36. Quoted by Origen in the *Contra Celsum*, VIII.2, 49 [*Origen: Contra Celsum*, Henry Chadwick, trans. (Cambridge: Cambridge University Press, 1965), 454, 488].

37. See Erik Petersen, "Der Monotheismus als politisches Problem," in *Theologische Traktate* (Munich: Verlag Heinrich Wild, 1951), 79.

38. Wright, *The New Testament and the People of God*, 355.

39. I say "may well be" since now any evaluation of the idea of "christendom" must take account of Oliver O'Donovan's powerful defense of it in his *The Desire of the Nations: Rediscovering the Roots of Political Theology* (Cambridge: Cambridge University Press, 1996). For an equally powerful critique of O'Donovan, see Stanley Hauerwas and James Fodor, "Remaining in Babylon: O'Donovan's Defense of Christendom," in Stanley M. Hauerwas, *Wilderness Wanderings: Probing Twentieth-Century Theology and Philosophy* (Boulder, Colo.: Westview Press, 1997), 197–222.

40. "Modernity" is, of course, a very problematic term of periodization. For a discussion of various periodizations and conceptualizations of "the modern," see Leszek Kolakowski, "Modernity on Endless Trial," in *Modernity on Endless Trial* (Chicago: University of Chicago Press, 1990), 3–13. There is also the vexing question of what one means by "feudalism." One might adopt a minimalist definition and restrict the term to relations of vassalage, or one that focuses on the manorial system of agricultural production. For a discussion of the problems with various definitions of feudalism and the way in which they affect how one views feudalism's decline, see M. M. Poston, "Feudalism and Its Decline: A Semantic Exercise," in *Social Relations and Ideas: Essays in Honour of R. H. Hilton*, T. H. Aston et al., eds. (Cambridge: Cambridge University Press, 1983), 73–87. As Poston points out, too narrow a definition of feudalism ends up

excluding time periods or places that historians normally count as "feudal." For my purposes I will employ a broader definition in which "feudalism" falls under the vague but useful notion of *mentalité* and that sees the relationship of lord and vassal as paradigmatic of all social relations within a society. Thus Marc Bloch defines feudalism: "A subject peasantry; widespread use of the service tenement (i.e., the fief) instead of salary, which was out of the question; the supremacy of a class of specialized warriors; ties of obedience and protection which bind man to man and, within the warrior class, assume the distinctive form called vassalage; fragmentation of authority—leading inevitably to disorder; and, in the midst of all this, the survival of other forms of association, family and State, of which the latter, during the second feudal age, was to acquire renewed strength—such then seem to be the fundamental features of European feudalism" (*Feudal Society*, 2 vols., L. A. Manyon, trans. [Chicago: University of Chicago Press, 1961], 446). One result of taking an approach to feudalism that sees it as a comprehensive term to describe a cultural matrix rather than as naming a mode of production is that I contrast feudalism with modernity, rather than with capitalism.

41. Castoriadis describes the radical imaginary as a "*doing* [that] posits and provides for itself something other than what simply is" and in which "dwell *significations* that are neither the reflection of what is perceived, nor the mere extension and sublimation of animal tendencies, nor the strictly rational development of what is given" (*The Imaginary Institution of Society*, Kathleen Blamey, trans. [Cambridge, Mass.: MIT Press, 1987], 146).

42. On the notions of "residual" and "emergent," see Raymond Williams, *Marxism and Literature*, 121–127.

43. The most influential work on this topic is Colin Morris, *The Discovery of the Individual: 1050–1200* [1972] (Toronto: University of Toronto Press, 1987). For a response and rejoinder, see Caroline Walker Bynum, "Did the Twelfth Century Discover the Individual?" in *Jesus as Mother: Studies in the Spirituality of the High Middle Ages* (Berkeley: University of California Press, 1982). Alan Macfarlane's *The Origins of English Individualism* (Oxford: Basil Blackwell, 1978) attempts a revisionist account of late medieval and early modern English society that portrays "individualism" as central to English character throughout the Middle Ages. For another account of the medieval "subject," one that criticizes certain "New Historicist" generalizations about the Middle Ages, see David Aers, "A Whisper in the Ear of Early Modernists; or, Reflections on Literary Critics Writing the 'History of the Subject,'" in *Culture and History 1350–1600: Essays on English Communities, Identities and Writing*, David Aers, ed. (Detroit: Wayne State University Press, 1992), 177–202.

44. See, for example, Étienne Gilson, "The Road to Skepticism," in *The Unity of Philosophical Experience* (New York: Charles Scribner's Sons, 1937), 61–91.

45. On nominalist theology in general, see Heiko Augustinus Oberman, *The Harvest of Medieval Theology: Gabriel Biel and Late Medieval Nominalism* (Durham, N.C.: Labyrinth Press, 1983). On Ockham in particular, see Marilyn McCord Adams' massive *William Ockham* (Notre Dame, Ind.: University of Notre Dame Press, 1987).

46. See, for example, Theodore Klauser, *A Short History of the Western Liturgy: An Account and Some Reflections*, John Halliburton, trans. (London: Oxford University Press, 1969), 94–116.

47. See John Bossy, *Christianity and the West 1400–1700* (Oxford: Oxford University Press, 1985), and Eamon Duffy, *The Stripping of the Altars* (New Haven: Yale University Press, 1992).

48. Janet Coleman, *Piers Plowman and the Moderni* (Rome: Edizioni di Storia e Letteratura, 1981), 192.

49. Christopher Dyer, *Standards of Living in the Later Middle Ages: Social Change in England c. 1200–1520* (Cambridge: Cambridge University Press, 1989), 223.

50. Barbara Hanawalt, *The Ties That Bound: Peasant Families in Medieval England* (Oxford: Oxford University Press, 1986), 4.

51. Helen Jewell, "*Piers Plowman*—A Poem of Crisis: An Analysis of Political Instability in Langland's England," in *Politics and Crisis in Fourteenth-Century England*, John Taylor and Wendy Childs, eds. (Gloucester: Alan Sutton, 1990), 59–80.

52. *The Vision of Piers Plowman* (B-Text), A. V. C. Schmidt, ed. (London: J. M. Dent and Sons, 1987), Passus XIX, line 330.

53. Bloch, *Feudal Society*, 446.

54. Maurice Keen, *English Society in the Later Middle Ages: 1348–1500* (London: Penguin Books, 1990), 6; Christopher Allmand, *The Hundred Years War: England and France at War c.1300–c.1450* (Cambridge: Cambridge University Press, 1989), 136–141. One should note, however, that the idea of English nationhood can already be found in documents from the beginning of the fourteenth century. See Thorlac Turville-Petre, "The 'Nation' in English Writings of the Early Fourteenth Century," *England in the Fourteenth Century*, Nicholas Rogers, ed. (Stamford: Paul Watkins, 1993), 128–139.

55. As R. N. Swanson puts it, "while the universal church struggled to assert its theoretical sovereignty over one of its fragments, in practice the sovereignty-seeking secular local authority asserted dominion through fragmentation and particularization of the church as a universality"

(*Church and Society in Late Medieval England* [Oxford: Blackwell Publishers, 1989], 90).

56. The term "organic," though widely used to describe premodern societies, is a problematic one precisely because it has embedded within it modern assumptions about societal change. Organicism is in fact a Romantic (and thus modern) concept that seeks to account for the way in which societies grow and change. Premodern societies, including medieval Europe, are generally noted precisely for their *lack* of an account of social change or growth. I am indebted to Reinhard Hütter for bringing this to my attention. Despite this caveat, I will follow convention in describing the self-understanding of medieval societies as organic, though perhaps "somatic" would be a better term.

57. John of Salisbury, *Politicraticus*, bk. 5, ch. 2 [*Medieval Political Theory—A Reader: The Quest for the Body Politic, 1100–1400*, Cary J. Nederman and Kate Langdon Forhan, eds. (London: Routledge, 1993), 38]. On medieval organicism, Otto Gierke, *Political Theories of the Middle Ages*, Frederic William Maitland, trans. (Cambridge: Cambridge University Press, 1900), 22–30, remains an excellent summary.

58. *Politicratus*, bk. 6, ch. 20 [43].

59. This has been argued by Georges Dumézil. For a brief account of Dumézil's work, see John Milbank, "Sacred Triads: Augustine and the Indo-European Soul," *Modern Theology* 13, no. 4 (October 1997): 451–474, esp. 451–453.

60. See G. R. Owst, *Literature and Pulpit in Medieval England*, 2d ed. (Oxford: Basil Blackwell, 1961), 548–593, and Roy Martin Haines, "Social, Political, and Religious Impressions from Some Late Medieval Sermon Collections," in *Ecclesia Anglicana: Studies in the English Church of the Later Middle Ages* (Toronto: University of Toronto Press, 1989).

61. *Mirk's Festial: A Collection of Homilies*, Theodore Erbe, ed., Early English Text Society, o.s. 96 (London: Kegan Paul, Trench, Trübner and Co., 1905), 65.

62. Thomas Brinton, Sermon 44: *Simul in unum, dives et pauper*, in *The World of Piers Plowman*, J. Krochalis and E. Peters, eds. (Philadelphia: University of Pennsylvania Press, 1975), 116.

63. Haines, "Social, Political, and Religious Impressions," 207.

64. In Krochalis and Peters, *The World of Piers Plowman*, 117.

65. Ernst H. Kantorowicz, *The King's Two Bodies: A Study in Medieval Political Theology* (Princeton: Princeton University Press, 1957). This point is one that is missed by modern interpreters who read the medieval distinction between "spiritual" and "temporal" power as equivalent to the modern distinction between "sacred" and "profane" or "secu-

lar." As Kantorowicz shows so well, during the Middle Ages "temporal" power was as theologically coded as "spiritual" power.

66. Mary Douglas, *Natural Symbols: Explorations in Cosmology* (New York: Pantheon Books, 1982), 65.

67. See the discussion in Duffy, *The Stripping of the Altars*, 91–95.

68. *Piers Plowman* (B) VI:207.

69. Recounted in Kantorowicz, *The King's Two Bodies*, 227, and in S. B. Chrimes, *English Constitutional Ideas in the Fifteenth Century* (Cambridge: Cambridge University Press, 1936), 68–69.

70. *The Sarum Missal in English*, part 1, F. E. Warren, trans. (London: De La More Press, 1911), 364.

71. This theme can be seen very clearly in the anonymous sermon from 1408 that serves as a prologue to the ordinances of the York Corpus Christi guild (edited and translated by Paula Ložar in "The 'Prologue' to the Ordinances of the York Corpus Christi Guild," *Allegorica* 1, no. 1 [1976]: 94–113). For a discussion (with many references to primary sources) of the patristic and medieval understanding of salvation as the restoration of unity, see de Lubac, *Catholicism*, esp. 25–81.

72. This was not an esoteric piece of eucharistic theology, but was a point that was included in popular instruction. See, for example, *Fasciculus Morum: A Fourteenth-Century Preacher's Handbook*, Siegfried Wenzel, ed. and trans. (University Park, Pa.: Pennsylvania State University Press, 1989), 409.

73. Gierke, *Political Theories*, 7–8.

74. Mervyn James, "Ritual, Drama and Social Body in the Late Medieval Town," *Past and Present* 98 (1983): 8–9.

75. *Sarum Missal in English*, part 1, 29.

76. Ibid., 31.

77. Ibid., 51–52.

78. *The Lay Folks' Mass Book* (T. F. Simmons, ed., Early English Text Society, o.s. 71 [London: N. Trübner and Co., 1879], 52) provides a prayer for the devout participant to pray during the pax and the priest's communion that asks for three types of love: love of God, love of self, and love of neighbor. The last is couched in terms of a universal love, but one observing a strict taxonomy so that it extends first to kin and thence outward to all members of the realm: "þo thrid loue is with-outen/to loue ilk neghtbur me aboute[n],/and of þat loue for no þing cese,/þerfore I pray þe, prince of pese,/þat þou wil make, als þou may best,/my hert to be in pese & rest,/& redy to loue alle maner of men,/My sib men namely, þen/Neghtburs, seruandes, & ilk sugete,/felouse, frendes, none to forgete,/bot loue ilk-one, bothe fer & nere,/als my-selue with hert[e] clere,/and turne hore hertis so to me,/þat we may fully frendis be,/þat I of hor gode, & þai

of myne/haue ay ioy with hert[e] fyne." For a discussion of the ceremony of the pax, see Duffy, *The Stripping of the Altars*, 125–127, and Miri Rubin, *Corpus Christi: The Eucharist in Late Medieval Culture* (Cambridge: Cambridge University Press, 1991), 74–76.

79. Certeau, *The Practice of Everyday Life*, 129. For a perceptive reading of the complex semiotics of concealment and revelation effected by the rood screen, see Duffy, *The Stripping of the Altars*, 111. Pamela Graves provides a less than perceptive reading of the division of space within the nave of medieval parish churches created by the chapels sponsored by various guilds. See "Social Space in the English Medieval Parish Church," *Economy and Society* 18, no. 3 (1989): 297–322. Despite a few valuable insights, Graves's analysis is hampered by a ham-handed and anachronistic distinction between "sacred" and "secular" interests.

80. For a description and analysis of the *Corpus Christi* procession, see James, "Ritual, Drama and Social Body." For another description, which takes issue with aspects of James's interpretation, see Rubin, *Corpus Christi*, 243–271.

81. This characterization of *communitas* is offered by Rubin (*Corpus Christi*, 2). Though she is critiquing Bossy and James, I believe her definition is accurate. For Victor Turner's own discussion of *communitas*, see *The Ritual Process: Structure and Anti-Structure* (Ithaca, N.Y.: Cornell University Press, 1977), 94–165.

82. Rubin, *Corpus Christi*; Sarah Beckwith, *Christ's Body: Identity, Culture, and Society in Late Medieval Writings* (London: Routledge, 1993); id., "Ritual, Church and Theatre: Medieval Dramas of the Sacramental Body," in *Culture and History 1350–1600*, 65–89. Duffy's portrayal of "traditional religion" in medieval England has been critiqued in particular for its tendency to downplay conflict, as evidenced by the almost total absence of the Lollards from his account of late medieval religion. See David Aers, "Altars of Power: Reflections on Eamon Duffy's *The Stripping of the Altars*," *Literature and History* 3 (1994): 90–102, and Katherine L. French, "Competing for Space: Medieval Religious Conflict in the Monastic-Parochial Church at Dunster," *Journal of Medieval and Early Modern Studies* 27, no. 2 (Spring 1997): 215–244.

83. Stories cited in Duffy, *The Stripping of the Altars*, 126–127.

84. For a sample of Lollard teaching on the Eucharist, in this case close to Wyclif's view, see *Selections from English Wycliffite Writings*, Anne Hudson, ed. (Cambridge: Cambridge University Press, 1978), 110–115. For Lollard polemic against religious dramas, see ibid., 97–104.

85. Ibid., 85.

86. Keen, *English Society in the Later Middle Ages*, 1.

87. Bloch, *Feudal Society*, 228.

88. Ibid., 225.

89. See Swanson, *Church and Society in Late Medieval England*, 16–26, 122–139.

90. This is a point at which one must tread a bit carefully. While it was common to stress the God-givenness of social status, the theological tradition, up until Aquinas in the thirteenth century, commonly held that private property and human inequality were a result of the Fall. This was used by Gregory VII during the investiture controversy to argue that temporal power was a result of sin and thus must be subordinated to the spiritual power of the church (see Gierke, *Political Theories*, 38). Aquinas, seeing the human person as a political animal, held that there was a prelapsarian exercise of *dominium*, but, in continuity with the earlier tradition, also held that in the state of innocence there would have been no lords or serfs, but only the lordship of governance necessary to human social life (*ST* 1.96.4).

91. R. H. Tawney, *Religion and the Rise of Capitalism* [1926] (New York: Mentor Books, 1947), 27.

92. On this "paradox of hierarchy" see Milbank, "Sacred Triads," 460.

93. Dyer, *Standards of Living*, 17.

94. Keen, *English Society in the Later Middle Ages*, 5.

95. The debates over both the terms "nominalism" and "*via moderna*" are seemingly interminable. In particular, there has been a shift in the past few decades with regard to the distinguishing characteristics of nominalism, as well as the degree to which it represented a break with the past. For a review of both traditional and revisionist positions on nominalism, see William J. Courtenay, "Nominalism and Late Medieval Religion," in *The Pursuit of Holiness in Late Medieval and Renaissance Religion*, Charles Trinkaus and Heiko Oberman, eds. (Leiden: E. J. Brill, 1974), 26–59. Recognizing the difficulties involved in both "nominalism" and "*via moderna*," I shall use them interchangeably to indicate those thinkers of the fourteenth and fifteenth centuries who take a certain inspiration from William of Ockham, particularly in their exploitation of the distinction between the absolute power of God (*potentia absoluta dei*) and the ordained power of God (*potentia ordinata dei*).

96. The significance of late medieval theology and philosophy for the emergence of modern thought is now widely accepted, though the exact nature of that significance is the subject of debate. See, e.g., Heiko Oberman, "Some Notes on the Theology of Nominalism with Attention to Its Relation to the Renaissance," *Harvard Theological Review* 53 (1960); Louis Dupré, *Passage to Modernity: An Essay in the Hermeneutics of Nature and Culture* (New Haven: Yale University Press, 1993); Amos Fun-

kenstein, *Theology and the Scientific Imagination: From the Middle Ages to the Seventeenth Century* (Princeton, N.J.: Princeton University Press, 1986); Hans Blumenberg, *The Legitimacy of the Modern Age*, Robert Wallace, trans. (Cambridge, Mass.: MIT Press, 1983); Frank B. Farrell, *Subjectivity, Realism, and Postmodernism: The Recovery of the World in Recent Philosophy* (Cambridge: Cambridge University Press, 1994); Michael Allen Gillespie, *Nihilism Before Nietzsche* (Chicago: University of Chicago Press, 1995).

97. As Marilyn McCord Adams puts it: "similarity is a two term relation between two things and not a three term relation between two things and a common nature." *William Ockham*, 111.

98. Oberman, "Some Notes on the Theology of Nominalism," 49–50. Cf. Harry R. Klocker, S.J., "Ockham and the Divine Freedom," *Franciscan Studies*, n.s. 45 (1985): 245–261, and Dupré, *Passage to Modernity*. For a dissenting view, which sees nominalism as primarily a position on philosophical logic that led to some theological conclusions that made even its adherents nervous, see George Lindbeck, "Nominalism and the Problem of Meaning as Illustrated by Pierre d'Ailly on Predestination and Justification," *Harvard Theological Review* 52 (1959): 43–60. Lindbeck's position has not found many adherents in current scholarship. For a critique of his essay, see Francis Oakley, "Pierre d'Ailly and the Absolute Power of God: Another Note on the Theology of Nominalism," *Harvard Theological Review* 56 (1963): 59–73. Another dissenter from the new consensus is David W. Clark, "Ockham on Human and Divine Freedom," *Franciscan Studies*, n.s. 38 (1978): 122–160.

99. Ibid., 54–55. Cf. Oberman, *The Harvest of Medieval Theology*, 4. Oberman delineates a "syncretist" school that mixed Ockham and Scotus (John of Ripa and Peter of Candia), a "left-wing" English school (Holcot and Woodham), a "right-wing" Augustinian school (Gregory of Rimini and in some respects Bradwardine), and a mediating school (Biel, Gerson, and Ockham himself). One must be careful not to ascribe to Ockham's thought in particular any kind of "normativity" for nominalism. In late medieval England, there is no evidence of any self-identified "ockhamist" school of thought. See William J. Courtenay, "The Reception of Ockham's Thought in Fourteenth-Century England," in *From Ockham to Wyclif*, Anne Hudson and Michael Wilks, eds. (Oxford: Basil Blackwell, 1987), 89–107. Louis Dupré goes so far—too far in my judgement—as to remove "Ockham from the nominalist flock" (*Passage to Modernity*, 277, n. 19).

100. For example, on the question of grace and merit, the left-wing tended toward the "pelagianism" with which nominalism is so often charged, while a right-wing nominalist like Gregory of Rimini held to a

strict Augustinian position of double predestination. On Gregory of Rimini's designation as a nominalist, see Oberman, *The Harvest of Medieval Theology*, 196–206.

101. For an overview of the modern rediscovery of the significance of the absolute-ordained distinction in identifying the *via moderna*, and the debates over what this distinction means, see William J. Courtenay, *Capacity and Volition: A History of the Distinction of Absolute and Ordained Power* (Bergamo: Pierluigi Lubrina Editore, 1990), 11–21.

102. Oberman, "Theology of Nominalism," 55.

103. See, for example, *ST* 1.25.5. For a survey of discussions of the absolute-ordained distinction (or analogous distinctions), see Courtenay, *Capacity and Volition*, esp. 25–114.

104. Adams, *William Ockham*, 1189–1190.

105. Ibid., 1193.

106. ["divina sapientia totum posse potentiae comprehendit."] *ST* 1.25.5.

107. Courtenay, *Capacity and Volition*, 92–95.

108. *Ordinatio* I, dist. 44, quoted in Courtenay, *Capacity and Volition*, 101.

109. Adams, *William Ockham*, 1194–1198.

110. For an enumeration of Ockham's different statements, see Adams, *William Ockham*, 1199–1207.

111. Courtenay writes: "Ockham's use of the distinction of the powers of God is a natural outgrowth of the thirteenth-century use, not a contradiction of it" ("Nominalism and Late Medieval Religion," 42). For a much expanded version of this argument, see Courtenay, *Capacity and Volition*, esp. 119–126, in which he presents Ockham as in fact opposed to Scotus's definition of the distinction.

112. For the view that Ockham sees the *potentia absoluta dei* as more than hypothetical, see Francis Oakley, "Medieval Theories of Natural Law: William of Ockham and the Significance of the Voluntarist Tradition," *Natural Law Forum* 6 (1961): 71–72. See also David W. Clark, "Ockham on Human and Divine Freedom," 152, n. 65.

113. William of Ockham, *Quodlibeta Septem* VI.1 [*Quodlibetal Questions*, 2 vols., Alfred J. Freddoso and Francis E. Kelly, trans. (New Haven: Yale University Press, 1991), 491].

114. *Quodl.* VI.1 [492].

115. David W. Clark, "Ockham on Human and Divine Freedom," 150–152.

116. See Francis Oakley, *Omnipotence, Covenant, and Order: An Excursion in the History of Ideas from Abelard to Leibniz* (Ithaca, N.Y.: Cornell University Press, 1984), 52, and Louis Dupré, *Passage to Modernity*, 176–177.

117. Ibid., 56. See also Courtenay, *Capacity and Volition*, 179.

118. Oberman, *The Harvest of Medieval Theology*, 45. Earlier, Oberman notes that Biel defines the *potentia absoluta* and *ordinata* of God "in exactly the same way as Duns Scotus and Occam had before him" (36). If Courtenay's argument in *Capacity and Volition* is correct, this would be true for Scotus, but not for Ockham.

119. *ST* 1.22.3–4; 1.23.6.

120. David B. Burrell, C.S.C., *Aquinas: God and Action* (London: Routledge and Kegan Paul, 1979), 123.

121. Heiko Oberman, "The Shape of Late Medieval Thought: The Birthpangs of the Modern Era," in *The Pursuit of Holiness in Late Medieval and Renaissance Religion*, Charles Trinkaus and Heiko Oberman, eds. (Leiden: E. J. Brill, 1974), 15; Oakley, *Omnipotence, Covenant, and Order*, 62–63. One should note that a figure such as Gregory of Rimini would be an exception to this.

122. Oberman, "The Theology of Nominalism," 63. Compare Hans Urs von Balthasar, *Theo-drama IV: The Action*, Graham Harrison, trans. (San Francisco: Ignatius Press, 1994), 147: "so long as God appears primarily in the form of power—omnipotence—the self can use this as an excuse, as a positive encouragement, to set itself up, likewise, as a 'power' over against God. After all, is it not the 'image' of God?"

123. Blumenberg, *The Legitimacy of the Modern Age*, 196. Cf. Oberman, "The Theology of Nominalism": "Using the *potentia absoluta* of God as the common denominator, this is related to the two mentioned characteristics [of nominalism]: the sovereignty of God and the quest for divine immediacy. Although these two seem to oppose autonomy, it is the *potentia absoluta* in the form of the dome-motif which creates the possibility for the *viator* to find his own way, unhampered by the supernatural world. With its voluntarism, Nominalism is a continuation of the Franciscan school tradition with a Scotistic turn toward individualism. While the miscalculations of the pagan philosophers proved the unreliability of human reason, the will (in the Occam-Biel line) is more independent and free than it ever was in the Franciscan-Augustinian tradition" (68).

124. Dupré, *Passage to Modernity*, 128.

125. On this point, see Oakley, "Medieval Theories of Natural Law," 80.

126. *Quodl.* VI.6 [506].

127. Funkenstein, *Theology and the Scientific Imagination*, 134.

128. *Sent.* bk. I, dist. 30, in *Philosophy in the Middle Ages: The Christian, Islamic, and Jewish Traditions*, 2d ed., Arthur Hyman and James J. Walsh, eds. (Indianapolis: Hackett Publishing Co., 1984), 680.

129. Blumenberg, *The Legitimacy of the Modern Age*, 150: "The universe as interpreted by atomism is ruled by the principle of the identity of

indiscernibles since the atoms and empty space are defined by the fact that they allow no rational action whatsoever but place reason in a position where all possibilities are indifferent, so that chance becomes the sole principle of reality. The nominalistic God is a superfluous God, Who can be replaced by the accident of the divergence of atoms from their parallel paths, and of the resulting vortices that make up the world. The concept of an absolute will is internally contradictory and consequently a chimera, a fiction."

130. See A. S. McGrade, *The Political Thought of William of Ockham: Personal and Institutional Principles* (Cambridge: Cambridge University Press, 1974), 173–206.

131. E. F. Jacob, *Some Notes on Occam as a Political Thinker* (Manchester: Manchester University Press, 1936), 21; Blumenberg, *The Legitimacy of the Modern Age*, 154.

132. See the remarks in McGrade, *The Political Thought of Ockham*, 199, n. 5. However, cf. Dupré, *Passage to Modernity*: "The obvious analogy between a royal edict and a decree of God's sovereign will is not coincidental: those who supported the latter in the spiritual order were the ones to promote the former in the temporal one" (137).

133. On Edward II and the Ordainers, see May McKisack, *The Fourteenth Century, 1307–1399* (Oxford: Oxford University Press, 1959), 1–31.

134. Dupré, *Passage to Modernity*, 124.

135. All this is nicely summed up by Herbert McCabe: "What makes a command a bad one? For the modern view it is essentially an unnecessary one, one that interferes, without proper cause or excuse, in the freedom of the subject. For the medieval view a bad command is a stupid one" ("Obedience," in *God Matters* [Springfield, Ill.: Templegate Publishers, 1987], 228).

136. Peter Fitzpatrick, *The Mythology of Modern Law* (London: Routledge, 1992), 54.

137. Ibid., 57.

138. McGrade, *The Political Thought of Ockham*, 118–119.

139. William of Ockham, *A Short Discourse on Tyrannical Government*, bk. 2, ch. 19 [Arthur Stephen McGrade, ed., John Kilcullen, trans. (Cambridge: Cambridge University Press, 1992), 61].

140. *Dialogus* II, I, i, fol. 230va, quoted in McGrade, *The Political Thought of Ockham*, 110.

141. See ibid., 170–171.

142. The complexity of this picture can be intensified when one considers the different forms that "modernity" took in England and on the Continent. Royal absolutism was not much of an issue in England, where

the political question of absolute sovereignty was short-circuited by the early development of a capitalist economy. To put the point briefly but cryptically, we might see this as a precocious elimination of a now irrelevent *potentia absoluta* by the well-regulated *ordinata* of the market. On the issue of how one relates continental absolutism and English capitalism, see Ellen Meiksins Wood, *The Pristine Culture of Capitalism: An Historical Essay on Old Regimes and Modern States* (London: Verso, 1991).

2. "I DESYRED A BODELY SIGHT"

1. Simone Weil, "The Love of God and Affliction," in *The Simone Weil Reader*, George A. Panichas, ed. (Mt. Kisco, N.Y.: Moyer Bell, 1977), 463. A shorter version of this essay, not containing the line quoted above, is found in *Waiting for God*, Emma Craufurd, trans. (New York: Harper and Row, 1951), 117–136.

2. To state this in another way, one might invoke Karl Rahner's dictum, "*The 'economic' Trinity is the 'immanent' Trinity and the 'immanent' Trinity is the 'economic' Trinity*" (Karl Rahner, *The Trinity*, Joseph Donceel, trans. [New York: Herder and Herder, 1970], 22).

3. As I have said, it is impossible with our present evidence to really know anything in detail about Julian's theological sources. However, Julian's overall theological perspective is perhaps attributable to an inherent conservatism in English piety, as opposed to the scholasticism of Oxford. J. P. H. Clark argues that the theology at Cambridge (which exerted particular influence in East Anglia) tended to be more conservative than that at Oxford, both on the question of nominalism and the theology of Wyclif. He notes in particular the more traditional view, over and against the nominalist view, of several Cambridge theologians by which grace is not simply divine acceptance of one who *fecit quod in se est*, but "an intrinsic principle of supernatural life within the soul." This, of course, is connected with the nominalist view of divine power. See Clark, "Late Fourteenth-Century Cambridge Theology and the English Contemplative Tradition," in *The Medieval Mystical Tradition in England: Exeter Symposium V*, Marion Glasscoe, ed. (Cambridge: D. S. Brewer, 1992), 1–16.

4. Dupré, *Passage to Modernity*, 222.

5. For an overview, see Ewert Cousins, "The Humanity and the Passion of Christ," in *Christian Spirituality: High Middle Ages and Reformation* (New York: Crossroad, 1988), 375–391.

6. Anselm, *Cur Deus Homo?* esp. bk. 2, ch. 6 ["Why God Became Man," in *A Scholastic Miscellany: Anselm to Ockham*, Eugene R. Fairweather, trans. and ed. (Philadelphia: Westminster Press, 1956), 150–151].

7. *ST* 3.62.5, ad 1.

8. See *Prayers and Meditations of St. Anselm with the Proslogion*, Benedicta Ward, S.L.G., trans. (New York: Penguin Books, 1973).

9. For an excellent description of *compunctio* in Gregory the Great, see Leclerq, *The Love of Learning and the Desire for God*, Catharine Misrahi, trans. (New York: New American Library, 1962), 38–40. On compunction in Anselm's *Prayers and Meditations*, see Benedicta Ward, "Anselm of Canterbury and His Influence," in *Christian Spirituality: Origins to the Twelfth Century*, Bernard McGinn et al., eds. (New York: Crossroad, 1992), 196–205. On the role of "horror of self" in Anselm's understanding of prayer, see R. W. Southern, *Saint Anselm: A Portrait in a Landscape* (Cambridge: Cambridge University Press, 1990), 104. One can see this horror vividly displayed in "Meditation 1: A Meditation to stir up fear," in Anselm, *Prayers and Meditations*, 221–224.

10. On the character and widespread influence of such texts, see Denise Despres, "Memory and Image: The Dissemination of a Franciscan Meditative Text," *Mystics Quarterly* 16, no. 3 (1990): 133–142.

11. On recollection and *imitatio*, see Karma Lochrie, *Margery Kempe and Translations of the Flesh* (Philadelphia: University of Pennsylvania Press, 1991), 27–37.

12. On the Franciscan Spirituals, see Malcolm Lambert, *Medieval Heresy: Popular Movements from the Gregorian Reform to the Reformation*, 2d ed. (Oxford: Blackwell, 1992), 189–214. On the Cathars and the Waldensians, see ibid., 44–175.

13. Aers and Staley, *Powers of the Holy*, 43–76.

14. Ibid., 41.

15. Ibid., 46.

16. *Anchoritic Spirituality: Ancrene Wisse and Associated Works*, Anne Savage and Nicholas Watson, trans. (New York: Paulist Press, 1991), 100.

17. For a recent representative of the older view, see Jacques le Goff, "Body and Ideology in the Medieval West," in *The Medieval Imagination*, Arthur Goldhammer, trans. (Chicago: University of Chicago Press, 1988), 83–85, and id., "The Repudiation of Pleasure," in ibid., 93–103.

18. *Ancrene Wisse*, 100.

19. Talal Asad, "On Discipline and Humility in Medieval Christian Monasticism," in *Genealogies of Religion: Discipline and Reasons of Power in Christianity and Islam* (Baltimore: Johns Hopkins University Press, 1993), 138.

20. Richard Rolle is a chief representative of the view that someone who had received the grace of God in the soul "mai als wele fele þe fyre of lufe byrnand in þaire saule, als þou may fele þi fynger byrn, if þou putt it in

þe fyre" (*The Form of Living* in *English Writings of Richard Rolle, Hermit of Hampole*, Hope Emily Allen, ed. [Oxford: Clarendon Press, 1963], 105). Rolle presents an interesting case of a male exemplar of a piety that is often associated with women.

21. See Caroline Walker Bynum, *Holy Feast and Holy Fast: The Religious Significance of Food to Medieval Women* (Berkeley: University of California Press, 1987), 122–123, 200–201, 210–211, 273–274.

22. *The Cloud of Unknowing* warns beginners in the contemplative life of overly material interpretations of spiritual languages: "& þan as fast þe deuil haþ power for to feyne sum fals liȝt or sounes, swete smelles in þeire noses, wonderful taastes in þeire mowþes, & many queynte hetes & brennynges in þeire bodily brestes or in þeire bowelles, in þeire backes & in þeire reynes, & in þeire pryue membres" (*The Cloud of Unknowing and the Book of Privy Counselling*, Phyllis Hodgson, ed., Early English Text Society, o.s. 218 [London: Oxford University Press, 1944], 96–97).

23. Caroline Walker Bynum, "The Female Body and Religious Practice in the Later Middle Ages," in *Fragmentation and Redemption: Essays on Gender and the Human Body in Medieval Religion* (New York: Zone Books, 1991), 194.

24. Joseph A. Jungmann, S.J., *The Mass of the Roman Rite: Its Origin and Development*, Francis A. Brunner, C.SS.R., trans. (London: Burns and Oates, 1959), 211.

25. See Caroline Walker Bynum, "Material Continuity, Personal Survival and the Resurrection of the Body: A Scholastic Discussion in Its Medieval and Modern Contexts," in *Fragmentation and Redemption*, 239–297.

26. See Colledge and Walsh, *A Book of Showings*, 286, n. 14, for the various possible corruptions of the long text manuscripts.

27. Robert Mannyng, *Meditations on the Supper of Our Lord, and the Hours of the Passion*, J. Meadows Cowper, ed., Early English Text Society, o.s. 60 (London: N. Trübner and Co., 1875), 22, lines 690–692. Cf. revelation 8 in the long text, where Julian writes: "in as mech as our lady sorowde for his paynes, as mech sufferde he sorow for her sorowse" (20.21–22).

28. The practice of presenting a dying person with a crucifix was a standard part of the *Ordo Visitandi* used with the dying. See Duffy, *The Stripping of the Altars*, 314.

29. Perhaps, like the lay people addressed by Walter Hilton in the second part of *The Scale of Perfection*, she aspired to a more advanced, contemplative spirituality.

30. Bk. 12, ch. 7 [St. Augustine, *The Literal Meaning of Genesis*, John Hammon Taylor, S.J., trans. (New York: Newman Press, 1982), 186]. If

Nicholas Watson is correct in his proposed dating of the composition of the short text as somewhere between 1382 and 1388 (see Watson, "The Composition of Julian of Norwich's *Revelation of Love*," *Speculum* 68 [July 1993]: 657–672), then a possible vernacular source for this Augustinian division would be chapter 18 of *The Chastising of God's Children*. See *The Chastising of God's Children and The Treatise of Perfection of the Sons of God*, Joyce Bazire and Eric Colledge, eds. (Oxford: Basil Blackwell, 1957), 169–173.

31. See, for example, Brant Pelphrey, *Christ Our Mother: Julian of Norwich* (Wilmington, Del.: Michael Glazier, 1989), 80–91, in which he attempts to offer an outline of the revelations that classifies each element. At first he seems able to follow the scheme Julian offers—using the categories of corporeal vision, mental vision, and lesson—but soon must add additional categories such as "translation" (i.e., out-of-body experiences), locutions, and teachings.

32. Nicholas Watson, "The Trinitarian Hermeneutic in Julian of Norwich's *Revelation of Love*," in *The Medieval Mystical Tradition in England: Exeter V*, 86.

33. Note that in describing the fourth showing, Julian speaks of how the blood from Christ's body vanishes before it touches the bed, whereas "if it had been so in kynde and in substance, for that tyme it shulde haue made the bedde all on bloude, and haue passyde over all about" (12.1–12).

34. This was first pointed out to me by Joan Nuth's book *Wisdom's Daughter: The Theology of Julian of Norwich* (New York: Crossroad, 1991), 12. Similarly, Denise N. Baker, in her *Julian of Norwich's Showings: From Vision to Book* (Princeton, N.J.: Princeton University Press, 1994), lists seven corporeal visions, all of which are of Jesus (48). Baker also notes the absence of the other figures who normally make up a passion "scene": "Her visions include none of the personages who play such a large role either as torturers or as compassionate witnesses in the serial Passion narratives and much of the devotional art of the late medieval period. Only Jesus appears in bodily likeness; even her visions of Mary at the time of the Incarnation and the Crucifixion are not corporeal" (48–49). Likewise, Frances Beer seems to indicate that she understands only the visions associated with the crucifix to be "bodily" (*Women and Mystical Experience in the Middle Ages* [Woodbridge: Boydell Press, 1993], 139). On the other hand, Christopher Abbot claims that "her vision . . . of the crucifix in a state of animation . . . belongs to (though it is not wholly definitive of) the category of bodily sight" ("His Body, The Church: Julian of Norwich's Vision of Christ Crucified," *Downside Review* no. 398 [January 1997]: 4). I am claiming that her visions of the

"animated" crucifix *are* in fact definitive of her use of the category of bodily sight.

35. Pelphrey, *Christ Our Mother*, 80.

36. Ibid., 90.

37. Watson, "The Trinitarian Hermeneutic," 84. Christopher Abbot says of the first showing that "[w]hat Julian presents herself as seeing here is not an independent vision of Christ's passion which makes the crucifix in front of her redundant, but the same crucifix mysteriously animated" (Abbot, "His Body, The Church," 4).

38. Note also that simply because something is a bodily sight, it is not immediately apparent to Julian that it is a "showing." See 10.33–36.

39. This view is not so much an epistemology shared by medieval writers as it is a shared image of that which is perceived coming to dwell within the perceiver. See, for example, Thomas Aquinas, *ST* 1.84.1, in which he speaks of how "the received [i.e., the species of that which is perceived] is in the receiver according to the mode of the receiver." Likewise, Bonaventure, who is generally taken to represent a more "Augustinian" (and therefore Platonist) perspective, says that "this world, which is called the *macrocosm*, enters our soul, the *microcosm*, through the portals of the five senses in so far as sense objects are apprehended, enjoyed, and judged" (*Itinerarium mentis in Deum* II.2 [*The Journey of the Mind to God*, Philotheus Boehner, O.F.M., trans., Stephen F. Brown, ed. (Indianapolis: Hackett Publishing Co., 1993), 11]).

40. See Dupré, *Passage to Modernity*, 39–41.

41. One finds a similar constellation of sickness, suffering, passion, and something like "bodily sight" in Margery Kempe: "Sumtyme, not-wyth-stondyng þe sayd creatur had gret bodily sekenes, ȝet þe Passyon of owr merciful Lord Crist Ihesu wrowt so in hir sowle þat fir þe tyme sche felt not hir owyn sekenes but wept & sobbyd in þe mend of owr Lordys Passyon as thow sche sey hym wyth hir bodily eye sufferyng peyne & passyon be-forn hir" (*The Book of Margery Kempe*, Sanford Meech and Hope Emily Allen, eds., Early English Text Society, o.s. no. 212 [Oxford: Oxford University Press, 1940], 138).

42. For example, compare long text 3.1–52 and short text ii.1–iii.11, or how in her long text account of the eighth showing Julian omits the mention of her mother's presence found at x.29–33.

43. This is the Sloane manuscript reading (taken from Marion Glasscoe's edition, *A Revelation of Love*, 3d rev. ed. [1993], ch. 51, p. 74). The Paris manuscript has "stode mykille in thre knowynges" (51.70). The variation here has been a central point of contention between the partisans of the different manuscript traditions. See Colledge and Walsh, *A Book of Showings*, 519, n. 70, where they cite this as "a clear example of P's

superiority to SS [i.e., the two Sloane manuscripts]." For the opposing view, see the (to my mind convincing) argument of Marion Glasscoe, "Visions and Revisions: A Further Look at the Manuscripts of Julian of Norwich," *Studies in Bibliography* 42 (1989): 116.

44. Watson, "Trinitarian Hermeneutic," 99.

45. A somewhat similar point is made by Edward Peter Nolan in *Cry Out and Write: A Feminine Poetics of Revelation* (New York: Continuum, 1994), noting that in the image of the bleeding Christ, Julian offers us "a complex verbal icon constructed of language that she hoped could trigger in our heads the *kind* of transformation that the original shewing triggered in hers" (146–147). I would simply note that the language of things occurring in Julian's head is extremely unfortunate, given the way in which Julian "sees" with her body. Also, I would not want to speak of a transformation that is tied to "the original shewing" for reasons that are by now, I hope, obvious.

46. The best known of these debates in recent years was engendered by Steven T. Katz's essay, "Language, Epistemology, and Mysticism," in *Mysticism and Philosophical Analysis*, Steven T. Katz, ed. (Oxford: Oxford University Press, 1978), 22–74. For a collection of responses that are in general critical of Katz's proposal, see Robert K. C. Forman, ed., *The Problem of Pure Consciousness: Mysticism and Philosophy* (Oxford: Oxford University Press, 1990).

47. See Simon Tugwell, "Faith and Experience III: Experience and its Interpretation," *New Blackfriars* 59, no. 702 (November 1978): 500.

48. As an anchoress, Julian presumably followed a regimen something like what is described in the *Ancrene Wisse*. If so, this would have included not only the prescribed fasts, but also the various postures prescribed for prayer. See the complex intertwining of vocal prayers, prostration, ablutions, clothings, etc. set out at the beginning of the *Ancrene Wisse* [53–54]. One should also not underestimate the significance of anchoritic isolation itself as a bodily practice.

49. For an explication of the way in which a "topography of places" is defined for a particular investigation by a combination of "interests," "sources," and "rules," see Michel de Certeau, "Christianisme et 'modernité' dans l'historiographie contemporaine: réemplois de la tradition dans les pratiques," *Recherches de science religieuse* 63, no. 2 (1975): 243–246.

50. Sloane text reading, ch. 8, p. 13. The Sloane text is closer to the short text here, while the Paris manuscript has "it is goddes wylle that ȝe take it with a grete ioy and lykyng, as Jhesu hath shewde it to yow [it is God's will that you receive it with a great joy and pleasure, because Jesus

has shown it to you]" (8.39–40). This perhaps makes a weaker connection between the reader and the "original experience."

51. Jean-Luc Marion, *L'Idole et la distance: cinq études* (Paris: Grasset, 1977), 37.

52. For an account of the apophatic tradition as a critique of "experientialism," see Denys Turner, *The Darkness of God: Negativity in Christian Mysticism* (Cambridge: Cambridge University Press, 1995).

53. See *The Cloud of Unknowing*, ch. 5, pp. 24–25.

54. Denise Baker notes: "the practice of meditation on Christ's passion, as a preparation for contemplation, was reserved in the twelfth and thirteenth centuries for those in religious life. In the fourteenth century, however, meditation was increasingly divorced from contemplation, with the former recommended as a devotional practice appropriate for those in the active life and the latter still primarily reserved for professed contemplatives" (*Julian of Norwich's* Showings, 29).

55. Simon Tugwell, O.P., *Ways of Imperfection: An Exploration of Christian Spirituality* (Springfield, Ill.: Templegate Publishers, 1985), 187. My reading of Julian as rejecting both affective and contemplative pieties is much indebted to Tugwell's interpretation. One might contrast Tugwell's view that Julian had "contemplative" aspirations with the view of Christopher Abbot, who argues that at the time of the visions Julian's piety was both individualist and affective. See Christopher Abbot, "Piety and Egoism in Julian of Norwich: A Reading of Long Text Chapters 2 and 3," *Downside Review*, no. 397 (October 1996): 267–282.

56. Colledge and Walsh posit a corruption of the short text here (*A Book of Showings*, 215, n. 45). I have tried to give a modern English rendering that makes sense of the text as it stands.

57. Tugwell, *Ways of Imperfection*, 192.

58. See Baker, *Julian of Norwich's* Showings, 25–39.

59. S. S. Hussey, "The Audience for the Middle English Mystics," in *De Cella in Seculum: Religious and Secular Life of Devotion in Late Medieval England*, Michael G. Sargent, ed. (Cambridge: D. S. Brewer, 1989), 117.

60. This is not to say that an "advanced stage of contemplation" cannot be understood as *gratias gratis data*, though unfortunately, contemplative experience is not usually understood as a grace given for the sake of others.

61. Tugwell, *Ways of Imperfection*, 188. Thus in Tugwell's eyes, Julian resolves a key difficulty in English piety. Speaking of *The Cloud of Unknowing*'s understanding of the role of the humanity of Christ, he writes: "This illustrates the doctrinal weakness of a whole tradition of spiritu-

ality: whereas devotionalism finds it hard to move on from the humanity of Christ to God, this more theocentric piety finds it difficult to ascribe to Christ anything more than a rather temporary significance" (ibid., 172).

62. As appears to have been the case with Margery Kempe, who, when offered the opportunity to marry the Godhead, "kept sylens in hir sowle & answeryd not þerto, for sche was ful sor aferd of þe Godhed & sche cowde no skylle [had no experience] of þe dalyawns [conversation] of þe Godhed, for al hir lofe & al hir affeccyon was set in þe manhode of Crist & þerof cowde sche good skylle [knew well from experience] & sche wolde for no-thyng a partyd þerfro" (*The Book of Margery Kempe*, 86). As might be expected, Margery's lack of response is taken by God the Father as an insult and the second person of the Trinity must step in to smooth things over. Fortunately things work out and, as in all comedies, the wedding happens in the end.

63. Julian only makes this explicit in the next chapter, where she says, "And in these thre wordes: It is a joy, a blysse and endlesse lykyng to me, were shewyd thre hevyns, as thus. For the joy, I vnderstode the plesannce of the father, and for the blysse the wurshyppe of the sonne, and for the endlesse lykyng the holy gost. The father is plesyd, the sonne is wurschyppyd, the holy gost lykyth" (23.2–6).

64. This is why Jesus says to Julian, "If thou arte apayde [satisfied], I am apayde" (22.4–5).

65. "[R]elation in God is not as an accident in a subject, but is the divine essence itself; and so it is subsistent, for the divine essence subsists" (*ST* 1.29.4).

66. On this, see Adams, *William Ockham*, 1264–1265.

67. Richard Rolle, *Meditations on the Passion* (Longer Meditations), in *English Writings*, 36.

68. *Fasciculus Morum*, 213. Cf. John Mirk's *Festial*, which speaks of how God the Father sends his only Son into the world "forto by man out of þe deueles þraldam" and how the Son "wyth his owne hert-blod wrot hym a chartur of fredome, and made hym fre for euer" (*Mirk's Festial*, 172). On the Charter of Christ in general, see Miri Rubin, *Corpus Christi*, 306–308.

69. *Fasciculus Morum*, 211.

70. There has not been much work done on the relationship between apophatic contemplation and the nominalist dialectic of the hidden and revealed God, though it seems to me that there are certain convergences. For a different reading of the relationship between nominalism and mysticism, one that sees close ties between nominalist theology and affective devotion, see Oberman, *The Harvest of Medieval Theology*, 323–360.

71. Sloane text reading, ch. 31, p. 42. P reads "the comyng of alle man kynde..." (31.11).

3. "A FEYER AND DELECTABLE PLACE"

1. de Lubac, *Catholicism*, 47.
2. See especially *Ancrene Wisse*, part 2. For a discussion of the way in which inner and outer are related in the *Ancrene Wisse*, see Janet Grayson, *Structure and Imagery in* Ancrene Wisse (Hanover, N.H.: University Press of New England, 1974). It is difficult to assess the importance of the influence of either anchoritic literature or the anchoritic life on Julian, since we do not know at what point she became an anchoress. The first mention of an anchoress named Julian in Norwich is found in a will dated 1394, and whether she was an anchoress prior to her visionary experience (which seems unlikely), or became one at some point between the experience and the writing of the long text, or entered the anchorhold only after her literary work was complete, is impossible to say. However, if Nicholas Watson is correct in his redating of the long text (see "The Composition of Julian of Norwich's *Revelation of Love*"), then this would clearly allow for the possibility of some influence of the anchoritic life. For a discussion of possible influences of anchoritic literature on Julian, see Denise N. Baker, "Julian of Norwich and Anchoritic Literature," *Mystics Quarterly* 19, no. 4 (1993): 148–160.
3. Walter Hilton, *The Scale of Perfection*, John P. H. Clark and Rosemary Dorward, trans. (New York: Paulist Press, 1991), 77–78.
4. "The Abbey of the Holy Ghost," in *Catholic England: Faith, Religion and Observance before the Reformation*, trans. and annotated by R. N. Swanson (Manchester: Manchester University Press, 1993), 97. For similar themes in preaching, see, for example, *Fasciculus Morum* VII.ii [648–655].
5. *Mirk's Festial*, 67.
6. Ibid., 172.
7. Often these conflicting tendencies are found within the same text. Thus the *Ancrene Wisse* speaks of "the wicked five senses, which should be at home and serve their lady. They serve their lady the anchoress well when she uses them well for her soul's needs—when the eye is on a book or some other good thing, the ear turned to God's word, the mouth in holy prayers" (part 3 [112]).
8. Mary Douglas, *Purity and Danger: An Analysis of the Concepts of Pollution and Taboo* (London: Routledge, 1966), 115. While one might hesitate to generalize too quickly about any universal symbolic value of

the body, it is clear that medieval societies saw the body as a system that mirrored larger systems, ranging from medieval political theory's deployment of somatic terms to medieval medical theory, which (drawing on a tradition stretching from Hippocrates) saw the body with its four humors as a microcosmic replication of the macrocosm made up of earth, air, fire, and water. See Robertson, "Medieval Medical Views of Women and Female Spirituality," 143.

9. Douglas, *Purity and Danger*, 121.

10. Third Lateran Council, canon 23, in *Decrees of the Ecumenical Councils*, vol. 1, *Nicaea I to Lateran V*, Norman P. Tanner, ed. (Washington, D.C.: Georgetown University Press, 1990), 222–223.

11. On heretics, Fourth Lateran Council, canon 3, in *Decrees*, 233–235. On Jews, canons 67–70, in *Decrees*, 265–267.

12. R. I. Moore, *The Formation of a Persecuting Society: Power and Deviance in Western Europe, 950–1250* (Oxford: Blackwell, 1987), 67.

13. Ibid., 64.

14. On the cult of St. William of Norwich and its persistence into the fourteenth century, see Benedicta Ward, *Miracles and the Medieval Mind: Theory, Record, and Event, 1000–1215*, rev. ed. (Philadelphia: University of Pennsylvania Press, 1987), 68–76.

15. "The Play of the Sacrament (Croxton)," *Medieval Drama*, David Bevington, ed. (Boston: Houghton Mifflin Co., 1975), 754–788. For a discussion of this text see Sarah Beckwith's essay "Ritual, Church and Theatre."

16. On the eucharistic inversion of the symbolism of nourishment, see Henri de Lubac, *Corpus mysticum: L'eucharistie et l'église au moyen age* (Paris: Aubier, 1948), 200–202.

17. See Kathleen Biddick, "Genders, Bodies, Borders: Technologies of the Visible," *Speculum* 68 (1993): 408–410.

18. Mikhail Bakhtin, *Rabelais and His World*, Hélène Iswolsky, trans. (Bloomington, Ind.: Indiana University Press, 1984), 19. Subsequent references in the text.

19. A division of "official" and "popular" such as Bakhtin makes is precisely what Eamon Duffy calls into question in his *The Stripping of the Altars*. Duffy writes, "It is my conviction, and a central plank of the argument of the first part of this book, that no substantial gulf existed between the religion of the clergy and the educated élite on the one hand and that of the people at large on the other. . . . [W]ithin the diversity of medieval religious options there was a remarkable degree of religious and imaginative homogeneity across the social spectrum, a shared repertoire of symbols, prayers, and beliefs which crossed and bridged even the gulf between the literate and the illiterate" (2–3). While medieval Christianity may not have

been quite so homogeneous as Duffy portrays (one might note his almost total neglect of Lollardy), he provides an important corrective to Bakhtin's claims.

20. See Nicholas Watson, "Censorship and Cultural Change in Late Medieval England: Vernacular Theology, the Oxford Translation Debate and Arundel's *Constitutions* of 1409," *Speculum* 70 (1995): 822–864.

21. John Bossy, "The Mass as Social Institution: 1200–1700," *Past and Present* 100 (August 1983): 53.

22. Moore exhibits a desire, similar to Bakhtin's, to exonerate the *plebes* from any enthusiastic participation in the formation of the persecuting society (see *The Formation of a Persecuting Society*, 124–153).

23. Peter Stallybrass and Allon White, *The Politics and Poetics of Transgression* (Ithaca, N.Y.: Cornell University Press, 1986), 193. See also 31–43.

24. Cf. Andrew Sprung's comment: "The moment of revelation is like the body of Christ in which Julian's understanding is endlessly born" ("'We nevyr shall come out of hym': Enclosure and Immanence in Julian of Norwich's *Book of Showings*," *Mystics Quarterly* 19, no. 2 [June 1993]: 56).

25. As Colledge and Walsh note, "The notion of God 'wounding' the loving soul is a commonplace among exegetes of Canticles 4.9, 5.7" (*Book of Showings*, 205, n. 51). There are interesting connections that can be made between Bakhtin's notion of the grotesque and Franciscan piety. Bakhtin writes of Francis: "[his] peculiar world outlook, his 'spiritual joy' (*laetitia spiritualis*), his blessing of the material bodily principle, and its typically Franciscan degradations and profanation can be defined, with some exaggeration, as a carnivalized Catholicism" (*Rabelais and His World*, 57).

26. Bakhtin, *Rabelais and His World*, 322.

27. *De Trinitate*, bk. 12, ch. 7 [*The Trinity*, Stephen McKenna, C.SS.R., trans. (Washington, D.C.: Catholic University of America Press, 1963), 351–355]. Augustine's intention seems to be to clear up exegetically a conflict between a passage from Genesis and a passage from Paul—and indeed to resolve it in a way that showed that woman, *qua* human nature, is an equal sharer with man in the image of God. However, the subsequent tradition seems to have become more enamored of the typological reading that Augustine employs than of the end for which he employed it.

28. *ST* 1.92.1. For a defense of Aquinas on this point, see Michael Nolan, "The Defective Male: What Aquinas Really Said," *New Blackfriars* 75, no. 880 (March 1994): 156–166. Nolan argues quite cogently that Aquinas's view is that a woman is "*occasionatum*" (translated above

as "misbegotten" but, according to Nolan, more accurately rendered "unintended") in terms of the microteleology of the male seed (which is what "the individual nature" in the above quotation refers to), but not in terms of the macroteleology of nature as a whole. However, modern scholars might well be forgiven for presuming that Aquinas was a man of his misogynist times.

29. On women's work in medieval England, Judith Bennett writes, "In the world of pre-industrial England, all people—men as well as women—worked hard, long and in difficult circumstances, but the working status of women—compared with that of men—was consistently lower: they received less training, they worked at less desirable tasks, they enjoyed less occupational stability and a weaker work identity, they received lower wages. This was true in the best of times (as perhaps in some locales after the plague) as in the worst of times" ("Medieval Women, Modern Women: Across the Great Divide," in *Culture and History: 1350–1600*, 163).

30. On the burning of Marguerite Porete, see Robert Lerner, *The Heresy of the Free Spirit in the Later Middle Ages* (Notre Dame, Ind.: University of Notre Dame Press, 1972), 71–78.

31. Joan Cadden, *Meanings of Sex Difference in the Middle Ages: Medicine, Science, and Culture* (Cambridge: Cambridge University Press, 1993), 280–281.

32. Bynum, "The Female Body and Religious Practice," 235–236.

33. See *The Book of Margery Kempe*, 28, 126. It should be noted, however, that for much of Julian's lifetime this would not have been the case, since it is only late in the fourteenth century that Lollardy comes to be perceived as a threat.

34. For a comparison of the number of extant copies of Julian's *Revelation* and Margery Kempe's *Book* with the much larger numbers of works by Rolle, Hilton, Langland, and the *Cloud* author, see S. S. Hussey, "The Audience for the Middle English Mystics," 115–116. I should note that it is also possible that the limited circulation of Julian's *Revelation* might have to do with shifting attitudes toward vernacular theological works. See Watson, "Censorship and Cultural Change."

35. Norman Tanner notes that Norwich differed from the rest of England both in its relatively large number of anchorites (both men and women) as well as the presence, shortly after Julian's time, of communities resembling continental beguinages. See Tanner, *The Church in Late Medieval Norwich: 1370–1532* (Toronto: Pontifical Institute of Medieval Studies, 1984), 58–66. On the relative lack of Lollardy in Norwich, see ibid., 162–166.

36. See, for example, *The Book of Margery Kempe*, 95.

37. This said, Julian's isolation should not be *over*emphasized. Felicity Riddy sketches a compelling picture of the kind of "speech community" of women to which Julian might have belonged. See "'Women Talking about the Things of God': A Late Medieval Sub-culture," in *Women and Literature in Britain, 1150–1500*, 2d ed., Carol M. Meale, ed. (Cambridge: Cambridge University Press, 1996), 104–127.

38. See *The Book of Margery Kempe*, 126, for Margery's account of how she handles a similar problem.

39. For a different reading of Julian's enclosed status, one that proceeds mainly in terms of archetypal psychology, see M. Diane F. Krantz, *The Life and Text of Julian of Norwich: The Poetics of Enclosure* (New York: Peter Lang, 1997), 13–29.

40. On Julian as a spiritual guide, see *The Book of Margery Kempe*, 42–43. For the (spurious) etymological connection between "anchorite" and "anchor," see *Ancrene Wisse*, 101. Ann Warren notes the true derivation of "anchorite" from the Greek *anachorein*, meaning "to withdraw" (Warren, *Anchorites and Their Patrons in Medieval England* [Berkeley: University of California Press, 1985], 8).

41. Warren, *Anchorites and Their Patrons*, 7.

42. Tanner, *The Church in Late Medieval Norwich*, 64.

43. On the Beguines as combining lay and religious characteristics, see Carol Neel, "The Origins of the Beguines," in *Sisters and Workers in the Middle Ages*, Judith Bennett et al., eds. (Chicago: University of Chicago Press, 1989), 244.

44. As Warren notes, while male anchorites tended to be clerics, female anchorites usually had *not* been nuns before their enclosure (*Anchorites and Their Patrons*, 22).

45. For a description of some medieval English enclosure ceremonies, see Warren, *Anchorites and Their Patrons*, 97–100. Cf. Francis D. S. Darwin, *The English Mediaeval Recluse* (London: Society for Promoting Christian Knowledge, 1944), 71–78, which gives a description of four different rites, three English and one German.

46. Duffy, *The Stripping of the Altars*, 313.

47. See Colledge and Walsh, *A Book of Showings*, 306, n. 35 for the derivation of "soule" from the Old English "sufol," meaning cooked or digested food. As Colledge and Walsh note, most translators have missed this meaning, and rendered the word as "soul."

48. Colledge and Walsh note that the word was "doubtless in Julian's time obsolescent, perhaps because of conflict with its homophone." See *A Book of Showings*, ibid.

49. From *Lollard Sermons*, translated in Swanson, *Catholic England*, 72–73. Swanson notes that he is skeptical about whether the collection

from which this sermon is taken is in fact a Lollard one. A similar interest in bodily orifices is found in a passage on humility in *Fasciculus Morum* I.xii [95]: "For if you consider, O man, what comes out of your mouth, your nose, and the other passages of your body, will you not find that you are worse than a dungheap."

50. It is worth noting that this passage occurs in the context of discussing the duties of the lowest of the three estates, the peasants. For a fuller treatment of the egalitarian semiotics of feces, see Taro Gomi, *Everyone Poops*, Amanda M. Stinchecum, trans. (Kane Millar Book Publishers, 1993).

51. Swanson, *Catholic England*, 73.

52. Julian makes, in passing, a similar point in chapter sixty: "For though it be so þat oure bodely forthbryngyng be but lytle, lowe and symple in regard of oure gostely forth brynggyng, yett it is he that doth it in the creaturys by whom it is done" (60.49–51). God is the primary agent, working through the secondary causality of human mothers, even in the "low" activity of giving birth.

53. Bakhtin, *Rabelais and His World*, 21. The genre of the grotesque fits well with the understanding of the *felix culpa* that Julian begins developing in the thirteenth revelation, which I shall discuss in the next chapter.

54. Note: "plentious" is the S reading, which is preferred by Colledge and Walsh to P, which has "pituous."

55. Nuth, *Wisdom's Daughter*, 74. Nuth offers a corrective to the view put forward by Sr. Anna Maria Reynolds that seems to associate "courtesy" almost exclusively with the courtly love tradition (see "'Courtesy' and 'Homeliness' in the *Revelations* of Julian of Norwich," *Fourteenth-Century English Mystics Newsletter* 5, no. 2 (June 1979): 12–20). As Nuth points out, the word is also used to describe specifically Christian virtues. See also Mary Olson, "God's Inappropriate Grace: Images of Courtesy in Julian of Norwich's *Showings*," *Mystics Quarterly* 20, no. 2 (June 1994): 47–59.

56. Nuth, *Wisdom's Daughter*, 76.

57. Ibid., 77.

58. Commenting on this text, Karma Lochrie writes, "Another meaning of familiarity is suggested by this vision: that of abjection, of the exposure of the interior of the body, and consequently, the infusion of exterior with interior. The vision is both terrible and sweet in that it 'corrupts' the boundaries which define the body; it introduces fissures as tokens of perfection and defilement as its means" (*Margery Kempe and Translations of the Flesh*, 129). It strikes me that Lochrie's term "abjection" is roughly equivalent to Bakhtin's "degradation."

59. See Nicholas Watson, "'Yf wommen be double naturelly': Remaking 'Woman' in Julian of Norwich's *Revelation of Love*," *Exemplaria* 8, no. 1 (Spring 1996): 1–34, esp. 12–29.

60. It is clear in the short text that what Julian sees are the marks ("semes") of scourging and not the scourging itself: "And aftyr this I sawe be haldande the bodye plentevouslye bledande, hate and freschlye and lyflye, ry3t as I sawe before in the heede. And this was schewyd me in the semes of scowrgynge" (viii.14–16). However, all of the long text manuscripts read "beholdyng the body plentuous bledyng in semyng of the scoregyng" (12.3–4), which *could* be read in a way consonant with the short text, though the more obvious meaning of "semyng" (as opposed to "semes") is some sort of imaginative representation of Christ's actual scourging. Colledge and Walsh make the very plausible suggestion that the short text reading represents what Julian wrote in both versions and that "we have in *semyng* editorial tampering in a long text common ancestor with Julian's *semes*, preserved in the short text" (*A Book of Showings*, 85). This point is important in supporting my contention that what Julian sees in the "bodily sights" is Jesus' body as it was physically present to her on the crucifix before her face, not realistic vignettes from the life of Jesus.

61. "... it is our owne kynde" (12.18).

62. Note that in chapter twelve's description of the descent into hell, many of the combat themes associated with the harrowing of hell are absent. Julian simply says of Christ's blood: "It descendyd downe in to helle and brak her bondes, and delyuerd them all that were there which belongh to the courte of hevyn" (12.22–24). Her later discussions of Christ's descent in chapter fifty-one, the *exemplum* of the lord and servant (which we shall look at in the next chapter) show even more clearly that her chief interest is not in a battle between Christ and Satan, but in the infinitely high being brought infinitely low, so as to make the low high.

63. I have altered slightly the punctuation given by Colledge and Walsh in their edition.

64. The short text (x.36–39) makes a distinction between the pain of hell (which, being despair, is "gastelye" [spiritual]) and the bodily pains of the crucifixion. By the time Julian composes the long text, she seems to have abandoned this distinction as too simple.

65. The short text only implies that she is referring to the darkness at the time of the crucifixion as the sun sharing in Christ's pains (xi.52–54), whereas the story she tells in the long text of "seynt Dyonisi of France" (18.27–35) makes this clear.

66. It is clear that if this was not a common theme in medieval piety, it was also not unheard of, particularly in monastic circles, where the abbot

was sometimes described as a mother. For an inventory of medieval texts, see the important early article by André Cabassut, O.S.B., "Une dévotion médiévale peu connue: la dévotion à 'Jésus Notre Mère,'" *Revue d'ascétique et de mystique* 25 (1949): 234–245. See also Caroline Walker Bynum, "Jesus as Mother and Abbot as Mother: Some Themes in Twelfth-Century Cistercian Writings," *Jesus as Mother*, 110–169.

67. See the remarks of Caroline Walker Bynum, ". . . And Woman His Humanity," *Fragmentation and Redemption*, 161–162.

68. There are certainly exceptions, such as 61.41–57, where Julian stresses what we today would call the mother's "parenting skills" as opposed to biological motherhood. Yet even here Julian's interest is not in "femininity" but in maternity. See the remarks of Lynn Staley, *Powers of the Holy*, 174.

69. See Cadden, *Meanings of Sex Difference*, 169–227.

70. "Et vir divinitatem, femina vero humanitatem Filii Dei significat." From the *Liber divinorum operum*, bk. 1, ch. 4, par. 100, quoted in Cadden, *Meanings of Sex Difference*, 191. Cf. Bynum, ". . . And Woman His Humanity," 171–172.

71. *Fasciculus Morum* III.xii [221]. Julian concurs with the typical medieval view that Christ's body was particularly sensitive to pain. See 20.2–7.

72. The question of the relative contribution of men and women to the generative process was not as clearly settled in medieval medical and philosophical thought as is often portrayed. For a discussion of the variety of opinions, see Cadden, *Meanings of Sex Difference*, 117–130.

73. Ibid., 171–173.

74. Beryl Rowland, ed., *Medieval Woman's Guide to Health: The First English Gynecological Handbook* (Kent, Ohio: Kent State University Press, 1981), 59, quoted in Robertson, "Medieval Medical Views of Women," 147.

75. Robertson, "Medieval Medical Views of Women," 146–147.

76. *Ancrene Wisse*, 109.

77. A well-known example is Thomas Aquinas's hymn *Adoro te devote*. One finds slightly less tender versions of the legend in the *Ancrene Wisse*, part 3 [93] and *Fasciculus Morum* III.x [209], in which the ill-tempered mother pelican first kills her offspring and then must pierce her own breast in order to revive them.

78. Robertson, "Medieval Medical Views of Women," 145.

79. This is particularly the case where Mary's milk and Christ's blood are associated. Speaking of Mary and Jesus at the time of the crucifixion, the thirteenth-century Beguine Mechtild of Magdeburg writes: "There they were both opened, his wounds and her breasts. The wounds poured

out and the breasts flowed, so that the soul quickened and was even cured" (*Ein vliessendes lieht der gotheit*, bk. 2, ch. 22 [*Flowing Light of the Divinity*, Christine Mesch Galvani, trans., Susan Clark, ed. (New York: Garland Publishing Company, 1991), 15]). One might note also visual representations that connect both Christ's flowing wounds and Mary's flowing breasts with heavenly intercession. See, for example, Bynum, *Holy Feast and Holy Fast*, pl. 28–29.

80. See *Fasciculus Morum* III.xvii [257]: "for our spiritual hunger Christ comes like a loving mother to nourish us. He himself says in John 6: 'I am the living bread that has come down from heaven.'" On woman's body as food, see Bynum, *Holy Feast and Holy Fast*, 269–276.

81. "Prayer to St. Paul," *Prayers and Meditations of Saint Anselm*, 153.

82. Cadden, *Meanings of Sex Difference*, 178.

83. Thus Julian never refers to Jesus as "she" but always uses the masculine pronoun, e.g., "oure precyous moder Jhesu, he may fede vs wyth hym selves" (60.30–31).

84. Robertson, "Medieval Medical Views of Women," 145, 154–155. While I think that Robertson is correct in claiming that the moisture of Christ's body codes that body symbolically as female, I am highly doubtful of her claim that "Julian of Norwich was a subtle strategist who sought to undo assumptions about women and to provide, in an Irigarayan sense, a new celebration of femininity through contemplation of Christ's 'feminine' attributes." While it is true that Julian is subtle, the truth of the rest of Robertson's claim would require that we read Julian's writings not as being about what they claim to be about (Julian's reflections on the love of God as revealed to her in her sixteen showings), but rather as an oddly familiar-sounding quest to realize her human potential, in which Christ functions as a helpful (but inessential) prop.

85. Cf. 63.23–25, 31–32.

86. E.g., 46.28–29, 59.32, 61.35–57.

87. The image is so striking that it is worth quoting: "*Disciplina pacis nostre* [sic] *super eum*, says Isaiah (Isa. 53:5)—'So our beating fell on him' because he put himself between us and his Father, who was threatening to strike us, as a compassionate mother puts herself between her child and the angry, stern father, when he is about to beat it. Our Lord Jesus Christ did this, took the death-blow himself, to shield us from it, thanks be to his mercy" (*Ancrene Wisse*, part 6 [182]).

88. For a different view, which focuses much more on what I would call the "femininity" rather than the "femaleness" of Jesus as mother, see Paula S. Datsko Barker, "The Motherhood of God in Julian of Norwich's Theology," *Downside Review* 100, no. 341 (October 1982): 290–304.

89. Krantz, *Life and Text*, 99–109.

90. Ibid., 111–124. One should note that Krantz makes her argument on this point very tentatively though, to my mind, convincingly.

91. Vincent Gillespie and Maggie Ross, "The Apophatic Image: The Poetics of Effacement in Julian of Norwich," in *The Medieval Mystical Tradition in England: Exeter V* (1992), 67.

92. Augustine, *Confessiones*, 1.1.1 [*Confessions*, Henry Chadwick, trans. (Oxford: Oxford University Press, 1991), 3]. Augustine elaborates this theme by means of his distinction between *uti* (use) and *frui* (enjoyment). In *De Doctrina Christiana* he writes: "To enjoy anything means to cling to it with affection for its own sake. To use a thing is to employ what we have received for our use to obtain what we want, provided that it is right for us to want it. . . . [W]anderers from God on the road of this mortal life, if we wish to return to our native country where we can be happy, we must use this world, and not enjoy it, so that the 'invisible attributes' of God may be clearly seen, 'being understood through the things that are made,' that is, that through what is corporeal and temporal we may comprehend the eternal and spiritual" (1.4.4 ["Christian Instruction," John J. Gavigan, O.S.A., trans., in *Saint Augustine*, The Fathers of the Church, vol. 2 (Washington, D.C.: Catholic University of America Press, 1947), 29–30]). In my understanding of this theme in both Augustine and (indirectly) Julian, I am indebted to Rowan Williams' reading of *De Doctrina*, which connects its discussion of "use" and "enjoyment" to its discussion of "things" (*res*) and "signs" (*signum*). See "Language, Reality and Desire in Augustine's *De Doctrina*," *Journal of Literature & Theology* 3, no. 2 (July 1989).

93. Cf. 10.36–38, which reads: "It was a fygur and a liyknes of our fowle blacke dede, which that our feyre bryght blessed lord bare for our synne." The corresponding passage in S reads: "It was a figure and likenes of our foule dede hame [outer covering], that our faire, bright, blissid lord bare for our sins" (ch. 10, p. 15). Both readings are possible.

94. *The Scale of Perfection*, bk. 1, ch. 54 [125]. Compare Catherine of Siena's statement, "We are your image, and now by making yourself one with us you have become our image, veiling your eternal divinity in the wretched cloud and dung heap of Adam." *The Dialogue*, ch. 13 [Suzanne Noffke, O.P., trans. (New York: Paulist Press, 1980), 50].

95. Bakhtin, *Rabelais and His World*, 317.

96. For example, "he led forth the vnderstandyng of hys creature" (24.4–5); "to this vnderstondyng was þe soule led by loue" (46.40); "now was my vnderstandyng ledde" (51.45).

97. As is typical, Julian is employing certain medieval conventions in an unconventional way. In the Middle Ages, such an elision between natu-

ral and moral evil was not unusual, but it was ordinarily in the direction of seeing sickness as a punishment for sin, rather than seeing sin as a kind of sickness that afflicts people. On sickness as punishment, *Fasciculus Morum* notes: "Now since the body and soul are partners in delights and sins, we see that the flesh, if it could, would like to steal away without punishment and leave all his debt with the soul. This would be quite unjust. Therefore . . . Christ, out of his love for our soul, takes the body and restrains it and sends it infirmities, and thus he forces it to pay the part of the debt which belongs to it" (II.vi [139]).

98. Sloane text reading, ch. 27, p. 38. P (27.15–24) reads "trybulation" for "nowtyng," a modernization that obscures Julian's meaning.

99. Julian notes that in her initial visionary experience, this was the only beholding of the passion which she had.

100. Julian later (71.25–43) reiterates these three ways of beholding the passion, in describing "th(re) manner of cherys [demeanor/attitude] of oure lorde." She notes that while the first two are "þe comyn [normal] cherys whych he shewyth to us in this lyfe," the third is "lyke in perty as [partly like] it shalle be in hevyn," and that in her revelation this is the aspect that was "oftenest shewyd and longeste contynuyd."

101. It is more appropriate to speak of "antecedent" and "consequent" than "before" and "after" or "preceding" and "following" because Julian is speaking of a nontemporal sequence, as shall be made clear in the example of the lord and servant.

102. Hans Urs von Balthasar, *The Glory of the Lord: A Theological Aesthetics*, vol. 5, *The Realm of Metaphysics in the Modern Age* (San Francisco: Ignatius Press, 1982–1991), 87.

103. In her discussion of the eighth showing Julian promises a later discussion of Christ's "dowbylle thurst, oon bodely and a nother gostly" (17.3–4). She does not discuss the spiritual thirst until chapter thirty-one.

104. In addition to the parallels listed by Colledge and Walsh (*A Book of Showings*, 418, n. 14), see *Ancrene Wisse*, part 2 [91], "His thirst is nothing but yearning for our soul's health," as well as the Sequence hymn in the Sarum Missal for the Mass of the five wounds of Christ: "O Jesu, wonder-worker, how dost thou this explain?/ Thou of the cross art silent, yet dost of thirst complain./ Didst thou feel thirst more keenly than all that bitter pain?/ Or rather, our salvation didst thou so thirst to gain?" (*The Sarum Missal in English*, part 2, 68).

105. Sloane text reading, ch. 31, p. 42. This is a bit clearer than P's reading ("loue longyng of vs, all to geder here in hym to oure endlesse blysse" [31.18–19]).

106. Cf. 39.11–17, where Julian expands the short text's injunction to accept the penance given by one's "domys man" (confessor) by noting that

this is one meekness that pleases God, as does acceptance of sickness and shame and all of life's spiritual and bodily grievances.

107. In modernity this theme sounds again in the writings of Thérèse of Lisieux, who writes of Jesus' thirst for souls, and of her own desire to slake that thirst, for which he rewards her by communicating his own thirst to her, thus increasing her desire: "I slaked His thirst and the more I gave Him to *drink*, the more the thirst of my poor little soul increased, and it was this ardent thirst He was giving me as the most delightful drink of his love" (*Story of a Soul: The Autobiography of St. Thérèse of Lisieux*, 2d ed., John Clarke, O.C.D., trans. [Washington, D.C.: Institute of Carmelite Studies, 1976], 101).

108. Simone Weil, "Reflections on the Right Use of School Studies with a View to the Love of God," in *Waiting For God*, 114.

109. Ibid., 111.

110. Ibid., 115.

111. Such a description of Christ's atoning work on the cross, stressing as it does his capacity to arouse an affective response in human hearts, would seem to put Julian in the "Abelardian" or subjectivist camp, according to the well-known scheme devised by Gustav Aulén in his book *Christus Victor: An Historical Study of the Three Main Types of the Idea of Atonement*, A. G. Herbert, trans. (New York: Macmillan, 1969). However, lest one think that one can belong to only one camp at a time on this point, see Oberman, *The Harvest of Medieval Theology*, 266–270, on the way in which the fifteenth-century theologian Gabriel Biel combined in his soteriology "Abelardian" elements, stressing imitation of Christ, with "Anselmian" themes of propitiation and "classic" themes of Christ as Victor.

112. Lynn Staley also characterizes Julian's theology as one that establishes "the inherent unity . . . between privation and plenty" (*Powers of the Holy*, 178).

113. See J.-L. Marion's claim that "the Son made human does not offer a reproduction of a god who is himself, by some other route, visible, according to a ratio of similarity or dissimilarity measurable by a norm other than his visage. He brings to pass in visibility the definitive invisibility of the Father, which remains all the more invisible because no other visage ever suits him except the face of his Christ" (*L'Idole et la distance*, 223).

114. Andrew Ryder, S.C.J., "A Note on Julian's Visions," *Downside Review* 96, no. 325 (October 1978): 304.

115. On the "enfolded" structure of the long text, see Baker, *Julian of Norwich's* Showings, 142–164, and Krantz, *Life and Text*, 49–66.

116. For Wyclif's views on the "invisible church" consisting solely of the elect, see *Tractatus de Ecclesia*, Johann Loserth, ed. (London: The Wyclif Society, 1886), 2–18.

117. On the various high jinks of Henry Despenser, both at home and abroad, see Tanner, *The Church in Late Medieval Norwich*, 160–162; McKisack, *The Fourteenth Century*, 429–433.

118. In seeing the relationship between divine immutability and divine agency, I have been greatly helped by Brian Davies' little essay "The Action of God," *New Blackfriars* 75, no. 879 (February 1994): 76–84. Davies' argument is summed up in his statement, *"the action of the agent lies in the patient"* (82, emphasis in the original), which helps us see that "God does nothing. Yet his action, notwithstanding, is all pervasive and very much to be reckoned with. For it is, we might say, the being and history of creatures" (83). I might also note that he concludes his essay with the remark that the view of divine agency that he has argued for, "[i]n the language of Julian of Norwich, . . . is something which allows us to say that 'God does everything that is done'" (83–84).

119. See Mirk's *Festial*: "for enchesen [because] holy chyrche ys modyr to all cristen pepull, scho [she] taketh hede to hyr chyldern as a good modyr ouyth forto do" (62).

120. Sloane text reading, ch. 61, p. 101. P reads "fastenyd and onyd" (61.63) and "flode of mercy" (61.64), which are plausible readings (the latter particularly in light of Julian's earlier emphasis on the great quantity of Jesus' blood), though less obviously eucharistic. P also reads "woundes" (61.65) in the plural rather than S's singular "wound." Again, a plausible reading, though if Julian is alluding to the blood and water which issued from Jesus' side in John 19:34, then P's reading weakens the allusion.

121. Cf. 39.2–17 on the role of confession and penance as a part of the "therapy" by which one is healed of sin.

122. S reads "for it is his holy church" (ch. 34, p. 47), making a weaker identification of God and the church. P, however, is in agreement with the short text, which reads "for he is haly kyrke" (xvi.3). On the other hand, in the immediately preceding part of the sentence S reads "al men and women that mytyly and mekely and wilfully taken the prechyng and techyng of holy church" (ch. 34, p. 47), which is closer than P to the short text's "alle men and womenn that myghttelye and mekelye and wyrschipfullye takes the prechynge and the techynge of haly kyrke" (xvi.1–2). Note that both S and the short text commend those who accept church teaching "mekely," whereas P commends those who take it "wysely." It is difficult to render judgement on which of the long text readings is to be preferred, though P seems the more theologically daring, both where it is like the short text—identifying God closely with the church—and where it departs—saying that the teachings of God/church must be taken "wysely" and not simply "mekely."

123. Julian is perhaps reiterating this point at 40.45, when she says that "Crist hym selves is ground of alle the lawes of cristen men."

124. S adds "He is the leryd [the taught]" (ch. 34, p. 47), for which P reads "he is the ende," seeming to connect to the following statement: "and he is the mede (reward) wherfore every kynde soule travelyth" (34.18–19). Note that in the apparatus of their edition of P, Colledge and Walsh give the reading of Sloane MS 2499 as "lend," which it is impossible to give any sense to except as a misreading of "end." However, Glasscoe and Crampton both reject this as a misreading of the manuscript. For a discussion, see Marion Glasscoe, "Visions and Revisions," 117. What Julian might have intended by saying this seems to be that God is not simply the *ecclesia docens* [the church that teaches] but also, in Christ, the *ecclesia discens* [the church that is taught]. In claiming that God is "the leryd," perhaps Julian means that God is not simply the teacher but, because in Christ he shares our "pilgrim" status, God is also the exemplary learner, "the pioneer and perfecter of our faith" (Heb. 12:2). Julian writes that God showed her Christ "in erth thus, as it were a pylgrymage, that is to sey he is here with vs ledyng vs, and shalle be tylle whan he hath brought vs alle to his blysse in hevyn" (81.6–8). Christ does not simply stand over and against the church, but identifies with it even as a believer in the promises of God. The divine pedagogy takes place in an exemplary manner with regard to the humanity of Christ. This issue will be discussed further in the next chapter.

125. In the short text she goes into greater detail on this point, recounting the specific instance in which she "harde a man telle of halye kyrke of the storye of saynte Cecylle" (i.47). This chapter in the short text also contains what appears to be an assurance with regard to Julian's desire for a bodily sight of the passion that it did not involve a rejection of the use of images "that er made be the grace of god aftere the techynge of halye kyrke to the lyknes of Crystes passyonn" (i.16–18).

126. In a passage from the short text that she does not include in the long text, Julian writes: "I say nought that me nedes na mare techynge, for oure lorde with the schewynge of this hase left me to haly kyrke, and I am hungery and thyrstye and nedy and synfulle and freele, and wilfully submyttes me to the techynge of haly kyrke with alle myne euencrystenn in to the ende of my lyfe" (xiii.47–51). For passages in the long text in which Julian reiterates her acceptance of church teachings, see 29.9–10, 33.4–5, 42.39–40, 51.32–35, 53.23–26, 67.22–24.

127. For a description of the way in which Julian's views on sin differed from that of the popular understanding of church teaching, see M. L. del Mastro, "Juliana of Norwich: Parable of the Lord and Servant—Radical Orthodoxy," *Mystics Quarterly* 14 (1988): 84–93, and Nicholas Watson, "Visions of Inclusion: Universal Salvation and Vernacular Theology in Pre-Reformation England," *Journal of Medieval and Modern Studies* 27, no. 2 (Spring 1997): 145–187, esp. 146–148.

128. *Cur Deus Homo?* II.xiv [163–164].

129. I shall bracket the question of whether the damnation of some (i.e., the "populated hell" thesis) *is* in fact an article of faith, not least because of the thorniness of the question of what constitutes an article of faith. What matters is that Julian clearly believes it to be an article of faith. For an argument against the *de fide* status of a populated hell, see Hans Urs von Balthasar, *Dare We Hope "That All Men be Saved"? With a Short Discourse on Hell,* David Kipp and Lothar Krauth, trans. (San Francisco: Ignatius Press, 1988).

130. Barbara Newman, *From Virile Woman to WomanChrist: Studies in Medieval Religion and Literature* (Philadelphia: University of Pennsylvania Press, 1995), 130. Careful readers of Julian have generally recognized that any "universalism" in her thought is an implied one. Thus, Nuth says "the doctrine that 'all will be well' . . . hints at universal salvation" (*Wisdom's Daughter*, 18) and "Julian's revelations strongly suggest that the 'all' that will be well in God's promise includes 'every particular' human being, although this is never stated absolutely" (ibid., 165). Denise Baker perhaps overstates the case when, in reference to chapter thirty-two of the long text, she says: "In explaining the secret meaning of the thirteenth showing, Julian cautiously refers to a deed that the Trinity will perform at the end of time to make all things well. The context makes clear that she is alluding to the promise of universal salvation" (*Julian of Norwich's* Showings, 79). Baker may be right, but the context does not really make this "clear."

131. Cf. 30.5–7: "Here to we be bounde of god and drawyn and connceylyd and lernyd inwardly by the holy gost, and outward by holy chyrch in the same grace."

132. Except the devil, because in the fifth showing "god shewde that the feende is dampnyd" (13.43).

133. See *Fasciculus Morum* I.xv [111]: "humility is brought about by considering the just damnation of the wicked."

134. Aquinas writes: "in order that the happiness of the saints may be more delightful to them and that they may render more copious thanks to God for it, they are allowed to see perfectly the sufferings of the damned" (*ST* Suppl. 3.94.1).

135. On the certainty of the damnation of unconverted Jews (and of Muslims as well), Walter Hilton writes, "For it is true that from the beginning of the world to the last end, no one was ever saved or shall be saved without having faith—either general or special—in Jesus Christ, coming or already come. . . . Since this is true, then it seems to me that these men are greatly and greviously in error who say that Jews and Saracens can be saved by keeping their own law, although they do not believe in Jesus Christ as holy church believes, inasmuch as they think their own faith is

good and sure, sufficient for their salvation, and in that faith they do, as it seems, many good works of righteousness. And perhaps if they knew that Christian faith was better than theirs, they would leave their own and take it: therefore they should be saved. No, this is not enough, for Christ, God and man, is both the way and the end, and he is mediator between God and man. Without him no soul can be reconciled or come to the bliss of heaven. And therefore those who do not believe in him, that he is both God and man, can never be saved or come to glory" (*The Scale of Perfection*, bk. 2, ch. 3 [197]). We find further testimony to the prevalence of this view, as well as an articulation of precisely the view which Hilton condemns, in Langland: "'alle thise clerkes,' quod I tho, 'that on Crist leven/Seyen in hir sermons that neither Sarsens ne Jewes/Ne no creature of Cristes likenesse withouten Cristendom worth saved.'/'*Contra!*' quod Ymaginatif thoo, and comsed for to loure,/And seide, '*Salvabitur vix iustus in die iudicii;/Ergo—salvabitur!*' quod he, and seide no moore Latyn..../'Ac truthe that trespased nevere ne traversed ayeins his lawe,/But lyveth as his lawe techeth and leveth ther be no bettre,/(And if ther were, he wolde amende) and in swich wille deieth—/Ne wolde nevere trewe God but trewe truth were allowed./And wheither it worth or noght worth, the bileve is gret of truthe,/And an hope hangynge therinne to have mede for his truthe'" (*Piers Plowman* (B) XII:275–280, 285–290; cf. (B) X: 344–348). On all of this, see Watson, "Visions of Inclusion."

136. Julian distinguishes this "grett prevyte" from those things that "are prevytes to vs for oure blyndhed and oure vnknowyng" (34.9).

137. One might contrast Julian with Margery Kempe, to whom God showed "many sowlys, sum for to ben sauyd & sum for to ben dampnyd." The sight of the damned was "a gret ponyschyng & a scharp chastisyng" for her, because "sche durst alle men to be sauyd, and, whan owr Lord schewyd to hir of any þat xulde be dampynyd, sche had gret peyn." Because of this, she refused to believe that it was God who showed her the damned, and God "blamyd her þer-for & badde hir beleuyn þat it was hys hy mercy & hys goodnesse to schewyn hir hys preuy cownselys, seying to hir mende, 'Dowtyr, þu must as wel heryn of þe dampnyd as of the sauyd.'" As punishment for this God took her visions of Christ's humanity and of Mary and the saints from her and she was subjected to demonic attacks, including "beheldyng of mennys membrys & swech oþer abhominacyons." She endured this for twelve days, after which she had learned her lesson. Such are the dangers of refusing God's "preuy cownselys" with regard to the saved and the damned. One can only imagine the consequences of refusing the more general counsel of God, contained in the church's teaching. See *The Book of Margery Kempe*, ch. 59, 144–146. For a discussion of this episode see Watson, "Visions of Inclusion," 152–153.

138. Newman, *From Virile Woman to WomanChrist*, 132–133.
139. O'Donovan, *The Desire of the Nations*, 175.
140. Alan of Lille, *Theological Rules*, n. 7 (PL 210, 627). Cf. Bonaventure, *Itinerarum* V.8 [31].
141. Newman, *From Virile Woman to WomanChrist*, 134–135. For an alternative account of the source of Julian's "universalism," one that ties it to her writing in a tradition of vernacular theology, see Watson, "Visions of Inclusion," 169–173. I must confess that I am dubious about Watson's claim that "writing in the vernacular *exerts pressure* toward a universalist understanding of the meaning of the Incarnation as the expression of the illimitability of divine love" (171, empasis in original), not least because of the parochialism fostered by the growth of national identity.
142. O'Donovan, *The Desire of the Nations*, 176.
143. Robert Adams, "Langland's Theology," in *A Companion to Piers Plowman* (Berkeley: University of California Press, 1988), 89.

4. "A CONTYNUANT LABORER AND AN HARD TRAVELER"

1. Ludwig Wittgenstein, *Culture and Value*, G. H. von Wright, ed., Peter Winch, trans. (Chicago: University of Chicago Press, 1980), 31e.
2. Douglas, *Natural Symbols*, viii, cf. ibid., 54–64.
3. An alternative approach would be to correlate feudal images of lordship with the social reality of rural communities and the ensemble of images of the social body as *corpus christi* with urban communities; the symbolic valence of Christ's body mirroring for the city the symbolic valence of lordship in rural communities. Thus Mervyn James notes: "Corpus Christi expresses the creative role of religious rite and ideology in urban societies, in which the alternative symbols and ties of lordship, lineage and faithfulness, available in countrysides, were lacking" (James, "Ritual, Drama, and Social Body").
4. Julian writes, "For twenty yere after the tyme of the shewyng saue thre monyths I had techyng inwardly" (51.86–87). Nicholas Watson argues cogently that in fact the long text was still a work-in-progress as late as 1415, and that it is impossible to separate Julian's writing about her showings from her meditations on them. See Watson, "The Composition of Julian of Norwich's *Revelation of Love*," 673–683.
5. Colledge and Walsh, *A Book of Showings*, 513, n. 3. Owst writes that the word "example" is "the general all-inclusive term for any kind of homiletic simile or illustration" (*Literature and Pulpit*, 152).
6. Colledge and Walsh, *A Book of Showings*, 132. The work by de Lubac to which they refer is his four-volume *Exégèse médiévale*.

7. See Owst, *Literature and Pulpit*, 56–97.

8. I should note that it is not at all clear that what Julian means by "gostly in bodely lycknesse" is the same as what she calls a "bodely sight." As noted, Julian's language is not nearly as precise as it first appears.

9. Colledge and Walsh seem to acknowledge this when they write, "What Julian has achieved in this chapter, through the contemplation of the parable against the background of the whole sequence of the revelations, is a unified spiritual exegesis in which the three senses, allegory, tropology and anagogy, are constantly and easily identifiable, but, none the less, inextricable" (*A Book of Showings*, 139).

10. Julian seems to anticipate herself here, incorporating into her account of the "bodely lycknesse" some insight gleaned from the "more gostly" meaning.

11. The meaning of P is extremely obscure here and in my translation I am following Colledge and Walsh's view that "whych" refers back to "vnderstandyng." See *A Book of Showings*, 517, n. 42.

12. Baker, *Julian of Norwich's* Showings, 91.

13. *Cur Deus Homo?* bk. 1, ch. 24 [142]. For a comparison of Julian and Anselm, see Joan Nuth, "Two Medieval Soteriologies: Anselm of Canterbury and Julian of Norwich," *Theological Studies* 53 (1992): 611–645.

14. Though it might also mean "fright."

15. S reading, ch. 51, p. 74.

16. This is Colledge and Walsh's gloss on "þe propertes and the condescions." See *A Book of Showings*, 520, n. 88.

17. See, e.g., 5.28, 35.15, 40.44, 46.31–35, and 58.59–63. These three attributes and their appropriations are fairly common in the Middle Ages, being found in Aquinas (*ST* 1.39.8) and in Bonaventure, who assigns them pride of place (*Breviloquium* 1.6). Aquinas mentions Augustine as a source for them, though they do not appear in exactly this form in Augustine, and the Marietti edition of the *Summa* (Rome, 1948) gives Hugh of St. Victor's *De Sacramentis* in the notes as the source. For medieval vernacular sources, see *Ancrene Wisse*, part 1 [56] and Walter Hilton, *The Scale of Perfection*, bk. 2, ch. 34 [265]. This triad was also an element of preaching. See *Fasciculus Morum*, II.iv [129–131], III.xv [239], and III.xxiii [303]. The attribute appropriated to the Holy Spirit is variously expressed as goodness, love, or mercy.

18. Julian's understanding of the soul as an image of the Trinity, which finds its ultimate source in Augustine, is explicitly stated in the fifty-fifth chapter: "oure soule is a made trynyte lyke to the vnmade blessyd trynyte" (55.40–41).

19. This troubles not only Julian, but some of her modern interpreters as well. Clifton Wolters writes of the godly will, "This is wishful thinking

and not the teaching of the Church" (Introduction to *Revelations of Divine Love* [Harmondsworth: Penguin Books, 1966], 37).

20. Julian uses "comprehended" here to mean both "included" and "understood."

21. Origen writes concerning the Old Testament: "But if the usefulness of the law and the sequence and ease of the narrative were at first sight clearly discernible throughout, we should be unaware that there was something beyond the obvious meaning for us to understand in the scriptures. Consequently the Word of God has arranged for certain stumbling-blocks, as it were, and hindrances and impossibilities to be inserted in the midst of the law and the history, in order that we may not be completely drawn away by the sheer attractiveness of the language, and so either reject the true doctrines absolutely, on the ground that we learn nothing worthy of God, or else by moving away from the letter fail to learn anything of the more divine element" (*De principiis* IV.ii.9 [*On First Principles*, G. W. Butterworth, trans. (Gloucester, Mass.: Peter Smith, 1973), 285]).

22. This is not unlike Origen's correlation of the tripartite division of the text into literal, moral, and spiritual senses with the division of the human person into *soma, psyche,* and *pneuma.* See Origen, *De principiis* IV.2.4 [275–276].

23. Which is why I believe the example is better understood as a drama rather than an allegory. See below.

24. "[T]he more typically Pauline use of flesh connotes natural, material, and visible human existence, weak and earthbound, the human creature left to itself: 'No flesh can boast of anything before God' (1 Cor 1:29). 'People controlled by the flesh think of what pertains to the flesh' (Rom 8:5); they cannot please God (Rom 8:8)." Joseph Fitzmyer, S.J., "Pauline Theology," in *The New Jerome Biblical Commentary,* Raymond Brown et al., eds. (Englewood Cliffs, N.J.: Prentice Hall, 1990), 83:103 (1406).

25. For the ways in which Julian develops and departs from Augustine in her views on the division of the soul, see Nuth, *Wisdom's Daughter,* 104–116. Nuth seems to implicitly identify Julian's use of substance with Augustine's use of *mens* and of sensuality with his use of *spiritus,* and if in fact she is making this identification, she is mistaken. The Augustinian *spiritus* is much closer to Walter Hilton's use of "sensuality" (see below) than it is to Julian's, which seems a combination of the lower part of *mens* and *spiritus.*

26. See Augustine, *De Trinitate,* bk. 12 [343–368].

27. Hilton, *The Scale of Perfection,* bk. 2, ch. 13 [213–214].

28. Tarjei Park, "Reflecting Christ: The Role of the Flesh in Walter Hilton and Julian of Norwich," *The Medieval Mystical Tradition in England: Exeter V,* 33.

29. Nuth, *Wisdom's Daughter*, 109.
30. *De Trinitate* 12.4.4 [345].
31. Nancy Coiner, "The 'Homely' and the *Heimliche*: The Hidden, Doubled Self in Julian of Norwich's Showings," *Exemplaria* 5, no. 2 (Fall 1993): 311.
32. For a perceptive discussion of this passage, see Denys Turner, *The Darkness of God*, 159–162. He points out that in Julian's case, "[l]anguage fails to mark the distinction [between created and uncreated] not because there is none but because the gulf is too wide" (161).
33. *Confessions* 3.6.11 [42].
34. S, ch. 45, p. 64. P reads, "And ȝytt I stode in desyer . . ." (45.32–33). Nicholas Watson notes that P's reading "seems an evasion of what is clearly the theological *difficilior lectio* here" ("'Yf Wommen Be Double Naturelly,'" 21, n. 37).
35. Colledge and Walsh argue that Julian recognizes the existence "not merely of the alternation of consolation and desolation, of which all the great masters of Western spirituality write . . . but of the co-existence of desolation and consolation, a theme much more rare" (*A Book of Showings*, 125–126).
36. S, ch. 10, p. 16. For "geynmakyng" P reads "awne makyng" (10.55–56).
37. Apart from any question of specific influences, there is a constellation of themes within Julian's writing, particularly themes of exemplarism and unity of creatures within Christ, that we might identify as "Franciscan." The connection between Christ as pattern both of creation and of redemption is a major theme in Bonaventure's theology. E.g., "As Christ the uncreated Word had formed all things in perfection, so Christ the incarnate Word must have reformed all things in the same perfection" (*Breviloquium* IV.10.2 [175]).
38. There are some exceptions to this: e.g., Baker, *Julian of Norwich's Showings*, 113–134, and Krantz, *Life and Text*, 119–124. See also the brief remarks in J. P. H. Clark, "Predestination in Christ According to Julian of Norwich," *Downside Review* 100, no. 339 (April 1982): 87, and Nuth, *Wisdom's Daughter*, 112, which mentions briefly the *exitus et reditus* theme.
39. Thus Proclus writes, "Every effect remains in its cause, proceeds from it, and returns to it" (*Elements of Theology*, E. R. Dodds, trans. and ed. [Oxford: Clarendon, 1963], 38). And Dionysius writes, "Inspired by the Father, each procession of the Light spreads itself generously toward us, and, in its power to unify, it stirs us by lifting us up. It returns us back to the oneness and deifying simplicity of the Father who gathers us

in" (*The Celestial Hierarchy*, ch. 1, in *Pseudo-Dionysius: The Complete Works*, Colm Luibheid and Paul Rorem, trans. [New York: Paulist Press, 1987], 145).

40. Ruusbroec writes: "By means of the relations of the Persons in the Godhead, there is an ever-new sense of contentment accompanied by a new outflow of love in a new embrace of Unity. This is beyond time, that is, without any before or after, in an eternal now. In this embrace in the Unity all things are brought to perfection; in the outflow of love all things are accomplished; and in the living, fruitful nature all things have the possibility of occurring" (*The Little Book of Clarification*, in *John Ruusbroec: The Spiritual Espousals and Other Works*, James Wiseman, O.S.B., trans. [New York: Paulist Press, 1985], 263). See also P. DeLetter, "Trinitarian Indwelling according to Ruysbroeck," *Heythrop Journal* 2 (1961): 48.

41. *Collationes in Haxaemeron*, I.17 [*Collations on the Six Days*, *The Works of Bonaventure*, vol. 5, José de Vinck, trans. (Patterson, N.J.: St. Anthony Guild Press, 1970), 10].

42. Augustine, *Confessiones* 7.10.16 [123].

43. *Collationes* XX.5 [301–302].

44. See the discussion in chapter 3.

45. *Collationes* XX.5 [302].

46. S, ch. 59, p. 96. P (59.38–42) reads "goodly wylle" for "godly will."

47. III *Sent.* d.11, a.1, q.2 ["On the Predestination of Christ," Zachary Hayes, trans., in *Franciscan Christology: Selected Texts, Translations and Introductory Essays*, Damian McElrath, ed. (St. Bonaventure, N.Y.: Franciscan Institute, 1980), 79].

48. III *Sent.* d.11, a.1, q.3 [85].

49. This may in fact bring her position a bit closer to Bonaventure's, who stresses that it is Christ's human nature and not his person that is elected. See III *Sent.* d.11, a.1, q.1 [73].

50. Here Julian's emphasis on the exemplarity of Christ's human nature leads her to draw a conclusion that Thomas Aquinas explicitly seeks to avoid. Aquinas argues that Christ could not have assumed human nature *per se*—i.e., human nature as it is in the divine intellect—since, "according to this, human nature would be in the Son of God from eternity" (*ST* 3.4.4).

51. Hans Urs von Balthasar is in essential agreement with Julian when he argues that "there is not a single moment when the Logos can be held to be *asarkos*, nor does the New Testament entertain such a view. There is no question of prescinding from his Incarnation. The assumption of 'flesh'— which, seen from eternity, is timeless—is already an integral part of

the original world plan" (*Theo-drama III*, 256). This and subsequent references are to volumes of *Theo-drama: Theological Dramatic Theory*, 5 vols., Graham Harrison, trans. (San Francisco: Ignatius Press, 1988).

52. Within the New Testament we find statements such as Colossians 1:15, that Christ is the firstborn of creation, and Ephesians 1:4, that God chose us *in Christ* before the foundation of the world. In Mechtild of Magdeburg we find the claim that "This same second person became one nature with Adam's humanity before he became spoiled by sin" (*Ein vliessendes liebt der gotheit*, bk. 4, ch. 15 [112]), but this does not develop into a major theme in her theology. Medieval scholastic theologians, in discussing the eternal predestination of Christ, saw the motive for the incarnation not primarily in the need for a remedy for sin (though in fact it *was* such a remedy), but in the eternal unifying headship of Christ over all creation, thus making the union of divinity and humanity in Christ part of the eternal decree of God. The belief that the final unity of all things under the headship of Christ requires the incarnation of the Word, apart from the need to atone for sin, is a theme in English Franciscan writings stretching from Robert Grosseteste (who was a patron and admirer of the order, as well as a professor at the Franciscan school at Oxford, though not himself a member) to John Duns Scotus. On Grosseteste, and on this issue in general, see James McEvoy's extremely helpful article, "The Absolute Predestination of Christ in the Theology of Robert Grosseteste," in *Sapientia Doctrina*, H. Bascour et al., eds. (Leuven, 1980), 212–230. On Scotus in relation to Julian, see J. P. H. Clark, "Predestination in Christ," 88–89, and id., "Time and Eternity in Julian of Norwich," *Downside Review* 109 (1991): 259–276, esp. 272–273. It should be noted that Bonaventure, whom Julian resembles in so many striking ways, differs from her here, holding that the need to atone for sins is the cause of the incarnation. See Clark, "Predestination in Christ," 91, n. 39. In modern theology the rejection of the *logos asarkos* in favor of the eternal election of the man Jesus Christ is articulated in its greatest depth and power by Karl Barth, who constantly reiterated the radical break he understood himself to have been making with prior theology in this regard. See Karl Barth, *Church Dogmatics*, vol. 2, pt. 2, G. W. Bromiley et al., trans. (Edinburgh: T. and T. Clark, 1957), 94–194.

53. Augustine, *De Trinitate* 2.5.9 [62].
54. Augustine, *Confessions* 11.7.9 [226].
55. Ibid., 11.26.33 [240].
56. Ibid., 11.29.39 [244].
57. Coiner, "The 'Homely' and the *Heimliche*," 317, n. 17.
58. Augustine, *Ennarationes in Psalmos*, 119.2 (PL 37, 1598), quoted in Clark, "Time and Eternity," 267.

59. See Clark, "Predestination in Christ," 83.

60. Augustine, *De Trinitate* 15.13.22 [485].

61. S, ch. 86, p. 135. This forms a conclusion to S, which may or may not be original to Julian. It is not found in P.

62. Pelphrey, *Christ Our Mother*, 131–133. While I believe Pelphrey is correct in noting the "dramatic" character of the example, his attempt to describe the action as if it were being performed on a medieval stage (including audience reaction to moments of slapstick) strikes me as somewhat forced.

63. Bradley, *Julian's Way*, 216.

64. Elizabeth Koenig, "Julian of Norwich, Mary Magdalene, and the Drama of Prayer," *Horizons* 20, no. 1 (1993): 23–43.

65. Ibid., 29, n. 18.

66. Ibid., 34–36. Koenig follows Colledge and Walsh in their claim that William of St. Thierry is a, if not the, major influence on Julian. See Colledge and Walsh, *A Book of Showings*, 109–110. This claim has been much criticized. See Baker, *Julian of Norwich's Showings*, 76–78.

67. Baker, *Julian of Norwich's Showings*, 49.

68. Donald MacKinnon, "Some Epistemological Reflections on Mystical Experience," in Katz, ed., *Mysticism and Philosophical Analysis*, 138.

69. For an overview of Balthasar's work, see Edward T. Oakes, *Pattern of Redemption: The Theology of Hans Urs von Balthasar* (New York: Continuum, 1994). To my knowledge, Balthasar's theology has not been utilized in interpreting Julian. Of recent works on Julian, the one with the most clearly "systematic" theological interest in Julian is Joan Nuth's *Wisdom's Daughter*, which works within a basically Rahnerian idiom (that to my mind hampers its interpretation more than it helps it) and does not mention Balthasar. Balthasar himself has a brief discussion of Julian in *The Glory of the Lord*, vol. 5, *The Realm of Metaphysics in the Modern Age*, 85–88, and in *Dare We Hope*, 101–102. Though he mentions the long text in a footnote to *Dare We Hope* (102, n. 13), he always quotes from the short text, which does not register either the many striking convergences with his own thought—such as the election of Christ from the beginning of creation as the *deus homo*—or the significant divergences—such as her teaching on divine wrath—that are found in the long text.

70. *Theo-drama II*, 271. Subsequent references to volumes of *Theo-drama* will be in the text, abbreviated *TD*, followed by a Roman numeral indicating the volume.

71. "If the Son is the Father's eternal Word, the world in its totality is created by this Word (Jn 1:3), not only instrumentally but in the sense that the Word is the world's pattern and hence its goal" (*Theo-drama II*, 261). Cf. *Theo-drama III*, 250–259.

72. Balthasar writes, "the circle of relationships between the two Adams is both tragic—the Cross is unavoidable—and anti-tragic (we cannot use the word 'comic' here), since he who is infallibly vanquished is also infallibly Victor" (*Theo-drama IV*, 473). Balthasar consistently distances himself from Hegel's "tragic" account of the Trinity, in which the *agon* of Father with Son is the precondition for the generation of the Spirit. He represents his trinitarian theology as an attempt to steer a middle course in which the trinitarian life of God can be seen "as the ground of the world process (including the crucifixion) in such a way that it is neither a formal process of self-communication in God, as in Rahner, nor entangled in the world process, as in Moltmann" (*Theo-drama IV*, 322–323). Rahner, for his part, felt that Balthasar had failed in this attempt, ending up with a "gnostic" doctrine of God in which "conflict, godlessness and death" were projected into God. See *Karl Rahner in Dialogue: Conversations and Interviews, 1965–1982*, Paul Imhof and Hubert Biallowons, eds., Harvey D. Egan, trans. (New York: Crossroad, 1986), cited in Oakes, *Pattern of Redemption*, 281–282, n. 11.

73. *ST* 1.43.2. As Aquinas puts it, mission "includes the eternal procession, with the addition of the temporal effect."

74. Colledge and Walsh, *A Book of Showings*, 529, n. 181. S omits "and an hard traveler."

75. See, e.g., *Fasciculus Morum* III.xviii.

76. Balthasar, *Dare We Hope*, 187.

77. For this reason I must disagree with Nicholas Watson's reading of Julian's resolution to the conflict between the lower and higher judgements. He suggests that the logic of Julian's position (whatever her explicit statements) is that the teachings of the church on sin "are merely *pastoral* truths" and "are so limited in application as to be ultimately—at least in any factual sense—untrue" ("'Yf Wommen Be Double Naturelly,'" 21; cf. "Visions of Inclusion," 164–165). In other words, the tension between higher and lower judgements collapses in favor of the former. While Julian *does* give a certain priority to the higher judgement—enough to justify a universal hope—it seems to me that Watson's reading on this point is uncharacteristically flat-footed and fails to appreciate the dramatic character of Julian's thought.

78. Cf. 79.32–38: "And than wylle he that we se oure wrechydnesse and mekely be it aknowen; but he wylle nott that we abyde therewith, ne he wylle nott þat we besy vs grely aboute oure accusyng, ne he wylle nott that we be to wrechydfulle on oure selfe. But he wylle þat we hastely entende to hym, for he stondyth alle aloone, and abydyth vs contynually, monyng and mornyng tylle whan we come."

79. Baker, *Julian of Norwich's* Showings, 86.

80. Ibid., 88.

81. For a chronology of events, see *The Peasants' Revolt of 1381*, 2d ed., R. B. Dobson, ed. (London: Macmillan Press, 1983), 36–44.

82. *Anonimalle Chronicle*, in ibid., 123.

83. Thomas Walsingham, *Historia Anglicana*, in ibid., 132.

84. Froissart, *Chroniques*, in ibid., 370.

85. Owst, *Literature and Pulpit*, 290–294.

86. Froissart, *Chroniques*, in Dobson, *The Peasants' Revolt*, 371.

87. Rodney Hilton notes that such communism would be "an unlikely peasant aspiration" ("Social Concepts in the English Rising of 1381," in *Class Conflict and the Crisis of Feudalism: Essays in Medieval Social History*, 2d ed. [London: Verso, 1990], 150).

88. For the view that the majority of the rebels had very pragmatic, perhaps even bourgeois, goals, see Rosmund Faith, "The 'Great Rumour' of 1377 and Peasant Ideology," in *The English Rising of 1381*, R. H. Hilton and T. H. Aston, eds. (Cambridge: Cambridge University Press, 1984), 65–68. For a counterview that ascribes to the rebels as a whole a more radical ideology, see Hilton, "Social Concepts."

89. Dobson, *The Peasants' Revolt*, 382. For a discussion of the rebel literature of 1381, see Steven Justice, *Writing and Rebellion: England in 1381* (Berkeley: University of California Press, 1994).

90. This is precisely the temptation that Kenneth Leech, abetted by scant evidence, succumbs to in "Contemplative and Radical: Julian Meets John Ball," in *Julian: Woman of Our Day*, Robert Llewelyn, ed. (London: Darton, Longman and Todd, 1985), 89–101.

91. On the economic changes wrought by the Black Death, see John Hatcher, *Plague, Population and the English Economy, 1348–1530* (London: Macmillan Press, 1977). For a discussion of bastard feudalism, see Keen, *English Society in the Later Middle Ages*, 19–23.

92. Olson, "God's Inappropriate Grace," 53.

93. *Ancrene Wisse*, 181. For an overview of the various allegorical uses of clothing in medieval writing, focusing especially on the *Ancrene Wisse* and *Piers Plowman*, see Janet Grayson, "The Eschatological Adam's Kirtle," *Mystics Quarterly* 11, no. 4 (1985): 153–160.

94. Dyer, *Standards of Living*, 176.

95. Sumptuary ordinance of 1363, in *English Historical Documents, Volume IV: 1327–1485*, A. R. Myers, ed. (London: Eyre and Spottiswoode, 1969), 1153.

96. Dyer, *Standards of Living*, 88.

97. *Chronicon Henrici Knighton*, 2.140–141, in Dobson, *The Peasants' Revolt*, 238.

98. In this understanding of interiority, Julian is thoroughly Augustinian, at least if one accepts the reading of Augustine that Denys Turner argues for in *The Darkness of God*, 50–101.

99. Nuth, *Wisdom's Daughter*, 113.

100. John Milbank, "Can a Gift Be Given: Prolegomena to a Future Trinitarian Metaphysic," in *Rethinking Metaphysics*, L. Gregory Jones and Stephen E. Fowl, eds. (Oxford: Blackwell Publishers, 1995), 120–161, esp. 131.

101. Ockham writes, "if we leave aside all authority and follow [just] natural reason, then it can indeed be proved evidently that every created thing is absolute and that among creatures there are no relations outside the soul distinct from absolute things" (*Quodl.* VI.15 [537]).

102. For a discussion, see Adams, *William Ockham*, 999–1007.

103. Ockham, *Quodl.* III.4 [184].

104. Colledge and Walsh note that Julian uses the term "forth spredyng" to translate the technical term *circumsessio*, which describes the mutual indwelling of the persons of the Trinity. See *A Book of Showings*, 157–158.

105. Milbank, "Can a Gift be Given?" 136.

106. Ockham, *Quodl.* VI.4 [500].

107. Adams, *William Ockham*, 1274.

108. Dyer, *Standards of Living*, 88.

CONCLUSION: PERFORMING THE BOOK

1. Balthasar, *Theo-drama III*, 25.

2. Colledge and Walsh, *A Book of Showings*, 731, n. 2. For a defense of the S rubric, see Watson, "The Composition of Julian of Norwich's *Revelation of Love*," 669–670.

3. Nicholas Lash, "Performing the Scriptures," in *Theology on the Way to Emmaus* (London: SCM Press, 1986), 41–42.

4. Ibid., 46.

5. See Benedicta Ward, "Lady Julian and Her Audience: 'Mine Even-Christian,'" in *The English Religious Tradition and the Genius of Anglicanism*, Geoffery Rowell, ed. (Nashville: Abingdon Press, 1994).

6. For a reading of Julian that shows how drastically she differs, particularly with regard to the humanity of Christ, from conventional affective piety, see Aers and Staley, *Powers of the Holy*, 78–104.

7. Thomas of Celano, *The First Life of St. Francis*, in *St. Francis of Assisi, Writings and Early Biographies: English Omnibus of the Sources for the Life of St. Francis*, 4th ed., Marion A. Habig, ed. (Chicago: Franciscan Herald Press, 1983), 250–251. On the eschatological character of Francis's consciousness, see Joseph Ratzinger, *The Theology of History in*

St. Bonaventure, Zachary Hayes, O.F.M., trans. (Chicago: Franciscan Herald Press, 1971), 39–40.

8. See David Aers' contribution to *Powers of the Holy* for an extremely interesting comparison of Wyclif (and later Lollards), Langland, and Julian on their subversive readings of Christ's humanity.

9. William of Ockham, *The Work of Ninety Days*, ch. 93, in *A Letter to the Friars Minor and Other Writings*, Arthur Stephen McGrade and John Kilcullen, eds., John Kilcullen, trans. (Cambridge: Cambridge University Press, 1995), 111.

10. On the distinction between "place" and "space," see Certeau, *The Practice of Everyday Life*, 117–118.

11. I have tried to address these issues in more detail in "Walking in the Pilgrim City," *New Blackfriars* 77, no. 909 (November 1996): 504–518.

12. *Regula Sancti Benedicti*, Prol. 45 [*RB 1980: The Rule of St. Benedict in Latin and English with Notes*, Timothy Fry, O.S.B., ed. (Collegeville, Minn.: Liturgical Press, 1980), 165].

13. As Augustine writes: "You are to love all men, even your enemies— not because they *are* your brothers, but in order that they may be; so that brotherly love may burn within you, whether for him who is already a brother, or for your enemy, that love may turn him into one" (*Homilies on I John*, X.7 [*Augustine: Later Works*, John Burnaby, ed. and trans. (Philadelphia: Westminster Press, 1955), 344]).

14. Dorothy Day (1897–1980) was a secular radical who converted to Catholicism in 1926. In 1933 she cofounded the Catholic Worker movement with Peter Maurin, a largely self-taught philosopher and itinerant laborer. The Catholic Worker was premised (not unlike the early Franciscans) on a literal living out of the commands of Jesus in the Gospels, and its basic outlook was anarchist, distributist, and pacifist, yet in general fiercely loyal to church teachings. The Catholic Worker movement became best known for its newspaper, *The Catholic Worker*, and its houses of hospitality, which gave food and shelter to the homeless.

15. Dorothy Day, *The Long Loneliness* (New York: Harper and Row, 1952), 188.

16. Julian's *Revelation* was one of the books Day kept at her bedside for devotional reading. On the influence of Julian on Day, see Brigid O'Shea Merriman, O.S.F., *Searching for Christ: The Spirituality of Dorothy Day* (Notre Dame, Ind.: University of Notre Dame Press, 1994), 179–180, 287–288, nn. 17, 18, 19.

17. See Pat Jordan, "Dorothy Day: Illuminating Dark Times," *The Catholic Worker*, December 1980, reprinted in *A Penny a Copy: Readings from* The Catholic Worker, rev. ed., Thomas C. Cornell et al., eds. (Maryknoll, N.Y.: Orbis Books, 1995), 288.

18. Dorothy Day, "Be Kind, Cain," *The Catholic Worker*, November 1947, quoted in Merriman, *Searching for Christ*, 179.

19. Dorothy Day, *The Catholic Worker*, September 1945, reprinted in *By Little and by Little: The Selected Writings of Dorothy Day*, Robert Ellsberg, ed. (New York: Alfred A. Knopf, 1983), 268.

20. On this, see Nicholas Lash, "All Shall be Well: Christian and Marxist Hope," in *Theology on the Way to Emmaus*, 202–215.

21. Dorothy Day, "Inventory," *The Catholic Worker*, January 1951, reprinted in *By Little and by Little*, 105.

22. Dorothy Day, "On Pilgrimage," *The Catholic Worker*, February 1960, reprinted in Dorothy Day, *On Pilgrimage: The Sixties* (New York: Curtis Books, 1972), 22.

23. Dorothy Day, *The Catholic Worker*, February 1942, reprinted in *By Little and by Little*, 264.

APPENDIX: WHO WAS JULIAN OF NORWICH?

1. One manuscript reads "viii" and another reads "xiii." Benedicta Ward argues that the latter date is preferable, since it is more likely that a copyist would mistake an x for a v than vice versa. See "Julian the Solitary," in *Julian Reconsidered*, by Kenneth Leech and Sister Benedicta (Oxford: Fairacres, 1988), 35, n. 41.

2. This would give Julian a birth date of late 1342 or early 1343.

3. The long text reads, "I haue brought the image of thy sauioir; looke ther vpon and comfort thee ther with" (3.20–26).

4. Both Colledge and Walsh and Marion Glasscoe argue for the liturgical hour. See Colledge and Walsh, *A Book of Showings*, 631, n. 39, and Marion Glasscoe, *English Medieval Mystics: Games of Faith* (London: Longman, 1993), 216.

5. See, e.g., George Tyrrell: "She probably belonged to the Benedictine nuns at Carrow, near Norwich" ("Julianna of Norwich," in *The Faith of Millions* [London: Longmans, Green, and Co., 1901], 9). Colledge and Walsh argue for her having entered religious life at an early age, but claim no certainty as to where she was a nun (*A Book of Showings*, 44). Denise Baker argues that Julian was by 1373 "already familiar with the devotional practices most common for those in religious or solitary life," and therefore "It seems probable . . . that she was a nun or anchorite at the time of her visionary experience in 1373" (*Julian of Norwich's* Showings, 33, 34).

6. See Benedicta Ward, "Julian the Solitary," and id., "Lady Julian and Her Audience: 'Mine Even-Christian.'" David Knowles also argues

that "there is considerable probability that she was still living at home when the 'shewings' of 1373 took place" (*The English Mystical Tradition* [New York: Harper and Brothers, 1961], 120).

7. Michael J. Wright, "Julian of Norwich's Early Knowledge of Latin," *Neuphilologische Mitteilungen* 95, no. 1 (1993): 42.

8. Edmund Colledge, O.S.A., and James Walsh, S.J., "Editing Julian of Norwich's *Revelations*: A Progress Report," *Medieval Studies* 38 (1976): 410. See also Colledge and Walsh, *A Book of Showings*, 43–59. Cf. Michael J. Wright, "Julian of Norwich's Early Knowledge of Latin," which supports and seeks to strengthen Colledge and Walsh's interpretation. The "maximalist" approach to Julian's education is taken even further by Julia Bolton Holloway, who claims that Julian knew not only Latin but Hebrew as well. See "Chronicles of a Mystic," *The Tablet*, 11 May 1996, 610–611.

9. Marion Glasscoe, Introduction to Julian of Norwich, *A Revelation of Love*, xviii. Cf. Brant Pelphrey, *Christ Our Mother*, 92–93, 262, nn. 1 and 2.

10. Marion Glasscoe, *English Medieval Mystics*, 223.

11. There is also the question of *where* Julian would have received her education. The obvious candidate would be the convent at Carrow, but as Benedicta Ward notes, in Julian's day this convent was "a house of no great pretensions to spirituality and certainly with no school, library or concern with education" ("Julian the Solitary," 19).

12. Colledge and Walsh, *A Book of Showings*, 47.

13. Duffy, *The Stripping of the Altars*, 3.

14. Santha Bhattacharji, "Independence of Thought in Julian of Norwich," *Word and Spirit* 11 (1991): 79–92.

15. I am not, obviously, claiming that Julian heard or read any of Mirk's sermons, but simply that the kind of thing we find in the *Festial* is likely to have been the kind of teaching heard from medieval English pulpits.

16. An exception to this is Julia Holloway, who claims that the Westminster manuscript (see below, n. 18), which has generally been thought to be a collection of excerpts from the long text, is in fact a work by Julian that is *prior* to her experience of 1370, which was later incorporated into the visionary text that comes down to us as the long text (and indeed the Westminster manuscript does not contain any explicit mention of the visions). She argues further that the short text is subsequent to the long text and is an abridgement of it designed to remove the radical theology of her first text, represented by the Westminster manuscript. The chief problem that I see with this thesis is that in the long text Julian ascribes the theology found in the Westminster manuscript (especially her understanding of

Christ as mother) to her years spent contemplating her visions. Thus Holloway's thesis entails a deliberate misrepresentation on the part of Julian, with her theology having little connection with the visions. For a presentation of Holloway's argument, see "Chronicles of a Mystic."

17. British Museum, Additional MS 37790. For a description of the manuscript, see Colledge and Walsh, *A Book of Showings*, 1–5.

18. Westminster Archdiocesan Archives MS. For a description of the manuscript, see Colledge and Walsh, *A Book of Showings*, 9–10.

19. Paris, MS Bibliothèque Nationale Fonds anglais 40. For a description of this somewhat unusual manuscript, see Colledge and Walsh, *A Book of Showings*, 6–8. There is also a printed edition, most likely based on P, which Serenus Cressy published c. 1670.

20. London, MS British Museum Sloane 2499, and MS British Museum Sloane 3705. The latter appears to be a copy made from the former, and thus is a less significant witness. For a description of the manuscripts, see Colledge and Walsh, *A Book of Showings*, 8–9.

21. Colledge and Walsh base their critical edition on P, arguing strongly for its superiority on the basis of its preservation of certain rhetorical figures. See *A Book of Showings*, 25–27. Marion Glasscoe argues equally strongly for S on the basis both of its preservation of fourteenth-century linguistic forms and of its preservation of theological claims that have been "tamed" by P. See "Visions and Revisions."

22. Watson, "The Composition of Julian of Norwich's *Revelation of Love*," 658.

23. The Lollards were the fourteenth- and fifteenth-century followers of John Wyclif, who were known for their critique of the use of religious images.

24. Watson, "Composition," 664.

25. According to Watson, this revelation—"What, woldest thou wytt [know] thy lordes menyng in this thyng? Wytt it wele, loue was his menyng"—is crucial for understanding the differences between the short text and the long text. See ibid., 669.

26. Ibid., 681.

27. Lynn Staley Johnson, "The Trope of the Scribe and the Question of Literary Authority in the Works of Julian of Norwich and Margery Kempe," *Speculum* 66 (1991): 833.

28. Aers and Staley, *Powers of the Holy*, 79, n. 4.

29. For a description of the contents of these wills, see Colledge and Walsh, *A Book of Showings*, 33–35.

30. On the dating of this visit, see Colledge and Walsh, *A Book of Showings*, 35.

31. *The Book of Margery Kempe*, 42–43.

32. For a description of anchoritic cells, see Warren, *Anchorites and Their Patrons*, 29–37.

33. Most of this is drawn from Robert W. Ackerman, "The Liturgical Day in *Ancrene Riwle*," *Speculum* 53 (1978): 734–744.

34. This may seem infrequent by modern standards, though one should bear in mind that in the late Middle Ages most lay people received communion only once a year, at Easter time.

35. See *Ancrene Wisse* I [53–65].

36. Ackerman, "The Liturgical Day," 743.

37. See *Ancrene Wisse* VIII [199–207]. As a document written by a man for women, the *Ancrene Wisse* is typical in urging moderation, which urging some medieval women emphatically rejected. See Caroline Walker Bynum, *Holy Feast and Holy Fast*, 237–244.

38. As a theologian rather than a historian I make such a claim cautiously, particularly in the face of Colledge and Walsh's massive erudition, displayed in the notes to their edition of P. I am grateful to Nicholas Watson, who, in private correspondence, has agreed with my instinct that Julian's theology can be accounted for on the basis of humbler sources than those adduced by Colledge and Walsh. Cf. Watson, "The Composition of Julian of Norwich's *Revelation of Love*," 674, n. 87.

39. See Bernard McGinn, "Introduction: Meister Eckhart and the Beguines in the Context of Vernacular Theology," in *Meister Eckhart and the Beguine Mystics*, Bernard McGinn, ed. (New York: Continuum, 1994), 1–14.

BIBLIOGRAPHY

Abbot, Christopher. "Piety and Egoism in Julian of Norwich: A Reading of Long Text Chapters 2 and 3." *Downside Review*, no. 397 (October 1996).
———. "His Body, The Church: Julian of Norwich's Vision of Christ Crucified." *Downside Review*, no. 398 (January 1997).
Ackerman, Robert W. "The Liturgical Day in *Ancrene Riwle*." *Speculum* 53 (1978).
Adams, Marilyn McCord. *William Ockham*. 2 vols. Notre Dame, Ind.: University of Notre Dame Press, 1987.
Adams, Robert. "Langland's Theology." In *A Companion to Piers Plowman*, edited by John A. Alford. Berkeley: University of California Press, 1988.
Aers, David. "A Whisper in the Ear of Early Modernists; or, Reflections on Literary Critics Writing the 'History of the Subject.'" In *Culture and History 1350–1600: Essays on English Communities, Identities and Writing*, edited by David Aers. Detroit: Wayne State University Press, 1992.
———. "Altars of Power: Reflections on Eamon Duffy's *The Stripping of the Altars*." *Literature and History* 3 (1994).
Aers, David, and Lynn Staley. *Powers of the Holy*. University Park, Pa.: Pennsylvania State University Press, 1996.
Allmand, Christopher. *The Hundred Years War: England and France at War c. 1300–c. 1450*. Cambridge: Cambridge University Press, 1989.
Anchoritic Spirituality: Ancrene Wisse and Associated Works. Translated by Anne Savage and Nicholas Watson. New York: Paulist Press, 1991.
Anderson, Benedict. *Imagined Communities: Reflections on the Origin and Spread of Nationalism*. Rev. ed. London: Verso, 1991.
Anselm. "Why God Became Man" [*Cur deus homo?*]. In *A Scholastic Miscellany: Anselm to Ockham*, translated and edited by Eugene R. Fairweather. Philadelphia: Westminster Press, 1956.
———. *Prayers and Meditations of St. Anselm with the Proslogion*. Translated by Benedicta Ward, S.L.G. New York: Penguin Books, 1973.
Aquinas, Thomas. *Summa Theologica*. 5 vols. Translated by the Fathers of the English Dominican Province. Westminster, Md.: Christian Classics, 1981.

Aristotle. *Politica*. In *The Basic Works of Aristotle*, edited by Richard McKeon. New York: Random House, 1941.

Asad, Talal. *Genealogies of Religion: Discipline and Reasons of Power in Christianity and Islam*. Baltimore: Johns Hopkins University Press, 1993.

Augustine. "Christian Instruction" [*De doctrina christiana*]. Translated by John J. Gavigan, O.S.A. In *Saint Augustine*, The Fathers of the Church, vol. 2. Washington, D.C.: Catholic University of America Press, 1947.

———. *Homilies on I John*. In *Augustine: Later Works*, edited and translated by John Burnaby. Philadelphia: Westminster Press, 1955.

———. *The Trinity*. The Fathers of the Church, vol. 45. Translated by Stephen McKenna, C.SS.R. Washington, D.C.: Catholic University of America Press, 1963.

———. *The Literal Meaning of Genesis*. Translated by John Hammon Taylor, S.J. New York: Newman Press, 1982.

———. *Confessions*. Translated by Henry Chadwick. Oxford: Oxford University Press, 1991.

Aulén, Gustav. *Christus Victor: An Historical Study of the Three Main Types of the Idea of Atonement*. Translated by A. G. Herbert. New York: Macmillan, 1969.

Baker, Denise Nowakowski. "Julian of Norwich and Anchoritic Literature." *Mystics Quarterly* 19, no. 4 (1993).

———. *Julian of Norwich's* Showings: *From Vision to Book*. Princeton, N.J.: Princeton University Press, 1994.

Bakhtin, Mikhail. *Rabelais and His World*. Translated by Hélène Iswolsky. Bloomington, Ind.: Indiana University Press, 1984.

Balthasar, Hans Urs von. *The Glory of the Lord: A Theological Aesthetics*. 7 vols. Various translators. San Francisco: Ignatius Press, 1982–1991.

———. *Dare We Hope "That All Men be Saved"? With a Short Discourse on Hell*. Translated by David Kipp and Lothar Krauth. San Francisco: Ignatius Press, 1988.

———. *Theo-drama: Theological Dramatic Theory*. 5 vols. Translated by Graham Harrison. San Francisco: Ignatius Press, 1990–1998.

Barker, Paula S. Datsko. "The Motherhood of God in Julian of Norwich's Theology." *Downside Review* 100, no. 341 (October 1982).

Barth, Karl. *Church Dogmatics*. vol. 2, pt. 2. Translated by G. W. Bromiley et al. Edinburgh: T. and T. Clark, 1957.

Bauerschmidt, Frederick Christian. "Walking in the Pilgrim City." *New Blackfriars* 77, no. 909 (November 1996).

Beckwith, Sarah. "Ritual, Church and Theatre: Medieval Dramas of the Sacramental Body." In *Culture and History 1350–1600: Essays on En-*

glish Communities, Identities and Writing, edited by David Aers. Detroit: Wayne State University Press, 1992.

———. *Christ's Body: Identity, Culture, and Society in Late Medieval Writings.* London: Routledge, 1993.

Beer, Frances. *Women and Mystical Experience in the Middle Ages.* Woodbridge: Boydell Press, 1993.

Bennett, Judith. "Medieval Women, Modern Women: Across the Great Divide." In *Culture and History 1350–1600: Essays on English Communities, Identities and Writing,* edited by David Aers. Detroit: Wayne State University Press, 1992.

Bhattacharji, Santha. "Independence of Thought in Julian of Norwich." *Word and Spirit* 11 (1991).

Biddick, Kathleen. "Genders, Bodies, Borders: Technologies of the Visible." *Speculum* 68 (1993).

Bloch, Marc. *Feudal Society.* 2 vols. Translated by L. A. Manyon. Chicago: University of Chicago Press, 1961.

———. *Land and Work in Medieval Europe: Selected Papers.* Translated by J. E. Anderson. Berkeley: University of California Press, 1967.

Blumenberg, Hans. *The Legitimacy of the Modern Age.* Translated by Robert M. Wallace. Cambridge, Mass.: MIT Press, 1983.

Bonaventure. *The Breviloquium.* Vol. 2 of *The Works of Bonaventure.* Translated by José de Vinck. Patterson, N.J.: St. Anthony Guild Press, 1963.

———. *Collations on the Six Days.* Vol. 5 of *The Works of Bonaventure.* Translated by José de Vinck. Patterson, N.J.: St. Anthony Guild Press, 1970.

———. "On the Predestination of Christ" [III *Sent.* d.11, a.1, q.1–3]. Translated by Zachary Hayes. In *Franciscan Christology: Selected Texts, Translations and Introductory Essays,* edited by Damian McElrath. St. Bonaventure, N.Y.: Franciscan Institute, 1980.

———. *The Journey of the Mind to God [Itinerarium mentis in Deum].* Translated by Philotheus Boehner, O.F.M. Edited by Stephen F. Brown. Indianapolis: Hackett Publishing Co., 1993.

Bossy, John. "The Mass As a Social Institution, 1200–1700." *Past and Present* 100 (August 1983).

———. *Christianity and the West 1400–1700.* Oxford: Oxford University Press, 1985.

Bradley, Ritamary. *Julian's Way: A Practical Commentary on Julian of Norwich.* London: HarperCollins, 1992.

Burrell, David B., C.S.C. *Aquinas: God and Action.* London: Routledge and Kegan Paul, 1979.

Bynum, Caroline Walker. *Jesus as Mother: Studies in the Spirituality of the High Middle Ages.* Berkeley: University of California Press, 1982.

———. *Holy Feast and Holy Fast: The Religious Significance of Food to Medieval Women*. Berkeley: University of California Press, 1987.

———. *Fragmentation and Redemption: Essays on Gender and the Human Body in Medieval Religion*. New York: Zone Books, 1991.

Cabassut, André, O.S.B. "Une dévotion médiévale peu connue: la dévotion à 'Jésus notre mère.'" *Revue d'Ascétique et de Mystique* 25 (1949).

Cadden, Joan. *Meanings of Sex Difference in the Middle Ages: Medicine, Science, and Culture*. Cambridge: Cambridge University Press, 1993.

Castoriadis, Cornelius. *The Imaginary Institution of Society*. Translated by Kathleen Blamey. Cambridge, Mass.: MIT Press, 1987.

Catherine of Siena. *The Dialogue*. Translated by Suzanne Noffke, O.P. New York: Paulist Press, 1980.

Cavanaugh, William T. "'A Fire Strong Enough to Consume the House': The Wars of Religion and the Rise of the State." *Modern Theology* 11, no. 4 (October 1995).

Certeau, Michel de. "Christianisme et 'modernité' dans l'historiographie contemporaine: réemplois de la tradition dans les pratiques." *Recherches de Science Religieuse* 63, no. 2 (1975).

———. *The Practice of Everyday Life*. Translated by Steven Rendall. Berkeley: University of California Press, 1984.

Chastising of God's Children and The Treatise of Perfection of the Sons of God. Edited by Joyce Bazire and Eric Colledge. Oxford: Basil Blackwell, 1957.

Chrimes, S. B. *English Constitutional Ideas in the Fifteenth Century*. Cambridge: Cambridge University Press, 1936.

Clark, David W. "Ockham on Human and Divine Freedom." *Franciscan Studies*, n.s. 38 (1978).

Clark, J. P. H. "Predestination in Christ According to Julian of Norwich." *Downside Review* 100, no. 339 (April 1982).

———. "Time and Eternity in Julian of Norwich." *Downside Review* 109 (1991).

———. "Late Fourteenth-Century Cambridge Theology and the English Contemplative Tradition." In *The Medieval Mystical Tradition in England: Exeter Symposium V*, edited by Marion Glasscoe. Cambridge: D. S. Brewer, 1992.

Cloud of Unknowing and the Book of Privy Counselling. Edited by Phyllis Hodgson. Early English Text Society, o.s. no. 218. London: Oxford University Press, 1944.

Coiner, Nancy. "The 'Homely' and the *Heimliche*: The Hidden, Doubled Self in Julian of Norwich's Showings." *Exemplaria* 5, no. 2 (Fall 1993).

Coleman, Janet. *Piers Plowman and the Moderni*. Rome: Edizioni di Storia e Letteratura, 1981.

Colledge, Edmund, O.S.A., and James Walsh, S.J. "Editing Julian of Norwich's *Revelations*: A Progress Report." *Medieval Studies* 38 (1976).
Connerton, Paul. *How Societies Remember.* Cambridge: Cambridge University Press, 1989.
Cornell, Thomas C., et al., eds. *A Penny a Copy: Readings from* The Catholic Worker. Rev. ed. Maryknoll, N.Y.: Orbis Books, 1995.
Courtenay, William J. *Capacity and Volition: A History of the Distinction of Absolute and Ordained Power.* Bergamo: Pierluigi Lubrina Editore, 1990.
Cousins, Ewert. "The Humanity and the Passion of Christ." In *Christian Spirituality: High Middle Ages and Reformation*, edited by Jill Raitt. New York: Crossroad, 1988.
Darwin, Francis D. S. *The English Mediaeval Recluse.* London: Society for Promoting Christian Knowledge, 1944.
Davies, Brian. "The Action of God." *New Blackfriars* 75, no. 879 (February 1994).
Day, Dorothy. *The Long Loneliness.* New York: Harper and Row, 1952.
———. *On Pilgrimage: The Sixties.* New York: Curtis Books, 1972.
———. *By Little and by Little: The Selected Writings of Dorothy Day.* Edited by Robert Ellsberg. New York: Alfred A. Knopf, 1983.
del Mastro, M. L. "Juliana of Norwich: Parable of the Lord and Servant—Radical Orthodoxy." *Mystics Quarterly* 14 (1988).
DeLetter, P. "Trinitarian Indwelling according to Ruysbroeck." *Heythrop Journal* 2 (1961).
Deleuze, Gilles, and Felix Guattari. *A Thousand Plateaus: Capitalism and Schizophrenia.* Translated by Brian Massumi. Minneapolis: University of Minnesota Press, 1987.
Despres, Denise. "Memory and Image: The Dissemination of a Franciscan Meditative Text." *Mystics Quarterly* 16, no. 3 (1990).
Dionysius the Areopagite. *Pseudo-Dionysius: The Complete Works.* Translated by Colm Luibheid and Paul Rorem. New York: Paulist Press, 1987.
Dobson, R. B., ed. *The Peasants' Revolt of 1381.* 2d ed. London: Macmillan Press, 1983.
Douglas, Mary. *Purity and Danger: An Analysis of the Concepts of Pollution and Taboo.* London: Routledge, 1966.
———. *Natural Symbols: Explorations in Cosmology.* New York: Pantheon Books, 1982.
Duffy, Eamon. *The Stripping of the Altars: Traditional Religion in England c. 1400–1580.* New Haven: Yale University Press, 1992.
Dupré, Louis. *Passage to Modernity: An Essay in the Hermeneutics of Nature and Culture.* New Haven: Yale University Press, 1993.

Dyer, Christopher. *Standards of Living in the Later Middle Ages: Social Change in England c. 1200–1520*. Cambridge: Cambridge University Press, 1989.
Epistle to Diognetus. In *The Apostolic Fathers*, vol. 2, translated by Kirsopp Lake. Cambridge, Mass.: Harvard University Press, 1950.
Faith, Rosmund. "The 'Great Rumour' of 1377 and Peasant Ideology." In *The English Rising of 1381*, edited by R. H. Hilton and T. H. Aston. Cambridge: Cambridge University Press, 1984.
Farrell, Frank B. *Subjectivity, Realism, and Postmodernism: The Recovery of the World in Recent Philosophy*. Cambridge: Cambridge University Press, 1994.
Fasciculus Morum: A Fourteenth-Century Preacher's Handbook. Edited and translated by Siegfried Wenzel. University Park, Pa.: Pennsylvania State University Press, 1989.
Fitzmyer, Joseph, S.J. "Pauline Theology." In *The New Jerome Biblical Commentary*, edited by Raymond Brown et al. Englewood Cliffs, N.J.: Prentice Hall, 1990.
Fitzpatrick, Peter. *The Mythology of Modern Law*. London: Routledge, 1992.
Florovsky, Georges. "Empire and Desert: Antinomies of Christian History." *Greek Orthodox Historical Review* 3 (1957).
Forman, Robert K. C., ed. *The Problem of Pure Consciousness: Mysticism and Philosophy*. Oxford: Oxford University Press, 1990.
French, Katherine L. "Competing for Space: Medieval Religious Conflict in the Monastic-Parochial Church at Dunster." *Journal of Medieval and Early Modern Studies* 27, no. 2 (Spring 1997).
Funkenstein, Amos. *Theology and the Scientific Imagination: From the Middle Ages to the Seventeenth Century*. Princeton, N.J.: Princeton University Press, 1986.
Gierke, Otto. *Political Theories of the Middle Ages*. Translated and edited by Frederic William Maitland. Cambridge: Cambridge University Press, 1900.
Gillespie, Michael Allen. *Nihilism before Nietzsche*. Chicago: University of Chicago Press, 1995.
Gillespie, Vincent, and Maggie Ross. "The Apophatic Image: The Poetics of Effacement in Julian of Norwich." In *The Medieval Mystical Tradition in England: Exeter Symposium V*, edited by Marion Glasscoe. Cambridge: D. S. Brewer, 1992.
Gilson, Étienne. *The Unity of Philosophical Experience*. New York: Charles Scribner's Sons, 1937.
Glasscoe, Marion. "Visions and Revisions: A Further Look at the Manuscripts of Julian of Norwich." *Studies in Bibliography* 42 (1989).

―――. *English Medieval Mystics: Games of Faith*. London: Longman, 1993.
Gomi, Taro. *Everyone Poops*. Translated by Amanda M. Stinchecum. Brooklyn, N.Y.: Kane Miller Book Publishers, 1993.
Graves, Pamela. "Social Space in the English Medieval Parish Church." *Economy and Society* 18, no. 3 (1989).
Grayson, Janet. *Structure and Imagery in* Ancrene Wisse. Hanover, N.H.: University Press of New England, 1974.
―――. "The Eschatological Adam's Kirtle." *Mystics Quarterly* 11, no. 4 (1985).
Haines, Roy Martin. "Social, Political, and Religious Impressions from Some Late Medieval Sermon Collections." In *Ecclesia Anglicana: Studies in the English Church of the Later Middle Ages*. Toronto: University of Toronto Press, 1989.
Hanawalt, Barbara. *The Ties That Bound: Peasant Families in Medieval England*. Oxford: Oxford University Press, 1986.
Hatcher, John. *Plague, Population, and the English Economy, 1348–1530*. London: Macmillan Press, 1977.
Hauerwas, Stanley, and James Fodor. "Remaining in Babylon: O'Donovan's Defense of Christendom." In Stanley M. Hauerwas, *Wilderness Wanderings: Probing Twentieth-Century Theology and Philosophy*. Boulder, Colo.: Westview Press, 1997.
Hilton, Rodney. *Class Conflict and the Crisis of Feudalism: Essays in Medieval Social History*. 2d ed. London: Verso, 1990.
Hilton, Walter. *The Scale of Perfection*. Translated by John P. H. Clark and Rosemary Dorward. New York: Paulist Press, 1991.
Holloway, Julia Bolton. "Chronicles of a Mystic." *The Tablet*, 11 May 1996.
Hudson, Anne, ed. *Selections from English Wycliffite Writings*. Cambridge: Cambridge University Press, 1978.
Hudson, Anne, and Michael Wilks, eds. *From Ockham to Wyclif*. Oxford: Basil Blackwell, 1987.
Hussey, S. S. "The Audience for the Middle English Mystics." In *De Cella in Seculum: Religious and Secular Life of Devotion in Late Medieval England*, edited by Michael G. Sargent. Cambridge: D. S. Brewer, 1989.
Hyman, Arthur, and James J. Walsh, eds. *Philosophy in the Middle Ages: The Christian, Islamic, and Jewish Traditions*. 2d ed. Indianapolis: Hackett Publishing Co., 1984.
James, Mervyn. "Ritual, Drama, and Social Body in the Late Medieval Town." *Past and Present* 98 (1983).
Jantzen, Grace. *Power, Gender, and Christian Mysticism*. Cambridge: Cambridge University Press, 1995.

Jewell, Helen. "*Piers Plowman*—A Poem of Crisis: An Analysis of Political Instability in Langland's England." In *Politics and Crisis in Fourteenth-Century England*, edited by John Taylor and Wendy Childs. Gloucester: Alan Sutton, 1990.

Johnson, Lynn Staley. "The Trope of the Scribe and the Question of Literary Authority in the Works of Julian of Norwich and Margery Kempe." *Speculum* 66 (1991).

Julian of Norwich. *A Book of Showings to the Anchoress Julian of Norwich*. Edited by Edmund Colledge, O.S.A., and James Walsh, S.J. Toronto: Pontifical Institute of Medieval Studies, 1978.

———. *A Revelation of Love*. 3d rev. ed. Edited by Marion Glasscoe. Exeter: University of Exeter Press, 1993.

Jungmann, Joseph A., S.J. *The Mass of the Roman Rite: Its Origin and Development*. Translated by Francis A. Brunner, C.SS.R. London: Burns and Oates, 1959.

Justice, Steven. *Writing and Rebellion: England in 1381*. Berkeley: University of California Press, 1994.

Kantorowicz, Ernst H. *The King's Two Bodies: A Study in Medieval Political Theology*. Princeton: Princeton University Press, 1957.

Katz, Steven T. "Language, Epistemology, and Mysticism." In *Mysticism and Philosophical Analysis*, edited by Steven T. Katz. Oxford: Oxford University Press, 1978.

Keen, Maurice. *English Society in the Later Middle Ages: 1348–1500*. London: Penguin Books, 1990.

Kempe, Margery. *The Book of Margery Kempe*. Edited by Sanford Meech and Hope Emily Allen. Early English Text Society, o.s. no. 212. Oxford: Oxford University Press, 1940.

Kittel, Gerhard, ed. *Theological Dictionary of the New Testament*. Translated by G. W. Bromiley. Grand Rapids, Mich.: Wm. B. Eerdmans Publishing Co., 1965.

Klauser, Theodore. *A Short History of the Western Liturgy: An Account and Some Reflections*. Translated by John Halliburton. London: Oxford University Press, 1969.

Klocker, Harry R., S.J. "Ockham and the Divine Freedom." *Franciscan Studies*, n.s. 45 (1985).

Knowles, David. *The English Mystical Tradition*. New York: Harper and Brothers, 1961.

Koenig, Elizabeth. "Julian of Norwich, Mary Magdalene, and the Drama of Prayer." *Horizons* 20, no. 1 (1993).

Kolakowski, Leszek. "Modernity on Endless Trial." In *Modernity on Endless Trial*. Chicago: University of Chicago Press, 1990.

Krantz, M. Diane F. *The Life and Text of Julian of Norwich: The Poetics of Enclosure*. New York: Peter Lang, 1997.

Krochalis, J., and E. Peters, eds. *The World of Piers Plowman*. Philadelphia: University of Pennsylvania Press, 1975.
Lambert, Malcolm. *Medieval Heresy: Popular Movements from the Gregorian Reform to the Reformation*. 2d ed. Oxford: Blackwell, 1992.
Langland, William. *The Vision of Piers Plowman* [B-text]. Edited by A. V. C. Schmidt. London: J. M. Dent and Sons, 1987.
Lash, Nicholas. *Theology on the Way to Emmaus*. London: SCM Press, 1986.
Lay Folks' Mass Book. Edited by T. F. Simmons. Early English Text Society, o.s. no. 71. London: N. Trübner and Co., 1879.
Le Goff, Jacques. *The Medieval Imagination*. Translated by Arthur Goldhammer. Chicago: University of Chicago Press, 1988.
Leclerq, Jean. *The Love of Learning and the Desire for God*. Translated by Catharine Misrahi. New York: New American Library, 1962.
Leech, Kenneth. "Contemplative and Radical: Julian Meets John Ball." In *Julian: Woman of Our Day*, edited by Robert Llewelyn. London: Darton, Longman and Todd, 1985.
Lerner, Robert. *The Heresy of the Free Spirit in the Later Middle Ages*. Notre Dame, Ind.: University of Notre Dame Press, 1972.
Lindbeck, George. "Nominalism and the Problem of Meaning as Illustrated by Pierre d'Ailly on Predestination and Justification." *Harvard Theological Review* 52 (1959).
Lochrie, Karma. *Margery Kempe and Translations of the Flesh*. Philadelphia: University of Pennsylvania Press, 1991.
Ložar, Paula, trans. and ed. "The 'Prologue' to the Ordinances of the York Corpus Christi Guild." *Allegorica* 1, no. 1 (1976).
Lubac, Henri de. *Corpus mysticum: L'eucharistie et l'église au moyen age*. Paris: Aubier, 1948.
———. *Catholicism: Christ and the Common Destiny of Man*. Translated by Lancelot C. Sheppard and Sr. Elizabeth Englund, O.C.D. San Francisco: Ignatius Press, 1988.
Macfarlane, Alan. *The Origins of English Individualism*. Oxford: Basil Blackwell, 1978.
MacKinnon, Donald. "Some Epistemological Reflections on Mystical Experience." In *Mysticism and Philosophical Analysis*, edited by Steven T. Katz. Oxford: Oxford University Press, 1978.
Manent, Pierre. *An Intellectual History of Liberalism*. Translated by Rebecca Balinski. Princeton: Princeton University Press, 1994.
Mannyng, Robert. *Meditations on the Supper of Our Lord, and the Hours of the Passion*. Edited by J. Meadows Cowper. Early English Text Society, o.s. no. 60. London: N. Trübner and Co., 1875.
Marion, Jean-Luc. *L'Idole et la distance: cinq études*. Paris: Grasset, 1977.

McCabe, Herbert. *God Matters*. Springfield, Ill.: Templegate Publishers, 1987.
McEvoy, James. "The Absolute Predestination of Christ in the Theology of Robert Grosseteste." In *Sapientia Doctrina,* edited by H. Bascour et al. Leuven, 1980.
McGinn, Bernard. "Introduction: Meister Eckhart and the Beguines in the Context of Vernacular Theology." In *Meister Eckhart and the Beguine Mystics*, edited by Bernard McGinn. New York: Continuum, 1994.
McGrade, Arthur Stephen. *The Political Thought of William of Ockham: Personal and Institutional Principles*. Cambridge: Cambridge University Press, 1974.
McKisack, May. *The Fourteenth Century, 1307–1399*. Oxford: Clarendon Press, 1959.
Mechtild of Magdeburg. *Flowing Light of the Divinity*. Translated by Christine Mesch Galvani. Edited by Susan Clark. New York: Garland Publishing Co., 1991.
Meeks, Wayne. *The First Urban Christians: The Social World of the Apostle Paul*. New Haven: Yale University Press, 1983.
Merriman, Brigid O'Shea, O.S.F. *Searching for Christ: The Spirituality of Dorothy Day*. Notre Dame, Ind.: University of Notre Dame Press, 1994.
Merton, Thomas. *Mystics and Zen Masters*. New York: Noonday Press, 1967.
Milbank, John. *Theology and Social Theory: Beyond Secular Reason*. Oxford: Basil Blackwell, 1990.
———. "Can a Gift Be Given: Prolegomena to a Future Trinitarian Metaphysic." In *Rethinking Metaphysics*, edited by L. Gregory Jones and Stephen E. Fowl. Oxford: Blackwell Publishers, 1995.
———. *The Word Made Strange: Theology, Language, Culture*. Oxford: Blackwell Publishers, 1997.
———. "Sacred Triads: Augustine and the Indo-European Soul." *Modern Theology* 13, no. 4 (October 1997).
Mirk, John. *Mirk's Festial: A Collection of Homilies*. Edited by Theodore Erbe. Early English Text Society, o.s. no. 96. London: Kegan Paul, Trench, Trübner and Co., 1905.
Moore, R. I. *The Formation of a Persecuting Society: Power and Deviance in Western Europe, 950–1250*. Oxford: Blackwell, 1987.
Morris, Colin. *The Discovery of the Individual: 1050–1200*. Toronto: University of Toronto Press, 1987.
Myers, A. R. *English Historical Documents, Volume IV: 1327–1485*. London: Eyre and Spottiswoode, 1969.

Nederman, Cary J., and Kate Langdon Forhan, eds. *Medieval Political Theory—A Reader: The Quest for the Body Politic, 1100–1400*. London: Routledge, 1993.

Neel, Carol. "The Origins of the Beguines." In *Sisters and Workers in the Middle Ages*, edited by Judith Bennett et al. Chicago: University of Chicago Press, 1989.

Newman, Barbara. *From Virile Woman to WomanChrist: Studies in Medieval Religion and Literature*. Philadelphia: University of Pennsylvania Press, 1995.

Nolan, Edward Peter. *Cry Out and Write: A Feminine Poetics of Revelation*. New York: Continuum, 1994.

Nolan, Michael. "The Defective Male: What Aquinas Really Said." *New Blackfriars* 75, no. 880 (March 1994).

Nolcken, Christina von. "Julian of Norwich." In *Middle English Prose: A Critical Guide to Major Authors and Genres*, edited by A. S. G. Edwards. New Brunswick, N.J.: Rutgers University Press, 1984.

Nuth, Joan. *Wisdom's Daughter: The Theology of Julian of Norwich*. New York: Crossroad, 1991.

Oakes, Edward T. *Pattern of Redemption: The Theology of Hans Urs von Balthasar*. New York: Continuum, 1994.

Oakley, Francis. "Medieval Theories of Natural Law: William of Ockham and the Significance of the Voluntarist Tradition." *Natural Law Forum* 6 (1961).

———. "Pierre d'Ailly and the Absolute Power of God: Another Note on the Theology of Nominalism." *Harvard Theological Review* 56 (1963).

———. *Omnipotence, Covenant and Order: An Excursion in the History of Ideas from Abelard to Leibniz*. Ithaca, N.Y.: Cornell University Press, 1984.

Oberman, Heiko. "Some Notes on the Theology of Nominalism with Attention to Its Relation to the Renaissance." *Harvard Theological Review* 53 (1960).

———. *The Harvest of Medieval Theology: Gabriel Biel and Late Medieval Nominalism*. Durham, N.C.: Labyrinth Press, 1983.

Ockham, William. *Quodlibetal Questions*. 2 vols. Translated by Alfred J. Freddoso and Francis E. Kelly. New Haven: Yale University Press, 1991.

———. *A Short Discourse on Tyrannical Government*. Edited by Arthur Stephen McGrade. Translated by John Kilcullen. Cambridge: Cambridge University Press, 1992.

———. *A Letter to the Friars Minor and Other Writings*. Edited by Arthur Stephen McGrade and John Kilcullen. Translated by John Kilcullen. Cambridge: Cambridge University Press, 1995.

O'Donovan, Oliver. *The Desire of the Nations: Rediscovering the Roots of Political Theology.* Cambridge: Cambridge University Press, 1996.

Olson, Mary. "God's Inappropriate Grace: Images of Courtesy in Julian of Norwich's *Showings.*" *Mystics Quarterly* 20, no. 2 (June 1994).

Origen. *Contra Celsum.* Translated by Henry Chadwick. Cambridge: Cambridge University Press, 1965.

———. *On First Principles.* Translated by G. W. Butterworth. Gloucester, Mass.: Peter Smith, 1973.

Owst, G. R. *Literature and Pulpit in Medieval England.* 2d ed. Oxford: Basil Blackwell, 1961.

Park, Tarjei. "Reflecting Christ: The Role of the Flesh in Walter Hilton and Julian of Norwich." In *The Medieval Mystical Tradition in England: Exeter Symposium V*, edited by Marion Glasscoe. Cambridge: D. S. Brewer, 1992.

Pelphrey, Brant. *Christ Our Mother: Julian of Norwich.* Wilmington, Del.: Michael Glazier, 1989.

Petersen, Erik. "Der Monotheismus als politisches Problem." In *Theologische Traktate.* Munich: Verlag Heinrich Wild, 1951.

"Play of the Sacrament (Croxton)." In *Medieval Drama*, edited by David Bevington. Boston: Houghton Mifflin Co., 1975.

Poston, M. M. "Feudalism and Its Decline: A Semantic Exercise." In *Social Relations and Ideas: Essays in Honour of R. H. Hilton*, edited by T. H. Aston et al. Cambridge: Cambridge University Press, 1983.

Proclus. *Elements of Theology.* Translated and edited by E. R. Dodds. Oxford: Clarendon, 1963.

Rahner, Karl. *The Trinity.* Translated by Joseph Donceel. New York: Herder and Herder, 1970.

Ratzinger, Joseph. *The Theology of History in St. Bonaventure.* Translated by Zachary Hayes, O.F.M. Chicago: Franciscan Herald Press, 1971.

RB 1980: The Rule of St. Benedict in Latin and English with Notes. Edited by Timothy Fry, O.S.B. Collegeville, Minn.: Liturgical Press, 1980.

Reynolds, Sr. Anna Maria. "'Courtesy' and 'Homeliness' in the *Revelations* of Julian of Norwich." *Fourteenth Century English Mystics Newsletter* 5, no. 2 (June 1979).

Riddy, Felicity. "'Women Talking about the Things of God': A Late Medieval Sub-culture." In *Women and Literature in Britain, 1150–1500*, 2d ed., edited by Carol M. Meale. Cambridge: Cambridge University Press, 1996.

Robertson, Elizabeth. "Medieval Medical Views of Women and Female Spirituality in the *Ancrene Wisse* and Julian of Norwich's *Showings.*"

In *Feminist Approaches to the Body in Medieval Literature*, edited by Linda Lomperis and Sarah Stanbury. Philadelphia: University of Pennsylvania Press, 1993.

Rolle, Richard. *English Writings of Richard Rolle, Hermit of Hampole*. Edited by Hope Emily Allen. Oxford: Clarendon Press, 1963.

Rubin, Miri. *Corpus Christi: The Eucharist in Late Medieval Culture*. Cambridge: Cambridge University Press, 1991.

Ruusbroec, John. *John Ruusbroec: The Spiritual Espousals and Other Works*. Translated by James Wiseman, O.S.B. New York: Paulist Press, 1985.

Ryder, Andrew, S.C.J. "A Note on Julian's Visions." *Downside Review* 96, no. 325 (October 1978).

Sarum Missal in English. 2 vols. Translated by F. E. Warren. London: De La More Press, 1911.

Schmitt, Carl. *Political Theology: Four Chapters on the Concept of Sovereignty*. Translated by George Schwab. Cambridge, Mass.: MIT Press, 1985.

———. *The Concept of the Political*. Translated by George Schwab. Chicago: University of Chicago Press, 1996.

Southern, R. W. *Saint Anselm: A Portrait in a Landscape*. Cambridge: Cambridge University Press, 1990.

Sprung, Andrew. "'We nevyr shall come out of hym': Enclosure and Immanence in Julian of Norwich's *Book of Showings*." *Mystics Quarterly* 19, no. 2 (June 1993).

Stallybrass, Peter, and Allon White. *The Politics and Poetics of Transgression*. Ithaca, N.Y.: Cornell University Press, 1986.

Stillingfleet, Edward. *A Discourse Concerning the Idolatry Practiced in the Church of Rome and the Hazzard of Salvation in the Communion of it: In Answer to Some Papers of a Revolted Protestant. Wherein a Particular Account is Given of the Fanaticisms and Divisions of the Church*. 2d ed. London, 1672.

Swanson, R. N. *Church and Society in Late Medieval England*. Oxford: Blackwell Publishers, 1989.

———, trans. and ed. *Catholic England: Faith, Religion, and Observance before the Reformation*. Manchester: University of Manchester Press, 1993.

Tanner, Norman P. *The Church in Late Medieval Norwich: 1370–1532*. Toronto: Pontifical Institute of Medieval Studies, 1984.

———, ed. *Decrees of the Ecumenical Councils*. Vol. 1, *Nicaea I to Lateran V*. Washington, D.C.: Georgetown University Press, 1990.

Tawney, R. H. *Religion and the Rise of Capitalism*. New York: Mentor Books, 1947.

Thérèse of Lisieux. *Story of a Soul: The Autobiography of St. Thérèse of Lisieux.* 2d ed. Translated by John Clarke, O.C.D. Washington, D.C.: Institute of Carmelite Studies, 1976.

Thomas of Celano. *The First Life of St. Francis.* In *St. Francis of Assisi, Writings and Early Biographies: English Omnibus of the Sources for the Life of St. Francis,* 4th ed., edited by Marion A. Habig. Chicago: Franciscan Herald Press, 1983.

Trinkaus, Charles, and Heiko Oberman, eds. *The Pursuit of Holiness in Late Medieval and Renaissance Religion.* Leiden: E. J. Brill, 1974.

Tugwell, Simon, O.P. "Faith and Experience III: Experience and its Interpretation." *New Blackfriars* 59, no. 702 (November 1978).

———. *Ways of Imperfection: An Exploration of Christian Spirituality.* Springfield, Ill. Templegate Publishers, 1985.

Turner, Denys. *The Darkness of God: Negativity in Christian Mysticism.* Cambridge: Cambridge University Press, 1995.

Turner, Victor. *The Ritual Process: Structure and Anti-Structure.* Ithaca, N.Y.: Cornell University Press, 1977.

Turville-Petre, Thorlac. "The 'Nation' in English Writings of the Early Fourteenth Century." In *England in the Fourteenth Century,* edited by Nicholas Rogers. Stamford: Paul Watkins, 1993.

Tyrrell, George. "Juliana of Norwich." In *The Faith of Millions.* London: Longmans, Green, and Co., 1901.

Ward, Benedicta. *Miracles and the Medieval Mind: Theory, Record, and Event, 1000–1215.* Rev. ed. Philadelphia: University of Pennsylvania Press, 1987.

———. "Julian the Solitary." In *Julian Reconsidered,* by Kenneth Leech and Sister Benedicta. Oxford: Fairacres, 1988.

———. "Anselm of Canterbury and His Influence." In *Christian Spirituality: Origins to the Twelfth Century,* edited by Bernard McGinn et al. New York: Crossroad, 1992.

———. "Lady Julian and Her Audience: 'Mine Even-Christian.'" In *The English Religious Tradition and the Genius of Anglicanism,* edited by Geoffery Rowell. Nashville: Abingdon Press, 1994.

Warren, Ann K. *Anchorites and Their Patrons in Medieval England.* Berkeley: University of California Press, 1985.

Watson, Nicholas. "The Trinitarian Hermeneutic in Julian of Norwich's *Revelation of Love.*" In *The Medieval Mystical Tradition in England: Exeter Symposium V,* edited by Marion Glasscoe. Cambridge: D. S. Brewer, 1992.

———. "The Composition of Julian of Norwich's *Revelation of Love.*" *Speculum* 68 (1993).

———. "Censorship and Cultural Change in Late Medieval England: Vernacular Theology, the Oxford Translation Debate and Arundel's *Constitutions* of 1409." *Speculum* 70 (1995).

———. "'Yf wommen be double naturelly': Remaking 'Woman' in Julian of Norwich's *Revelation of Love*." *Exemplaria* 8, no. 1 (Spring 1996).

———. "Visions of Inclusion: Universal Salvation and Vernacular Theology in Pre-Reformation England." *Journal of Medieval and Modern Studies* 27, no. 2 (Spring 1997).

Weber, Max. "Politics as a Vocation." In *From Max Weber: Essays in Sociology*, edited and translated by H. H. Gerth and C. Wright Mills. New York: Oxford University Press, 1946.

Weil, Simone. *Waiting for God*. Translated by Emma Craufurd. New York: Harper and Row, 1951.

———. "The Love of God and Affliction." In *The Simone Weil Reader*, edited by George A. Panichas. Mt. Kisco, N.Y.: Moyer Bell, 1977.

Williams, Raymond. *Marxism and Literature*. Oxford: Oxford University Press, 1977.

Williams, Rowan. "Language, Reality and Desire in Augustine's *De Doctrina*." *Journal of Literature & Theology* 3, no. 2 (July 1989).

Wittgenstein, Ludwig. *Culture and Value*. Edited by G. H. von Wright. Translated by Peter Winch. Chicago: University of Chicago Press, 1980.

Wolters, Clifton. Introduction to *Revelations of Divine Love*. Harmondsworth: Penguin Books, 1966.

Wood, Ellen Meiksins. *The Pristine Culture of Capitalism: An Historical Essay on Old Regimes and Modern States*. London: Verso, 1991.

Wright, Michael J. "Julian of Norwich's Early Knowledge of Latin." *Neuphilologische Mitteilungen* 95, no. 1 (1993).

Wright, N. T. *The New Testament and the People of God*. Minneapolis: Fortress Press, 1992.

Wyclif, John. *Tractatus de Ecclesia*. Edited by Johann Loserth. London: Wyclif Society, 1886.

Index

Abbey of the Holy Ghost, 65
Abbot, Christopher, 230 n.34,
    231 n.37, 233 n.55
Ackerman, Robert W., 211,
    265 n.33
Adam, 114, 118, 132–136 passim,
    138, 141–143 passim, 152,
    153, 160–161, 172, 175–179
    passim, 199, 200, 244 n.94,
    258 n.72
Adams, Marilyn McCord, 24–25,
    187–188, 218 n.45,
    224 n.110, 233 n.97
Adams, Robert, 122
Aers, David, 35, 208, 214 n.8,
    217 n.43, 221 n.82, 260 n.6,
    261 n.8
affective spirituality, 34–35, 37–38,
    51–57, 62, 65, 228 n.20,
    229 n.22, 231 n.41, 233 n.54
allegory, 162, 172–173, 179,
    252 n.9, 259 n.93
Allmand, Christopher, 218 n.54
anchoresses, 64–65, 77–78,
    209–211, 232 n.48,
    235 nn. 2, 7, 238 n.35,
    239 nn. 40, 44, 45, 265 n.32
Ancrene Wisse, 37, 64, 91, 94, 171,
    178, 210–211, 232 n.48,
    235 nn. 2, 7, 242 n.77,
    243 n.87, 245 n.104,
    252 n.17, 265 n.34
Anderson, Benedict, 5
Anonimalle Chronicle, 175
Anselm of Canterbury, 34, 92, 114,
    132, 252 n.13

apophatic theology, 51–52, 56, 62,
    97, 234 n.70
Aristotle, 215 n.26
Asad, Talal, 37
asceticism, 37–38, 232 n.48
atonement: "asseeth makyng," 114,
    119; "onyng," 56, 62, 88–89,
    108, 110, 118, 122, 159, 165,
    187, 192
Augustine of Hippo, 2, 42, 73, 85,
    97–99 passim, 117, 146–147,
    148, 159, 160, 161, 173–174,
    182, 207, 237 n.27, 244 n.92,
    252 n.18, 253 n.25, 259 n.98,
    261 n.13
Aulén, Gustav, 246 n.111

Baker, Denise Nowakowski, 132,
    163, 173–174, 214 n.8,
    230 n.34, 233 n.54, 235 n.2,
    249 n.130, 254 n.38,
    257 n.66, 262 n.5
Bakhtin, Mikhail, 69–73, 74,
    81–82, 100, 106–107, 122,
    187, 236 n.19, 237 n.25
Ball, John, 174, 175–176, 258 n.90
Balthasar, Hans Urs von, 102, 127,
    164–173 passim, 191,
    225 n.122, 249 n.129,
    255 n.51, 257 n.69, 258 n.72
Barker, Paula S. Datsko, 243 n.88
Barth, Karl, 256 n.52
Beckwith, Sarah, 20, 221 n.82,
    236 n.15
Beer, Frances, 230 n.34
Beguines, 77, 238 n.35, 239 n.43

283

Benedict of Nursia, 197
Bennett, Judith, 238 n.29
Bhattacharji, Santha, 206
Biddick, Kathleen, 236 n.17
Biel, Gabriel, 27, 225 n.118, 246 n.111
Birgitta of Sweden, 75
Black Death, 175, 176, 238 n.29, 259 n.91
blindness, 48–49, 134, 136, 138–139
Bloch, Marc, 1, 14, 21, 217 n.40
blood of Christ, 41, 44, 47, 82, 84–87, 93, 230 n.33, 241 n.62, 242 n.79, 247 n.120
Blumenberg, Hans, 27–28, 29, 223 n.96, 225 n.129
bodily sight, 38, 41–46, 48, 72, 88, 187, 230 nn. 31, 34, 231 nn. 38, 41, 232 n.45, 241 n.60, 248 n.125, 252 n.8
body, human, 37–38, 64–73, 79–81, 142–143, 146, 147, 228 n.17, 235 n.8, 239 n.49, 240 n.52
body, mystical 197–198, 199–200
body of Jesus, 17–18, 35, 43, 49, 51, 60–62, 84–95, 103, 106–109, 118–121, 125–126, 160, 237 n.24, 240 n.58, 242 n.71, 251 n.3; church as, 103–104, 119, 121–123, 151, 186, 189; eucharistic, 65–66, 68–69. *See also* drying of Christ's body, humanity of Jesus
body politic, 15–23, 66–73, 121–123, 125–126, 176, 189, 235 n.8, 251 n.3
Bonaventure, 154–157, 231 n.39, 252 n.17, 254 n.37, 255 n.49, 256 n.52
Bossy, John, 20, 71, 218 n.47
Bradley, Ritamary, 163, 214 n.10
Brinton, Thomas, 16–17
Burrell, David, 27

Bynum, Caroline Walker, 38, 74, 217 n.43, 242 nn. 66, 67, 243 n.79, 265 n.37

Cabassut, André, 242 n.66
Cadden, Joan, 74, 92, 242 n.72
carnival, 70–72, 85–88 passim, 120, 184
Castoriadis, Cornelius, 12, 217 n.41
Catherine of Siena, 75, 212, 244 n.94
Cavanaugh, William T., 4
Celsus, 11
Certeau, Michel de, 19, 232 n.49, 261 n.10
christendom, 11–12, 22, 67–68, 72, 86, 120, 123, 193–195, 216 n.39
church, 4, 7, 9–12, 13–14, 22, 40, 77–78, 105, 108–113, 115–116, 118–119, 125, 144, 149, 153, 168–169, 170, 180–181, 182, 192, 196–198, 216 n.32, 218 n.55, 247 n.122, 248 n.124. *See also* body of Jesus, church as
civil society, 7, 8–9, 30–31
Clark, David W., 223 n.98, 224 n.112
Clark, J. P. H., 227 n.3, 254 n.38, 256 n.52
clothing and status, 177–178, 188, 259 n.93
Cloud of Unknowing, 52, 229 n.22, 233 n.61
Coiner, Nancy, 147, 160
Coleman, Janet, 13
Colledge, Edmund, and James Walsh, 1, 127–128, 163, 191, 192, 205–206, 213 n.2, 214 n.8, 231 n.43, 233 n.56, 237 n.25, 239 nn. 47, 48, 240 n.54, 241 n.60, 248 n.124, 252 nn. 9, 11, 16, 254 n.35, 257 n.66,

260 n.104, 262 nn. 4, 5, 264 n.21, 265 n.38
compassion, 40–41, 44, 56, 62, 105–106, 110, 120, 122, 123, 182–183, 185, 187, 196
composition, dates of, 207–209, 229 n.30, 251 n.4, 263 n.16
Connerton, Paul, 215 n.21
contemplative life, 52–53, 204, 233 nn. 54, 60
Corpus Christi, feast of, 17, 18, 19–20, 65, 174, 251 n.3
Courtenay, William J., 25, 222 n.95, 223 n.99, 224 nn. 101, 103, 111
courtesy, 83–84, 98, 112, 176, 177, 182, 240 n.55
Cousins, Ewert, 227 n.5
Crampton, Georgia Ronan, 213 n.5, 248 n.124
creation, 82, 85, 97–99, 153, 154–155, 158, 160, 161, 164–168 passim, 254 n.32. *See also* re-creation
Croxton Play of the Sacrament, 68, 72

Darwin, Francis, 239 n.45
Davies, Brian, 247 n.118
Day, Dorothy, 198–201, 261 n.14
death, 41, 78, 80
defecation, 79–81, 240 n.50
degradation, 70, 72, 81–84, 89–90, 94–95, 237 n.25, 239 n.49
Deleuze, Gilles, and Felix Guattari, 215 n.27
demons, 43, 55, 114–115, 178–179, 250 n.137. *See also* devil
desire, 91, 95, 98, 105, 107, 110, 150, 151, 246 n.107
Despenser, Henry, 109, 180, 247 n.117
Despres, Denise, 228 n.10
devil, the, 85–86, 93, 234 n.68, 249 n.132

Dionysius the Aeropagite, 154, 254 n.39
Dostoyevsky, Fyodor, 200–201
Douglas, Mary, 17, 66–67, 69, 125
drama, 70, 72, 122, 126–127, 162–173 passim, 183, 187, 188, 191, 221 n.84, 257 n.62
dread, 83, 120, 123, 192
drying of Christ's body, 84, 86–89
Duffy, Eamon, 20, 78, 206, 218 n.47, 221 nn. 78, 79, 82, 236 n.19
Dumézil, Georges, 219 n.59
Dupré, Louis, 28, 30, 33, 222 n.96, 223 nn. 98, 99, 226 n.132
Dyer, Christopher, 13, 178, 188

education, Julian's, 204–207, 263 nn. 8, 11
Epistle to Diognetus, 10–11
eternal perspective, God's, 152, 156, 158–161, 255 n.51
Eucharist, 17–21, 92, 93, 110–111, 122, 171, 221 n.84, 236 n.16, 243 n.80, 247 n.120, 265 n.34. *See also* body of Jesus, eucharistic; sacraments
evil, 85, 98–103, 116, 123, 138–139, 245 n.97. *See also* sin
exemplarism, 144, 154–161 passim, 248 n.124, 255 n.50

faith, 48, 55, 115–116
Faith, Rosmund, 259 n.88
fall, 132–133, 134, 135, 140, 142, 152, 154, 160–161, 174, 187, 222 n.90. *See also felix culpa*
Farrell, Frank, 223 n.96
Fasciculus Morum, 60–61, 90–91, 127, 220 n.72, 240 n.49, 242 n.77, 243 n.80, 245 n.97, 249 n.133, 252 n.17
felix culpa, 96, 103, 142, 240 n.53

feudalism, 14, 83, 127, 176–177, 178, 184, 187, 188–189, 196, 216 n.40, 251 n.3, 259 n.91
Fitzmeyer, Joseph, 253 n.24
Fitzpatrick, Peter, 30
Florovsky, Georges, 10
forgiveness, 123, 140
Forman, Robert K. C., 232 n.46
Francis of Assisi, 36, 193–194, 237 n.25
Franciscans, 34, 35, 193–194, 225 n.123, 228 nn. 10, 12, 254 n.37, 255 n.52, 261 n.14
freedom, 27–28, 164–166, 168, 170, 188, 196, 225 n.123, 226 n.135, 234 n.68
French, Katherine L., 221 n.82
Froissart, Jean, 175–176
Funkenstein, Amos, 28, 222 n.96

Gierke, Otto, 219 n.57, 222 n.90
gift, 168, 183–189, 195–197 passim
Gillespie, Michael Allen, 223 n.96
Gillespie, Vincent, 97, 106
Gilson, Étienne, 218 n.44
Glasscoe, Marion, 205–206, 213 n.2, 232 n.43, 248 n.124, 262 n.4, 264 n.21
godly will, 134–135, 149, 155–156, 160, 166, 182, 252 n.19
Goff, Jacques le, 228 n.17
grace, 55, 59, 156, 187, 227 n.3, 228 n.20, 233 n.60
Graves, Pamela, 221 n.79
Grayson, Janet, 235 n.2, 259 n.93
Grosseteste, Robert, 256 n.52

Haines, Roy Martin, 16–17, 219 n.60
Hanawalt, Barbara, 13
Hatcher, John, 259 n.91
Hauerwas, Stanley, and James Fodor, 216 n.39
"hazelnut," 42, 43, 52, 97, 181
Hegel, G. W. F., 258 n.72

hell, 85, 88, 93, 114–115, 116, 121, 135–136, 241 nn. 62, 64, 249 n.129
heresy, 21, 22, 67–68, 75, 118, 120, 193
Hildegard of Bingen, 90
Hilton, Rodney, 259 nn. 87, 88
Hilton, Walter, 52, 64, 71, 99, 146–147, 229 n.29, 249 n.135, 252 n.17, 253 n.25
Holloway, Julia Bolton, 263 nn. 8, 16
homeliness, 55, 81, 83–84, 98, 112, 182
hope, 88, 171, 198, 199–200, 262 n.20
humanity of Christ, 34–36, 40, 41, 51–62 passim, 76, 81, 85, 89, 90, 93, 108, 110, 119, 123, 151, 153, 155, 157–159, 160, 167, 234 n.62, 248 n.124, 260 n.6, 261 n.8. See also body of Jesus
Hussey, S. S., 55, 238 n.34
Hütter, Reinhard, 219 n.56

image of God, 134, 139–140, 149, 153, 225 n.122, 237 n.27, 244 n.94, 252 n.18
imagination, 5–6
Imitatio Christi, 35, 39, 199, 228 n.11
incarnation, 50–51, 54, 81, 84, 95, 108, 121, 141–142, 151, 152, 153, 160, 165, 168, 181–182, 195, 199, 255 n.51, 256 n.52
intermediaries ("meanes"), 42, 53–54, 81, 157, 180

James, Mervyn, 20, 221 n.80, 251 n.3
Jantzen, Grace, 214 n.9
Jews, 22, 67–68, 71, 72, 116, 120, 249 n.135
John-Julian, Father, 214 n.5

John of Salisbury, 15
judgement ("doom"), 128, 138,
    144, 148–153, 159, 172,
    189–190, 197–198, 258 n.77.
    See also secret, God's
Justice, Stephen, 259 n.89

Kantorowicz, Ernst H., 219 n.65
Katz, Steven, 232 n.46
Keen, Maurice, 21, 23, 218 n.54,
    258 n.91
Kempe, Margery, 75, 206, 209,
    210, 231 n.41, 234 n.62,
    238 n.34, 239 nn. 38, 40,
    250 n.137
Klauser, Theodore, 218 n.46
Klocker, Harry R., 223 n.98
Knowles, David, 262 n.6
Koenig, Elizabeth, 163
Kolakowski, Leszek, 216 n.40
Krantz, M. Diane F., 95, 239 n.39,
    244 n.90, 254 n.38

Lambert, Malcolm, 228 n.12
Langland, William, 13–14, 35, 71,
    122, 128, 250 n.135,
    261 n.8
Lash, Nicholas, 192, 262 n.20
last rites, 78, 203
Lateran Council III, 67
Lateran Council IV, 67
Lay Folks' Mass Book, 220 n.78
Leclerq, Jean, 228 n.9
Leech, Kenneth, 259 n.90
lepers, 22, 67–68, 120
Lerner, Robert, 238 n.30
Lindbeck, George, 223 n.98
Lochrie, Karma, 228 n.11, 240 n.58
Lollards, 20–21, 35, 38, 68, 75, 81,
    194, 208, 221 n.84,
    238 nn. 33, 35, 239 n.49,
    261 n.9, 264 n.23
lord and servant, example of, 47,
    125–145 passim, 147, 149,
    150, 162–163, 168, 169–170,
    172–174, 176–179, 183, 187,
    188–189, 200, 241 n.62,
    245 n.101, 257 n.62
Love, Nicholas, 192
Ložar, Paula, 220 n.71
Lubac, Henri de, 10, 63, 128, 197,
    215 n.31, 220 n.71, 236 n.16

Macfarlane, Alan, 217 n.43
MacKinnon, Donald, 163
Manent, Pierre, 4
Mannyng, Robert, 38–39
manuscripts of *A Revelation of*
    Love: description of, 207;
    differences between, 231 n.43,
    232 n.50, 240 n.54, 241 n.60,
    245 n.98, 247 nn. 120, 122,
    248 n.124, 254 n.34,
    263 n.16, 264 n.21
Marion, Jean-Luc, 51, 246 n.113
Marxism, 5, 215 n.19
Mary, mother of Jesus, 38–39, 42,
    43, 53, 82, 91, 157, 183,
    229 n.27, 230 n.34, 242 n.79
Mary Magdalene, 38, 123
Mastro, M. L. del, 214 n.5,
    248 n.127
McCabe, Herbert, 226 n.135
McEvoy, James, 256 n.52
McGinn, Bernard, 211
McGrade, Arthur Stephen, 30–31,
    226 nn. 130, 132
McKisack, May, 226 n.133,
    247 n.117
Mechtild of Magdeburg, 212,
    242 n.79, 256 n.52
Meeks, Wayne, 216 n.32
Merriman, Brigid O'Shea, 261 n.16
Merton, Thomas, 1
Milbank, John, 9, 184, 187, 207,
    214 n.11, 219 n.59, 222 n.92
Mirk, John, 15–16, 65, 67, 127,
    234 n.68, 247 n.119,
    263 n.15
modernity, 5, 23, 31, 127, 216 n.40,
    226 n.142, 232 n.49
Moore, R. I., 67–68, 237 n.22

Morris, Colin, 217 n.43
motherhood: of Christ, 59, 76, 89–95, 110–111, 126, 155–156, 160, 170, 241 n.66, 242 n.68, 243 nn. 80, 83, 84, 87, 88; of the church, 181, 247 n.119

nation-state, 4–9, 14, 30, 67, 71, 198, 218 n.54
nature ("kynd"), 59, 95, 196
Neel, Carol, 239 n.43
Neoplatonism, 154, 254 n.38
Newman, Barbara, 114, 118, 121
Nolan, Edward Peter, 232 n.45
Nolan, Michael, 237 n.28
Nolken, Christina von, 213 n.5
nominalism, 14, 23–31, 45, 58–60, 119, 123, 164–165, 187, 218 n.45, 222 n.95, 223 nn. 98, 99, 100, 225 nn.123, 129, 227 n.3, 234 n.70 *See also* William of Ockham
noughting, 98, 101–106, 120. *See also* privation
Nuth, Joan, 83, 147, 182, 230 n.34, 240 n.55, 249 n.130, 252 n.13, 253 n.25, 254 n.38, 257 n.69

Oakes, Edward, 257 n.69
Oakley, Francis, 223 n.98, 224 n.112, 225 n.125
Obermann, Heiko, 24, 27, 100, 218 n.45, 222 n.96, 223 n.99, 225 nn. 118, 123, 234 n.70, 246 n.111
O'Donovan, Oliver, 120, 121, 216 n.39
Olson, Mary, 177, 240 n.55
Origen of Alexandria, 253 nn. 21, 22
orthodoxy, Julian's, 109, 110, 112–119, 132, 135, 138, 142, 170, 205, 208
otherness of God, 46, 166–167

Owst, G. R., 219 n.60, 251 n.5, 252 n.7

Park, Tarjei, 147
Paul, Saint, 51, 121, 123, 146, 253 n.24
Peasants' Revolt of 1381, 174–176, 180, 259 nn. 87, 88, 89
Pelphrey, Brant, 43, 162–163, 230 n.31, 257 n.62, 263 n.9
penance, 104–105, 122, 149, 192, 245 n.106, 247 n.121
persecution, 67–68, 120, 121, 123, 237 n.22
Petersen, Erik, 216 n.37
Pierre d'Ailly, 26–27
pilgrim, Christ as, 169–170, 194–195, 248 n.124
Pliny the Younger, 11
Porete, Marguerite, 74
Poston, M. M., 216 n.40
power, divine, 23, 24–31, 33, 36, 58–59, 61–62, 83–84, 85, 119, 122–123, 164–165, 166, 183, 184, 187–188, 219 n.65, 222 n.95, 224 nn. 101, 103, 225 n.123, 226 nn. 132, 142, 227 n.3
prayer, 53–54, 140, 232 n.48
predestination, 155–159, 185, 223 n.100, 256 n.52
privation, 85, 96–97, 99, 102–106 passim, 120, 139, 147, 196, 246 n.112

Rahner, Karl, 172, 227 n.2, 258 n.72
Ratzinger, Joseph, 260 n.7
realism, metaphysical, 22
re-creation, 107, 122, 160, 254 n.37
resurrection, 38, 109, 110, 142–143, 161, 178, 189, 229 n.25
Reynolds, Sister Anna Marie, 240 n.55

Riddy, Felicity, 239 n.37
Robertson, Elizabeth, 214 n.9, 236 n.8, 243 n.84
Rolle, Richard, 60, 228 n.20
Ross, Maggie, 97, 106
Rubin, Miri, 20, 221 nn. 78, 80, 81, 82, 234 n.68
Ruusbroec, John, 154, 255 n.40

sacraments, 65, 110–111, 180–181, 183, 196. *See also* body of Jesus, eucharistic; Eucharist
salvation, 10, 79, 88, 89, 96, 102, 105, 108, 118–119, 145, 151, 168, 170–171, 200
Savage, Arnold, 18
Schmitt, Carl, 4–5, 214 n.17, 215 n.25
Scotus, John Duns, 25–26, 224 n.111, 225 nn. 118, 123, 256 n.52
secret, God's, 63, 96, 99–100, 116–117, 119, 121, 127, 171, 189–190, 197, 250 nn. 136, 137
secularity, 4, 6, 31, 123, 219 n.65
self-knowledge, 134, 148, 152, 169–170
sensuality. *See* substance and sensuality
sickness, 39, 100, 102, 203–204, 231 n.41, 244 n.97, 245 n.106
sin, 10, 39, 96, 98–103, 105, 113–114, 121, 132, 135, 136, 138, 150, 155–156, 167–168, 187, 244 n.97, 248 n.127
Skinner, John, 214 n.5
Southern, R. W., 228 n.9
Sprung, Andrew, 237 n.24
Staley, Lynn, 208, 214 n.9, 242 n.68, 246 n.112, 260 n.6
Stallybrass, Peter, 71–72
Stillingfleet, Edward, 1

substance and sensuality, 144–149, 152–153, 159–160, 162, 165, 172, 180–182, 192, 195, 198, 253 n.25
suffering, 34–35, 38–39, 45–46, 56–57, 58, 62, 64, 84, 88–89, 92, 93–94, 99–102, 104–106, 109, 136, 142, 149, 151, 196, 200, 231 n.41
Swanson, R. N., 218 n.55, 239 n.49

Tanner, Norman, 77, 238 n.35, 247 n.117
Tawney, R. H., 22
teacher, Christ and church as, 111–113, 115, 119, 149–150, 172, 247 n.122, 248 nn. 124, 126, 258 n.77
temptation, 37, 55, 64–65
Thérèse of Lisieux, 246 n.107
thirst, Christ's, 62, 103, 105, 109, 110, 118, 147, 151, 245 nn. 103, 104, 246 n.107
Thomas Aquinas, 12, 24–25, 27, 34, 58, 73, 168, 222 n.90, 231 n.39, 234 n.65, 237 n.28, 242 n.77, 249 n.134, 252 n.17, 255 n.50, 258 n.73
Thomas of Celano, 194
three estates, 15–16, 22, 23, 188, 240 n.50
time, 159–160, 163–164, 258 n.73
Trinity, 41, 48, 50–51, 57–58, 59, 62, 97, 107–108, 134, 139, 141, 153, 154, 155–156, 157–158, 160, 166–168, 170–171, 172, 183–189, 197, 227 n.2, 234 n.63, 252 nn. 17, 18, 255 n.40, 258 nn. 72, 73, 260 n.104
Tugwell, Simon, 52, 54, 57, 232 n.47, 233 nn. 55, 61
Turner, Denys, 233 n.52, 254 n.32, 259 n.98
Turner, Victor, 20, 31, 221 n.81
Turville-Petre, Thorlac, 218 n.54

Tyler, Wat, 174
Tyrrell, George, 262 n.5

universalism, 114–119, 121, 159, 170–171, 200, 248 n.127, 249 nn. 129, 130, 135, 250 n.137, 251 n.141, 258 n.77

vernacular theology, 71, 194, 208, 211, 237 n.20, 238 n.34
violence, 6–9, 22, 31, 73, 195, 196

Walsh, James. *See* Colledge, Edmund, and James Walsh
Walsingham, Thomas, 175
Ward, Benedicta, 204, 211, 228 n.9, 236 n.14, 262 n.1, 263 n.11
Warren, Ann, 77, 239 nn. 40, 44, 45
Watson, Nicholas, 42, 44, 48, 208–209, 211, 229 n.30, 235 n.2, 237 n.20, 238 n.34, 241 n.59, 248 n.127, 250 nn. 135, 137, 251 nn. 141, 4, 254 n.34, 258 n.77, 260 n.2, 264 n.25, 265 n.38
weal and woe, 54, 86, 139, 152, 254 n.35

Weber, Max, 6–8, 31, 215 n.25
Weil, Simone, 33, 106
White, Allon, 71–72
William of Ockham, 12–13, 25–26, 28–31, 184–185, 187–188, 194–195, 222 n.95, 223 n.99, 224 nn. 111, 112, 225 n.118, 260 n.101
William of St. Thierry, 163, 257 n.66
Williams, Raymond, 5–6, 215 n.19, 217 n.42
Williams, Rowan, 244 n.92
wisdom, 82, 94, 139, 154, 155, 159, 161, 188
Wittgenstein, Ludwig, 125
Wolters, Clifton, 252 n.19
women, status of in Middle Ages, 73–76, 90–95, 121, 205, 235 nn. 27, 28, 236 n.29, 240 n.52, 242 n.72
Wood, Ellen Meiksins, 227 n.142
wrath, 94, 113, 125, 132, 139–140, 171–172, 243 n.87, 257 n.69
Wright, Michael J., 204–205, 263 n.8
Wright, N. T., 11
Wyclif, John, 20, 35, 108, 180, 194–195, 227 n.3, 246 n.116, 261 n.8

About the Author

Frederick C. Bauerschmidt is Associate Professor of Theology at Loyola College in Maryland. He has published essays in *Modern Theology, New Blackfriars, The Journal of Medieval and Early Modern Studies, Philosophy and Theology, Communio,* and *The Journal of Literature and Theology.*

www.ingramcontent.com/pod-product-compliance
Lightning Source LLC
Chambersburg PA
CBHW030335240426
43661CB00052B/1644